ALTERNATIVE CHRISTIANITIES VOLUME II

THE VALIDITY OF TODAY'S CHRISTIAN TEACHINGS AND THE LOST GOSPELS OF THE OTHER DISCIPLES

A TREATISE

CHALLENGING TODAY'S CHRISTIANITY WITH THE RECENT DISCOVERIES OF:

THE SUPPRESSED GOSPELS OF: JAMES, PETER, PHILIP, THOMAS, JUDAS, AND MARY

MANY LOST GOSPELS: HEBREWS, EBIONITES, EGYPTIANS, NAZAREANS, AND TRUTH

THE SECRET SAYINGS OF JESUS: THE GOSPEL OF THOMAS (THE FIFTH GOSPEL)

THE LEGEND AND BANNED GOSPEL OF JUDAS WHICH CHANGES EVERYTHING

THE GOSPEL OF MARY MAGDALENE, THE PREMIER DISCIPLE OF JESUS

THE ANCIENT GNOSTIC CHRISTIAN PREACHERS, FOLLOWERS, AND BELIEFS

These are texts as old and valid as the four Gospels that were put in the New Testament

The sequel to:
Alternative Christianities – Volume I: Early Christian Sects and the Formation of the Bible

WARNING:
This is not a Religion book but a factual History book that will CHALLENGE your current beliefs!

By Vince Nicolas

authorHOUSE®

AuthorHouse™
1663 Liberty Drive
Bloomington, IN 47403
www.authorhouse.com
Phone: 1 (800) 839-8640

Published by AuthorHouse 12/28/2018

ISBN: 978-1-5462-4407-3 (sc)
ISBN: 978-1-5462-4406-6 (e)

Print information available on the last page.

Dedicated to my wonderful Husband, Tony
For his patience through my years of
Research and Writing of two volumes

TABLE OF CONTENTS

PART IV – THE PAUL FACTOR

PREFACE

Welcome to Volume II of **Alternative Christianities**. For those that have read **Alternative Christianities – Volume I: Early Christian Sects and the Formation of the Bible**, Welcome Back and I hope you enjoy **Alternative Christianities – Volume II: The Validity of Today's Christian Teachings and the Lost Gospels of the Other Disciples**. If you have not read Volume I, I do hope you pick it up or order it. It is well-worth reading.

For those new readers to whom I have not introduced myself in Volume I: I am Vince Nicolas. I am a "historian" not a "theologian." I am writing these books as a "historian" not as a "theologian." I want to make that very clear.

My four-year language major in High School was Latin. We spent a lot of time translating ancient Latin books. Having an Italian heritage, I loved the history of it all. I have visited Rome and Italy many times. The history of Christianity is intricately intertwined with the history of the Roman Empire and Emperors. Most notably with Emperor Constantine who personally forced the formation of the unified Christian Church, or the Catholic (universal) Church.

I also want to point out that both these volumes are part of a larger "treatise," a work to prove a point, which I have undertaken to do. As much as there are some people that will love my work, I am sure that many more of today's conservative evangelical Christians will hate it. It will be called by them blasphemous and the work of the devil. I am neither, nor alone on this subject. I have read dozens of the hundreds of published books by a plethora of authors who are theologians, clergy, Biblical scholars, and university Religious Studies professors. I have only scratched the tip of the iceberg with the voluminous information they have published. I can write so many more volumes from the unbelievable wealth of information on this subject.

For those who are more visceral, I happening upon several series and videos by The History Channel, National Geographic, and other documentaries such as "***Banned from the Bible***" or ***"The Gospel of Judas Iscariot"***. The latter was a game changer for me. It destroyed everything we were ever taught about the Disciple Judas Iscariot. Judas was a hero not a traitor! He did what Jesus commanded him to do. The other Disciples were more cowards and traitors. There are many more books and shows on the "lost" **Gospels of Peter, James, Philip, Thomas, Judas,** and **Mary Magdalene.** They were all left out of the ***New Testament***! Why? Because these Gospels contradicted the four Gospels in the ***New Testament*** **the bishops wanted** to be included. It would have completely changed Christianity as we know it today.

.

I am hoping my treatise will open many more eyes among theologians, clergy, professors, and students. It would be great if these **Alternative Christianities** become an integral part of a well-rounded Religious Studies curriculum. This was not meant to destroy anyone's specific faith or religious affiliation but hopefully, enhance and expand upon it. I hope this do not show any favoritism, partiality, or hostility toward any particular religion or denomination. There are some denominations that disrespect those who do not subscribe specifically to their brand of Christianity. Let us remember that Jesus Christ did not establish a religion. Although He could have, He allowed for it to go out in many different directions. It was formalized and stifled by the new Roman Emperor Constantine in the 4th Century who used it to consolidate the Roman Empire. Mere men decided what would be "Holy Scriptures" going forward and which ones would be destroyed.

This is an ambitious effort as a first-time author trying to balance and convey a mountain of information, please forgive any imperfections.

Enjoy, Vince Nicolas

INTRODUCTION AND TREATISE SCOPE

This is Volume II of **Alternative Christianities.** Volume I was about the **Early Christian Sects and the Formation of the Bible**. Volume II expands on the subject matter touched upon in Volume I with **The Validity of Today's Christian Teachings and the Lost Gospels of the Other Disciples**. Volume II includes so much more information and insight about the unpublished Gospels of Jesus' Disciples James, Peter, Philip, Thomas, Judas, and Mary. There are also many "secret Gospels" written by Jesus' Disciples, such as Mark and John, which went unpublished because they contained the "secret teachings" of Jesus which were not spoken to the masses but only to those in His "Inner Circle." They were too "**gnostic"** or "mystical." Plus, the unheard of Gospels with names like the Hebrews, Truth, Ebionites, Egyptians, and Nazareans. There is so much information, and contradictory information, I could easily write a third and fourth volume. I know for me this has been a fascinating and mind-expanding journey for which I cannot get enough information. I hope I have inspired many to carry the torch and keep digging and exclaiming this subject. Maybe, millennia of Christianity that has gone wrong can be righted for further generations. I am only a relayer of the information I have learned and compiled from the best and most educated biblical scholars, clergy, educators, and authors. This is only a small token of my gratitude to them enough for inspiring me.

Before I go further, I must apologize for the repetitions. One, I must take into account people that may be reading Volume II who have not read Volume I. To my readers of Volume I, please forgive me. For those who have not read Volume I, I strongly suggest reading it. Two, there are times information is repeated between Chapters. One of the audiences I hope to attract is Religious Studies educators and students. I wanted to make each Chapter somewhat autonomous and can be used independently to discuss a specific subject or lesson.

First, **I am a historian NOT a theologian**. These are the historical facts for your consideration. **I am not a preacher** and this book is not meant to "convert" anyone; there is nothing to convert you to. I am a life-long, educated, and practicing mainline Christian. I am not an "evangelist," religious fanatic, an agnostic, nor the devil. I believe Jesus Christ came to this earth as our Lord and Savior. He preached a wonderful message of love, good works, compassion, and everything that is good. He was arrested and put to death. **AT THAT POINT THINGS GETS "*VERY FUZZY!*"** Who was behind His arrest and why? The four ***published*** Gospels each relay a **completely different story about His arrest, trial, persecution, death, and resurrection.** The Evangelical ministers are committed to arguing it and they do everything to prove the Gospels are infallible. Adding to the chaos, you can read the Gospels, Epistles, and other texts **not published,** in fact, banned and ordered destroyed which were just as revered and just as valid attributed to Jesus' other Disciples: **Peter, James, Philip, Thomas, Judas, and Mary Magdalene.** This Volume is dedicated to those works. Many **Alternative Christianities**

evolved around those works and not the four published Gospels. They live and are practiced today deep inside the **Catholic Coptic** and **Orthodox Coptic Churches**. They exist in Asia Minor and the U.S. today.

Second, everyone should understand this Volume Two is also a "**Treatise.**" A Treatise is similar to a Thesis but is defined as "a formal and systematic discourse written on a subject, generally longer and treating the subject more in-depth than a thesis or essay but it is more concerned with investigating and exposing the principles of a subject, or an argument, for specific issues, philosophies, or trains of thought."

In the Treatise Scope, with the groundwork laid in Volume I, I will continue to discuss how Christianity from almost its very beginning took off in the wrong direction, or at least since the 4th Century. Then it has been misdirected further through the centuries up to and including present-day Christianity as it is preached and practiced. Because of this, we need to look back at the "original" and most "real" Christianity or Christianities that are present in some of the **Alternative Christianities.** Through my research the paths many times lead to the ancient "**Gnostics**," their "**Gnosticism,**" and the "**Gnostic Gospels**." The "***Secret Gospels***" most times contain teachings from Jesus that the early Church Leaders felt were too **"Gnostic"** for the general public. There were many "**Gnostic Christian**" sects among the early Christians in the first centuries. They were squashed and banned by the early Church Leaders who were in charge of developing the emerging Christian Church in the 2nd through 4th centuries. Today, as in past centuries, these ancient **Gnostic beliefs** can be found deeply rooted in some Eastern religions or taught quietly underground.

Third, it is important to remember and reiterate that Christianity spread out in different directions and regions producing "**Christianities**" with different versions of Jesus' life, teachings, and death. Remember, the twelve Disciples scattered to different regions of the world. Their followers were very diverse in their practices but unified in their fundamental beliefs thanks to the Apostles Creed which was agreed upon and considered passed down from The Twelve.

Fourth, Constantine was converted to Christianity by his mother and became the new Emperor of Rome. He used Christianity to unite the Roman Empire under his rule. He called together all the bishops from around the Roman Empire to Nicaea, Turkey in order to come to an agreement regarding the differing "Christian beliefs." In 325 A.D. these men vastly expanded the original "Apostles' Creed" and published "Nicene Creed" which established the "one, holy, catholic (universal), and apostolic church." The purpose was to extinguish all the **Alternative Christianities** and establish the Catholic Church. They added more dogma again to the Nicene Creed later in that century while formalizing the "accepted" Christian beliefs then choose the "canon" or "official" texts which would be in the Christian Bible.

Fifth, before that there are innumerable religions, denominations, sects, and cults who all call themselves "**Christians**" and all consider themselves to be the "**real**" Christians. There are only **FOUR GOSPELS** (out of ten Apostolic Gospels) "chosen" by these Bishops at a subsequent Council in Nicaea. They mainly followed the recommendation championed by one man in A.D. 180, Irenaeus, to be the only "true ones" and as such should be the only ones included in the New Testament. According to Irenaeus, there should be only **four** Gospels, no more, no less. All other "Sacred Scriptures" were banned and ordered destroyed. Alternative Christians were considered heretics. ***You would think that true Christians would want to read EVERYTHING written about Jesus Christ!***

Sixth, this Volume II is a continuation and expansion of Volume I. According to my publisher, my manuscript was entirely too much information to put into one volume. This Volume II is divided into four major groupings. Part I, Christianity and Sex (Marriage and Homosexuality in the Bible). Part II, The Gnostic Christians, Part III, The Gnostic Gospels (text and commentary of the some of the banned Gospels, and Part IV, The Paul Factor about the main reason Christianity was led astray by following Paul's Epistles. "Paul was a Fraud" and his Epistles should be completely stricken from the Bible. Many of the **Alternative Christianities** knew Paul was completely wrong and did not include his Epistles in their Sacred Scriptures. Many Biblical scholars and linguistic experts agree that some of Paul's Epistles were NOT written by him and some that they felt were written by him were left out. Regardless, he never knew or was instructed by Jesus. Paul had his own brand of Christianity, while several writings from Jesus' Inner Circle of Disciples were discarded.

Warning: I know that this Treatise and its contents will be highly criticized by the Evangelist and Fundamentalist Christians who believe in a strict interpretation of the Bible (ignoring its human evolution) considering it hand-delivered by God himself to us here on Earth in a shrink-wrapped tamper-proof package (like Tylenol ®) to be believed and followed **to the letter** and under **penalty of eternal damnation**. **This is not for those people – their views are immutable and they will challenge anyone with even the simplest differing viewpoint.** Let me say to them: That's nice, Good for you, Enjoy, Peace be with you, and Good Luck with that. But then maybe this book is something you

SHOULD read! If you are <u>not</u> interested in expanding your mind, please close this book now!

<u>Finally</u>, my research led me to believe that Jesus came to SAVE us from the mean and vengeful "God of the Old Testament" and correct the course of what came before Him. Remember, the Jews at that time did not believe there was eternal life after their physical death. Jesus preached the Good News that there was "no death" but "everlasting life." However, then for two thousand years since He walked on this Earth, His teachings were derailed and we have been misled down the wrong path. Jesus' mission and the real Christianity has been a failure. **<u>What a horrible thought!</u>**

REFERENCE AND DEFINITIONS

ABRAHAMIC RELIGIONS: One issue that goes unnoticed by many, there are three Abrahamic Religions, that is, the three major religions are direct descendants of the God, faith, and sons of Abraham, chronologically: Judaism, Christianity, and Islam. Yes, all three believe in the same Almighty Heavenly Father though they may refer to him by their own native names: Yahweh, Jesus' Father, or Allah (which only means "God" in Arabic, not a different God). To put Christianity into perspective, the worldwide adherent statistics are:

21% Muslim (almost all the countries from Africa east to Indonesia)

21% All Roman Catholic rites [fairly equal to Islam at 1.2 Billion each] (i.e. all approx. 30 Catholic rites that report to the Pope in Rome)

19% Hindu, Buddhist, and Shinto (from India, through China, to Japan)

12% Protestant (all non-Catholic and non-Orthodox denominations)
10% Orthodox, Anglican, and all other non-Roman Catholic denominations
1% Jewish

CHRISTIANITY Christians and Christianity encompass a wide variety and iterations of belief-systems with the only common thread being that they all consider Jesus Christ a deity who is their Lord and Savior. [***Alternative Christianities Volume I*** goes into much more detail.] Christianity breaks **dogmatically** breaks into three major branches: Catholic, Orthodox, and Protestant; and these three branches breakdown further in subsects or denominations. Christians (mainly Roman Catholics) account for approximately 1/3 of the world's population and Islam account equally for 1/3 of the population. The last 1/3 include Protestant, Hindu, Buddhist, Shinto, atheist, agnostics, and other indigenous religions.

CATHOLIC: When used with a small "c" it means the "universal" Christian Church before any breaks or schisms. When used with a capital "C" usually means the "Roman Catholic Church" or any dogmatically Catholic Church that may or may not report to the Pope in Rome. When used in the phrase "One, Holy, Catholic, and Apostolic Church" it means the unified Christian Church established by Roman Emperor Constantine at the Council of Nicaea in A.D. 325. The Great Schism of 1054 formed the Roman Catholic Church and the Eastern Orthodox Church. Note: the Anglican/Episcopal Churches dogmatically align with the Catholic Church but does not report to the Pope in Rome.

ORTHODOX: When used with a small "o" means the teachings or the emerging and established one, unified, universal (or catholic) Church on or before the Council of Nicaea in 325. When used with a capital "O" refers to the "Orthodox" or "Eastern Orthodox Churches." They independently report to a local Patriarch in charge of a branch such as the Greek Orthodox Church, Russian Orthodox Church, etc. They are dogmatically very close to the Roman Catholic Church with only a very few exceptions.

PROTESTANT: Applies to all the religions that came out of the Protestant Reformation initiated by Martin Luther in 1595 breaking away from the Roman Catholic Church with several specific dogmatic differences. This includes all subsequent "reformations" and "splits" from their initial first tier "mainline/mainstream Protestants" such as Lutheran, Baptist, Methodist, Presbyterian, etc. and most other non-Catholic/Orthodox religions. Today there are tens of thousands of Protestant "Christian" denominations in the world.

BORN-AGAIN CHRISTIANS: Offshoots from the "mainline Protestants" are Bible-centric sects which include "reborn" or "born-again" Christians who claim to have a "personal relationship" with Jesus Christ (not to be confused with a "religious order" who takes life-long vows of poverty, chastity, and obedience). These "born-again Christians" firmly believe that they are saved and will go to heaven because they have confessed their sins and have accepted Jesus Christ as their Savior. They usually refer to themselves generically as just "Christians." Some use it as if no one that came before them were true "Christians."

EVANGELICALS: A stricter forms of these “born-again” Christians (above) share some other conditions:

1. Professing their faith in Jesus is the most important thing in their daily lives.
2. Believe they have a personal responsibility to share their Christian beliefs with others.
3. Believe that Satan is a living force that is presently working in the world today.
4. Believe that salvation is only attained by the grace of God and not by doing good works. A belief that stems from “Calvinism” or your salvation is decided the day you were born.
5. They are sublimely constantly begging Jesus to save them from eternal damnation.
6. Believe Jesus was a good and perfect during His time here on earth.
7. The Bible is 100% historically accurate and inerrant in its every word and teaching.
8. Jesus is the all-powerful, all-knowing, all-perfect deity who created this world today.
9. Evangelical, fundamentalist, or “born again” Christians do not require church attendance.

10. Ironically, this movement began in the U.S. in the early 1900's. It is barely 100 years old.

CHRISTIANS: Conversely, I sometimes spell "christians" in the lower case for those who purport to be "Christians" but they do not act very Christian-like. Many are referred to as "cafeteria christians" or those that pick and choose what parts of the Bible pertain to them and which parts in the Bible pertain to other people and not them (like remarriage is adultery).

WORLDVIEW: From the perspective of the Outsiders, the mainly-American, loudly-vocal and highly-visible Evangelical, Ultra-Conservative, Fundamentalist, Born-Again Christians, Political Right-Wingers who are basically outside the mainline Christian religions and denominations are the ones who cast the dark cloud over the more mainstream worldwide tolerant and loving mission of Jesus Christ and the real Christianity.

THE BIBLE: There are many quotes in this book. You may not be able to find it, or find it where it referenced. This is because there is one "Catholic Version" but multiple "Protestant Versions" of the Bible (see ***Alternative Christianities – Volume I***).

As a result of the Councils of Nicaea, in 382 Pope Damasus I commissioned Jerome, a renowned multilinguistic, to translate the Gospels and other Sacred Scriptures into Latin, the official language of the Rome. Called the "Latin Vulgate," it is still in use today by the Catholics. In 1611, King James commissioned the King James Version (KJV), although it is the most popular version in use today, it has been deemed by Biblical scholars as the poorest translation of the Latin texts they had. The big difference is the Catholic version has 73 books but the Protestant version has only 66 books. Missing are Tobit, Judith, 1 and 2 Maccabees, Wisdom of Shoman, Sirach (or Ecclesiasticus), and Barach. Extra chapters and verses were put in the Books of Daniel and Esther. The Protestants deleted the verses in Maccabees which had the doctrine of Purgatory and the importance of prayers and sacrifices for the dead. Also deleted were verses in Tobias on the importance of doing Good Works in God's eyes. The Protestant version in Luke 2:14 changed "men of good will" to read "good will towards men." There are many versions of the Bible caused by translation errors, transcription errors, accidental errors, and purposeful theological or political motives.

This is discussed in depth in ***Alternative Christianities – Volume I.*** Regardless; many of Protestant denominations have the unwavering belief that the Bible is in its entirety the 100% direct or inspired word of God and 100% historically accurate.

DISCIPLES vs. APOSTLES: A "***Disciple***" is someone who is taught by the Master. Disciple with a capital "D" refers only to the Twelve Disciples of Jesus, His Inner Circle, including Mary Magdalene and His constant companions who were taught directly and consistently by Jesus Christ when He was on this earth. An "***apostle***" is a "missionary," someone sent out, an emissary. A Disciple can be called an Apostle designated with a capital "A" but otherwise, an apostle who is not also a Disciple is shown with a small "a." Many times I and others state that Paul was neither a disciple nor an apostle (in capital or small letters).

JESUS AND THE FATHER: All **He, His, My,** etc. referring to Jesus, His Father, or the Almighty God are capitalized not only for reference purposes but out of my respect for the Higher Power.

PART I - CHRISTIANITY AND SEX

CHAPTER 1

THE PERCEPTION OF TODAY'S CHRISTIANITY

CHRISTIANITY HAS AN IMAGE PROBLEM

As I begin ***Alternative Christianities – Volume*** 2, it is probably appropriate to give a perspective of Christianity in today's world. Basically, Christianity has a serious image problem. Christians are supposed to represent Jesus Christ to the world. It was put very well by, I believe, Gandhi, who said to the effect: ***"I like your Christ, it is just a shame your Christians are not more like your Christ."***

According to the latest surveys, today's Christianity has gone terribly wrong. Words like "hypocritical," "insensitive," and "judgmental" are used to describe today's Christianity and Christians by the American youth. They more or less express the same impression as put forth by Gandhi. The research reveals that the perceptions of 16- to 29- year olds believe that Christianity and Christians have taken several **giant steps backward.** Recent research describes reputation of Christians as becoming **increasingly negative** among young Americans.

Today's Christians seem now to be best known for what they are against. They now are considered all to be about being judgmental, antihomosexual, and **much too political**. Young people quick admit ***Christianity is no longer as Jesus preached or intended.*** **It is the antithesis of Christ and Christianity.** It is a shame that it has gone that way.

What caused this? Probably it is the overzealous, overconfident, and uncompromising Christian ministers and the Christians that they are producing causing Christians and Christianity to boomerang retrograde in the wrong direction.

RANKING OF WORLD'S RELIGIONS:

First, it is probably appropriate to repeat from ***Volume I*** where "Christianity" stands with the world population:

33% **Christian** (There are three major dogmatic divisions: Catholic, Orthodox, and Protestant)
21% Roman Catholic
7% Protestant
5% Eastern Orthodox, Anglican and Other Non-Protestant but non-Roman dogmatically Catholics.

21% **Islam**

45% **Other**
13% Hindu

6% Buddhist

26% Indigenous Religions, Atheists, and Others

Credit: Wikipedia for these statistics

THE STATISTICS

I am an old-fashioned "numbers person," so show me the numbers. These statistics were compiled, published, and copyrighted in 2007 by **David Kinnaman** and **Gabe Lyons** in their book "***UnChristian***" (Baker Books, Grand Rapids, MI 49516-6287 www.bakerbooks.com) as a result of their **Fermi Project** by the **Barna Group**.

David Kinnaman is the president of the **Barna Group** which has provided over 500 research studies for a variety of churches, corporations, nonprofit organizations. You can find **David Kinnaman** and **George Barna's** research reports online at www.barna.org. Christians seem to need to be knocked down a few pegs for their own good before they self-destruct and extinguish themselves.

I. How Outsiders (non-Christians) Perceive Christians, Evangelicals, and Born-Again Christians:

(Among 440 16-29-year-olds)

	Christians	Evangelicals	Born-Again Christians
Have a **BAD** impression	38%	49%	35%

Have a **NEUTRAL** impression	45%	48%	55%
Have a **GOOD** impression	16%	3%	10%
	99%	100%	100%

II. How (non-Christian) Outsiders and Churchgoing Christians Perceive Christianity:

(Among 440 16-29-year-olds)

	Outsiders	Churchgoing Christians
Antihomosexual	91%	80%
Too Judgmental	87%	52%
Hypocritical (saying one thing, doing another)	86%	47%
Old-fashioned	78%	36%
Too Involved in Politics	75%	50%
Out of Touch with Reality	72%	32%
Insensitive to Others	70%	29%
Boring	68%	27%
Not Accepting of Other Faiths	64%	39%
Confusing	61%	44%

IMPORTANT NOTE: It is just not surprising why Christianity does not have more adherents or converts.

III. Expanding on the Perceptions on the (mainly Evangelical and Born Again) Christians:

1. **Hypocritical.** Outsiders consider Christians to be very hypocritical, or otherwise preaching one thing and personally not practicing what they preach. Worse, they think Christians put forth a morally superior attitude toward Outsiders. Christians profess their religion is the only true religion in the world, which does not do anything to endear 2/3 of the world's population.
2. **Too Focused on Getting Converts.** Outsiders feel that Christians do genuinely care about them but they are just treated as scoring points in attaining **their own salvation.** They question those Christians' motives more when they keep trying to "save" those that might have already tried "Jesus" or "Christianity" before; maybe that counts for extra "points."
3. **Homosexuality.** Many Christians and non-Christians (Outsiders) alike feel the most conservative Christians are innately bigoted with all the disdain they show for gays and lesbians; even those who profess to be practicing "Christians." These Christians are more fixated on curing the homosexuals and doing everything to leverage American politics against these people.
4. **Sheltered.** Many Christian religions are thought to be archaic and completely out-of-touch with the reality of the modern world. Many Christians cannot handle today's complex world problems but instead still try to take the most simplistic parochial approaches of yesteryear. Their responses and solutions no longer are the answers to today's people's lives, relationships, and well-being.

5. **Too Political.** Many Christian sects have stepped outside their religious realm and into the political arena, profess a strictly political agenda, and promoting their ultra-conservative religion, interests, and values with total disregard to the multi-cultural diversity of the American people. With all due respect to their humble beliefs, it is as if the Amish and Mennonite take over the American political system and then force everyone in the U.S. to adopt shunning modern conveniences like electricity, cars, airplanes, etc. and return to farming and self-sufficiency.
6. **Judgmental.** Christians are very quick to judge other people or are not completely upfront in letting their attitudes and perspectives be known about other people different than themselves. But to the more astute, their true selves are transparent. Some of the Outsiders are quick to point out their doubt that the Christians really do NOT love or care for people as much as they say they do.

HOMOSEXUALITY

Although all the above perceptions can be very subjective and all may be equally serious in many people's eyes, the aforementioned one that seems to be the real hot-button issue both religiously and politically in the United States (admittedly, more or less in other countries of the world). So I will single this out for further discussion.

The #1 Perception is: Many Christians show limitless contempt for all gays and lesbians.

The research indicates the highest perception was that Christians are totally against all gays and lesbians, objecting to their "**deviant," "perverse"** and **"immoral**" lifestyle. Many go a step further and have an irrational fear and scorn everyone and everything even hinting at homosexuality. The "gay issue" has become the main negative image of today's Christianity. As Americans became more and more accepting of gays and lesbians as active contributing members of society, conservative Christians became more and more hostile towards the gay segment of American society. Acerbating the issue more is that the United States and many of the world's major countries allow a same-sex couple to get legally married. This is disastrous: they want these homosexual burned at the stake or similar, not be welcomed in their churches and married in the presence of God. A thorn in their side which needs to be rectified was when the United States Supreme Court ruled that it is "***every American citizen's right***" to "***equal rights and protections under the United States Constitution"*** and ***"states cannot legislate discrimination***" (14th Amendment).

Never has American's conservative Christians turned into the most "**unChristian**" people. They became MORE vocal, political, prejudice, bigoted, hateful, ambiguous, and negative. The Outsiders view the Christian hostility and disdain toward gays and lesbians virtually a prerequisite dogma to be a "Christian." It is so severe that it is causing divisions, more divisions than the thousands already, within Christianity. All the other factors put aside, 91% of the Outsiders said that "anti-homosexuality" describes the Christianity of today. When a person calls themselves a "Christian," they are automatically labeled as an anti-homosexual, gay-hating homophobe. These Christians must wake up to this issue in the evolving world and review themselves "objectively." Many "Christians," notably the White Anglo-Saxon Protestants

(WASP's), still are seething over the 1960's Supreme Court Rulings that gave Equal Rights to all citizens regardless of race, and worse allowed interracial marriages which were banned in most states until then.

Instead of coming across as arrogant and self-righteous, they should treat everyone like Jesus did. Here are some examples of the ridiculous things that have been said or done by these "conservative" Christians:

- God's hatred for homosexuals has caused His wrath with the 9/11 attacks and numerous natural events.
- Christian pastors routinely publically berate homosexuals and incite their congregations to take action.
- Christians unfoundedly oppose gays in public positions, government positions, or any positions of authority.
- There are many Christian websites with "God-hates-gays" themes full of "select" Biblical verses.
- The current U.S. President has signed an order to allow businesses to openly discriminate against gays.

Some sects profess more inconsistencies and much deeper biases than originally imagined:

- "**Born-again Christians**"[1] disapprove more of homosexuality than they do of divorce. The vast majority of the "born-again Christians" do not consider same-sex relationships legitimate lifestyles and even strongly object to same-sex church-sanctioned weddings. Whereas, Jesus said **NOTHING** about homosexuality, they got to reach back to the 5000-year-old Hebrew texts which ban many things like eating pork or shellfish, or women wearing clothes of two different fabrics, which are all in the same sentence but they conveniently ignore and do anyway. Worse, these born-again Christians ignore **Jesus' DIRECT preaching that divorce is a major sin and anyone who remarries commits adultery** (see ***Matthew*** 5:32). Guess that makes many or most of them the big sinners. At least the Catholic Church abides by Jesus' teaching "***what God has joined together, let no man put asunder***" and prohibits divorce and prohibits remarriage like Jesus instructed in the ***New Testament***.

- Almost 80% of "**born-again Christians**" want legal restrictions placed on homosexual behavior and that same-sex relationships between two consenting adults should be made illegal (just like Islamic Sharia law).
- Approximately 60% of "**born-again Christians**" feel that school boards should fire teachers who they find out are homosexuals (Hitler and others style witch hunts); gays and lesbians should NOT EVER be near children. This is despite the fact that over 90% of child molestations done by heterosexuals on the opposite sex and minors.
- Many Christians continue to be very skeptical and uncaring about HIV/AIDS victims, even outside the United States citing **the idea that this inevitable-fatal disease is deserved and a punishment by God** for their personal decisions and deviant lifestyle. This is despite the fact that 99% of AIDS are heterosexually transmitted in Africa.

NOTE 1: About 2/3 of the self-proclaimed "conservative" Christians beliefs qualify them as "**born-again Christians,**" while evangelicals (self-proclaimed "Christianity" preachers) are a subset of Born-again Christians.

All these attitudes disgust the Outsiders and youth of America who many say, "***I cannot imagine Jesus really treating gays and lesbians like these Christians are doing today in His name.***" The Outsiders realize more than these Christians that God gave everyone a purpose, God created and gave life to everyone, and expects everyone to be a conduit of Himself in their treatment and compassion towards His other creations, whether they are straight, gay, lesbian, bisexual, or transgender. To quote Gandhi again, "***it is just a shame your Christians are not more like your Christ.***"

WE ARE ALL SINNERS

Many times Society under the guise of religion considered **SEX** to be a particularly destructive force in people's lives. This was true of ALL sex and sexual acts. Especially to these "**born-again Christians**" **WE ARE ALL SINNERS!** According to these Christian sects and their interpretation of the Bible, sin is a rebellion against the will of God. Sex is evil – sex is a sin. It did not matter whether that sex is between people of the same sex or people of the opposite sex. We all fall short of God's expectations of us. We are all lowly creatures undeserving God and without His Grace, we cannot attain eternal salvation in the Kingdom of Heaven. This has its roots in one of the original Protestant reformers, John Calvin, and his doctrine of "**pre-destination**;" we are all born to be damned to Hell and few will escape that fate but only at His will, ***"...there but for the Grace of God go I..."*** (See ***Volume I***). God did love this world and tried to make peace with us. He sent His Son Jesus to die on the cross

(***John*** 3:16). According to the "**born-again Christians,**" a person's salvation depends on their personal relationship with Jesus. Either you commit to Him or are considered rejecting Him.

IMPORTANT NOTE: The Bible makes hundreds of references to inappropriate and sinful heterosexual activity. However, there are only three direct or indirect (depending on whom you ask) references to homosexuality:

Leviticus 18:22, ***Romans*** 1:26-27, and ***1 Corinthians*** 6:9-10 (one "***Old Testament***" and two letters allegedly written by Paul – see discussions on the veracity of "Paul's" epistles in ***Alternative Christianities – Volume I***).

One of the most respected Christian leaders in modern day America, Billy Graham, makes these statements about homosexuality in a press conference, "***I'm going to quote the Bible now, not myself, that it*** [homosexuality] ***is wrong, it's a sin. But there are other sins. Why do we jump on that sin as though it's the greatest sin? The greatest sin in the Bible is idolatry, worshipping other things besides the true and living God. Jealousy is a sin. Pride is a sin. All of these things are sins."*** This was so well phrased. WE ARE ALL SINNERS; "***let he who is without sin, throw the first stone.***"

It is one thing to say you "personally" are against ***"homosexuality"*** but it is quite another thing to voice your feelings and words ***"against homosexuals"*** as people and by default your same creator. Again, as Lady Gaga's song ***Born This Way*** repeatedly says "***God makes no mistakes!***" To imply God does make mistakes is downright blasphemy and surely no way to endear Him for your own salvation.

Do NOT forget Jesus' greatest commandment to love one another.

THE COMMON CHRISTIAN ARGUMENTS AGAINST HOMOSEXUALS

Many Christians are easily alarmed by their ministers who instill fear in them against homosexuals by exaggerating or fabricating the dangers of gays and lesbians in American society. Most who have gay or lesbian relatives, friends, co-workers, business associates, or vendors have all those alleged fears and misconceptions quickly dissipated into thin air. However, there will be some persons who have their minds made up and nothing will change it no matter what. But for most, their same "christian" bigotry, prejudices, and hatred can apply to the gamut of people different than themselves whether it is color, race, nationality, sex, and especially "creed" all in the name of Jesus Christ. For example:

1. ***"Homosexuals are immoral."***

    For anything allegedly about same-sex relationships, these "christians" need to resort to the "Old Testament" or the "Hebrew Bible" whereas NOTHING at all is said by Jesus Christ, you know, the Christ that these "christians" purport to follow and preach. Meanwhile, the Hebrew Bible is littered with same-sex love and relationships. If it was such an abomination Jesus would have mentioned it at least several times **but did not even once**. There are a hundredfold more admonishments against heterosexual sexuality, divorce, and adultery which they avoid because it pertains to them personally. It is ironic that in so many of the "christian" churches gays and lesbians have been forced out calling them immoral. But ***"Who abandoned who?"*** Many gays and lesbians still go to those Churches and pray beside those hypocrites. There is a Dignity organization for Catholics to worship and an Integrity group for Episcopalians. Many just go to another Christian Churches that accept them such as the Congregationalist or Unitarian-Universalist. Studies show that 1/3 of gays and lesbians attend church regularly and a much higher percentage on a less frequent basis. Not all the mainline Protestant churches can boast an equivalent percent. Homosexuals are no more "immoral" than their heterosexual counterparts, in fact with all those admonishments about virginity, divorce and adultery, gays actually may be MORE moral.

2. ***"Homosexuals are determined to destroy conservative Christianity."***

First of all, <u>not</u> ALL gays and lesbians are Christians. Some are Jewish or Muslim. They ALL do <u>not</u> feel the same about the issues facing society today, or ALL have the antagonism toward their religion. Gays and lesbians are almost as diverse in their feelings as their heterosexual counterparts. Although they can be more skeptical towards conservative Christianity, this is not true of ALL homosexuals. Most of the gays and lesbians in America consider themselves "Christians"; about 1/6 of gays and lesbians are in the "**born-again Christian**" category.

3. ***"Homosexuality is a choice issue."***

Homosexuality is NOT just a "simple life choice." Again as Lady Gaga's song by the same name says, we were "***Born this Way***." Psychologists and psychiatrists (which include "Christian" pastors) 100% agree that human sexuality, whether it is homosexual or heterosexual, comes from a very complex compilation of intangible factors. The same type factors that determine whether that same person likes chocolate ice cream over vanilla, or likes blonds over redheads.

Most gays have no problem with their homosexual lifestyle, in fact, prefer it; others struggle their whole life their homosexual attractions and hid them by living or marrying heterosexually; some go through only brief period of experimentation; some live a veiled double life; some "come out" late and destroy their wives and family; some are forced because of their religious families and society to internally anguish over their repressed homosexuality and resent their heterosexual life; while other accept their religious beliefs and are comfortable with themselves and their heterosexual life.

4. ***"It is best to avoid the homosexuals."***

Many "christians" believe that homosexuals should be avoided and condemned; this is what they claim Jesus Christ would want them to do. The acronym the "christians" like to use is "**WWJD**" or "***What Would Jesus Do?***" Well, not exactly. Jesus did NOT avoid or condemn anyone;

He went out of His way to befriend the sinners or those less fortunate. The youth and adults of today are exposed to gays and lesbians every day in their personal inactions and on their television programs. It is hard to find a high school or college student, a young adult or a married couple who do not have personal friends in their daily lives who are gay, lesbian, bisexual, or even transgendered; this is a new generation that does not have the same prejudices as their parents or grandparents.

5. "***Homosexuality is an abnormality of nature***."

   This is usually the belief among "christians" who have willfully spent little time or energy to try and get to know any gays or lesbians in their lives. First of all, some individual animals of every species exhibit same-sex love and have long-term relationships. Again I have to quote Lady Gaga's song ***Born This Way:*** "***God makes no mistakes…"*** It is really blasphemy by any real "Christian" to imply "***God made a mistake***" when He created these people. It contradicts their professed beliefs unequivocally that God is an all-good, all-loving, all-knowing, all-merciful, and all-powerful God who is the creator of the universe and human beings over which He rules.

THE TIMES ARE CHANGING

Much to the dismay of generations of conservative Christians past, the new and upcoming generations accept homosexuality and favor same-sex civil rights, same-sex civil unions, recognized marriages, and same-sex church weddings. Studies compiled a decade ago shows that people and voters under 26 do not have any opposition at all, and every year that age gets higher and today is probably over 35. As the longtime saying goes: "***the times they a-changin'.***"

Author's Note: This Book and Treatise are a compilation from many sources on the same subject. See the Complete List of Bibliographies, References, and Suggested Readings in Appendix II

CHAPTER 2

SEX AND MARRIAGE IN THE BIBLE

What does the Bible really say about Sex and Marriage? This chapter will surprise you.

We hear virtually daily from our local pastors to the omnipresent ultra-conservative evangelical fundamentalists: "***the Bible says***" or "***God commands***" and similar admonishments. This chapter will discuss what the Bible actually does – or does not – say about marriage, monogamy, polygamy, homosexuality, the role of women, and sexual relations between opposite and same-sex couples.

WARNING: This chapter will totally infuriate most of the religious clerics and laymen alike in the world from our local pastors to the Bible-banging televangelists. I am sure the lynching mobs are tracking me down and the stakes are being fired up.

IMPORTANT POINT: The Bible was not meant to be a sex manual but it sure turned out that way. It is practically a steamy romance novel. In all honesty, practically all the explicit and implicit sex stories are found in the ***Old Testament*** while the ***New Testament*** Gospels are practically completely devoid of any sex.

THE BIBLE AS A SEX GUIDEBOOK

The Bible tells us of premarital sex (without admonishment).

The Bible tells us of extramarital sex (without admonishment).

The Bible tells us of prostitution (without admonishment).

The Bible tells us of polygamy (without admonishment).

The Bible tells us of homosexuality (without admonishment).

The Bible tells us of lust (without admonishment).

The Bible tells us of flagrant sexual activity (without admonishment).

BIBLE STUDY: Patriarch Judah solicited a prostitute while he was away from home on a business trip. The prostitute was Tamar who turned out to be his daughter-in-law. Tamar became pregnant with her father-in-law's babies. She had twin sons, Perez and Zerah. They were in King David's lineage. Jesus was an ancestor of King David. That makes Jesus an ancestor of bastards, the illegitimate children of a prostitute. That tarnishes the family pedigree of Jesus.

"Marriage is between one man and one woman." How many times have you heard that line preached at the top of a conservative's voice? How many times have you heard, "***The Bible says marriage is between one man and one woman***"? What about those that say, "***We must protect the sanctity of marriage***," or "***sexual intercourse should only be between a husband and his wife***," or "***sexual intercourse is only for procreation within the sanctity of marriage.***"

BIBLE STUDY: It surely seems in both ***Exodus*** and ***Deuteronomy*** polygamy is the norm. Men not only have multiple wives, they also have concubines (common law wives) and multiple extramarital sexual partners. ***Exodus*** 21:10 explicitly says that if a man takes another wife, "***he shall not diminish the food, clothing, or marital rights of the first wife.***" ***Deuteronomy*** says if a man has two wives that ***he must treat sons born to each wife equally***.

Adultery, polygamy, and concubines are commonplace in the Bible, at least in the ***Old Testament***:

- **Abraham** fathered children with Hagar, Keturah, and Sarah.
- **Jacob** marries sisters Rachel and Leah and then takes two slave concubines, Bilhah and Zilpah.
- **David** was married to Abigail, Ahinoam, Maacah, Haggith, Albitah, Elogah, Bathsheba, among others.
- **Solomon's** harem supposedly included 700 princesses and 300 concubines, according to ***1 Kings.***

GOOD NEWS FOR MEN: Tell your wives that polygamy is sanctioned by the Bible so go marry that girlfriend, or at least ask her to move in with you and your wife, and have sex with both of them! Start a harem!

BAD NEW FOR WOMEN: Sorry, women are permitted only to be married to one husband.

BIBLE STUDY: ***Deuteronomy*** permits Jewish men to stone to death any young woman who they discover is NOT a virgin when they get married. If a woman does not bleed on her wedding night by him penetrating her hymen, he is to take her to the doorstep of her father and stone her "***because she committed a disgraceful act in Israel by prostituting herself in her father's house.***" (***Deut***. 22:21)

GOOD NEWS FOR MEN: According to the Bible, there is a full money-back guarantee that if your wife is NOT a virgin (previously used goods) on your wedding night; you can bring her back to her father's house, stone her, and leave her there. In this day and age, I would think most husbands will be returning their wives and annulling their marriages after the wedding night. Side Note: I wonder how many women whose hymens have been broken by non-sexual activity (e.g. horseback riding) that were returned to their fathers' houses and stoned erroneously?

BAD NEWS FOR WOMEN: Sorry it is all bad news because "***the Bible says so.***"

WHAT DOES THE NEW TESTAMENT SAY ABOUT SEX?

The biggest opponent of any sexual activity is Paul. Whether you know him as Saint Paul, the Apostle Paul, or the Disciple Paul, I will only refer to him as "Paul." For those who have read ***Alternative Christianities – Volume I*** knows why. We don't know much about Paul other than he had a vision or dream 10 years after the death of Jesus and went from executioner of Christians to Christianity promoter, albeit "his version" of Christianity against the repeated "cease and desist" orders from James, John, Peter and the other real Disciples in Jerusalem. Paul is not a good representative of Christianity or the Gospels but he surely has a lot to say about it, especially when it comes to sex.

We don't know much about Paul's history. Was he married? Did he have a wife and children? Was he a reformed homosexual? Did he have one or several bad sexual experiences? [There is an unauthenticated story written about the latter scenario for which he was repenting.] We **DO KNOW** that Paul did not approve of **ANY** sexual activity, including marriage or childbearing. He vehemently preaches that the followers of Jesus should avoid any sexual activity including inside marriage. Sex distracts the converts, including husbands and wives, from their main goal in life commanded by Jesus. Celibacy demonstrates self-control and a commitment to Christianity.

BIBLE STUDY: There are some ***New Testament*** Gospels that marginally agree with Paul's preaching. The Gospels of ***Matthew, Mark,*** and ***Luke*** instruct a Christian's commitment to Jesus Christ has to be held in a higher priority than their families. The ***Gospel of Luke*** quotes Jesus as saying, "***Whoever comes to me and does NOT hate father and mother, wife and children, brothers and sisters, yes, and even life itself, cannot be my disciple***" (14:26). It seems that spreading the good news about Jesus and His teaching is more important than marriage and families. Jesus did not marry nor was He a family man. Marriage is presented as a waste of time, though once married, divorce is not permitted.

<u>IMPORTANT POINT:</u> Jesus never preached about the "***sanctity of marriage or families***." Nor did He object to the local people's attitude toward marriage, fidelity, polygamy, homosexuality, prostitution, or any of the arrays of flagrant sexual activities of modern day Judea or the Greco-Roman Empires in which He lived and preached. Nor did Jesus condemn those same activities that were practiced by His Jewish predecessors as described in the Hebrew Bible, or the Christian ***Old Testament,*** which He knew so very well.

<u>WHO SAYS WHAT?</u>

Anyone who has read ***Alternative Christianities – Volume I*** already knows the answer to that question; or that there are MULTIPLE answers to that question. The Bible, in this case, the ***Old Testament,*** is full of inconsistencies and contradictions; there is not ONE stance regarding marriage, the status of women, or sexual proprieties. In ***Genesis***, the woman who has sex with her father-in-law and bears his child is a heroine [maybe because her bastard children are the predecessors of King David and thus predecessors of Jesus]. Prostitution is perfectly acceptable according to ***Exodus*** and ***Deuteronomy***. The Bible is pretty much clear that sex is a male privilege and women are the subservient property of men. While women must guard their virginity until they are married in order to save the reputation of her father and then remain absolutely faithful to the man she marries; however, men can have sex with as many women as they like before and after they are married. Paul's epistles in the ***New Testament*** tell the faithful that they should avoid sex and marriage to keep themselves pure in anticipation of the afterlife. This is just some examples of the many inconsistencies and contradictions not only between the ***Old*** and ***New Testaments*** but also between the books in each. More times than not, the same morals apply still today, thousands of years later.

MISINTERPRETING THE BIBLE

Never has anything written in black and white been so misinterpreted. Never has the innumerable flaws of any book been so overlooked as if none of them ever existed. I can't get over how supposedly well-educated ministers are able to conveniently pick and choose words and phrases to push their selective Christianity. There is NO way they can possibly act like the Bible is absolutely straightforward and simple to understand and follow. Makes you wonder if ANY OF THESE MINISTERS EVEN BOTHERED TO READ THE BIBLE IN ITS ENTIRETY. Anyone who has unbiasedly read the Bible in total can see its numerous inconsistencies, falsehoods, contradictions, and historical impossibilities. Different Biblical books take sides, are at odds with each other, downright disagree with one another, contradict earlier teachings, making physically impossible claims about human beings (e.g. ages) and the human nature of God (e.g. anger). There are cases where the narratives by today's standards are patently immoral.

One thing that is consistent is that the Biblical teachings regarding sexual desire, marriage, monogamy, and so much surrounding the human body are entirely inconsistent. Some Books condone and approve of polygamy while subsequent books highly recommend celibacy. Some books espouse the wonders of erotic desire, even homoeroticism; then subsequent books strongly warn us that sexual desires are evil. Some books place their women on pedestals, and practically the very next book tells women to remain silent and fade into the background. Your children and property are your most important assets to be protected and passed on; later books tell you to cast away your family and worldly possessions in order to gain admittance to Heaven. Contrary to the teachings of many fundamentalist ministers, the Bible does not offer a clear set of teachings or instructions for life but is a constant flux of inconsistencies and contradictions. Meanwhile, these self-proclaimed evangelists attempt to define Biblical sexual morality to specific people or groups of people all in the name of God. Worse, they condemn the violators to eternal damnation.

So what side of the issues, both today and yesteryear, is the Bible ***irrefutably*** on? Is it for or against slavery, polygamy, same-sex committed relationships, masturbation, abortion, submission of women to their fathers and husbands, pre-marital chastity, post-marital abstinence, and women as productive members of society? Can God's call to serve Him come to everyone, irrespective of their gender or sexual orientation? Does God prohibit gays and lesbians to serve as ordained ministers, priests, and rise to the office of bishop, cardinal, or even Pope?

IMPORTANT POINT: There is nothing explicitly or implicitly stated anywhere in the ***New Testament*** Gospels that prohibits any of these things, or that Jesus Christ spoke against them.

A FEW HIGHLIGHTS OF SEX STORIES FOUND IN THE BIBLE

- The ***Song of Songs*** is a very erotic poem found in one of holiest books in the Bible with a vivid wording of lovers' sexual desires for each other.
- The ***Book of Ruth*** contains stories about King David who engages in sexual intercourse outside of his marriage and is blessed for committing adultery.
- Polygamy is considered to be accepted and normal in ***Exodus*** and ***Deuteronomy;*** it even goes as far as giving instructions on how to have a "good marriage" with slave concubines and second wives.
- Jesus NEVER neither "corrected" or "admonished" these practices; nor said, as some evangelicals claim, that marriage should be ONLY between one man and one woman. During Jesus' time, sexual desires and practices were NOT a problem that needed to be addressed otherwise we assume He would have at least spoke to it.
- ***Leviticus, Joshua,*** and ***Revelation*** espouse that sexual indulgences and deviations are worse than worshiping a false god other than one true God. Passages were used to depict outsiders as abhorrent to Yahweh.
- The worst form of sexual deviance in the Bible was not adultery, incest, or bestiality, but was sex with angels.
- Also abhorrent was Jewish men have sex with foreign women.
- The Bible has strong teachings against regarding men avoiding the impure blood of menstruating women, the spilling of precious semen, and mandatory circumcision of all males. Advances in later medical

sciences have changed these attitudes, but if the Bible is supposed to take precedence over secular science then why are these prohibitions not still followed by "the people of the Book" under penalty of damnation?

- There were major concerns to keep the temple pure from the pollution of menstrual blood. Men were warned to avoid menstruating women. Today, menstruating women can now attend synagogues full of men.

IMPORTANT POINT: Apparently the Bible is a lot more liberal in its attitude and acceptance of sex than the strict evangelical and fundamentalist Christian ministers would preach, allow, or let us know about. They like to pick and choose which passages and interpretations of the Bible they will enforce; some are called "**Cafeteria Christians**."

TIGHTENING THE BIBLE BELT

In the "Bible Belt" of the United States, one of the prudist areas of the Western world, sex is still severely restricted by strict evangelical ministers – albeit in accordance with their selected passages in the Bible.

In these ministries abstinence-only programs, Girls are told that every time they have sex they are playing Russian roulette with their lives, their health, and their reproductive organs. You may get very sick, you may never be able to have children, you may die, and you can infect your future spouse and your children – you may even kill them.

Abstinence-only educators preach to boys to control their animalistic impulses, of course with the assistance of God. Boys need strong Christian parenting and good Christian girl to marry. Parents are responsible for overseeing their daughters and their sexual desires, and protect them from those uncontrollable boys who want to touch them and have sex with them. Parents must watch their daughters closely to ensure their bodies remain pure for their future husbands. If either the parents or children fail, the abstinence-only educators warn that disasters of Biblical proportions will follow. These ministers claim that the Bible supports them, especially in the case of their daughters. The only part that is missing is the command to take a bride who is not a virgin to her father's house and stone her in front of it; someone should remind them of that passage and insist upon it being enforced to the fullest degree.

Men just have to wait until marriage then they are free to have sexual escapades. There are so many passages in the Bible celebrating finding sexual pleasures outside the bonds of marriage. There are no repercussions, no diseases to be had, and no one dies. A fact not touted is that many of Jesus' ancestors were adulterers and adulteresses – Ruth, Solomon, King David, Boaz, Naomi, and Bathsheba, to name a few – whose extramarital sexual relations received God's blessing, not God's curse, and a long, productive, and positive life. Jesus does not have many ancestors of whom He can be proud.

SEX STORIES IN THE BIBLE

THE *SONG OF SONGS*

The ***Song of Songs*** is a biblical love poem tells of towering breasts, flowing black locks, kissable lips, and the joy of sexual fulfillment. No other Biblical passage is as blunt and forthright – so much so it is surprising that this book made it into the Bible at all. However, the ***Song of Songs*** is one of the most widely read and studied of all the Hebrew Bible books. The ***Song of Songs*** was found circa A.D. 73 among the Dead Sea Scrolls which were hidden in caves in the desert outside of the city of Jerusalem. It was mentioned by name by 1st-century Jewish historian Josephus in his list of sacred books as important [***The Complete New Testament***, Nashville, Nelson 2006]. A Greek translation of the ***Song of Songs*** is found in 4th and 5th century Christian Bibles. It was included among the sacred Christian books by well-known 4th century Alexandrian Bishop Athanasius. Apparently, the risqué ***Song of Songs*** has always been accepted as being holy.

JONATHAN AND DAVID – A SAME-SEX LOVE AFFAIR

David was a very handsome man. He was brought to Saul where he pleased everyone. We all know that he defeated the Philistine giant, Goliath. More importantly, David developed a "strong bond" with Saul's son and heir, Jonathan. The bond between David and Jonathan was so strong that Jonathan gave David his robe, armor, and sword. This extravagant gesture could suggest there was more than just a friendship. The Scriptures say that Jonathan was willing to transfer his right of succession to David whom "***he loved... as his own soul.***" Jonathan takes "***great delight in David.***" Saul even attempted to arrange for David's death. Jonathan repeatedly chose his friend over his own father (19: 1-7; 20:1-42). Jonathan made a formal covenant with David to remain faithful to him and his descendants. The covenant was sealed with an oath in which David swears with his love for Jonathan, who "***he loved him as he loved his own life***" (20:17).

When Jonathan is killed by the Philistines, David laments for Jonathan: "***I am distressed for you, my brother Jonathan; greatly beloved were you to me; your love for me was wonderful, passing the love of women***" (***2 Sam***. 1:23-26). Jonathan's homosexual love for David also surpassed his heterosexual love of women. Both ***1*** and ***2 Samuel*** is full of the intimacy between these two men that went well beyond friendship to the point of homo-eroticism. Saul was embarrassed by his son Jonathan's love for David that appeared also to be sexual. Of course, most evangelical ministers do everything to avoid concluding this was a homosexual relationship.

THE ADULTERESS AFFAIR OF DAVID AND BATHSHEBA

David succeeded Saul when Jonathan died. David always kept the covenant he made with Jonathan. With the help of Ishbaal, David triumphantly wins the loyalty of all the leaders of Israel and he is installed as the new King in Jerusalem. Now as the new King of Israel, David displays his new status by taking on wives and concubines. He is successful in his military and sexual conquests. One of his conquests was Bathsheba, the wife of one of his commanders.

The ***Song of Songs***, the ***Book of Ruth***, and the stories of King David show how a person's relationship with their immediate family and their sexual desires are mutually exclusive. It is obvious that sex and desire are NOT just confined to the marriage bed of a husband and his wife. The traditional family of today is far from the families of Biblical times. As described in the ***Song of Songs,*** Ruth, Naomi, and Obed were a family with a mutual love for each another.

King David's idea of marriage is nothing remotely consistent with marriages today. His first erotic attachment is homosexual with the son of the King at the time; then he marries several women and ultimately has an extramarital affair with the wife of one of his generals. David has a child with Bathsheba while she was still married to Uriah.

The lovers in the ***Song of Songs*** all had sex long before any marriage ceremony took place. If Ruth, Naomi, Boaz, Jonathan, David, or Bathsheba had listened to today's Christian educators Obed and Solomon may never have been born and history would be completely different if not strategically devoid of influential people.

"PERMISSIBLE MARRIAGES" DEFINED

The people in "Biblical times" were a lot more liberal with the definition of marriage than in the more recent eras. It seems like current day people were more arbitrarily denied the right to get married. Most people today do not realize that it not that long ago, a marriage between men and women of different races were downright against the laws in the United States. It was not until the Supreme Court ruled in 1967 in the famous ***Commonwealth of Virginia v. Loving*** [Loving being an interracial couple married in the District of Columbia who returned to their home in the State of Virginia] that resulted in the antimiscegenation [interracial] laws were struck down as unconstitutional. Not only were the prevalent laws against white and black marriages affected, but the twelve states that had laws outright prohibiting a marriage between a white person and a Native American, and the fourteen states that banned a marriage between white people and Asians. The laws in California were more encompassing prohibiting marriages between "white persons" and "Negroes,

Mongolians, members of the Malay race, or mulattoes" which were in effect from 1850 until 1948. All those prohibitions were struck down by the U.S. Supreme Court.

Those pages in history are all behind us, much to the celebration of many Americans who now can marry outside their race. Now in the 21st century, the U.S. Supreme Court has included "same-sex marriage" as a right under the Equal Rights Amendment. Regardless, it still remains a thorn in the claw of conservative fundamentalist Christians.

Their insistence of the propriety of heterosexual marriages over homosexual marriages is just the continuance of the WASP (White Anglo-Saxon Protestants) exclusionary marriage rules and their feeble attempt to define what the sole "legitimate" marriage is supposed to be. The Bible is the source quoted in their arguments; the same source they used in their miscegenation arguments of the past centuries to justify their rights to own slaves. The evangelicals like to look to ancient Biblical Scriptures in order to solve the problems of the world, which includes defining which marriages that civil government should or should not certify. The Bible does not contain any explicit solutions; there is no single Biblical example of marriage. If anything adultery, polygamy, concubines, and homosexuality are the most common themes in the Bible; therefore, they all should be considered legitimate "marriages" according to the permissiveness in the Bible.

IMPORTANT POINT: Nowhere in the Bible does it explicitly say that "marriage is between one man and one woman;" and very seldom does one man in the Bible just have a relationship and sex with just ONE woman.

This all is just a good argument for the need to have a separation of church and state in a multi-philosophical society. No matter how much politicians and pastors might argue their viewpoint, marriage is a "civil right" – it is NOT a "religious right." It is NOT a privilege allowed for some persons but denied to others. The Marriage License is a "civil document" obtained at a town hall not at a church, unlike a baptismal certificate. If churches or religious leaders could decide who can marry, will Christians be allowed to marry Jews or other non-Christians? If Christianity was allowed to rule over marriages, can they deny Muslims to marry, or Buddhists and Hindus? Ultimately, they all collectively can deny Deists and Atheists to marry?

WOMEN HAVE NO RIGHTS IN THE BIBLE

One consistent theme throughout the Hebrew Bible, the ***Old Testament,*** is that women have NO RIGHTS! Women have always been the property of the men at the absolute disposal of their fathers and husbands. The ***Song of Songs*** is a good example of how sex is not restricted just to marriage, especially for women. The ***Book of Ruth*** and the story of David imply that the only function of marriage is to continue the male lineage. In ***2 Samuel***, David is accused of violating Uriah's property rights when he seduces Bathsheba, not her rights. Many times in the Bible women are bartered in the negotiations between men. Men actually demonstrate their success and wealth by the number of wives, concubines, and children they have. Polygamy is the accepted norm, along with extramarital sexual relations.

IMPORTANT POINT: Why then do today's evangelical, fundamentalist, conservative, strict Bible-thumping Christian ministers NOT demand concurrence to these same time-honored Biblical multiple sexual guidelines **today**? They preached that the Bible is the direct word of God and must be followed. Guess there are some exceptions!

These principles of female property, marriage, and genealogical were never emphasized or even mentioned by Jesus or His Disciples. By default, we can assume that Jesus and His Disciples concurred with the Biblical relationships.

THE *BOOK OF GENESIS*

Does the ***Book of Genesis*** define marriage or not? Or does it define marriage different than we define it today?

Genesis **allludes** to the definition of marriage "***Therefore a man leaves his father and mother and clings to his woman, and they become one flesh***" (2:24). I said "**allude**" because it surely is not practiced anywhere in the Old Testament as a "one man – one woman" relationship. What is practiced is the command to the woman: "**your desire shall be for your man, and he shall rule over you**" (3:16). Stories attest to Eve not being Adam's first and only wife.

Genesis is really the story of two creations. Elohim (YHWH) created all of mankind at the same time: "***God created Adam in his own image; He created them male and female, and both were made in God's image.***" Why was then a need to create the female later from the rib of Adam? Some theorize that the word ***adam*** is properly translated as "humankind" not the proper name Adam. The original human beings were both male and female, or were the first human beings were neither a man nor a woman but lacked any discernible gender. Such is believed to be the nature of the angels who are without a demonstrative sexual gender. Male and female may be one flesh because they are both made of the same material (***ad amah*** = fertile soil). Or that they are considered one flesh because God formed the female from Adam who was already created by Him. These theoretical but plausible explanations discredit that marriage is between one man and one woman if they were formed from the same flesh.

These creation stories show that human sexuality is a "gift" from God. He did not have to lead us down that path; some of His living things and creatures are asexual or able to reproduce without the need for another's intervention. He has taken humans out of the animal kingdom sexually. It is not just an occasional primordial instinct but is based on a physical and emotional attraction. Maleness and femaleness are the basis for sexual desire of the opposite sex. As in the animal kingdom, humans can be attracted to someone of the same sex whether it is sexual or purely platonic. Yes, God's animals can be homosexual. Sometimes, a person's friendships with people of the same sex are stronger than with their spouse. Then a person's sexual desires can sometimes be a hindrance to a productive friendship.

The creation stories in ***Genesis*** are preached by ministers as purportedly describing what God intended marriage to be, conveniently overlooking the differences between ***Genesis 1*** and ***Genesis 2.*** Then they fail to take into consideration the implications of heterosexual marriage in ***Genesis 3*** when Yhwh says, "***I will greatly increase your pangs in childbearing, in pain you shall bring forth children, yet your desire shall be for your husband, and he shall rule over you***" (3:16). So does this means then is that a woman's sexual desire for her husband is not a blessing from God but a punishment! A woman is subject to a man's sexual whims and pregnancies. It must also be realized that childbirth has always been a dangerous proposition and risk to lives of women, a thousand-fold worse in the ancient millennia past.

Ask any Sunday school teacher, what is the hardest question they are inevitably asked. If Adam and Eve had three sons, with whom did these sons have sexual intercourse to produce the subsequent human race? There are stories not cited often enough of how Eve was Adam's second wife. The first wife who bore the girls did not get along with Adam and offended God. She was banished from the Garden. This first and second wife story seems to make more sense than Adam and Eve's sons having no one with whom to mate; less incestuous than their sons mating with their blood sisters.

THE THEORIES ABOUT THE ADAM'S SEXUALITY

Some Jewish rabbis interpret "***in the image of God He created them, male and female***" to mean humans were created not as two different sexes but as one gender. Rabbi Samuel bar Nahman explained in ***Genesis Rabbah*** in the 5th century C.E. "***When the Holy One created the first man He created him with two faces. Then He split him and made two bodies, one on each side, and turned them about***." The Rabbi is saying that the first human being was androgynous meaning that Adam possessed the genitals of both sexes. Then it was in ***Genesis 2*** that God took the rib from Adam and made the androgynous Adam into two beings from one. There are many that find this interpretation plausible.

Some followers of Paul shared this same view of an androgynous being that was divided. This comes from Paul's epistle to the Church in Galatia: [in Christ] "***there is no male and female***" (3:28).

THE GOSPEL OF PHILIP

The ***Gospel of Philip*** states, "***If the female had not separated from the male, she and the male would not die.***" The Disciple Philip goes on to say that Christ came to reunite the male and female giving life to those who understand the truth **(*Gospel of Philip* 70)** [Bently, Layton, trans., ***The Gnostic Scriptures: Ancient Wisdom for the New Age,*** Anchor Bible Reference Series, New York, Doubleday, 1987, p.343]. The 3rd century ***Gospel of Philip*** gives a different version of creation; however, it was ultimately rejected by emerging Christian Church. It was retained by the Gnostic theologians.

They claim that the stories about creation were **modern inventions** of the origins of Christianity and Judaism which were necessary to establish the Biblical need for heterosexual love and marriage. The rabbis in ancient times interpreted the separation of the female from the male as a way to justify male-female sexual intercourse. This was never intended to take away from considering that the original human form had dual sexuality. Some Christians in ancient times considered the separation of the primitive androgyny was not that marriage and sexual relations are both natural and good but that they preferred sexual abstinence altogether. Such abstinence was preparing humans for their heavenly fate in which they would not be married. It also replicated the pure non-sexual lives of Adam and Eve before they were expelled from the Garden of Eden which implies that Adam and Even never engaged in sexual activity before then.

IMPORTANT POINT: It is worth noting that no pre-Christian writings had any mention of the nature of marriage before the 1st century B.C., very long after these supposed stories were first told.

IS *GENESIS* REALLY ABOUT FARMING?

The stories about creation in ***Genesis*** may not be as straightforward as they are made out to be. As much as it may seem the stories in ***Genesis*** are used to make Biblical statements about marriage and sex, they can also be used as commandments to protect the humans from the perils of the frail ancient agriculture. Farming and fertility storylines can be interchangeable. The first humans were put in charge of every creature and every plant with the command "***to be fruitful and multiply.***" This can be interpreted as commanding the humans to care for the land and make the food grow. Successful cultivation of food in those primitive times was hard work. If they failed, they would starve. Although producing children was also important, it was also a very dangerous activity for these ancient humans. There were very high infant mortality rates and also high rates of maternal deaths in the process of childbearing; thus making the "***to be fruitful and multiply***" a difficult proposition to try to fulfill. At the beginning of the human race, it was the fertile land that "multiplied" and "fruitful" yield that caused men to prosper. Men had to sow their seeds in both the fertile land and the childbearing (fertile) females. Like the land, women have no choice but to dedicate their bodies to childbearing.

There are numerous stories in the Bible of patriarchs and their liberal marriage arrangements which are not considered acceptable or legal today. All the patriarchs seem to have been married to more than one wife, take concubines in their homes who were essentially unmarried (common-law) wives, and spread their seed among these women in order to father as many children as he could (considered another source of wealth).

- Abraham, the father of "Abrahamic" religions of Judaism, Christianity, and Islam married Sarah she bears him a son late in her life, Isaac.
- Before Isaac when Sarah failed to conceive Abraham fathers a son with Sarah's slave Hagar.
- Near the end of Abraham's life, he takes a second wife named Keturah and fathers four more sons.
- Isaac has twin sons, Esau and Jacob, and they both had multiple wives and concubines.
- Jacob marries two sisters, Leah and Rachel, along with their two maids, Bilhah and Zilpah.
- Jacob fathers twelve sons with his multiple wives and concubines.
- Esau marries three women, Adah, Oholibamah, and Basemath with whom he has five sons.

IMPORTANT POINT: We don't know whether all these revered ancestors were in complete defiance of God's instruction that "***marriage is between ONE man and ONE woman***" and all can be found in the flames of eternal damnation, **OR** these instructions were probably **made by man** many subsequent generations and centuries later.

It is worth keeping in mind that when these stories in ***Genesis*** were put in writing they were in the context of their civilization and the demands of agriculture. These stories, laws, and instructions were intended to address the unique circumstances faced by these ancient human beings NOT the Christian and Jews of the 21st century.

THE MARRIAGE LAWS OF MOSES

The Law of Moses found in the Hebrew Bible (the ***Old Testament***) does have many commandments to the Jewish men with strict guidelines about the handling of women, slaves, and property. They were commanded not to commit adultery, not to covet a neighbor's wife, slaves, ox, donkey, or other property. Judaism believed in honoring marriage arrangements, the equitable treatment of wives and concubines, the paying the full price to a father for an unmarried daughter he seduced, the execution of adulterous men and women, and a man was forever cursed if he had sex with the wife of his father (***Deut***. 22:30). Under Biblical law, a girl can only be wed and avail of herself sexually to the Jewish man that has been chosen for her by her father. Virgin daughters were one of the most valuable properties of fathers; fathers were injured and rob of their price when a daughter's virginity was lost before she was married.

Conversely, if a man falsely claimed that his bride had premarital sex to which her parents proved otherwise by producing evidence of her virginity by the blood on the sheets they saved from the wedding night, the groom would be heavily fined. However, if the charge proves to be true that the woman was not a virgin on their wedding night, then she would be stoned to death by the village folk at the entrance to her father's house. This also punishes and embarrasses the father for his negligence in failing to properly supervise his daughter as required by the Judaic law.

IMPORTANT POINT: Now for all those proponents who condone and want a return to the "**traditional Biblical definition of marriage**," there it is all laid out in the preceding paragraph. A girl was the property of her father to be disposed of at his will; a girl's husband can only be chosen by her father; a man's multiple wives and concubines should all be treated equally; a man who takes a girl's virginity must pay the price demanded by the father; a man who finds his bride not to be a virgin on their wedding night should take his bride to her father's house and stone her to death; and any adulterous man or woman should be executed! **Let us all return to what is says is acceptable in the Bible!**

BIBLICAL MARRIAGE UNDER JESUS CHRIST

According to the Gospels that were included in the ***New Testament***, Jesus said nothing or very, very little about marriage. In fact, Jesus tends to play down marriage and family relationships. Jesus does not encourage the "***be fruitful and multiply***" commandment given to them. Why if they are so important does Jesus not stress the obligation of men to supervise and take care of their wives, daughters, and slaves? Jesus seems to promote that His followers be beholding to each other, "***love thy neighbor***," forsaking the ties to their families and their obligations to marry and produce children.

Jesus Christ portrays a different attitude than His predecessors; especially in the ***Gospels of Matthew*** and ***Luke***. Jesus turns sons against fathers, fathers against sons, sons against mothers, daughters against mothers, and mothers against daughters. Jesus warns those against loving their fathers, mothers, sons, or daughters more than they love Him for they will not be worthy of Him. In the ***Gospel of Luke,*** this is clearly stated: "***Whoever comes to Me and does not hate father and mother, wife and children, brothers and sisters, yes, and even life itself, cannot be My disciple***" (***Luke*** 14:26)

In the ***Gospel of Matthew***, Jesus is even more emphatic when His mother and brothers come to the temple to retrieve Him and He responds: "***Who is My mother and who are My brothers? Here are My mother and My brothers! For whoever does the will of My Father in Heaven is My brother and sister and mother.***" (***Matthew*** 12:48-50).

It would appear from Jesus' viewpoint that your family is your fellow believers, not your blood kinfolk. People are not united by birthright, blood, or marriage but by connecting with others who share and follow the teachings of Jesus.

IMPORTANT POINT: The evangelical fundamentalist Christians and their ministers, who incessantly quote the Bible, **CONVENIENTLY** overlook **Jesus' direct teachings**: "***He who divorces his wife and marries commits adultery... She who leaves her husband and marries commits adultery... What God has joined together, let no man put asunder"*** [which is said by all Christian ministers after the couples exchange their solemn vows at every marriage ceremony]. Only the Catholic Church strictly enforces the "no divorce" rule, ALL OTHERS conveniently ignore Jesus.

BIBLE STUDY: For those that may not have read Volume I, or as a quick refresher, the ***Gospels of Matthew, Mark,*** and ***Luke*** all appear to relate the same stories in the same order probably because WHOEVER wrote ***Matthew*** and ***Luke*** used the previously-written ***Mark*** as their source. Biblical scholars refer to these three Gospels as the **Synoptic Gospels;** derived from a Greek term meaning "***to see together***" (***syn*** = "together" + ***optic*** = "to see"). This explains why the narratives and structure of these three Gospels are so coincidentally similar. ***Matthew*** and ***Luke*** contain sayings of Jesus that are not found in ***Mark***. Also,

WHOEVER wrote ***Luke*** actually acknowledges in his first lines: "***many have undertaken to set down an orderly account of the events that have been fulfilled among us... I too decided to write an orderly account.***" All three Gospels share many of the sayings of Jesus which can be found almost verbatim in the previously written ***Gospel of Thomas.*** Although it was known about since the 2nd, 3rd, and 4th centuries, the lost ***Gospel of Thomas*** which was re-discovered 1945 is considered to be by Biblical scholars **"The Fifth Gospel"** and is believed to be the source document for three synoptic Gospels. The ***Gospel of John*** is completely different from ***Matthew, Mark,*** and ***Luke*** and is considered to be more aligned with the **Gnostic Gospels** of ***Peter, James,*** and ***Philip***.

THERE IS NO SEX OR MARRIAGE IN THE AFTERLIFE

Jesus does make is apparent there is no sex or marriage in the afterlife. The Gospels suggest we should look forward to the benefits of having androgynous bodies in heaven with no need for sex or marriages: "***When they rise from the dead, they neither marry nor are given in marriage, but are like angels in heaven***" (***Mark*** 12:25).

A saying of Jesus found in the ***Gospel of Matthew*** makes a similar point, and even more dramatically:

> "***Not everyone can accept this teaching, but only those to whom it is given. For there are eunuchs who have been so from birth, and there are eunuchs who have been made eunuchs by others, and there are eunuchs who have made themselves eunuchs for the sake of the kingdom of heaven.***

> ***Let anyone accept this who can.*" (*Matthew** 19:11-12)

The ***Gospel of Matthew*** goes as far as implying that voluntary castration is a good option for those wanting to enter the Kingdom of Heaven. Some Christians apparently took Matthew seriously, such as 2nd century Justin Martyr who tells of a Christian man seeking to castrate himself in order to guarantee his celibacy. Third-century Origen was believed to have removed his testicles to comply but then in his later years, he realized Jesus was more concerned with sexual self-control. The 4th-century assembly at the Council of Nicaea in A.D. 325 actually forbade the Christian clergy to castrate themselves. Jesus' recommendation of celibacy did not mean the need for physical castration but instead just a sex-free lifestyle. This could be by avoiding sexual relations altogether or by not remarrying after a spouse dies.

THE SANCTITY OF MARRIAGE

There was one thing that Jesus and His teachings were very strict about and that was the "sanctity of marriage." In fact so much so that Jesus regularly contradicted the ancient Hebrew practices of His predecessors. Jesus REPEATEDLY forbade extra-marital sex, i.e. divorce, adultery, illicit sexual desires, and outright lust.

> "***You have heard that it was said, 'You shall not commit adultery,' but I say to you that everyone who looks at a woman with lust has already committed adultery with her in his heart***" (***Matthew*** 5:27-28).

Jesus felt the same strict way about divorce. Although Hebrew covenant specifically allowed their men to divorce their wives, the ***New Testament*** Gospels more than implying that divorce should be forbidden and remarriage is "adultery." When the Pharisees specifically asked Jesus, "***Is it lawful for a man to divorce his wife?***" (***Mark*** 10:2), Jesus replied from ***Genesis*** 1:27 and 2:24:

> ***"God made them male and female."***
>
> ***"For this reason, a man shall leave his father and mother and be joined to his wife, and the two shall become one flesh."***

To which Jesus added:

> ***"So they are no longer two, but one flesh. Therefore <u>WHAT GOD HAS JOINED TOGETHER, LET NO ONE SEPARATE</u>."***

When the Pharisees told Jesus that the Law of Moses permitted divorce initiated by Jewish men, **Jesus forbade remarriage** for either the husband or the wife. In His instructions to the Disciples, Jesus equated divorce and remarriage the same as committing adultery:

> ***"Whoever divorces his wife and marries another, commits adultery against her, and if she divorces her husband and marries another, she commits adultery"*** (vv. 10-12)

The only exception is found in the ***Gospel of Matthew*** as well being put in a very different way:

> ***"Whoever divorces his wife, except for unchastity, and remarries commits adultery."*** (v.9) ***"But I say to you that anyone who divorces his wife, except on the ground of unchastity, causes her to commit***

> ***adultery; and whoever marries a divorced woman commits adultery"*** (v. 32).

Unlike ***Mark***, Jesus offers an exception directed at men with sexually immoral wives. Also different than in ***Mark***, Jesus said these things publicly in front of the Pharisees and others; rather than to the Disciples alone. Basically, according to ***Mark***, **remarriage is impossible**, whereas in ***Matthew*** **remarriage is an option for some men if the divorce from their wife is due to her adultery.**

The ***Gospel of Luke*** also tells Jesus' teachings regarding marriage and divorce slightly differently:

> ***"Anyone who divorces his wife and marries another commits adultery, and whoever marries a woman divorced from her husband commits adultery"*** (***Luke*** 16:18).

So according to Luke, divorce in and of itself is not forbidden so Jesus does not contradict the ancient Hebrew laws; however, remarriage is not permitted, in other words, separation is acceptable but remarriage is not allowed.

IMPORTANT POINT: As previously noted, as much as the evangelical fundamentalist Protestant ministers are always quoting and like to enforce the text of the Bible **verbatim**, it is ONLY the Roman Catholic Church that strictly enforces Jesus teachings that divorce and remarriage are NOT allowed; and furthermore enforces Jesus' commandment, "***what God has joined together, let no one separate.***" Although Roman Catholic couples can separate, and even in some cases may get their marriage annulled, but if they get divorced (which is not recognized by the Church) and if they remarry they are excommunicated, i.e. no longer considered a Roman Catholic and can no longer partake of any the Church's sacraments.

BIBLE STUDY: For the readers of ***Alternative Christianities - Volume I***, there is no surprise that there are many discrepancies and contradictions among versions of these same narratives in the Gospels in the ***New Testament***. Scribes have altered and edited passages trying to harmonize what was said in one Gospel with what was said in other Gospels.

THERE IS NO SINGLE VIEW ON MARRIAGE IN THE BIBLE

In summary, one thing we can be sure of is that whether it is ***Genesis, Exodus, Deuteronomy***, or ***Mathew, Mark, Luke***, there simply is no consensus as to sanctity or purpose for marriage. We CAN say that the union of a man and a woman serves for **procreation**. In ***Exodus*** and ***Deuteronomy,*** men can have sexual intercourse with multiple wives, concubines, and as many of their slaves as they like. The ***New Testament*** Gospels do not mention procreation at all; they are more concerned with the resurrection of deceased bodies. The Hebrew laws as recorded in ***Exodus*** and ***Deuteronomy***, although they may differ in detail, suggest that marriage is an arrangement to protect the property and interests of the free Israeli men. In the accounts of ***Genesis,*** the emphasis is not only on the procreation of the humans but also the importance of the fertility of the land and production of food for the humans to live. ***Genesis*** punishes Eve's ambition and all future generations of females with the extreme labor pains of childbirth. Jesus' teachings in the ***New Testament*** Gospels are quite different than found in the Hebrew Bible.

For many of the modern day Protestant ministers, married hetero-sex is not only wonderful but the only permissible type of sex. It is what God has given to us and as such the only acceptable form of sex. Many of these evangelical ministers have gotten into trouble by voicing their belief that wives should be totally submissive to their husbands and his desires in marital bed. Marital sexual intercourse in their eyes is raised to a religious act.

Not all of original Christians in ancient times would agree with these modern-day ministers. For some of the ancients although sexual intercourse was considered by some as a gift from God, for others it was to be avoided as an "evil" human impulse and shortcoming that, except for producing children, nothing good can come from having sex.

PAUL: SEX IS EVIL

PAUL: ONLY PUT YOUR PENIS IN THE RIGHT PLACE

Paul is famous, or infamous, for his epistles denouncing sex. Paul in his letter to his followers in Rome warned them that inappropriate sexual desires will lead to their spiritual and physical death. Claiming that they have given themselves over to false gods, the one true God punishes them by giving them unacceptable passions which lead them to perform "unnatural" sex acts:

> ***"Their females exchanged their natural use for that which is against nature, and in the same way the men, having given up the natural use of females, were consumed with desire for one another, men in men achieving the shame and dishonor***

> ***which, having received [it], bound their error to themselves.*** (1:26-27)

This passage of Paul may be difficult to understand; however, the meaning of Paul's message is unmistakable. Paul's considers "natural" sex as the "nature-intended" use by men of female bodies in the sexual act. In ***I Romans*** "***exchanged their natural use***" means the desire to forgo natural sex between men and woman is "exchanged" for sex with women by women or men by men. Paul mirrored the ancient view that "maleness" is equated with "penetration" and "femaleness" is equated with "being penetrated." Although homosexuality was freely and naturally practiced in the Greek and Roman Empires (and some homoerotic episodes are told in the ancient Hebrew Bible), Paul insists that God will abandon those who succumb to "***unnatural***" desires and acts, and they deserve to be put to death.

MALE AND FEMALE ROLES

Paul assumed that women were the "natural" passive recipients of a penis during sexual intercourse; therefore, it was "unnatural" for men to penetrate other men. Roman and Greek men were "naturally" dominant by nature and status and, as such, they usually were the dominant player in the sexual act; but to Romans and Greeks, it did not matter whether they were having sex with women, boys, or slaves. Adult free men who were penetrated could lose his honor and status.

IMPORTANT POINT: Paul seems to be alone in his preaching whereas no one and nowhere else in the ***New Testament***, **including Jesus**, preached against homosexuality, especially if it is supposed to be such a damning sin.

Paul was definitely in the minority in relation to the attitude of many of Greeks and Romans of his time. They did not diminish the stature of men who engaged in sexual relations with other men, it was commonplace. The penetrated man kept his manliness and preserved his honor as long he was penetrated by someone a higher status. There was always that sexual attraction of mature men to youthful beautiful boys. This was so common and accepted that it was often found in Roman and Greek literature and art: young adolescent boys was idolized in poetry, immortalized in statues, pictured on vases, and commonly found in mosaics and frescos. Of course, then there are numerous stories of the god Zeus' love for his young male companion, Ganymede. For the Greeks and Romans, the loyalty of a beautiful willing boy was a treasured possession and source of praise or jealousy from their friends. It was "**perfectly natural**" for men to have sexual relations with both women and boys.

Roman god Priapus puts it bluntly:

> "***Grant me a flowering youth; grant that I may please good boys and girls with my naughty prick, and that with frequent fun and games I may chase away the worries that harm the soul, and that I may not fear old age too much***."

Apparently, the Roman gods also felt that it is appropriate for adult males to desire both girls and boys to be receivers of their "***naughty pricks***." In fact fun, games, and homoerotic sex are good for the soul and fend off old age.

PAUL: THE END IS NEAR

One of Paul's major preaching was for his followers and all Christians to prepare themselves spiritually for the **imminent** end of the world, the second coming of Jesus Christ, and the resurrection of the dead. Part of that preparation was to be "sexually pure" in order to be admitted into the Kingdom of Heaven.

Paul strongly felt that the unmarried remain unmarried and celibate, "***In whatever condition you were called, brothers and sisters, there remain with God***" (***1 Cor***. 7:24); "***Our Lord, comes!***" (***1 Cor***. 16:22); and "***the day of the Lord will come like a thief in the night***" (***1 Thess***. 5:2).

Paul also applied this principle of "***in whatever condition you were called*** ... ***there remain***" to divorce, "***to the married I give this command – not I but the Lord – that the wife should not separate from her husband, but if she does separate, let her remain unmarried or else she reconcile to her husband, and the husband should not divorce his wife***" (***1 Cor***. 7:10-11). On this point, Matthew and Luke independently agreed with Paul that any divorce is forbidden.

Even decades after Paul's death in the early 60's his followers perpetuated these teachings of purity not only in Rome but also in the churches in Asia Minor. Included were Paul's expectation that the end of the world is near, God's judgment would happen, and pure would be resurrected. In case nobody has noticed, almost 2,000 years have passed and the world is still here, Jesus has not returned, and the pure ones have not been resurrected.

In Paul's defense, there is a series of letters falsely written in his name. His disciples continued his teachings and emphasized control of one's desires which they felt coincided with having an orderly household and having firm control over their wives, children, and slaves. These false letters of Paul are firmly placed in the ***New Testament*** and considered to be written by Paul. These letters have been discredited by several Biblical scholars as **"pseudepigraphical,"** i.e. attributed to one author, in this case Paul, but obviously not written by him. These pseudepigraphical letters include ***Colossians, Ephesians, 2 Thessalonians, 1 Timothy, 2 Timothy, Titus, and Hebrews***.

The ancient Christians suspected that every letter claimed to be written by Paul was **not** written by him. Origen's treatise about ***Hebrews*** says:

> "***The diction*** [of Hebrews] ***does not exhibit the characteristic roughness of speech of phraseology admitted by the Apostle*** [Paul] ***himself, the construction of the sentences is closer to Greek usage, as anyone capable of recognizing differences of style would agree."***

THE PASTORAL EPISTLES

Some decades after Paul's death, another author took it upon himself to interpret Paul's teachings. He is commonly referred to as the "Pastor." He focused on ***1 Timothy, 2 Timothy,*** and ***Titus*** that are often referred to as the "***Pastoral Epistles.***" They were directed to church leaders such as bishops, priests, and deacons who must defend against misleading and downright false teachings. The "Pastor" presented himself as Paul in his writings giving advice to these church leaders that they needed to be strong leaders and strong men. He warns that without them the Christian community would crumble, physical desires would take over, and women and the youth would go astray. Only virtuous men should be chosen by the Church basis on how well they are able to control their sexual desires and those of their underlings.

Women MUST be kept in check otherwise their desires will surely get the best of them. The Pastor preaches that women must avoid excessive adornment: avoiding gold, pearls, and flashy clothes; otherwise such women are an embarrassment to their families and the Church. Women are prone to sin and bad desires.

A man's wife must live in silence and under full submission to their husband demands. Eve's sin is the cause for every woman's submissiveness and as such, every descendant of Eve is inherently dangerous and needs to be controlled by their husbands. It is only through marriage that women can save themselves by childbearing and living lives with holiness and, above all, modesty. Paul was actually stricter; he commanded both women and men to remain virgins. Paul even preferred they remained unmarried.

This put the Pastor in contradiction with Paul and the teachings of Jesus found in the Gospels of ***Matthew, Mark,*** and ***Luke***. Women were not the only ones lectured by the Pastor. Young men are especially motivated by their intense innate sexual passions. The Pastor "urge the younger men to be self-controlled" (***2 Tim*** 2:6) and "shun youthful passions" (***2 Tim***. 2:22). The Pastor admits that he was formerly controlled by his uncontrolled passions. Like Paul, he overcame these worldly shortcomings by living a highly disciplined life and forming a strong relationship with Jesus Christ and His

Church. The Pastor also outlined the guidelines for the high standards that the Church officials should be held. The overseers, or "***episkopoi,***" must remain above reproach, married only once, temperate, and respectable. Their own households and children must be submissive and respectful. The "***diakonoi***" or deacons must be "serious and never indulge in too much wine." The "***presbyteroi***" or elders should be above reproach and married only once.

A COMPARISON OF PAUL'S AND THE PASTOR'S VIEWS ON SEX

Paul's Letters:	**Desires** must be controlled. Lack of control indicates your abandonment of God.
The Pastor:	**Desire** is extremely dangerous, especially for women and young men.
Paul's Letters:	**Sexual Intercourse** must be avoided; if married have sex regularly to avoid temptation. A man should never submit to penetration whereas a woman must always submit to penetration.
The Pastor:	**Sexual Intercourse** is required to be submitted by women for procreation in order to be saved by God. Widows must remarry to avoid temptation. Husbands should control their subordinates.
Paul's Letters:	**Marriage** is intended for the weak that are not able to control their sexual desires. Married men should keep their wives under control. Wives, children, and slaves always should obey the male head of their household.

The Pastor — **Marriage** may only be entered into once by church leaders. Virgins and widows must marry and are not allowed to remain celibate. Ineligible men cannot be leaders in the Church.

IMPORTANT POINT: The Pastor, like Paul, were "over the top" in their teachings about "Christianity;" both preaching things that were never mentioned by Jesus Christ while He was on this earth. In other words, they were preaching their own brand of Christianity.

ILLICIT SEXUAL UNIONS

Leviticus, for those of you that follow the ***Old Testament*** or the Hebrew Bible, has a whole host of illicit sexual acts, unions, and prohibitions. These include but are not limited to incest, intercourse at particular times, sex with some people, or in certain ways. ***Leviticus*** never gives any logical rationale for these prohibitions. It seems to expect semen to be deposited only in the appropriate receptacle, i.e. a woman's vagina.

So if the receptacle is deemed "unclean" (i.e. menstruating), the property of another man (i.e. married), a barren woman (i.e. unable to produce children), a non-Israeli woman, or an angel, then a man is having sexual intercourse with a receptacle that is not permitted. Semen was considered all too important for the purpose of procreation to be wasted on a receptacle that would not produce a child, produce a child out of wedlock, an illegitimate child, or have a mixed lineage. ***Leviticus*** is very clear, the seed (semen) of a man must never be wasted, or ever spilled upon the ground (masturbation).

Leviticus 18 expressly forbids:

1. Intercourse with a woman who is menstruating (18:19),
2. Intercourse with the wife of a relative or another (18:20),
3. Lying with another man in the same manner as with a woman (18:22), and
4. Bestiality (18:23).

These same prohibitions are reiterated in ***Leviticus*** 20 but this time with specified punishments:

1. In the case of adultery with the wife of a neighbor [which can apply also to divorce and remarriage]: "***both the adulterer and the adulteress shall be put to death***" (20:10);
2. In the case of a man lying with another man in the manner as with a woman: "***both of them have committed an abomination; they shall be put to death***" (20:13); and
3. Bestiality: "[the man] ***shall be put to death, and you shall kill the animal... you shall kill the woman and the animal; they shall be put to death***" (20:15-16).

Following their perceived logic:

- Intercourse with a woman who is menstruating is considered a waste of semen because the man has ejaculated into a woman who cannot become pregnant at that time.
- Ironically, adultery is punishable by death in ***Leviticus*** despite all the adulterous affairs of their Biblical ancestors and heroes. A wife is the property of her husband and is forbidden to have sex with other men. And a man who has intercourse with another's wife is

seen as stealing his property. Similarly, by injecting his semen into another man's wife can lead to unwanted pregnancy, and worse the mixing of semen of the two men can lead to confusion as whose child and heir is born.

- The "lying with a man as with a woman" and "bestiality" also involves the waste of one man's semen into another man or into an animal, or vice versa, the animal's semen into a woman, all of which cannot result in pregnancy.

LYING WITH A MAN AS WITH A WOMAN

Given the present obsession by evangelical fundamentalist ministers with this one repeated line in the ***Old Testament,*** **AND NONE OF THE OTHER AFOREMENTIONED PARTS OF LEVITICUS,** is worth an extended discussion. First, it is well-worth noting that the admonishment against "***lying with a man as with a woman***," is found **NOWHERE ELSE** in the ***Old Testament*** or ***New Testament.*** To the contrary, there are other references through the Bible forbidding incest, adultery, and bestiality. Prohibitions against bestiality are found in ***Exodus*** and ***Deuteronomy;*** incest is also condemned in ***Deuteronomy*** and ***Ezekiel;*** and adultery is forbidden in ***Exodus, Deuteronomy,*** and ***Numbers***. These two references in ***Leviticus*** to "***lying with a man as with a woman***" are entirely isolated **but command the most energy of these ministers!**

IMPORTANT POINT: It also calls into question as to the actual translation of the Hebrew words (***miskeba a***) which gave us the English translation of "***lying with a man as with a woman***." These words are used nowhere else in the

Hebrew Bible so we have no reference as to its accurate literal translation or is it just an uneducated guess?

As has been discussed several times previously in this series, male-male bromances, homoeroticism, or even sexual liaisons were strewn throughout the Hebrew Bible, and furthermore, they were considered commonplace, socially acceptable, and the norm in the Judaic, Greek, and Roman cultures. Many times adult men sought out and desired to dominate and penetrate slaves or beautiful young women (or men) as an assertion of their masculinity. The thing the Hebrew Bible really considered a real "perversion" was the mixing of species, i.e. acts of sex with animals.

BIBLE STUDY: The one prominent and revered Biblical man guilty of this damning offense of a man who "***lies with a man as with a woman***" or "***when one man uses another man as he would a female***" was King David himself who is a direct ancestor of Jesus Christ. According to ***1 Samuel***, Jonathan's love for David surpassed his love for women. He chose David to be his life partner. It was implied that Jonathan was the receptive sexual partner in their love relationship. It was said that Jonathan was so loved by David as if he was his "wife." This seemed acceptable in ***2 Samuel*** because it was implied that David was the "man" to Jonathan's "woman." Meanwhile, Jonathan was King Saul's son and his heir.

IMPORTANT POINT: For the writers of ***1*** and ***2 Samuel,*** the abominations cited in ***Leviticus*** were conveniently overlooked. David's affair with Jonathan was used to secure his position as King. It was illegitimate and as such, it delegitimized the royal lineage of Jesus Christ.

THE POLITICS OF THE BIBLE

Some Biblical scholars interpret ***Leviticus*** as condemning the perverse sexual practices of the non-Israelites; at the same time justifying their failure to observe the sexual morals of their Judeo-Christian-Islamic patriarch Abraham, the prophet Moses, Solomon, and the royal lineage of King David. Such immoral behavior goes all the way back to ***Genesis*** to Cain killing Abel, the shameful behavior of Ham, or Joshua in the story of ***Rahab***. ***Exodus, Deuteronomy, Judges***, and other Biblical books prohibit the pagan gods of the outsiders, and illicit flagrant sex and prostitution. The Hebrew Bible warns that suffering will be inflicted on those who participate in illicit sexual behavior (at least maybe some participants).

However recent decades have seen the opposite unfold. Many ultra-conservative, evangelical, fundamentalist ministers blame the violence and ills of the modern world as God's retribution for secular society's acceptance of atheism, abortion, liberalism, women's rights, non-Christians, and gays and lesbians. Some go to the extreme by calling for the execution of those that do not convert and conform to Christianity. Reminiscent of the shameful eras of killing the infidels during the Inquisitions and Holy Crusades of the Middle Ages. Today, most of the blame for violence is on Muslims, conveniently ignoring their violent Christian past. Violence is encouraged by the modern "christian" preachers (like killing abortion doctors) while criticizing the Muslims for their holy wars and threats to kill the infidels. The Christians consider anything done in the name of Christ is justified as in the Middle Ages; whereas non-Christian's acts of violence are an abomination. Of course, the non-Christians have the same opinion of the violent acts perpetrated by Christians.

<u>Author's Note: This Book and Treatise are a compilation from many sources on the same subject. See the Complete List of Bibliographies, References, and Suggested Readings in Appendix II</u>

##

CHAPTER 3

HOMOSEXUALITY IN THE NEW TESTAMENT

There are stories galore written on same-sex love and homosexuality in the Bible. There are so many more stories of same-sex love and homosexual relationships in the ***Old Testament*** but we will forego repeating them here but try to keep this treatise more about Christianity and the ***New Testament.*** Jesus even seems at times to be anti-family.

Christian churches have no problem, or even conspicuously, quietly pass over any passages in the Bible which references or positively portray homoerotic desires and homosexual relationships. It is amazing how evangelical and fundamentalist "christians" (sorry, I have a hard time capitalizing that "c" when referring to them) love to quote ***Leviticus*** ignoring many sentences full of abominations, to decry homosexuality (which is in itself a "stretch"); however, they ignore all the homoerotic references and obvious homosexual relationships throughout the ***Old Testament***. Again, I will restrict my treatise to the ***New Testament***; this does not imply that the ***Old Testament*** does not have homoerotic references and homosexual relationships abound. More importantly, I refer to these evangelicals as "**cafeteria christians**," picking and choosing which passages are more important to them about others while ignoring the ones that pertain to their sins.

Then one of the passages these "**cafeteria christians**" love to quote to justify their salvation is:

> "***For God so loved the world that He gave His only begotten Son, that whosoever believeth in Him should not perish, but have everlasting life."*** (***John*** 3:16)

However, they have their own interpretation of that succinct line. They like sitting as Judge and Executioner in place of God Himself claiming that this same God that created homosexuals exempted them from that same salvation. Good News! This promise is for ALL God's children, not just the heterosexuals! I think a lot of people are going to be very surprised when "they" are the ones who will be denied admission through Heaven's pearly gates. Whole books have and can be written on the subject of this chapter but I will limit it to some poignant highlights.

SEXUAL ORIENTATIONS

JESUS

It is so rarely talked about, but over time there have been certain passages in the ***Gospel of John*** about the "Beloved

Disciple of Jesus" which can be interpreted as proposing that Jesus actually may have been gay, or at least had a proclivity leaning towards a homosexual or bisexual orientation. He hung out exclusively with twelve men and was never married unless you believe like some that He was married to Mary Magdalene.

ST. AELRED

St. Aelred was a 12th century English abbot in Rievaulx. His feast day is celebrated by the Catholic Church every January 12th. He professed that a loving relationship between males was a perfectly natural and beautiful phenomenon. The following passage of Aelred describes the joy of being in love with another man:

> ***"It is no small consolation in this life to have someone you can unite with you in intimate affection and the embrace of a holy love, someone in whom your spirit can rest, to whom you can pour out your soul, to whose pleasant exchanges, as to soothing songs, you can fly in sorrow.... with whose spiritual kisses, as with remedial salves, you may draw out all the weariness of your restless anxieties. A man who can shed tears with you in your worries, be happy with you when things go well, search out with you the answers to your problems, whom with the ties of charity you can lead into the depths of your heart.... where the sweetness of the spirit flows between you, where you so join yourself and cleave to him that soul mingles with soul and two become one."***

Not surprisingly, St. Aelred and this passage has become a gay manifesto.

The use of the words '***cleave to***' and '***two become one***' are a direct reference to the same text in Genesis:

> ***"Therefore shall a man leave his father and his mother, and shall cleave unto his wife; and they shall be one flesh"*** (***Genesis*** 2:24)

It seems Aelred deliberately used these same words to put the relationship between two men the same as a husband and wife.

CHRISTOPHER MARLOWE

Christopher Marlow was an English playwright born in 1564. He is well known for writing acclaimed dramas such as ***Tragical History of Doctor Faustus*** and ***Edward II.*** This known gay man might have perceived some gay undercurrent in the ***Gospel of John***. The story goes that he was killed in 1593 in an apparent drunken tavern brawl but some are suspect that his murder was actually more complex and covert. His murder, Richard Baines, said that Marlow deserved to die because he had blasphemed about Jesus and the Beloved Disciple saying:

> "***St. John the Evangelist was bedfellow to Christ and leaned always in his bosom, that he used him as the sinners of Sodoma."***

KING JAMES

This is the same King James that commissioned the Bible named for him the ***King James Version***. It was noticed that from an early age the future King showed a marked propensity towards homosexuality and male companionship. One of his great lovers was George Villiers who was the Duke of Buckingham. George rose to this important royal position from the lowly job as a cupbearer thanks to his "relationship" with James. The King James of the ***King James Version*** fame equated the Biblical story of Jesus and the Beloved Disciple to his homosexual relationship with his lover George:

> ***"I love the Earl of Buckingham more than anyone else, and more than you who are here assembled.... Jesus Christ did the same and therefore I cannot be blamed. Christ had his John, and I have my George."***

BISHOP HUGH MONTEFIORE

In 1967, Hugh Montefiore gave a speech at Oxford that caused quite an outrage, even though he went on to become the Bishop of Birmingham in the Church of England. He questioned why Jesus never got married:

> ***"Men usually remain unmarried for three reasons: either because they cannot afford to marry or there are no girls to marry (neither of these factors need have deterred Jesus); or because it is inexpedient to marry in light of their vocation (this has also been ruled out); or because they are homosexual in nature in as much as women hold no special attraction for them. Of course,***

> ***the homosexual explanation is one which is completely ignored. According to the Gospels, women were his friends but it is the men whom he is said to love."***

Bishop Montefiore felt that Christians needed to get over their willful blindness at the idea that Jesus was gay and just acknowledge the simple evidence in front of their faces.

THE RICH MAN

Jennings (2003) indicate that Jesus may have had a gay eye when in the ***Gospel of Mark*** Jesus' attention is turned toward a "***rich young man***." When this man approached Jesus to ask what was necessary to attain eternal life, Jesus told him to keep the commandments and then:

> ***"Jesus, looking at him, loved him and said, 'you lack one thing, go sell what you own, and give the money to the poor, and you will have treasure in Heaven; then come, follow me."*** (***Mark*** 10:17-22)

But why did Mark say that Jesus "***loved him***"? Jesus did appear to have known this young man before that meeting? What can this mean that Jesus "***loved him***"? And what did Mark mean when he said: "***Jesus, looking at him***." What can that mean? The original Greek word used was "***emblepein."*** This word suggests that Jesus "***scrutinizes his appearance.***" Translated into a contemporary language it could be construed that Jesus was "***eyeing him up.***" Was Jesus taking delight in this man's physical beauty? Were Jesus' sexuality and desires being aroused? This "***looking***" and "***loving***" would be strongly consistent with Jesus being "***fully human***," and as such, a "***sexual***" human being.

THERE WAS A NAKED YOUTH IN THE GARDEN OF GETHSEMANE?

Also in the ***Gospel of Mark,*** there is another story of a young man, a naked young man, who was with Jesus in the Garden of Gethsemane the night He was arrested. Mark tells us:

> ***"And they all forsook Him and*** [the Disciples] ***fled. And a youth accompanied Him, clothed in a linen cloth over his nudity. And they seized him. And he left the linen cloth fled nude."*** (***Mark*** 14:50-52)

The original Greek words that were used to describe the boy cloaked in just a linen cloth would imply that the boy was a male prostitute which was commonplace in the Hellenistic culture of that era. Jeremy Bentham is firm in his belief that there was some sort of a homoerotic incident taking place that night in the Garden of Gethsemane. Amazing that all His "faithful" Disciples ran off (maybe they were more of "traitors") while Jesus and the boy were arrested. The boy narrowly escapes because of the loose linen clothing. Who was this boy and what was he doing there? It is more remarkable that Mark thought this boy being there was significant enough that he included it in his Gospel.

THE SECRET GOSPEL OF MARK

A "***Secret Gospel of Mark***" is known because it is referenced in a letter by Clement of Alexandria believed to have been written about A.D. 200, and it was actually discovered in 1958. In it is a story of a woman who came to Jesus asking Him to raise her brother from the dead. Jesus goes to the tomb, rolls away the stone, and calls him to life.

> ***"But the youth, looking upon Him, loved Him, and began to beseech Him that he might be with Him. And going out of the tomb they came into the house of the youth, for he was rich. And after six days Jesus told him what He wanted him to do and in the evening the youth comes to Him wearing a linen cloth over his naked body. And he remained with Him that night, for Jesus taught him the mystery of the Kingdom of God."*** (Jennings 2003 p.115)

Clement's letter is clear that the earlier versions of the ***Gospel of Mark*** were more open about Jesus' gayness. Of course, these versions were called heretical and suppressed by the Church leaving only one acceptable ***Gospel of Mark.***

JESUS' HEALS THE GAY CENTURION'S LOVER

Remember the Sunday school story about Jesus healing the Centurion's "***servant***." Biblical scholars and linguistic experts lean toward this servant that Jesus healed was, in fact, the Centurion's "***male lover***."

The story is found in two places in the New Testament, Matthew (8:5-13) and in Luke (7:1-10); although not identical. In the ***Gospel of Matthew***, Jesus entered Capernaum and a Gentile Roman centurion came up to Him. Centurions were powerful and brutal high-ranking Roman military leaders who were key players in keeping the Jews in-line. It surely would be highly unusual for a Roman centurion to beg for help from a lowly Jewish preacher.

This centurion asks Jesus, "***Lord, my servant is lying at home paralyzed, suffering dreadfully***." Jesus immediately promises to go to the centurion's home and heal him. However, the centurion humbly replied, "***Lord, I am not worthy to have you under my roof; only say the word and my servant will be healed.***" Jesus, amazed at the centurion's faith, responds, "***You may go; as you have believed, let it be done for you.***" Matthew assures us that "***at that very hour the servant was healed.***"

This same story is different (really different) in the ***Gospel of Luke***. Luke relays that the centurion would not leave the side of his sick boy servant who he dearly loved. The boy is so near death that the centurion sends the Elder of the Jews to plead with Jesus to cure his "***servant***." The Elders tell Jesus that the Roman centurion, although he is a Gentile, is a good man who has built a synagogue for them. Jesus agreed to go to with the Elders to the centurion's home. Right before they arrive at the home, the centurion sends friends out to stop Him, with the same basic message, "***Lord, trouble not thyself, for I am not worthy that thou shouldst enter under my roof, wherefore neither thought I myself worthy to come unto thee, but say in a word, and my servant shall be healed"*** (***Luke*** 7:6-7). Luke then tells us that when the Elders returned to the centurion's home they "***found the servant whole that had been sick***."

How do you know that the Centurion and his servant were in a homosexual relationship? There are two different Greek words used when referring to servants. The "common" Greek word is "***doulos***" which more succinctly means a "servant" or "slave." However, in the ***Gospel of Matthew,*** the centurion uses the Greek word "***pais***" in referring to his servant that primarily means "boy;" but can also secondarily mean slave, servant, or even one's son. The difference is that the latter term refers to a person who is young, endeared, or not the equivalent of an adult. "***Pais***" was also the word for "boy slaves" who were used for sex, which was not only common but fairly normal among the Greeks and Romans. Because in the ***Gospel of Luke*** the only word used is "***doulos,***" it is very unlikely that the boy is the centurion' son. It is noteworthy that "boy" can be used derogatorily in referring to an adult male who is considered socially inferior; such was common in the South as late in the mid-20th century.

The ***Gospel of Luke*** gives us more hints about the relationship between the centurion and the sick boy when Luke used the Greek word "***entimos.***" That term definitely infers that the boy was indeed very dear to the centurion; they were in a close emotional relationship. Let's face it, slaves die all the time and are just property replaced by their owners.

The descriptive Greek word also used was "***parakaloon.***" From how that word was used in other areas of the Bible it clearly means "real desperation" such as when a person is helplessly watching the life leave the body of a lover. This pretty much indicates that this boy was a sexual partner with whom the centurion had grown very fond. There was nothing to indicate anything to the contrary that the centurion was not a homosexual.

Considering that Jesus Christ was God, or at least the Son of God, He would not to be naïve to their relationship. We hope the possibility that the centurion's relationship with the boy was a homosexual one would not have escaped the intellects of Jesus, Matthew, or Luke. So it could be assumed, much to the dismay of today's conservative religious leaders, that Jesus did encounter a gay man, a Roman Gentile Centurion, and cured his homosexual lover. And then Jesus remarked that this Roman Gentile had more faith in Him than many of the pious Jews, and Jesus said the centurion should be emulated by those who truly accept His teaching. In the ***Gospel of Matthew***, Jesus uses this opportunity as a clear lesson: "***And I say unto you, that many shall come from the East and the West, and sit down with Abraham, and Isaac, and Jacob, in the Kingdom of Heaven. But the children of the Kingdom shall be cast into outer darkness; there will be weeping and gnashing of teeth"*** (***Matthew*** 9:11-12). When Jesus speaks of the ***"many who shall come from the East and the West"*** He is referring to the "Gentiles" who are good people and follow Jesus will surely "***sit down with Abraham, Isaac, and Jacob in the Kingdom of Heaven."*** Whereas, many who believe they are the rightful "***children of the Kingdom"*** **<u>will be disappointed</u>**."

Jesus did NOT distinguish between Jews or Gentile, Israelis or Romans, heterosexuals or homosexuals. Jesus did not exclude but praised the Roman centurion, who was in a homosexual relationship, it was important to Jesus that the centurion had faith in Him. Jesus did not hesitate for even a moment to cure the sick servant but He cared more about the centurion's love for his dying servant. Jesus' tribute to the gay centurion is not surpassed anywhere else in the Gospels.

Jesus shocked the chief priests and elders when he told them: "***Verily I say unto you that the tax collectors and the prostitutes*** [will] ***go into the Kingdom of God before you. For John came unto you in the way of righteousness, and you believed him not; but the tax collectors and the prostitutes believed him"*** (***Matthew*** 21:32).

In an ironic twist, thousands of times every day and every Sunday at Mass for the past 2000 years in the Catholic, Anglican, Episcopalian, and Orthodox churches around the world, right after the bread and wine has been consecrated as the body and blood of Christ at the high point and most solemn moment in the liturgy, the congregation is required to repeat thrice aloud the words of the gay Roman centurion:

"Lord, I am not worthy to receive you but only say the word and I shall be healed."

Christ seems to make it abundantly clear that His mission on Earth was to extend His hope of eternal salvation to all of humanity. But it seems that the Christian Church through the ages and in today's world adamantly has resisted this universal salvation and has arbitrarily excluded different minority factions of His human creations. Whereas, it seems that Jesus actually went out of His way to cure the Gentile Roman Centurion's "boyfriend."

IMPORTANT POINT: There has never been a recorded instance that Jesus condemned homosexuality.

WE WERE BORN THIS WAY

The Lesbian, Gay, Bisexual, and Transgender (LGBT) community is faced every day with Christian churches and preachers failing to recognize them as part of God's creation of His beautiful and diverse children. Lady Gaga says it best in her hit song "***Born This Way***,": "***God makes no mistakes! ...We were born this way.***"

These narrow-minded preachers believe that God created everybody to be heterosexual and that therefore homosexual behavior is just another sort of evil crime just like murder and stealing. As such, homosexuals deserve to be condemned and eternally punished. They love to **misquote** the Bible to say God created a man and a woman. Well technically

God created a man, Adam, and then from that man's rib, he created a woman, Eve. There is nowhere in the Bible that it is explicitly said men and woman were created as pairs. Jesus Himself never mentioned that all people should marry a person of the opposite sex; something He never did.

These so-called "christians" preachers just grasp at straws because it is easier to coalesce their congregations around principles of hate instead of love. And they call themselves "christians" or "followers of Jesus Christ"! No wonder they have image problems (covered in a preceding chapter).

In the ***Gospel of Matthew*** Jesus sets forth God's view of heterosexual marriage to some Pharisees with His famous line, "***what therefore God hath joined together, let not man put asunder,"*** and "***And I say to you, whoever divorces his wife, except for immorality, and marries another woman commits adultery"*** (***Matthew*** 19:3-12).

IMPORTANT POINT: It is so utterly amazing how these ultra-conservative evangelical christians love to quote ***Leviticus*** from the ***Hebrew Bible***, what they call the "***Old Testament,"*** about what is an "abomination" but they **COMPLETELY IGNORE** the words of Jesus Christ when it comes to divorce that re-marriage is committing adultery!! **WORSE** is that when they get married and take their so-called "solemn vows" in a Christian church officiated by a Christian minister before God and a room full of Christian witnesses, and the Christian minister proclaims **JESUS' WORDS**: "***what therefore God hath joined together, let not man put asunder,"*** but still they have no problem with 50% of those couples getting divorced and most getting remarried. I guess Jesus' words in the ***New Testament***, or the ***Christian Bible***, are of much lesser importance than

Leviticus? Funny how that works! Could you imagine how many they will lose from their congregations if they forbad divorce and remarriage just like the Catholic Church does?

Jesus appears to make it clear that heterosexual marriage may not be for everyone: ***"Not all men can accept this teaching, but only those to whom it has been given. For there are eunuchs who were born that way from their mothers' womb; and there are eunuchs who were made eunuchs by men, and there are also eunuchs who made themselves eunuchs for the sake of the Kingdom of Heaven. He who is able to accept this, let him accept it."***

Let us sidestep to understand the meanings of the word ***"eunuch."*** According to many Biblical glossaries, a "***eunuch***" is a "chamberlain" or men who do not have sex with women or who were unable to procreate. Obviously, they were considered the safest to be left around women such as alone in a harem. Also, they had no need to leave their wealth to their children because they did not have any children. As such, they were the safest to be employed in private or government services with the least fear that they would be financially dishonest to support their wives or families.

There are three types of eunuchs:

1. **Castrated men** – men and boys who become eunuchs at the hands of other men, or in essence, men and boys who have their testicles intentionally cut off so that they can work in certain sensitive capacities.

2. **Voluntary celibates** – men and boys who make themselves eunuchs in order to enter the Kingdom of Heaven. These essentially are religiously devout men and boys who voluntarily abstain from sex such as Catholic priests and all Catholic monastic religious orders as they are required to do.
3. **Homosexuals** – boys who are born eunuchs into this world from their mothers' wombs, or otherwise men who have no interested in having sexual intimacy with any women.

IMPORTANT POINT: On its face, it seems that Jesus acknowledged that homosexuality was an intentional creation by God ("***God makes NO mistakes…***") and an integral part of God' plan ("***we were born this way***")! So that means that all these Christian preachers who condemn lesbian and gay people for their "evil lifestyle choice" are in reality condemning God and His plan along with His teachings in His name whose words they claim to be relaying.

Obviously, depending on what type of eunuch you are, does not completely rule out you having any sexual relationships. A eunuch can be a man who does not want to have sex with a woman, but he could be sexually active with other men. There are also eunuchs who were castrated so that they would remain young and pretty while at the same time still able to have sex, such as famously Bagoas, the Persian Boy, and the lover of Alexander the Great.

Another famous case was Daniel with Ashpenza under King of Babylon, Nebuchadnezzar, where it was reported: ***"Now God had brought Daniel into favor and tender love with the prince of eunuchs"*** (***Daniel*** 1:9).

One of the most infamous cases was the castration of Alan Turing who was the brilliant mathematician who was able to break the German Code in Second World War and, as a result, saved countless lives and possibly won the war. Afterward, he was prosecuted because he was a homosexual and sentenced to castration. He committed suicide.

Even in the 21st century, the "anti-gay" ministries who are claiming (albeit wrongly) that homosexuality was never part of God's creations or plan, they damage innocent lives through useless "conversion" programs of prayer.

IMPORTANT POINT: There is absolutely no Biblical reason for this. It really was not all that long ago all physical defects such as being blind, deaf, or mute were believed by such religious fanatics caused by evil and sin.

Like in the case of the blind man, Jesus may have been saying that gay people are just in God's plan. There is no evil or sin involved. Sex is just a normal biological function of human beings the same as eating or defecating. Doctors and scientists all agree that homosexuality is just a normal human predisposition such as liking blonds or chocolate ice cream. It is those same religious fanatics who refuse to believe this scientific truth due to their own ignorance or feel their religious beliefs override scientific evidence (like the age of the earth), or purposely do so to hide their motive to use homosexuality to rile up and coalesce their congregations around hate.

JESUS WAS DEFINITELY NOT A FAMILY MAN

Much to the evangelicals' dismay, Jesus had a very ambiguous attitude to the family, if not downright arrogant:

"If anyone comes to me and does not hate his own father and mother and wife and children and brothers and sisters and even his own life, that one cannot be my disciple. Whoever does not bear the cross and come after me cannot be my disciple" (***Luke*** 14:26-27). This could be construed as a definite anti-family statement by Jesus.

"Hate" is a very strong term; it is usually reserved to define your strong adverse emotion to somebody. Jesus' message here and in other texts seem to contradict all these modern Christian "family value" evangelists who preach the need for "family values." It is almost as if Jesus' is making you choose between your "family values" or the salvation He is offering. It may go as far as being so mutually exclusive and you may have to choose between them.

Is it possible that today's conservative evangelical Christians have actually to turn Jesus' "family values" message inside out? They preach "family values" is needed for salvation. If this is contrary to Jesus' philosophy, does that make promoting "family values" a sin? Taking it a step further, if "family values" has nothing to do with salvation does that mean preaching "family values" is the same as worshipping a false idol in violation of the first Commandment?

Jesus' whole life seems to be completely devoid of any "family values." He never married, He never had any children, and He shows disrespect for His mother and brothers. On a day when Jesus was busy preaching and is told that His family has come for Him, the ***Gospel of Mark*** tells us:

"Your mother and your brothers and your sisters are outside asking for you." And He replied, "who are my mother and my brothers?" And looking at those who

sat around Him, He said, "Here are my mother and my brothers! Whoever does the will of God is my brother and sister and mother." (***Mark*** 3:1-55)

The **only** family that seems to matters to Jesus is not blood (or step) relatives but rather the "family" that has "chosen" to follow Him and do His work. He required His Disciples to leave their family, home and work behind to follow Him. Although some or most of Jesus' Disciples were married and probably had children; they left those families behind. Not exactly a very "family-values-minded" thing of Jesus to do to those Disciples' wives and children.

At one point Peter said to Jesus, ***"Look, we left everything and have followed you."*** Jesus replied, ***"Truly I say to you, there is no one who left house or mother or father or brothers or sisters or children or fields for my sake and for the sake of the Gospel, who does not receive, now in this time, a hundredfold houses and brothers and sisters and mothers and children and lands, with persecutions, and in the coming age life everlasting."*** (***Mark*** 10:28-30)

It appears that Jesus considers families as embracing material assets and wealth. Families are mainly a social and economic structure. This may be why Jesus and His Disciples rejected their families. It also involves the responsibility of securing and passing possessions and wealth from current to future generations. Usually, that includes the home, any real property, and the family business. All must be secured, kept up, and passed to the next generation. All this takes most of your time and leaves you no time to do God's work and prepare for His coming Kingdom. It seems from the quotes of Jesus, He would prefer if you removed yourself from these material responsibilities and commit yourself completely to following Him. You then will have many more mothers, fathers, brothers, sisters, cousins, and family in His Kingdom.

Jesus seems to claim that there is nothing special about your immediate family or relatives; even His relationship to His own mother Jesus is remarkably detached. A woman had shouted to Him, ***"Blessed is the womb that bore you and the breasts that you sucked!"*** To which He replied, ***"Blessed rather are those who hear the word of God and keep it."*** (***Luke*** 11:27-28)

In fact, Jesus never addressed Mary as "***mother***" but always as "***woman.***" Such is the case when at the wedding in Cana when Mary tells Jesus that the host just ran out of wine; Jesus' response to her is abrupt: ***"Woman, what concern is that to you and me?"*** (***John*** 2:3-4) When He is dying on the cross His only comment to Mary is: ***"Woman, behold thy son"*** (***John*** 19:26). Jesus always seems to be so cold to His mother. He is not exactly a loving son to her.

Jesus' has an even a lesser respect for fathers and their part in "family values." Jesus seems to be opposed the domination that fathers represent; considering it counterproductive to His "values" of equality and justice for all. He goes as far as telling Christians that they have only one Father and that is their Creator who is their loving and merciful Father:

"And call no man your father upon the earth, for one is your Father, which is in Heaven." (***Matthew*** 23:9)

Jesus seems to be against all temporal positions of distinction, power, and wealth. He also tells His Disciples not to be called "rabbi" or other such titles. Nobody has a claim to authority over another. Jesus tells us, ***"The first shall be last, and the last first."*** However, the Christian churches amassed themselves in hierarchal titles of authority.

Jesus and the Lesbian, Gay, Bisexual, and Transgender Community

Jesus' lack of favor for the traditional family is really good news for the LGBT community. It debunks the claim by evangelical fundamentalist ministers that LGBT community poses a "threat" to Christian families and "family values."

Besides even sounding so ridiculous, it should be blatantly obvious that gays and same-sex marriages are definitely NOT a threat to opposite-sex marriages and traditional families [unless one or both of the people in an opposite-sex marriage prefer to be with someone of the same sex and now realizes they can make that choice]. This demonization of gay people and their lifestyle is just a ploy to unite Christians by using "hate" to pull them together instead of the "love thy neighbor" commanded by Jesus towards all peoples. Ironically, these conservative Christians have the nerve even to call themselves "christians" whereas they are really less "christian" than the people they are demonizing. It is kind of farfetched that the 10% of the population that are homosexuals are going to cause heterosexuals to stop marrying each other, having heterosexual sex, and making babies. Jesus never said anything plus or minus about preferring either one lifestyle over the other. Jesus meant for respect to apply towards ALL families: opposite-sex couples, same-sex couples, single-parents, straight parents, gay parents, Christian families, Jewish families, Muslim families, Hindu families, Native-American families, Italian families, French families, Chinese families, Korean families,

Japanese families, tribal families, etc. ***These evangelical fundamentalist "christians" should learn to be more like Christ!***

So many LGBT people follow Jesus' example and leave their "blood family" and join a new adopted family of their choosing based on friendship, love, and commonality. These are the "families" and the "values" the way Jesus lived His life. He not only wanted us to look after our own immediate family but also it is our responsibility to look after all our human brothers and sisters in the world. You will find that because of their more extra-familiar lifestyle, the LGBT community does so much for people both locally and worldwide with no regard for race, color, creed, or sexual orientation. There are many instances the LGBT community is at the forefront of Jesus' mission of doing good works.

IMPORTANT POINT: Jesus NEVER preached or endorsed anything about the socio-economic unit called a "family" or an ideology called "family values." His teachings were about "ethical and moral values" to attain salvation.

Jesus did not promote the historical Hebrew law, or Moses' Law, as a requirement for salvation. Eventually, the Disciples abandoned Hebrew Law altogether. The earliest Christians were free to eat pork and shellfish, wear clothes made of different fabrics, and prohibitions on "lying with a woman" outside of wedlock (or menstruating woman). **It was Paul** who urged his followers to avoid sex as much as they could or all together. Paul also prohibited "male-male" sexual intercourse (which technically is impossible) but strangely makes no mention of "female-female" sexual relations.

The time has long past for gays to be welcomed into the "Christian" fold; the same way the Roman Gentiles were welcomed into the Jewish fold and the "Christian" fold. It is time these fundamentalist "christians" realize that God does welcome into His fold the LBGT people which He created with no conditions attached or repentance needed.

It is ironic that the Christian Churches from their inception became patriarchal institutions defining strict gender roles which excluded women. This went without question or contest. The world has changed tremendously in this regard after 2,000 years. Many today feel that many conservative Christian churches' anti-woman and anti-gay stance not only goes against the teachings of Jesus but also goes against His all-inclusive actions while He was on earth. Jesus knows that the whole concept of gender will not exist in the Kingdom of Heaven as sexuality and reproduction do not exist there. For Jesus Christ there are no males or females, no husband or wives, no heterosexual sexuality or gay sexuality – we are all one in eyes of Jesus Christ and the Father Almighty. Jesus never acknowledged any social and sexual distinctions. For those saved, in the Kingdom of Heaven there are no social or political distinctions whether it be along the divisive lines of gender, race, color, creed, class, wealth, ethnicity, nationality, or sexual orientation. All these socio-cultural-economic distinctions are only temporary and transient in our material world but have no place in the hereafter.

IMPORTANT POINT: In the ancient Roman and Greek world at the time of Jesus there was the full acceptance of homosexuality, bisexuality, lesbianism, and long-term same-sex loving relationships. It wasn't until 19th century Western Europe that the concept of homosexuality was defined and condemned. In our brave new 21st century evolving world, the stigmatism of homosexuality, bisexuality, lesbianism, and long-term same-sex loving relationships have gone the way of the kingdoms, serfdoms, and fiefdoms of the Dark

Ages. Like with so many other practices of the mid to late centuries, we now look upon these past generations as being antiquated and at times downright barbaric civilizations.

CHAPTER SUMMARY

Certain facts and issues were discussed in this chapter and are well worth repeating and reinforcing:

1. Nowhere in the ***New Testament*** Gospels, originally known as the "Memoirs of Our Savior," is homosexuality, bisexuality, lesbianism, or same-sex love and marriage mentioned. As discussed in ***Alternative Christianities – Volume I*** and Chapter 15, the Epistles of Paul do not count; Paul was not a Disciple, never met Jesus – a one-time vision is not the same; nor was trained by Jesus. Many of Paul's Epistles were not written by him but are forged.

2. Lesbian, Gay, and Bisexual lives and relationships are found throughout the Old Testament without contest.

3. The anti-gay bias of the evangelical fundamentalist conservative so-called "christian" churches are based on their own personal bigotry and prejudices; in no way are they based on the Bible or any ***New Testament*** texts.

4. The rare admonishments against homosexuality in the Bible are subject to interpretation. Such as condemning male to male sexual intercourse which cannot exist but saying nothing about female to female sexual relations.

5. These same conservative christian leaders of yesteryear used the Bible to sanction Slavery (***Ephesians*** 6:5-9; ***Colossians*** 3:22-4:1; ***Timothy*** 6:1-2; ***Peter*** 2:1). Why don't these same conservative Bible-quoting christian leaders not actively promote slavery in the United States today? Or maybe they are covered in white sheets?

6. These same "christian" churches choose to ignore that the Biblical expressly forbid and condemns "usury" or the taking of interest in order to make a profit (***Exodus*** 22:25; ***Psalms*** 15:15; ***Proverbs*** 28:8; ***Ezekiel*** 18:13, 17, 22:12). Do "christians" picket banks? Do "christian" churches not use banks? Why do these same conservative "christian" preachers not preach from their pulpits a condemnation of banks and credit card companies? Why are they selective in enforcing Biblical passages and who they want to condemn?

7. More importantly, why do these same conservative Bible-banging "christian" leaders (excluding the Catholic Church) ignore a commandment **that Jesus Christ himself gave us** regard to divorce, "***What God had joined together, let no man put asunder,"*** **and any man that divorces his wife and marries another woman commits adultery?** Why do these sanctimonious self-righteous "christian" leaders just like to preach, forbid and condemn only the things in the Bible which do NOT pertain to them or the majority of their congregations?

8. These evangelical fundamentalist ministers ***conveniently*** ignore or adamantly deny all the Biblical stories about homosexuality and same-sex love, such as: Samuel's account of the same-sex love between

David and Jonathan; the lesbian love between of two women in the Book of Ruth; and the highly probable gay Roman centurion who begged Jesus to cure his boy lover (a/k/a "male servant"). These ministers are **willfully blind** to the obvious fact that these are Biblical stories involving homosexuality.

9. When it comes to Jesus Himself as much as these churches profess that He is "fully human" at the same time they deny that He has any human sexual desires. The ***Gospel of John*** relates the strong loving relationship between Jesus and **His beloved Disciple**. Biblical scholars for centuries have not hesitated to describe this as a homoerotic, if not a full-blown homosexual, relationship. As previously discussed, much to the appalling consternation of the evangelicals, there are some factions that believed that Jesus was a homosexual.

10. These evangelical ministers conveniently misrepresented Jesus as being as the biggest proponent of "family values" whereas that is furthest from the truth. Jesus was not an example in His own life nor did His teachings have any mention of "family values," or what some ministers like to narrow it down to "Christian values."

11. Jesus gave preference to the sinners, outcasts, poor, sick, and deprived as candidates for the Kingdom of Heaven; whereas today's evangelical fundamentalist churches prefer to exclude everyone except themselves especially "those" people. However, their sanctimonious ideology turns out to be blasphemous and disingenuous to the teachings and message of

Jesus Christ. They may not be first but last, if at all, in line at the Pearly Gates.

12. These ministers work diligently in their marketing and advertising to tap into people's prejudices, bigotry and hatred to win them over to their erroneous version "Christianity."

13. They say things like God said marriage is between one man and one woman. HE NEVER SAID THAT! NOWHERE DOES IT SAY THAT! <u>But it is OK for several Biblical men to have several wives and concubines</u>. Seems like polygamy, as in Biblical times, should be allowed and be the norm. Also, women are the property of their fathers until they are sold to a man in a pre-arranged marriage. And if you marry a woman who is not a virgin, you should bring her to the front of her father's house and stone her in front of all his neighbors

14. They like to quote ***Leviticus***, especially "man shall not lie with another man as with a woman" which technically a man CANNOT lay with another man as he does with a woman because a man does not have a vagina.

15. But in the same set of admonishments and abominations in ***Leviticus***, they "choose" to ignore: thou shall not eat pork or shellfish, or "mark their bodies" such as with taboos, or have sex with a menstruating woman, or wear clothes of two different fabrics, or plant fields with different crops, etc. etc. etc. <u>**Personal Note:**</u> There must be a humongous traffic jam of people in line waiting who are condemned to Hell.

IMPORTANT POINT: It seems that these "christian" preachers are really "cafeteria-christians" being selective as to what texts they want to preach, and "willfully" ignoring the sins that pertain to them or their congregations (divorce, adultery, etc.); or "altering" their obvious meanings. How is it possible for strict Bible-believing Christians to ignore some of the teachings and passages on a host of subjects while demanding the enforcement of others? It just seems that they like to quote the Bible when they want it to be used to put down other people as sinners, but are "willfully blind" when they "choose" to ignore the more succinct sections that pertain to their own sins. Sorry, I consider that to be the same as the sin of "blasphemy," that is, misusing or taking the name of God in vain. And as it has been said in the banned Gospels, maybe by Jesus Himself, the one sin that will NOT be forgiven is the sin of blasphemy. These so-called "christian" ministers may find themselves standing on a long line with their peers bottlenecked at the Gates of Hell.

Sociologists are quick to point out that homosexuality is not exactly a crime against nature when the God-created innocent animals are approximately the same percentage homosexual as humans.

IF it was such a grave sin like these evangelical fundamentalist ministers make it out to be, then surely Jesus would have renounced it on more than one occasion (like He did about adultery). The fact still remains He never did mention it at all. It is just a ruse by these "false ministers" who use "hate" to preach "their version" of Christianity, not Jesus' message of love.

This is all blatant BLASPHEMY! "***Beware of the false ministers for their wells are empty... and they will lead***

you to Hell along with them." (Jesus to Peter in the ***Gospel of Peter***)

FINAL THOUGHT

It is best put by Lady Gaga in her song ***Born This Way*** when she says: "***We were born this way and God makes NO mistakes.***" To say God makes mistakes is blasphemy. We are all put here with a purpose and are part of His plan.

BIBLIOGRAPHY, REFERENCES, AND SUGGESTED READINGS

Boswell, J. (1980) ***Christianity, Social Tolerance, and Homosexuality: Gay People in Western Europe from the Beginning of the Christian Era to the Fourteenth Century*** (Chicago Press)

Boswell J. (1994) ***Same-Sex Unions in Premodern Europe*** (New York, Villard Books)

Comstock, GD (1993) ***Gay Theology Without Apology*** (Cleveland, The Pilgrim Press)

Hanway, DG (2006) ***A Theology of Lesbian and Gay Inclusion*** (London, Haworth Press)

Helminiah, D (2000) ***What the Bible Really Says About Homosexuality*** (Alamo Square Press)

Horner, T (1978) ***Jonathan Loved David: Homosexuality in Biblical Times*** (Philadelphia, Westminister Press)

Jennings, TW (2003) ***The Man Jesus Loved*** (Cleveland, The Pilgrim Press)

Marks, J (2008) ***Exchanging the Truth of God for a Lie*** (London, Courage UK)

Martin, D (2006) ***Sex and the Single Saviour*** (Westminster, John Knox Press)

McNeil, J (1976) ***The Church and the Homosexual*** (London, Darton, Longman and Todd)

Scroggs, R (1983) ***Homosexuality in the New Testament: Contextual Background for Contemporary Debate*** (Philadelphia, Fortress Press)

Sharp, K (2011) ***Gay Gospels, The: Good News for Lesbian, Gay, Bisexual, and Transgendered People***

(O-Books, John Hunts Publishing, Hants, U.K.) www.thegaygosples.com

Stuart, E (2003) ***Gay and Lesbian Theologies: Repetitions with Critical Difference*** (Aldershot, Aldgate Press)

Vasey, M (1995) ***Strangers and Friends: A New Exploration of Homosexuality and the Bible*** (London, Hodder and Stoughton)

Veyne, P (1985) ***Homosexuality in Ancient Rome, in Aries and Bejin*** (Eds) ***Western Sexuality*** (Blackwell, Oxford)

Wilson, N (1995) ***Our Tribe: Queer Folks, God, Jesus, and the Bible*** (Harper San Francisco)

Author's Note: This Book and Treatise are a compilation from many sources on the same subject. See the Complete List of Bibliographies, References, and Suggested Readings in Appendix II.

PART II – THE GNOSTIC CHRISTIANS

CHAPTER 4

WAS JESUS REALLY GOD?

Before we get into the subsequent chapters, there are some Religions, including some Christian followers of Jesus Christ, do NOT believe that He was actually God incarnate consubstantial with His Father, but a prophet or an emissary. Just so you know, I do personally believe, or would like to believe, that Jesus was God. In my worship, I do profess the Christian Creed, or properly called the "Nicene Creed" issued in A.D. 325 and subsequently amended. Although there are so many valid logical arguments made to the contrary and believed by other Christians and non-Christians worldwide:

> ***I believe in One God, the Father Almighty,***
> ***Maker of Heaven and Earth, of all things visible and invisible.***
> ***I believe in one Lord Jesus Christ,***
> ***The only begotten Son of God,***

> ***Born of the Father before all ages.*** [*i.e. Jesus eternally existed*]
> ***God from God, Light from Light, True God from True God,***
> ***Begotten, not made, consubstantial*** *[i.e. one Being]* ***with the Father;***
> ***Through Him all things were made*** *[i.e. Jesus created the Universe and this world].*
> ***For us men and for our salvation He came down from Heaven;***
> ***And by the Holy Spirit was incarnate of the Virgin Mary,***
> ***And became man…*** *[etc. etc. etc.].*

Ironically, their source was the "***Apostles' Creed***" which needed to be professed from memory by anyone wanting to be baptized as a Christian up to that time, supposedly passed down from the Apostles themselves, **did not say all that:**

> ***I believe in God, the Father Almighty,***
> ***Creator of Heaven and Earth,***
> ***And in Jesus Christ, His only Son, our Lord***
> ***Who was conceived by the Holy Spirit,***
> ***Born of the Virgin Mary…***

Many more facts and dogma **were added** to the "***Apostles' Creed***" by the bishops in 325 at the Council of Nicaea; and even more facts and doctrines to the Apostles' Creed in subsequent Councils by the Bishops.

At the very heart of Christianity are the required beliefs:

- Jesus of Nazareth was God incarnate – meaning that He was God and was "made man."

- Jesus of Nazareth was Jesus Christ – that He was the "Christ" child, a title meaning "the anointed one."
- Jesus Christ was the long-awaited Jewish Messiah and He fulfilled all the prophecies as stated: "***in accordance with the Scriptures***" – the Hebrew Bible (the only reason the Hebrew Bible was incorporated into the Christian Bible was to prove Jesus was the Messiah while dropping every other tradition contained in the Hebrew Bible).

The indisputable facts are:

- Jesus was born in a manger into a lower-class Jewish family whose stepfather was a carpenter in Galilee.
- Jesus was rebellious and was condemned to death for crimes against the state and crucified for sedition.
- It was some time after His death that His followers started claiming that Jesus was a divine being or God.
- Eventually, His divinity was expanded to say that Jesus was God Himself and existed for all eternity.

However:

- Jesus never claimed that He was God. At most, He said, "***YOU say I am...***"
- The twelve Disciples never considered Jesus to be God during His time on earth. They never referred to Jesus as God.
- The real nature of Jesus was debated for centuries. Was He God, or human, or both?
- The Council of Nicaea in the 4th century was called by Constantine to finally decide this debate. The "He was both God and Man consubstantial (one) and

indivisible" faction won out and it became official Christian dogma.

- Not every Christian Church concurred with the Nicene Creed. Some remained with the new Catholic (universal) Christian Church, while others separated from it. These "**Alternative Christianities**" were called "heretics" and were banned and suppressed by the new official Roman state-sanctioned Catholic (universal) Christian Church.
- Sixteen centuries later, the Protestant Reformation caused more religions to splinter from the Catholic Church.

IMPORTANT POINT: In light of the above, how historically and factually was it decided in A.D. 325 unequivocally that Jesus was God incarnate (made man) maintaining both natures "fully man" and "fully God" equally while being eternally consubstantial (one) with His Almighty Father? Especially since He never said any such thing about Himself? If Jesus was God, consubstantial with His Father, how could He suffer and be put to death?

This all seems to make the logic and reason in your brain short-circuit. For some immediately run and hid behind the façade of "it is faith" and the "mystical trinity." This may work within some inner religious circles but does nothing to convince or convert the "outsiders" of Christianity looking in. It causes quite the contrary among outsiders.

Questions:

- So when then did Jesus Christ go from a human prophet/preacher to being the "Son of God"?
- Then when did Jesus Christ go from being the "Son of God" to being "God" Himself consubstantial with His

Father the Almighty, the Creator of the Universe and all things visible and invisible, etc.?

- Who made the decision to require this belief for all Christians, even the dissenting ones, in A.D. 325?
- Was this only said after it was claimed that He ***resurrected Himself bodily*** from the dead; or at least this was ***assumed*** when they found an ***empty tomb***? Some thought it was the Disciples' task or grave robbers.
- In the Nicene Creed, Jesus was <u>now</u>: ***"Born of the Father before all ages."*** Though the Disciples' and Gospels said: ***"Born of the Virgin Mary"***? The Nicene Creed goes on to contradict itself and say: ***And by the Holy Spirit was incarnate of the Virgin Mary, and became man…***

<u>IMPORTANT POINT:</u> Putting theology aside (we know the ambiguous "faith-based" theological answer), from a verifiable and historically factual viewpoint: "***When did this human-born man become divine or even God Himself?***"

DIVINE BEINGS IN ANCIENT GREECE AND ANCIENT ROME

Whether you want to believe it or not, Jesus' story is not unusual or unique. Divine beings and divine humans were common and abound in Ancient Greece and Ancient Rome at, before, and after the time of Jesus.

<u>Jesus had one remarkable life:</u> His mother had a visitor from Heaven in the form of an angel who told her that she was with child although she never had sex with a man and that it would be a male child. Her son would be special as he would be divinely sent from Heaven. His birth and youth were remarkably unusual as if he was truly divine. When he became an adult he began preaching. He went from village to village preaching to anyone who would listen; he gathered throngs due to his dynamism and magnetism. His message was to be less concerned about their material goods in this earthly life but need to live for spirituality and eternity. He did miracles by healing the sick, casting out demons, and raising the dead. His followers were convinced that He truly was a divine being, even the Son of God. He annoyed the authorities of Rome, put on trial, and was executed. However, He would not die but bodily ascended to Heaven where He would live on. To prove that He lives, He would appear to His doubting followers. Many would write books about him.

However, there was another great miracle-working Son of God named Apollonius from the town of Tyana. He was a pagan, a polytheistic worshiper of the Roman gods, and a well-known respected philosopher. His followers knew that he had to be one of the immortals. A book written by his devotee Philostratus, ***Life of Apollonius of Tyana,*** is eight volumes and was written around A.D. 220 or 230 in the early 3rd century A.D. (3 centuries after Jesus). Philostratus' book was largely based on the eyewitness accounts of companions of Apollonius. Apollonius lived years after another miracle-working Son of God, Jesus of Nazareth. Some of the followers of these two divine men were considered in competition with each another.

A century after his death, a holy shrine was dedicated to Apollonius in his home city of Tyana by the Roman Emperor Caracalla, who ruled the Roman Empire from A.D. 198 to 217. Roman Emperor Alexander Severus who ruled the Empire from A.D. 222 to 235 honored Apollonius and kept an image of him among his household gods. Roman Emperor

Aurelian who ruled from A.D. 270 to 275 revered Apollonius as a god.

In the same era that Jesus was being called God, so were the Romans claiming Apollonius was a deity. Regardless, whether this was just coincidental or if it was intentional; **it was a competition.** Who was the ***real*** deity? Was it Jesus or Apollonius? Did the Christians purposely elevate Jesus to a level of a God in response to the Romans elevating Apollonius to the level of a deity? Or was just their competitive environment to prove whose leader was more exalted?

DIVINE BEINGS IN ANCIENT JUDAISM

The first people to speak openly about Jesus as being God incarnate were not pagans but were Jews from Palestine. It could have been because these Jews were confronted with the exaltation of the Roman emperor so there was a need for them to simultaneously place an emphasis on Jesus; Jesus was God rather than the Roman emperor. This posed another problem for the Jews, unlike the Romans, they were monotheists believing in only ONE God. But it became difficult for them to explain how the man Jesus was God while not diminishing their long worshipped God, Yahweh. If Yahweh was God and Jesus was God, wouldn't that be ***two distinct*** Gods?

Having two God was also in violation of the First Commandment which states: "***I am the Lord thy God, who brought you out of the land of Egypt, out of the house of slavery; you shall have no other gods before me***" (***Exodus*** 20:2-3). And the book of ***Isiah*** which is unequivocal in asserting monotheism: ***"I am the Lord, and there is no other; besides me, there is no god"*** (***Isiah*** 45:5)

<u>IMPORTANT POINT:</u> A constructive solution: if the Jews are committed to there being only one God, and the converted Christians now claiming that Jesus is "also" God, to solve this dilemma, they invent The Holy Trinity (three persons in One God). ***To many, this is just another divine mystery that has to be taken on pure faith alone.*** When this dogma was proclaimed by the Catholic Church, the Eastern Orthodox Church (as they started calling themselves) did not go along with this "Trinity Doctrine," which was not found in any of the Sacred Scriptures, started a schism with Rome.

Another possibility is a "divine pyramid." Can monotheism encompass lesser divine beings to comprise the whole divine realm? Such as lesser Gods, superhuman beings, or spirits with superpowers. Well, honestly, that has always existed in the Hebrew and Christian theological cultures: archangels (Michael, Gabriel, and Rafael), angels, cherubims, seraphims, and hosts of lesser angels who administered the will of the Almighty. We are told these beings have divine or supernatural powers beyond us beings, but less than the Almighty Himself to whom they are subservient. Angels in Judaism, Christianity, and Islam were always the superhuman messengers of God who were disguised as humans or in angelic forms. Both also acknowledge there are higher ranks of angels or those who are called archangels. It has been well established in Judaism, Christianity, and Islam that a "divine realm" exists composed of divine beings with different levels of divine powers. Coincidentally, this also is fully compatible with the divine realms of the pagan Roman and Greek gods who were also on different levels with different spectrums of powers. ***<u>Coincidental?</u>***

There are many examples both in the Hebrew and Christian Bibles where angels are considered Gods and angels who functioned as human beings. It is believed by many people in a variety of world religions that when they die, and they have lived good lives, they will become angels or some form of a higher being. In the Hebrew Bible's ***2 Baruch*** state that believers will morph "***into the splendor of angels... for they will live in the heights of that world and they will be like angels and equal to the stars. And the excellence of the righteous will then be greater than that of the angels"*** (***2 Baruch*** 51.3-10). There are other Hebrew Biblical texts which tell of people who upon their death will transform into angels, such as in Enoch. It was not unusual to hear of divine beings that can temporarily become humans, and have spawned "semi-divine" offsprings.

DID JESUS EVER SAY THAT HE WAS GOD?

The answer to that question is **NO!** He may have skirted around the issue, or the most He ever said when asked on different occasions if He was God, He would respond to the effect, "***so it is you that says I am.***" Besides, NEVER saying He was "***God***" or the "***Son of God,***" he repeated said He was the "***Son of Man***"! The latter statement seems to be very clear that He claimed to be the "son of a man" like we are all "sons of men." ***Jesus claimed to be a human man***.

Taken at face value, not intentionally reading into the Gospels and formulating what is not there, many Biblical scholars and theologians have called into question some fundamental basics of the Christian faith: the divinity of Jesus. Contributing to this is the realization that Jesus is very rarely ever, if ever, EXPLICITLY referred to as "God" in the

New Testament. Apparently, most of the authors of the ***New Testament*** never thought that Jesus was really "God."

If you read my ***Alternative Christianities – Volume I,*** you will see how I, along with many others, discount anything "claimed" to have been written by one-vision-wonder Paul [some of his Epistles are thought by Biblical scholars to be forged while some real ones have been left out of the ***New Testament***]. The ONLY place where **He claimed to be God was in the *Gospel of John,*** the most "theological" of the four Gospels. You would think that ***if Jesus was always referring to Himself as "God" it would be important enough for the other Gospels at least include that fact?***

These facts raise so many questions and doubts among Biblical scholars and educated theologians. Why did Jesus never explicitly and repeatedly say that He was God? At least say that He was the "Son of God"? Likewise, did He ever say that He came down from Heaven, or was sent from His Father, to lead us humans to the Father? Did Jesus ever claim to be equal with the Almighty Father? Did Jesus ever imply that He existed forever and was the Creator of Heaven and Earth? Why are the Church fathers claiming that Jesus IS God and IS ONE with the Father if He never said anything to that effect? Why are Christians forced to believe all these things that appear nowhere in the four Gospels? Are we being told to believe these undocumented dogmas? Or is it because the ancient Christians wanted, or needed, to believe these things?

IMPORTANT POINT: Ironically, evangelical Protestants hang onto the words of ***John*** 14:6: "***I am the way, the truth, and the life; no one comes to the Father but by me."*** Ironically, that is UNQUESTIONABLY IMPORTANT to their faith, however logically, if you needed to go through

Him to get to the Father then obviously Jesus was NOT God (you wouldn't need to go through HIM to get to God if He was God) and furthermore He then would **NOT** be ***"consubstantial"*** with the Father for **ALL** eternity and the Creator of Heaven and Earth as we are forced to believe in the Nicene Creed.

IMPORTANT POINT: Many prominent Biblical scholars such as Bart D. Ehrman have done exhaustive studies on Jesus from purely a "historically factual" instead of "purely religious" aspect. Volumes have been written on this specific subject of "divinity." Of course, you will find books professing different viewpoints all with the same claim of being true. The one thing they all MUST agree upon: **Jesus did not spend His ministry declaring Himself to be divine!**

Most educated "non-fundamentalist" Biblical scholars teach that **the Gospels cannot simply be taken "verbatim" as being reliable accounts of what Jesus said and did**. The ***New Testament*** is NOT a perfectly dictated record of Jesus' words as they were being said by Him, NOR an accurate account of His life and death. All these words and actions were relayed by word of mouth from generation to generation before they were even initially written down. ONLY the evangelists and fundamentalists really believe that the Bible is in its entirety is the inerrant word of God. This is extensively discussed in ***Alternative Christianities – Volume I: Early Christian Sects and the Formation of the Bible.*** Differences abound for anyone who can read these stories in the oldest ancient Greek and Hebrew manuscripts; and that does not take into account the differences from the real original manuscripts in Aramaic, Koine, and Coptic.

A WORD ABOUT PAUL

Many Christians, especially Protestant evangelists, like to quote Paul. Ironically, early Christians converted by Jesus' inner circle Disciples had nothing to do with Paul. Why would they? They were converted by a Disciple who was taught by Jesus Himself why would they listen to anyone else? You must realize that Paul's epistles do NOT tell us anything, or very little, about Jesus' teachings. The first writings done by Paul were his letters to his outlying congregations. It has to be taken into account that Paul did not convert to Christianity until 10 years after the death of Jesus, 10 years after Jesus' Disciples had been preaching and spreading the word of Jesus, and 10 years after he worked as a Roman soldier who killed Jews who converted to Christianity.

Paul never met Jesus or was instructed by Him. He is a "one-time, one-vision" wonder who claimed in his Epistles he understood Jesus better than "***those so-called authorities in Jerusalem***." Paul did not even meet any of Jesus' "inner circle" of Disciples until 3 years into his ministry, and only when he was summoned to Jerusalem. The result of their meeting was the Disciples telling Paul to "***cease and desist***" preaching his own personal brand of Christianity. Paul, of course, did not comply which angered the Disciples. Jesus' brother James, the real first head of the Christian movement sent Peter to Antioch to "re-convert into the proper teachings of Jesus" those who have been converted by Paul. This caused many public fights between Peter and Paul, even one that got physical between them (they were mortal enemies; they were never friends). Paul was summoned back to Jerusalem by James and the other Disciples. Again, this meeting did not end well. This is all documented in Paul's Epistles. When he returned Paul told his followers to the effect "***to follow only him and anyone that follows those***

***frauds in Jerusalem deserve to be damned forever to Hell.*"** **This is a very terse statement to be made by a self-professed true believer.**

IMPORTANT POINT: Paul's epistles do not belong on the same level or alongside the Disciples' Gospels.

THE GOSPELS

Obviously, the closest best sources we have for "historical" accuracy are the four Gospels in the ***New Testament.*** Also, to the dismay of some, you do need to include the six Gospels attributed to Peter, James, Philip, Thomas, Judas, and Mary Magdalene. The four Gospels that were included are riddled with errors because of the numerous discrepancies and contradictions between their accounts. Ironically, the six additional Gospels that were NOT included are much closer in agreement with each other in their accounts and teachings of Jesus. I have to repeat the kudos I gave to the Roman Catholic Church in ***Alternative Christianities – Volume I*** for still using the Latin Vulgate Bible that was written by St. Jerome in the 390's in which they preface each Gospel with ***The Gospel According to Matthew, The Gospel According to Mark, The Gospel According to Luke, The Gospel According to John.*** In doing so, the Catholics revere each account independently without having to turn a willful blind eye like the evangelists to the discrepancies, contradictions, falsehoods, and historical inaccuracies. The Catholics have three Biblical passages in every Mass and priests use them for homilies. The Bible is not a perfect book, it is a very human book, but it is the best source for Jesus' teachings that we have.

Those who have read **Volume I** are very familiar with the scenario, for those who aren't – these are the facts: **NONE of the Gospels were written by eye-witnesses! The names assigned to the Gospels were not the authors!** The Disciples were uneducated and functionally illiterate. Biblical scholars generally agree that the texts that eventually comprised the ***New Testament*** were put into writing in the latter part of the 1st century way after those Disciples were dead. If we assume that Jesus died around A.D. 33 (or very close to it), the 1st Gospel, ***Mark***, was probably put in writing about A.D. 65-70. The next Gospels, ***Matthew*** and ***Luke,*** were probably put in writing about 15-20 years later between A.D. 80-85. These three Gospels are called the "synoptic," or similar, Gospels because ***Matthew and Mark*** were probably copied from their predecessor ***Mark*** (they are in too many respects almost identical to ***Mark***). The last Gospel, ***John,*** was probably put into writing about A.D. 90-95. In the 1st century with a very barbaric system of communication, a gap of 35 to 65 year in which Jesus' teachings and words are passed from generation to generation by memory and word of mouth, **is much too long.** The authors of these Biblical texts were very far removed from personally knowing anything firsthand about Jesus. Worse yet, all these texts were written **anonymous** never indicating the source. When the official books were being compiled for the ***New Testament*** at the end of the 4th century, a ***best guess*** had to be made as to which Disciple, or apostle, was the originator of the story they are reading. Disciples Matthew and John, and apostles Mark and Luke, were arbitrarily assigned. If correct, only the first two personally knew Jesus. Mark is believed to be possibly a secretary to Peter, and Luke is believed to be possibly a traveling companion of Paul – they themselves never met or knew Jesus.

Also taking into consideration, the oldest known manuscripts of the Gospels are written in Greek. We know that the Disciples and followers of Jesus were uneducated and poor Jewish laborers who were Palestinians who spoke only Aramaic. Thus these manuscripts were definitely not written by any of the Disciples or any immediate apostles. The initial authors would have to have been highly-educated Greek-speaking Christians from later generations who could write well and professionally for the period. Even the English language did not begin to receive formal structure until Shakespeare.

IMPORTANT POINT: Oral transmission from memory has inherent embellishments, falsehoods, historical inaccuracies, discrepancies, and personal interpretations as it was passed from generation to generation. Consequently, the Gospels cannot be taken accurate and inerrant. At the best, they contain ***sketchy*** information about the most admired man of all time.

WHAT WAS JESUS CALLED?

First, let us clarify: it is amazing that most people think "Christ" is Jesus' last name, Jesus Christ. It is not; it is a title. Few people at that time had last names; they more had a descriptive title, such as Jesus of Nazareth, Jesus of Galilee, Jesus the carpenter's son, Jesus son of Mary, Mary the Magdalene, John the Baptist, James brother of Jesus, etc. "**Christ**" is a title. It a Greek word which is the translation of the Hebrew word "***messiah***" or "***the anointed one.***" Jesus' followers believed He was the long-awaited Jewish Messiah. The Messiah was expected to be a human king like David to save them from oppression. The Messiah was never expected to be God Himself, nor divine in any way other than a holy High Priest. Many people called Him, "Rabbi;" the Disciples frequently called Him, "Rabbi;" even the thief on the cross next to him called Him "Rabbi." Jesus from a very young age was well versed in the Hebrew Scriptures so it is not inconceivable that Jesus became a Rabbi; albeit a modern progressive Rabbi.

IMPORTANT POINT: I think ALL rabbis HAD to be married. Maybe Jesus was married? Some think that the Marriage Feast at Cana was Jesus' own wedding to Mary Magdalene?

Those were very turbulent times for the Jews. They were persecuted and make subservient to their Roman leaders. This was another time they needed a "savior" to help them. There were ample reasons and hopeful expectations for the Jews to believe that their long-awaited and promised "Messiah" or "Savior" had arrived with the appearance of Jesus. Many people referred to Him by His given name of Jesus; fewer called Him "Christ" meaning the "anointed one." Of course, the fact is that Jesus NEVER did anything to warrant that title. It was expected for the Jewish Messiah to form an army, drive the suppressers out of Judea, and establish the "promised land." Jesus did NONE of these things.

In reality, Jesus' life and teachings were quite the contrary to what the Jews expected of their long-awaited "Messiah" which caused many Jews to reject Jesus, even thousands of years later. It should go without saying that the Jews never expected their "messiah" and "savior" to be allowed to be captured, publically humiliated, physically tortured, and put to death by public crucifixion. They NEVER expected that He would be "God" Himself. They DID expect him to be an admired leader, a fierce warrior, defender, a man wiser than

Solomon, and revered High Priest of their faith. **JESUS WAS NONE OF THESE THINGS**. Jesus was an embarrassment easily overpowered by the Romans.

The only reason the Christians adopted and included the Hebrew Bible was to "claim" that Jesus fulfilled all the prophecies of the expected Messiah. They included the major feat that the Messiah would die and rise from the dead (***Isaiah*** 53 and ***Psalm*** 22). This was only done to give validity to Christianity that was really floundering. Jewish scholars claim the contrary saying that those passages do not make any references to the expected "messiah."

IMPORTANT POINT: Even that many may refer to Jesus Christ as the "***Messiah***," possibly **YES**; but "***God***," definitely **NEVER.** Jesus never referred to Himself as "***God***." When anyone asked Him, He ambiguously replied, "***So you say I am,***" or "***I am the Son of God,***" [guess He was **NOT** God but only a "product" of God like angels and us]. Or worse yet "***I am the Son of Man***" [meaning He is a product of human sexual reproduction between a flesh and blood man and woman?]. It is hard to make a case the Jesus was really "God" going by what He Himself said and not His post-death subsequent followers say. We like to believe that He was God but that brings us to subjective "matter of faith."

THE RESURRECTION SCENARIO

Theologians, scholars, and historians all have difficulty discussing the Resurrection of Jesus scenario. That is because the four canonical Gospels in the ***New Testament*** virtually disagree on every detail of Jesus' resurrection. Even to the point that using the word "disagree" is in itself an understatement. ***Alternative***

Christianities – Volume I has a whole chapter devoted to what is more accurately described as the dozens of "***discrepancies, inconsistencies, contradictions, forgeries, and downright falsehoods***" in the ***New Testament.*** This has a lot to do the Gospels in the ***New Testament*** being written 40 to 65 years after the events happened during which time these stories were passed down from memory by word of mouth by fallible and forgetful human beings. Also, these accounts were probably written in the ancient languages of that day Aramaic or Coptic. The most-original manuscripts we have in an ancient Greek which came many years later.

For example, these are narratives that are related differently in ***Matthew*** 28, ***Mark*** 16, ***Luke*** 24, and ***John*** 20-21:

1. ***Who was the first person to go to Jesus' tomb and discovered the "empty tomb"?***
   Mary by herself (***John***)?
   Mary along with another Mary (***Matthew***)?
   Mary along with another Mary and Salome (***Mark***)? or
   Mary, Mary, Joanna, and a number of other women (***Luke***)?

2. ***Was the stone of the tomb already rolled away when they arrived?***
   Yes (***Mark, Luke,*** and ***John***)? or
   No. (***Matthew*** only)?

3. ***Who did they see?***
   An angel (***Matthew***)?
   A man (***Mark***)? or
   Two men (***Luke***)?

4. ***Did they immediately go to tell the Disciples what they had seen?***
   Yes (***John***)? or
   No (***Matthew, Mark, and Luke***)?

5. ***What were the women instructed to do at the gravesite?***
   Tell the Disciples that Jesus will meet them in Galilee (***Matthew*** and ***Mark)?*** Or
   Tell the Disciples to remember what Jesus told them to do when He was in Galilee (***Luke***)?

6. ***Did the women then do what they were told?***
   Yes (***Matthew*** and ***Luke)***? or
   No (***Luke***)?

7. ***Did the Disciples also see Jesus?***
   Yes (***Matthew, Luke,*** and ***John)***? or
   No (***Luke***)?

8. ***Where was it that they saw Him?***
   Only in Galilee (***Matthew***)? Or
   Only in Jerusalem (***Luke***)?

This is only the discrepancies in the resurrection narratives. There are more discrepancies regarding Jesus' arrest, trial, passion and death between the four Gospels in the ***New Testament.***

<u>IMPORTANT POINT:</u> According to some people, this is the single more important event to happen in the history of Western Civilization and we don't have a straight story on what ***<u>REALLY</u>*** happened? A religion of over 2 Billion followers has sprung up mainly because of this one event and there is no one, clear, concise, or definitive narrative.

Obviously, if you are an evangelical fundamentalist who believes without any leeway in the 100% inerrancy of the Bible as being written, even word for word, by God Himself or with His direct inspiration.... You got some explaining to do. With no offense to the Almighty, either God was senile and forgetful in what He told the different authors?

The Catholics, much to the criticism of the Protestants, are able to show their reverence for the Sacred Scriptures without getting weighted down in irrelevant word-for-word details but in the underlying lessons to be learned. To the ultimate consternation of the evangelists and fundamentalists, an interesting fact from my ***Volume I*** is that the ***Qur'an*** [***Koran***] explicitly claims it was dictated word-for-word directly from above to Muhammad. In fact, Muhammad was made to read it back word-for-word to make sure it was all taken down accurately. There is no such claim, explicitly or even remotely implied, about the words appearing in the ***New Testament***!

Some point out: If Jesus had really had rose from the dead, it would have been a spectacular event that would resound around at least the Roman Empire. Jesus Himself would want to proclaim the greatest feat of all time to everyone. Why would Jesus NOT want to appear to thousands of witnesses? That would have surely jumpstarted Christianity. Why would Jesus let Christianity flounder almost to the point of extinction? Why wouldn't Jesus want His words and teachings to be heard from His own mouth? How could He let His words and teachings get distorted into thousands of iterations?

IMPORTANT POINT: There really are NO good counterarguments. NO good answers to those questions.

Because of these ambiguities, it is much easier for people to say Jesus was NOT God, NOT even the Son of God, NOT even remotely related to the Almighty Father, and Christianity is NOT the one true religion. It does seem, at the least, maybe these self-righteous sanctimonious re-born Christians should ease up on their aloofness in their dealings with the subscribers to the other major non-Christian religions of the world. Many have better roots than Christianity does.

The fact remains, historians cannot factually prove or disprove that Jesus actually rose from the dead. Of course, you can hear the evangelicals decry "anti-supernatural bias." However, it is not uncommon for these same evangelicals to criticize and profess doubt about others' supernatural events? There was the claim that more than a dozen Roman senators that actually saw King Romulus ascend up into the heavens right from among their midst. There have been groups of Roman Catholics who have witnessed an appearance of the Blessed Virgin Mary. These same evangelicals claim there is absolutely no truth to these apparitions and demand to see the "proof." But it is alright for these evangelicals who refuting other peoples' claims while at the same time expect people to believe in a bodily resurrection that had NO eyewitnesses.

This applies to all the major religions. Historians can only deal with verifiable facts; they cannot say whether a miracle happened or NOT without eyewitnesses. For the adherents of any religion, much is taken on "**pure faith**" by the "**truly faithful**" as "**immutable truths,**" while for others "**their assertions**" are only "**legendary fables**." For example:

- Historians cannot factually establish that the angel Moroni spoke to Joseph Smith.

- Roman Catholics, Unitarian-Universalists, Congregationalists, Orthodox Jews, and Buddhists could care less.
- Likewise, 2/3 of the world's populations who belong to non-Christian religions feel the same way about Jesus Christ and Christianity.
- Deities and supernatural events only have meaning and importance within their own religion.
- Historians are fact-finders. They do not believe in "acts of God." They are the impartial factual observers.

IMPORTANT POINT: This is not to put down Christians, really, not at all. It is just to make a shock-value point that Christians, now and throughout the past ages, should be more ecumenical and tolerant of other world religions. Maybe a lot more about life and spirituality can be learned from other cultures and religions which could serve to enhance Christianity. Some of the "other" Gospels claim Jesus spent His lost years learning the Eastern religions of which traces could be found in His teachings. Jesus was ecumenical welcoming peoples from all cultures and backgrounds.

WHAT THE GOSPELS TELL US

There is no real certainty, consistency, or agreement of ***when*** the belief took root that Jesus was God after His supposed resurrection which is traditionally placed on the 3rd day after Jesus was crucified. However, this is still just conjectured not based on any shred of factual evidence. It was more likely to be decades, if not a whole century, after His death the claim of His deity was being made. We really don't know when other than it surely was not immediately.

If you subscribe to the accounts that the Disciples fled Jerusalem in fear for their own lives and ran home to Galilee as soon as Jesus was arrested, the whole timetable changes. **IF** they left Jerusalem on Friday, they couldn't have been able to go very far initially because they would be forbidden to travel on the Sabbath, Saturday. Then it would take them at least a week traveling on foot to go the approximate 120 miles. The same would apply if they followed one of Jesus' supposed orders for them to meet Him in Galilee "***as they previously discussed.***"

The Disciples that say they "saw" Him might not have seen Him on "Easter Sunday" morning but may have been weeks later. However, as declared by Paul "***according to the fulfillment of Scriptures***" they saw Him on "***the 3rd day***"

Then you have several accounts to contrary that say the Disciples went into hiding in Jerusalem for "***fear of their lives***" and being hunted down to be killed for being the Disciples of Jesus. Funny how everyone calls Judas the Traitor but when **ALL** the Disciples denied him, deserted him, ran away, were not around for His trial and crucifixion, and went into hiding. They are **ALL** the ones we called "***saints.***" Later we will discuss how Judas was really the "saint."

IMPORTANT POINT: It is casually overlooked that there was no universal agreement among the early Christians that Jesus even had been raised from the dead. And for those who did believe He did, there was NO further agreement as what "***raised from the dead***" exactly meant. Early Christians right up to the time of the Council of Nicaea and after the dogma put in the Nicene Creed of A.D. 325, there were continuously heated debates about the nature of "Jesus' resurrection." Specifically, the word resurrection is defined as a dead body returning to a living human being again. Jesus preached that our soul and spirit will live on forever, not our bodies. That was squashed in Nicaea.

For those who follow or revere Paul [***see Volume I***], in ***1 Corinthians*** he emphatically claims that **Jesus was *bodily* raised from the dead.** Then further along Paul states as fact: **all resurrected believers will be like the resurrected body of Jesus… it is a *bodily* event**.

IMPORTANT POINT: Not ALL Apostolic Christians read, follow, believe, or revere Paul. Although Paul's letters were the first writings, however, Paul never met Jesus and converted 10 years after Jesus' death [***see Volume I***].

Early Christians especially in the Eastern Churches did not agree with or ever entertained Paul's version of Christianity. Many modern Christians have found Paul's views to be too confusing or even contradictory, and that is even assuming what you are reading is not one of the forged epistles only written in the name of Paul. Several ancient ***Alternative Christianities***, especially among the **Gnostic Christian** sects, take a completely different stand than expressed in Paul's ***1 Corinthians:*** Jesus' human body **NEVER** rose from the grave; it was His spirit that was raised to show us that it is our internal spirit that lives on forever. Remember, the Jews at the time of Jesus did not believe in eternal life. Only an "empty grave" was found which is not proof that His body resurrected or someone had taken it.

The ***Gospel of Luke***, written approximately A.D. 80-85, says that when Jesus appeared to the Disciples they had trouble believing that they were actually seeing Him in His human flesh: "***While they were saying these things, Jesus Himself stood in their midst and said to them, 'Peace be***

with you.' They were startled and afraid, and thought that they were seeing a 'spirit'."

This bewildered many. Why were they surprised and startled? Why would they be afraid of their Lord with whom they had just spent three years of their lives? If Jesus was in His unchanged human body, would they not run to Him and hug Him. Did Jesus look **<u>different</u>** than the man they ate, slept, and traveled with for the last three years? Maybe Jesus was blurred around His edges? If the Disciples became convinced that Jesus WAS really God, would they not run up to Him and throw themselves down at His feet saying "***you are the true God, the expected Messiah!***"

<u>IMPORTANT POINT:</u> For an excellent different perspective read the Gnostic ***Coptic Apocalypse of Peter.***

JESUS' VARIOUS APPEARANCES

First, we don't know if the usual definition of an "appearance" is really the correct word to use in describing Jesus after His death. An "appearance" usually means a "physical and tangible" presence. That would coincide with a "bodily resurrection" from the dead after three days in a tomb. As has been discussed, we cannot be sure from all the differences and contradictions in the known texts that Jesus appeared in his pre-death flesh and blood body. "Visions," "apparitions," or "dreams" may be more accurate terms in describing seeing God, Mary, a saint, an angel, a spirit, or a ghost. Basically, it gets down to which Bible you read and which Bibles or Sacred Scriptures you believe (or what you **<u>want</u>** to believe).

- Paul in ***1 Corinthians*** conveniently says nothing about the "empty tomb" (that is if Paul ever realized the tomb was discovered "***empty***;" he wasn't around.) Paul just says that Jesus "***appeared***" to the Disciples which he insinuates Jesus "bodily" resurrected from the grave and continually credits Jesus with that feat.
- The ***Gospel of Mark*** states that the tomb was empty but considers it proof that Jesus had been resurrected.
- The ***Gospel of Luke*** considers the empty tomb to be just "an idle tale" (24:11). Upon seeing Jesus, the Disciples consider that He must have resurrected Himself from death.
- Mary Magdalene is confused when she discovers the tomb was empty. At first, she assumes that Jesus' body had been moved elsewhere; only considered "resurrection" when Jesus appears to her (20:14-18).
- The Jews credited "grave robbers" or a hoaxed staged by His Disciples.

IMPORTANT POINT: In that period, no one considered Jesus to be God; not even His own Disciples.

THE PART THAT ULTIMATELY DEFIES EXPLANATION

More important than the bodily resurrection of Jesus, which defies any explanation by every scholar, historian, and physician, is how did Jesus spend His supposed "**40 days**" on this earth before His ascension to Heaven? For those that claim that Jesus spent the whole of these "**40 days**" with His Disciples; however, their writings **DO NOT** confirm this "theory." You would think the Disciples' Gospels would overflow with His teachings during that **40 day** period.

Next theory is that Jesus was in seclusion for "**40 days.**" ***Why***? Would Jesus not want more people to see Him and convert more people with His amazing feat? If not in seclusion, why did more people not see Him over those "**40 days**"?

Why did His Disciples have trouble recognizing Him? Why did Mary Magdalene think she saw a gardener outside the empty tomb? Was it so far beyond her possibilities that the person could be Jesus? Why would a "stranger" walk among previous companions and go a long distance without them realizing much later the "stranger" was Jesus?

MAJORITY WORLDVIEW

Only 1/3 of the world's population is Christian; another 1/3 of the world's population is Muslims who do revere Jesus Christ but do not consider him to be God but just another prophet. The other 1/3 of the world's population does not acknowledge Jesus Christ as someone religiously important at all. 1/3 is not a good or convincing ratio of believers. Some Christians and all non-Christians do NOT believe Jesus ever rose from the dead and appeared to anyone. There is no compelling evidence that He did. His divinity and His "resurrection" has been fiercely debated and debunked since that first Easter Sunday starting with Mary Magdalene and the Disciples. Those who call themselves conservative "Christians" obviously tend to take the strict "Christian" position on this, albeit **on pure faith alone**.

Prominent ***New Testament*** scholar, Gerd Ludermann in his "***The Resurrection of Christ: A Historical Inquiry"*** (New York, Prometheus, 2004, p.19) firmly argues that visions of Jesus were "***psychologically induced***." Gerd firmly states that "***when Jesus died his body decomposed like any other body***" and consequently since Christianity is based on Jesus' bodily resurrection from the dead which never happened, the "***Christian faith is a dead as Jesus***."

Another ***New Testament*** British scholar, the late Michael Goulder, reminds us about numerous past and present natural (e.g. tides and solar eclipses) and supernatural (e.g. meteors and solar flares) occurrences for which there were no logical explanations. Many which over time modern scientists have been able to explain (like tides) and some still lack explanation. In ancient times, many of these occurrences were given "divine" attributions. Relatively not that long ago in the Middle Ages and up to maybe a century ago, mental illness, hysterical tantrums, bodily shakes, fainting, epilepsy, and so many more explainable and curable conditions were treated and condemned by Christians and Christian Churches to be obvious evidence of demonic possession requiring exorcisms. Nowadays we no longer attributed them to works of Satan.

For non-Christian non-believers, a similar argument is leveled against the appearances of Jesus to His Disciples. Without any physical tangible explanation, many times there are only non-physical intangible supernatural theories. Even today when someone says they saw or felt the presence of their dead spouse, or died and were revived, or saw a U.F.O, they are considered to be hallucinating or a nut job; unless of course it happened personally to you.

FINAL THOUGHTS

Jesus was a very popular preacher with throngs of followers who have persisted for two thousand years. He never said He was God (why would He NOT say it?) nor that He was part of the Holy Trinity consubstantial with His Father who existed forever and created the universe and this world (why would He NOT want us to know that?). Both would gain Him more followers; was that not His mission on Earth? Apparently, that was not important to Him, then why should it be important to us? Like Him, maybe it should not be as important as we think it is? Maybe, we are missing the gist.

For this greatest person who has ever lived on this Earth, it is His message that should be important; not where He came from, who He was, and to where He returned. An important Gospel that was left out of the ***New Testament*** was ***The Gospel of Thomas.*** It does not contain any narratives but just 114 raw statements that were said by Jesus. This Gospel may be the most important of all the Gospels; its sayings can be found in the Gospels written at later dates. This is the only Gospel credited to the Disciple Thomas and it is a terrible shame the early Church powers chose to ban the ***Gospel of Thomas*** and order all the copies destroyed. Maybe there were some of Jesus' sayings they did not want us to hear while others are found word-for-word in the four canonical Gospels. Ironically, the ***Gospel of Thomas*** is validated as one of the first Gospels and among the oldest Scriptures. What else did Jesus say that we are being deprived of reading? ***Why?***

IMPORTANT POINT: Further into this volume we will discuss these banned and ordered destroyed Gospels.

Beyond the ***Gospel of Thomas,*** we seem to have made Christianity more complicated than Jesus intended it to be. Jesus had simple recurring commandments. His response to ***"Lord what is the Greatest Commandment"*** was: "***Love your neighbor as yourself,***" "***Do unto others as you***

would have them do unto you," and "***What you do to the least of my brothers, you do unto me."*** He just asked us to love one another, be kind, have mercy and compassion, and do good deeds. Jesus obviously never intended to establish a formal religion or otherwise He would have done it Himself. Jesus obviously never intended to put His words in writing or otherwise He would have written the Bible Himself. He just would not have left all that to chance, especially if He was God and was able to foretell the future of how disorganized and scattered Christianity turned out to be.

This all wasn't supposed to be SO complicated. I can't help keep imagining that Jesus in Heaven, holding His forehead, shaking His head, and saying, "***Those earthlings are not too swift; they just don't even get the simplest instructions. What do they not understand? I thought I was being perfectly clear.***"

Maybe Jesus came to earth to correct Judaism and tell them that there was an eternal life after this cruel and material world; but then His new theology, Christianity, in the hands of fallible human beings veered off His intended course correction. Maybe the Council of Nicaea in A.D. 325 permanently took Christianity in the wrong direction with the ***erroneous*** Nicene Creed and by ***banning and destroying*** important Gospels, Epistles, and other Sacred Scriptures. Then the Protestant reformers continued to steer Christianity distinctly further in the wrong direction with their Sola Scriptura giving the wrong canonical Gospels and Epistles more credence and infallibility.

##

BIBLIOGRAPHY, REFERENCES, AND SUGGESTED READING

Baigent, Michael, ***Jesus Papers, The: Exposing the Greatest Cover-up in History*** © 2006 HarperCollins, New York

Bolton, David, ***Who on Earth Was Jesus? The Quest for the Jesus of History*** © 2008 A Books-John Hunt Publishing, Hants, United Kingdom

Boyd, Gregory A. and Paul Rhodes Eddy, ***Lord or Legend? Wrestling With the Jesus Dilemma*** © 2007 Baker Books, Grand Rapids, Michigan

Cook, Michael L. S.J., ***Responses to 101 Questions About Jesus*** © 1993 Paulist Press

Copan, Paul, ***How Do You Know You're Not Wrong? Responding to Objections That Leave Christians Speechless*** ©2005 Baker Books

Gibson, David and Michael McKinley, ***Finding Jesus: Faith, Fact, Forgery, Six Holy Objects That Tell the Remarkable Story of the Gospels*** © 2015 St. Martin Press, New York

McLaren, Brian D., ***Secret Message of Jesus, The: Uncovering the Truth That Could Change Everything*** © 2006 W. Publishing, Nashville, Tennessee

Pagels, Elaine, ***Gnostic Gospels, The: A Startling Account of the Meaning of Jesus and the Origin of Christianity based on the Gnostic Gospels and Other Secret Texts*** © 1989, 1979 Vintage Books-Random House, New York

Schofield, Hugh J., ***Passover Plot: New Light on the History of Jesus*** © 1965 Hutchison, London, England

Stark, Rodney, ***Rise of Christianity, The: Obscure, Marginal Jesus Movement Became the Dominant Religious Force in the Western World in a Few Countries*** © 1996 Princeton University Press © 1997 First HarperCollins

Ranke-Heineman, Uta, and Peter Heinegg, ***Put Away Childish Things: The Virgin Birth, the Empty Tomb, and Other Fairy Tales You Don't Need to Believe to Have a Living Faith*** © 1994 HarperSanFrancisco, San Francisco, CA

Author's Note: This Book and Treatise are a compilation from many sources on the same subject. See the Complete List of Bibliographies, References, and Suggested Readings in Appendix II

CHAPTER 5

EARLY CHRISTIANITY

From almost the precise moment of Jesus' ascension, His Disciples took off in all directions with sometimes differences in their interpretation of Jesus' life, mission, and teachings. That led to numerous "Christian" sects in the first centuries A.D. (in the year of our Lord) all founded by one of Jesus' inner circle of twelve Disciples. By the end of the 4th century, the 300's, most of these Apostolic-Christianities were condemned and called heretics by the emerging state-sanctioned Church of the Roman Empire, which was the unified, catholic (meaning "universal") church which evolved into today's Roman Catholic Church. Unfortunately, most of these early Alternative Christianities were eradicated or went underground. That is until the 1945 discovery of the banned and ordered destroyed ancient sacred Gospels of these Disciples which were brought back to public awareness. There were different Christian sects we never heard of before: Valentinians, Marcionites, Encratites, Sethians, and Montanists…all valid Christian religions. These Christian religions had the same basic beliefs, maybe with some minor theological differences. Some more than others challenged the new teachings laid out in the Council of Nicaea and the emerging Church, such as the Hermeticists, the Manicheans, and the Neoplatonists. But now we have before us many new thought-provoking sacred texts such as the ***Gospel of Peter,*** the ***secret Gospel of Mark,*** the ***Gospel of Philip,*** the ***Gospel of Thomas*** (sometimes called the Fifth Gospel), the ***Gospel of Mary Magdalene,*** the ***Gospel of the Savior***, etc. Over 50 ancient texts were found. Biblical scholars have always known about these lost texts and Christianities thanks to them being documented by Irenaeus in A.D. 180.

This chapter will not only discuss the early iterations of Christianity that were snuffed out and did not survive but also enlighten the readers as to the different directions Christianity could have taken if it wasn't for the establishment of the official state religion of the Roman Empire. Of course, conversely, Christianity itself could have been snuffed out if it wasn't for the conversion of Constantine. Right now we could all be worshipping the ancient Roman Gods.

Thanks to great educators and authors whose books brought these discoveries to the public such as Elaine Pagels and her best-selling books ***The Gnostic Gospels*** and ***Beyond Belief*** in which she discussed the different versions of Christianity. She excellently compares the ***Gospel of Thomas*** with the ***Gospel of John.*** Professor Bart Ehrman authored many books on the subject, especially the early Christian diversities in ***Lost Christianities,*** such as for example:

- **VALENTINIAN CHRISTIANS** an elite 2nd century intellectual group who had a sophisticated metaphysical and spiritual interpretation of Jesus' mission.
- **MARCIONITE CHRISTIANS** a 2nd century group who completely rejected the Hebrew Bible (what is now called the "Old Testament") and along with it the **God of the Jews.** They were the first pre-Nicaea council to suggest a group of scriptures consisting of a highly edited version the ***Gospel of Luke*** and set of Paul's epistles.
- **MONTANIST CHRISTIANS** were a 2nd and 3rd century woman's charismatic spiritual group that ordained women as bishops, priests, and deacons.
- **DONATIST CHRISTIANS** a 4th-century group against the Roman Empire during the mass persecution of the 300's.

Many Christian sects had to struggle with their conflict of beliefs:

- Is the Bible to be literally interpreted only or can it be interpreted metaphorically?
- How can Christians live in a non-Christian Roman environment which is radically different than their Christian vision? Is Christianity primarily about an inner spiritual freedom that can adapt itself to any dominant culture, or if necessary, can it give resistance to a dominant culture such as the Roman Empire?
- Should the Hebrew Bible be incorporated into the new Christianity? Many sects distinguished the God of the Old Testament as a strict and wrathful God to

the new God of the New Testament as a loving and merciful God.

THE HISTORY OF ALTERNATIVE CHRISTIANITIES

If nothing else, I hope this treatise gets across to the readers, there has never been *ONE* SINGLE FORM of Christianity from its beginning, i.e. the ascension of Jesus Christ into Heaven and the dispersion of the Disciples...

Some mistakenly think that Christianity became fractured in more recent history when Protestant Reformation took place in the 16th century. Some credit the fracture in unified Christian Church with the Great Schism of 1054 which created the Roman Catholic Church in the west and Orthodox Catholic Church in the east. The schism of 1054 was just the final schism after several earlier ones. The 1054 schism broke the Catholic Church into two schools of thought but both were still basically Catholic in beliefs. However, it was the Protestant Reformation of the 16th century that broke away from the Roman Catholic Church and spawned dozens of Protestant denominations, and those dozens broke into hundreds of denominations which in today's world has resulted in more than 30,000 Protestant denominations. In effect, there were more and more Protestant Reformations of Protestant Reformations resulting in thousands of independent denominations all professing a return to the "true" Christian beliefs.

Today, the denominations try to avoid the word "Protestant" as it has negative undertones, but the fact remains their roots are derived from their heritage religions which were "protesting" and "reforming" from the One, Universal, Apostolic, Christian Church and its beliefs which were established by Council of Nicaea in A.D. 325. Instead, they like to call themselves "Christians" as if they are the original and true "Christians" although they had "broke away" from the established "Christian Church." However, as previously discussed in Volume I, many scholars feel they have conversely steered Christianity more and more ***away*** from the original teachings of Jesus. To them (no matter how far away they are chronologically from Jesus and His Disciples) they consider themselves to be the "real Christians." As the Vatican put is, besides the ***New Testament*** there are other written documents and traditions on which the original universal Christian Church was based. The further away the thousands of denomination spread out, the further away from the original Christian Church they strayed. Obviously, no one can claim to be the sole definitive "Christian;" and no one denomination of thousands of Christian denominations can be the "only" true arm, the only "right" way. Obviously, there are some that "definitely" are NOT Christians or follow the teachings and examples of Jesus Christ. Technically, they should not refer to themselves as "Christians" at all. The term "Christian" does not belong to any one denomination; it is a generic, all-encompassing term. The moniker "Christian" should be appropriately qualified: Catholic, Orthodox, Anglican, Episcopalian, Lutheran, Methodist, Presbyterian, Baptist, Assembly of God, or at least by differentiation of beliefs.

It turns out that the diversity of Christianity, or Alternative Christianities, goes back even before the Council of Nicaea in A.D. 325. The reason for the council was to consolidate all the various Christian beliefs abound in the 1st, 2nd, 3rd, and 4th centuries, 300 years of Christians, most followers of one of Jesus' Disciples. There was the problem of the central and most important issue of the Council of Nicaea in A.D. 325, the main reason that council was called however it was never fully resolved: **What is the true nature of Jesus Christ? Was He man or God? Or both?**

At both ends of the issue were two powerful Christian leaders of the early 4th century, Arius and Athanasius. Was Jesus one with the eternal God the Father, consubstantial as one being with the Father, and part of the eternal Trinity: as according to Athanasius? Or although Jesus was of the utmost importance, could He have been a little bit less of a God than God the Father, created by God the Father, "His Father," and thus did not exist for all eternal with God the Father: as according to Arius ca. 250-336. He was a Libyan-born priest who was a deacon in Alexandria and was eventually condemned and removed by the Bishop of Alexandria. Arius' idea still quickly spread and was kept alive in many parts of the Christian world. There was a third narrative: also plausible, but was the first to be discarded by the Bishops at the Council: Jesus was born a human man and at His baptism was taken over by His Father or the Holy Spirit. He preached and performed miracles until His crucifixion when the spirit left Him. There is support for this in the ***New Testament***.

IMPORTANT POINT: As it turned out, Athanasius' consubstantiation position won out "**politically**" with the Bishops and would thereafter be professed by all Christians in the "Nicene Creed." This does not mean it was/is the truth.

Many of the diverse "Christian" beliefs and practices that existed in the first centuries are very different from the Christianity that we know today. Some of these well-respected and well-established sects at that time held "Christian" beliefs that considered this an evil world created by an inferior God who manifested himself as the mean and wrathful God of the Jews and the Old Testament. Conversely, Jesus may have been a mere mortal man created and send to us from the good, all-loving, all-merciful Almighty Father. It is important to believe in the salvation He brought us; i.e. salvation from this mean and wrathful God of the Jews and the promise of a perfect eternal life after death.

This is not old news, it continues today and is even elevated to a higher more intellectual level with the ideas and works of **highly regarded scholars, professors, and authors like Marvin Meyers, Elaine Pagels, Bart Ehrman,** and so much more like them. Not only in academic books but also in recent blockbuster novels and movies like ***The Da Vinci Code*** or ***The Matrix*.** These authors have raised the Alternative Christianities bar to astronomical heights of thought, perception, and intellectual possibilities.

You see, any Alternative Christianities is only considered to be an "alternative" when it is seen as competing, or "trying to compete," with the form(s) of Christianity that became dominant which we are familiar with today. As a historian, I cannot help but wonder what Christianity and the world would be like today if one of these other iterations of ancient Christianity had taken hold, or if Christianity had remained pluralistic as it was in ancient times. I wonder what if any or one of the numerous **Gnostic Christianities** had become the dominant "orthodox" Christianities going forward. How different would the world be today and the centuries past? Would the world have been, or be, a better place?

The **Gnostic Christians** believe in the superiority of the spiritual world; they distrust and belittle the material world as evil and corrupt. The Gnostic scriptures they revered provided them the instructions needed to transcend this material world and raise themselves into God's divine realm. **<u>These books that don't appear in Catholic or Protestant Bibles today as they were banned and suppressed by the dominant Christian Church</u>** such as the ***Gospels of Peter, James, Philip, Thomas, Judas,*** and ***Mary;*** the ***Secret Gospel of Mark*** and the ***Secret Gospel of John*** (with different theological concepts); and epistles of other Disciples that were not included in the canon. **<u>Maybe the "real" Christianity that was preached by Jesus and given in private to His Disciples has been dismissed and banned!</u>**

<u>SOME VARIATIONS ON CHRISTIANITY</u>

<u>SETHIAN GNOSTICS</u>

They are closest to the Christians of ancient and modern day. The considered themselves to be **Gnostics** while still part of the mainline Christian community. They believe in meditation on the Sacred Scriptures (both accepted and banned) and even "group meditations" in their established churches. The Sethians were highly mystical and boast a more "mature" and advanced spiritual life. **<u>They can find spiritually deeper and possibly hidden meanings in everyday Bible passages.</u>** They were creative in their worship liturgies.

<u>VALENTINIANS</u>

Different from the **Sethians**, the Valentinians who reserved their worship services for only the most "mature" spiritual members of their community who have been initiated. Valentinius invented the catechism which held the tenets of their "Christian-beliefs."

MARCIONITE CHRISTIANS

Marcion was another type of **Gnostic Christian**. He and his followers were big believers that **there are two Gods**: one who was the mean, evil, and fallen creator of this material world (like the fable of the fallen Archangel Lucifer) and the real God is the all-good, all-loving, and all-merciful Almighty Father who sent us His son, Jesus. Many references and whole books about this evil God were intentionally deleted from the ancient Bibles. Conversely, those who follow the dominant "orthodox" Christianity believe that Lucifer, or the generic Satan, exist on this earth today. When it came to Marcion, he did NOT acknowledge the ***Old Testament*** to be part of Christianity and thus excluded it from their Holy Scriptures. Also, they only included the ***Gospel of Luke*** in their canon and exclude the ***Gospels of Matthew*** and ***Mark*** which they considered *obviously copied structurally* from ***Luke***, their "synoptic" source.

ENCRATITE CHRISTIANS

The **Encratites** were a completely different type of **Gnostic Christian.** They were more in line with the teachings of the "Gnostic" side of Paul. "***Encratite***" means "self-controlled" or "self-regulated." Their followers practiced penitent fasts and intense prayer sessions. They rejected marriage and sex because they believe salvation was only for those pure of body. **The Encratites *thrived within* Churches founded by Peter, James, John, or some other of Jesus' Disciples.**

IMPORTANT POINT: This is just a few of the variations of Christianities and **Gnosticism** which gives an indication of **the gamut of possibilities that might have become**

the dominant Christian Church and evolved into the traditional Christian Church of today. There were more diverse Christianities, with a wide variety of beliefs, many of which claim to be founded by one of Jesus' Disciples.

The universal (catholic) Christian Church formed by the Council of Nicaea in A.D. 325 began to schism less than 700 and 1300 years later, initially into the Catholic, Orthodox, and Protestant branches respectively. The Protestant branch allowing free and individual interpretation of the Bible almost immediately split into further divisions such as Lutherans, Presbyterians, Methodists, Baptists, and Episcopalians – all with radically different beliefs on dogma and major theological issues. These mainstream branches broke further into innumerable denominations within denominations, with over 30,000 Protestant denominations in the United States alone, and rapidly growing.

More recently, with the 1945 Nag Hammadi discoveries and other discoveries before and after, there is a resurgence of the ancient **Gnostic** sects in a well-deserved revitalization two millennia later. IRONICALLY, these Protestant denominations are distancing themselves from the original ancient Christianities of the first three centuries.

THE "BIG BANG" THEORY OF CHRISTIANITY

The formation of one Christian religion had more of a political motivate than a theological one; and how we ended up with the Christianities of today. Constantine was a newly converted Christian and new Roman Emperor. His mother had previously converted to Christianity and was a driving force behind him. This new Christian movement served a convenient purpose for him. **HE USED CHRISTIANITY** to be doctrinally uniform the movement from its disarray and make it an organized institution just like the Roman Empire and Roman militia. In turn, **this "divine" union would help him unite his vast and far-flung Roman Empire.** One of his first acts as emperor in the 4th century, Constantine summoned about 300 bishops to the Turkish resort city of Nicaea from around his empire: Rome, Gaul, Alexandria, Athens, Constantinople, Jerusalem, Greece, Persia, Egypt, and Syria. The Christian beliefs were as varied as the languages. He instructed them to formulate one set of beliefs about Jesus Christ and **ONE creed** that all Christians could recite to affirm themselves as Christians. Constantine, the only non-clergy, supervised the council and approved their final product, **The Nicene Creed**. The ***Nicene Creed*** was an expansion of the original "**Apostles' Creed**." He ordered the bishops to consolidate into **ONE catholic** (meaning "universal") Church as the Church of Jesus Christ and His Disciples.

The bishops were empowered to excommunicate anyone deviating from this newly established Christian Church and any dissenting beliefs were considered to be heretical. It should be noted that the word "***heretic***" comes from the Greek word meaning "***to choose for oneself***." The word "heresy" is many times taken to mean "wrong" or "not true" but in reality it is the antithesis of the word "orthodox" which does not mean "true" but what is "accepted." In this case it was the beliefs "accepted" by the newly established Catholic (universal Christian) Church. Anyone not in compliance with the new "state-sanctioned" religion of the Roman Empire was ostracized and many sects eventually vanished. When they did not get rid of all the dissenting groups, more "beliefs" were added to the original ***Nicene Creed*** a few decades later especially regarding the origin and nature of Jesus Christ. The original "***Apostle's Creed***" nearly tripled in size

IMPORTANT NOTE: Neither Jesus Christ nor His Disciples ever established a religion. His Disciples spread out to different regions and established individual churches or congregation of believers. Traditional Christianity today is the product of mere human beings: the apostles (missionaries) of Jesus' Twelve Disciples, their apostles (missionaries), a select set of bishops chosen by Constantine, and beliefs sanctioned by Roman Emperor Constantine. Several of the Religion Studies professors say that "***Religion is a human invention***." That seems to be very true!

BISHOP IRENAEUS

Constantine and the Council of Nicaea were not the first to tackle supposed heretics. Most notably was Irenaeus (ca. 130-202) who was one of the first to get disgusted with the varied beliefs. He decided UNILATERALLY what was true or not true; or what he considered "orthodox" and "heresy." He compiled the various writings and published his famous book "Against Heresy" (which officially has a longer Latin title) in A.D. 180. He was especially very **vile and cantankerous in his writings against Gnosticism (mysticism) and any form of alternative Christianity.** He sent his multi-volume work to Rome and got what he was hoping for, he was elevated to be the Bishop of Lyons in Gaul [present day France]. His real ambition was to become Pope. He should be considered the first major heresiologist setting the stage for every subsequent "heresy hunter" or "witch hunter." Irenaeus really outlined the basis for the Council of Nicaea's "orthodox" Christianity. Irenaeus' work became a major contributor when the time came for the Bishops of Nicaea to pick and choose which books would be allowed in the ***New Testament***. Irenaeus believed there should only be four Gospels because four is a "natural number" as there are <u>four</u> corners of the earth, <u>four</u> directions of the wind, and <u>four</u> pillars of the Church. This angered those congregations founded by, and had Sacred Scriptures based passed down from, one of the Twelve Disciples other than Matthew or John such as ***Gospels of Peter, Philip, James, Thomas, Judas,*** or ***Mary Magdalene.*** Some of them were written before and are believed to be more authentic than the ***Gospels of Matthew, Mark, Luke,*** and ***John,*** who also had were some "secret" Gospels that were banned because they were too "gnostic."

The **Gnostic Gospels** were more on a mystical, intellectual, and ascetic level. Some Christian sects put more faith in them than the four chosen Gospels, such as the **Sethians, Valentinians, Marcionites, Encratites, and Montanists.** They inherited Scriptures which lead them to a deeper spiritual relationship to Jesus and His Kingdom. These **Gnostic Gospels** taught a different, challenging, and fascinating theology about experiencing the Christian God.

JESUS BELIEVED IN DIVERSITY

This may come as a shock to many people: **<u>Jesus never founded a religion! Jesus believed in diversity.</u>**

Another bigger shock for many: **<u>Jesus was NOT a Christian; Jesus was a Jew</u>** who was born a Jew, was anointed as a Jew, studied the Hebrew Bible, was a rabbi, went to synagogue, died a faithful Jew, and was received a Jewish burial. **<u>Jesus was a dark-skinned Arab-Palestinian Jew</u>** who lived in a region occupied by Roman soldiers. It was two very different cultures and religions forced to live side by side. At the minimum, the Jews and Romans lived in relative peace. Three different languages were spoken in the region: Aramaic was the ancient Arabic language spoken by Jews; Latin was obviously the official language of the Roman Empire and the soldiers; and Greek was spoken by the elite and educated in the region. Jesus spoke Aramaic with His Disciples and to the local people. We might assume Jesus knew and spoke Greek if He received a formal education because all of the literature of the region was primarily in Greek. Greek had been the language of the intellectuals since Alexander the Great for about three centuries by that time.

Another bitter pill people may have to acknowledge is that **Jesus never said He was God!** Although Christians affirm in their **Nicene Creed** that ***Jesus is God***, it is something that Christians claimed for Him – it is **not anything that Jesus ever said about Himself.** He usually referred to Himself as the "**Son of God** or more often the "**Son of Man**." You would think He was telling us that He was a human flesh-and-blood being just like us. This may have been to show that all humans, all races, and all colors, are welcome in the Kingdom of His Heavenly Father.

Obviously, Jesus' main focus was proclaiming the Kingdom of God. He never defined His own role in the Kingdom of His Father. He never said where this Kingdom was. He never said what was needed to get into the Kingdom of God, except to believe Him. Jesus just appeared to be a ***divine messenger*** **but He NEVER claimed Himself to be divine!** This claim that Jesus was God was made by everyone who came after Him.

Besides Aramaic, if Jesus preached in Greek it was probably intended to communicate with the vast population in the region and empire who understood the language. Paul we know was a Roman so his native language was Latin; if he was educated he may have also spoken Greek. However, he would have had no reason to be fluent in Aramaic, the native language of Jesus and the Disciples, although Paul was converting the Gentiles in the area. Most Biblical scholars agree, Paul taught his own brand of Christianity in conflict with the message the Disciples were preaching. Paul took it upon himself to denounce all the Jewish religious rites and rituals for sake of converting the Gentiles. Although initially, this did not meet with the approval of the Disciples, in the long run, it was a major step for Christianity to exist and grow.

Jesus was trying to tell us everyone can enter the Kingdom of God. Jesus said many things like: "***the Kingdom of God is close to you!***" (***Luke*** 10:9); "***the Kingdom of God is within you***" (***Luke*** 17:21); "***Blessed are the poor for the Kingdom of God is yours***" (***Luke*** 6:20); and Jesus began many of His parables with, "***the Kingdom of God is like....***"

We can be sure that the Kingdom of God which Jesus has proclaimed is understood by many to include all the peoples of the world in it. It will be comprised of people from different backgrounds, races, cultures, and faiths. The Kingdom will be as diverse as the different people in it. Some people strictly followed Jewish law, others were more lenient when it came to Jewish Law, some people revered the ***Old Testament***, while some revered the ***New Testament***, others revered both books, but the major portions of the world revered neither book. Some insisted that men be circumcised for religious reasons, while many others did not follow that custom.

Even within Christianity, many of the Christian communities are different in their interpretation of Jesus' teachings. Many Christians regard Him as truly the Son of the Father, not just a messenger, but definitely divine in His own right. Jesus Christ was to them the savior of the world because of His death and resurrection. Others believed differently: Jesus was just a man who was infused with divinity at His Baptism (***"This is My Son in whom I am well pleased"***) who left His Body at His death (***"Father, into Thy hands I commend My spirit"***). The salvation Jesus offered in His preaching was one in an eternal Kingdom where our spirit will live forever (remember, Jews did not believe in an afterlife), and was a welcomed escape from this evil and horrible world.

IMPORTANT POINT: The ***New Testament*** is full of diversity and as a result Christianity has a multitude of beliefs. The way Jesus Christ left His mission is probably the way He envisioned Christianity as being diverse as His people that populate the world.

PAUL WAS DIVERSE.... MAYBE TOO DIVERSE

Paul's letters to the Churches he founded are revealing as to his diversity. Maybe Paul took diversity to an extreme by not being on the same page as the Twelve Disciples. It was to the point that Paul on more than one occasion was told to "cease and desist" his preaching as it did not fall into line with the teachings of Jesus Christ. In fact, to many then and now, the teachings of Paul are mutually exclusive from the teachings of Jesus' Twelve Disciples. This distinction also caused diversity in Christian believers.

Paul began almost every one of his letters with "***Paul, an apostle of Jesus Christ.***" This was a title Paul took upon himself. We know Paul was not one of The Twelve Disciples.

Paul differed from the Disciples because the Disciples actually had known Jesus personally for years, whereas Paul knew Him only in a vision. Ten years after killing Christians, the Roman soldier Paul claims he had a vision of Jesus that was so overwhelming that he proclaimed himself to be a "Christian" and went around Asia Minor to preach his version of Christianity about Jesus and the Kingdom of God. Paul took it upon himself without consulting with the Disciples to declare that non-Jews did not need to follow Jewish law.

Refresher on terms: a Disciple is someone who was taught by the Master. Disciple with a capital "D" refers directly back The Twelve Disciples of Jesus, His Inner Circle. An apostle is a "missionary" sent out, an emissary. A Disciple can be an Apostle with a capital "A" but rarely is an apostle with a small "a" also a Disciple.

Paul tells us himself about his falling out with the Disciples on their first meeting in ***Galatians*** 1:11-2:14. Paul actually relates how he was having problems with the local missionaries so Paul went to Jerusalem to meet with James, John, and Peter who were the supposed leaders of the "Jesus Movement." This first meeting did not go well at all. The Disciples who lived and knew Jesus personally were insistent that a "Christian" had to follow Jewish law: circumcision, dietary rules, and all the laws of the Old Testament which Jesus and they had done their whole lives.

Paul was totally outraged by this requirement for his Gentiles and insisted Jesus revealed something different to him. Paul claimed that Jesus wanted him to bring the Gentiles into His fold – but said nothing about complying with Jewish law. Paul insisted that the law was probably just for Jews and the Gentiles could enter the Kingdom by their faith in Jesus alone. This was the first of many radically different interpretations of Christianity documented in the ***New Testament***. **<u>The Disciples finally acquiesced for the sake of converting non-Jews and Paul left.</u>** The Disciples in Jerusalem now had two strains Christianity, Jewish and Gentile, which would have to coexist.

It was not that simple. **<u>That was just the beginning of the animosities and fighting between the Disciples and Paul</u>**. James, as the brother of Jesus was their chosen leader, sent Peter on a mission to the Jews of Antioch. While Peter was there he visited one of the Gentile churches founded by Paul. Peter and Paul were invited to a dinner with both Jew and Gentile Christians. Peter refused to violate the Jewish dietary laws and began to depart. A furious Paul went after a hot-tempered Peter and confronted him. It did not end well; they became mortal enemies. Peter started re-converting Paul's Gentiles into the correct teachings of Jesus Christ. Needless to say, this infuriated Paul. One incident got physical between them in front of a congregation. A subsequent meeting with the Disciples in Jerusalem went even worse when they asked Paul again to cease and desist. This you can find in Paul's letters when he informed his followers that "the reputed leaders in Jerusalem are phonies....and anyone following them deserves to spend eternity in Hell..."

Many of the ancient Christian sects and subsequent Alternative Christianities did not include Paul's letters in their canon of Sacred Scriptures. Many Biblical scholars concur because Paul's letters are HIS preaching and teaching with few inclusions of the preaching and teachings of Jesus Christ. Many of these sects did not include the Hebrew Bible, what is now called the ***Old Testament.***

Although Paul's inclusion and conversion of the Gentiles was a major feat for Christianity, his preaching really caused the first schism in Christianity. Judea is part of Asia Minor and there were too many Christian sects sprouting up around the region. This was one of the reasons Roman Emperor Constantine called the Council of Nicaea in the 4th century to establish a uniform set of beliefs and practices to make the universal ("catholic") Christian Church.

GNOSTIC CHRISTIANITY

Gnosticism appeals to real life and serious-minded people who enjoy the intellectuality, mysticism, and intense spirituality. **Gnosticism** can be very subtly sophisticated while dazzling the imagination of the mind of the intellectually curious spiritual elite. **Gnosticism** has its own varieties of thought and ideas. **Gnosticism can make the conventional Christian Church look mundane and boring in comparison.** This dismayed the bishops whose congregations were looked upon as being dull lacking spiritual maturity. Thus, the Christian Church's quick opposition to **Gnosticism** began as early as the 2nd century and continues to the present day.

Unfortunately, **Gnosticism** was erroneously defined by its critics who had a vested interest in suppressing and eradicating it. Ironically in a way they did **Gnosticism** a favor, their writings validated its existence in the earliest days of Christianity. Most of what we know about it comes from arguments against it, written by its enemies in the second, third, and fourth centuries. Irenaeus (130-200 C.E.), Tertullian (160-240), Hippolytus (170-236), and Epiphanius (310-403) were the most prominent of the critics of **Gnosticism**. Still, many **Gnostic** adherents existed.

When these Gnostic Gospels, Epistles, Apocrypha, letters, and other old codices (books written on papyrus) were discovered in 1945 in the Egyptian desert near the town of Nag Hammadi (and at other times in other places before and after 1945) preserved in large red earthenware jar, we know they all existed in the early centuries of Christianity. They were probably put there to preserve them when the Church ordered them destroyed by the monks in a nearby monastery.

Biblical scholars identified these works as authentic Coptic (an ancient Egyptian language) **Gnostic** texts believed to have been translated from originals written in Greek. This was a goldmine of historical works that were suppressed by the emerging universal Christian Church as it gave a different perspective on Jesus Christ and His message such as: ***The Gospel of Thomas, The Gospel of Philip, The Apocryphon of John, The First and Second Apocalypse of James, The Gospel of Truth, On the Origin of the World, The Sophia of Jesus Christ***, and over 50 other texts.

For the most part, ***gnosis*** was accepted and considered positive in the early days of Christianity especially among the Coptics in Egypt. Bishop Clement of Alexandria (ca. 150-215) was a prominent 2nd century Christian theologian. He frequently used the term **"true Gnostic"** in referring to a legitimate category of Christian life. Irenaeus had documented the difference between "true" and "false" ***gnosis*** in his writings. Of course, the opposing Church bishops claimed they had the true knowledge ***which is what they taught***; any deviation from that, such as what was being taught by the **Gnostics,** was complete heresy.

The **Coptic Christians** seem to be the major preserver of **Gnosticism.** Luckily, there still exists in the world and in the United States **Coptic Catholic Churches** (under the Pope in Rome) and **Coptic Orthodox Churches** (in the Eastern Orthodox tradition).

WHAT IS GNOSTICISM?

The Greek word ***"gnosis"*** means "knowledge." It not only connotes knowledge but also understanding, perception, and insight of this world and the afterlife. In the most general terms, the **Gnostics** are people who oriented their earthly lives to attaining the required knowledge, understanding, and perception of this worldly life and the afterlife. **Gnosticism** is the various associations and movements founded in the 1st centuries of the Christianity. **Gnosticism** is not isolated to Christianity but to other religions and cultures around the world. This treatise limits its discussion to **Christian Gnostics** as an **Alternative Christianity.** In the early centuries, and today, the **Gnostics** were able to be with and mingle among other Christian religions, denominations, and sects unchallenged – at least until they were banned from doing so by the emerging universal Christian Church. Admittedly, in every generation there are some people who could not understand or accept the ideas and beliefs of the **Gnostics,** sometimes referring to them slyly as the "elite Christians." Many times the **Gnostics** would refer to themselves superiorly as the "spiritually mature Christians," meaning they believed the same as the "orthodox" Christians just on a higher more spiritual, mystical, or esoteric level.

The **Gnostics** are always seeking to get a deeper understanding. By doing so, they embrace science while seeking to understand further the physical and the spiritual realms. Many do not understand the knowledge the **Gnostics** seek while the **Gnostics** love having access to information that is reserved only for the few who do understand it on an intellectual and spiritual level.

Gnostics very much exist in today's world. They believe that the world they live in is really an illusion and intrinsically evil. This is represented in the movie ***The Matrix*** in which the main character finds out that his present day world is actually an illusion that was created by a force who wanted to enslave human beings by keeping them asleep. Similar themes could be found in popular movies such as ***Minority Report, Blade Runner,*** and ***Total Recall***. Formal **Gnostic** religions are rarely found, but the **Gnostic** beliefs surely are. **Gnosticism** and Christianity coexist as in ancient times.

THE CHRISTIAN GNOSTICS BELIEFS

We know that the **Gnostics** of the first centuries after Christ felt that they were imprisoned inside their bodies, in the physical world, and it was a hindrance for them to attain the true knowledge, or the "***gnosis***," of their existence. They needed to escape their bodies and this material existence which were evil. They needed to understand the relationship between the distinct and separate material world and the spiritual realm. **Gnostics** understood that we were trapped in the material world and we need to get to the spiritual world to be completely free.

Many of the **Gnostics** share the same belief about of the creation of this world. The **Gnostics** feel an evil demiurge was the one who created this evil world and human beings in it. The term "demiurge" comes from the creator in Plato's ***Timaeus.*** The real true God is the "Supreme Deity" who created the universe and the spiritual realm; who put the spirit and the divine spark in those humans. The demiurge, like Lucifer, is in a battle with the true God for the humans.

The demiurge preys on the ignorance and weaknesses of humans, entrap them in their mortal bodies, and force them to live in his evil and material world. His ultimate mission was to prevent people from realizing the truth about their enslavement and his evil world of suffering and pain, and not realizing a higher spiritual realm awaits them ruled by the True God. It makes fundamentalist preachers cringe when we say the **Gnostics** do believe that Jesus Christ is their Lord and Savior sent from His Father, the one True Almighty God, but to save us from this evil fallen god. This mortality vs. immortality, materiality vs. spirituality, and this world vs. the divine realm is the foundation of the **Gnostic** beliefs.

IMPORTANT POINT: This is the same as when the conservative Christian preachers lecture us about Satan, the fallen archangel Lucifer and his band of devils, who are leading us into temptation, steering us away from the True God, and making us do bad, evil, sinful, and hurtful acts.

The **Gnostics** believe in the good spiritual world created by the one True God, and realize that the demiurge created this material and evil world which distracts humans from finding the true Supreme God so that they think he is the True Supreme God. Humans must attain the **Gnosis** and overcome the demiurge's power over them. This required a savior who could save the people with the **Gnostics** to release them from the material world of the demiurge. The Savior's job was to proclaim the existence of the spiritual world and the reality of the True Almighty God. The "mighty" excluded **Gnostic Gospels** because they contained the **Gnosis** in Jesus' private teachings to His Disciples. Many of those **Gnostic Gospels** are called the "Secret Teachings." Jesus did imply the same in His parables to the general masses, but He entrusted the more complicated teachings to His private sessions with His Inner Circle of Twelve. The **Gnostics** continued this practice by divulging these elite teachings to the "spiritually mature."

IMPORTANT POINT: Many Gnostic sects did not include the Hebrew Bible, or ***Old Testament,*** as part of their Bible with that mean, vengeful, and mass-murderer of innocent people, God. Jesus was their Lord and Savior who told them about His Father who was the all-powerful, all-loving, all-merciful, and all-good Supreme God. Such is the basis of His parables in the ***New Testament*** Gospels. Jesus did save us and introduced His Father, the True God, to us.

GNOSIS UNLOCKS THE INNER SPIRIT

Now everyone should be asking how the **Gnostics** are able to transcend this material world and embrace the higher spiritual realm. The **Gnostics** have the key to the secret and mysterious knowledge. First of all, the realization that the material world and their human bodies are hindrances that need to be overcome in order to know their inner spiritual selves and their One, True God in the divine realm.

Where is this secret knowledge found? **In the Sacred Scriptures: the Bible**. Much of the **Gnostics'** knowledge comes **from their deeper mystical interpretation of specific Biblical passages in the *Old Testament*** such as in regard to the creation of the world and mankind. Of even higher importance are numerous parables of Jesus in the ***New Testament***. These biblical passages when properly interpreted provide the **Gnostics** with the knowledge about the divine realm and the courage to thwart enslavement of humans by the demiurge. The human mind needs to be awakened from its veiled stupor so that it can connect instead to the spiritual world and Supreme Divine being.

Many theologies have similar beliefs as to the nature of human beings. **Humans consisted of a flesh and blood mortal body** (***hyle*** meaning "matter"), **a soul** (***psyche*),** **and our spirit** (***persona*** or ***pneuma*** meaning "personality," "spirit" or "mind). The latter two elements are immortal. **Gnostics believe that the spirit, not the soul, is the most important component that will live on forever in the divine realm**. The body needs to submit to the immortal soul, and the soul, in turn, needs to submit to the spirit. It is the spirit that connects the human being to the Supreme God. **Gnostics** refer to this process the **"divine spark"** which resides inside every person. It is the **"divine spark"** that is the umbilical cord that connects us to God.

For humans to defeat the hold the demiurge has on them and instead gain direct access to the divine realm, **Gnostics** use "cosmic" and "scientific" knowledge found in astronomy, cosmology, astrology, Christology, demonology, angelology, mathematics, physics, geometry, geology, and all the physical sciences. To the knowledge of the aforementioned, and more, add a sophisticated interpretation of the Scriptures, their understanding of this world and beyond starts to coalesce. This is grouped by many together as "metaphysics." The **Gnostics** have mastered their application of the sciences of the physical world and universe to assist them in advancing from this material world into the ethereal divine realm.

The Gnostics were keenly aware of how the good and evil supernatural entities affected human beings.

The **Gnostics** particularly study the effects of angelology and demonology; consequently, the **Gnostics** were able to manipulate these forces to release the human body from its material restraints. This knowledge usually is out of the normal mental sphere for most people; it is made available to only a select few who seek it and accept the Savior's calling. Of course, they need to possess the intellectual and spiritual maturity to respond to His calling. The **Gnostics** have always considered themselves to be the people elected to attain the understanding of the divine spark which is deeply implanted inside them.

They also had enough knowledge of the universe to follow their divine spark through the cosmos to connect to the divine realm of the One, True God. This knowledge constitutes almost a doctoral-level education in theology and spirituality. The **Gnostics** understood the nature of human existence and the ultimate goal to be attained. They not only knew from where they came but also to where they were going. Many outsiders resented the **Gnostics'** smugness and elitism. Their arrogance intensified opposition and eventually drove many of their sects underground.

The following saying (Saying #50) from the ***Gospel of Thomas*** is like a **Gnostic** creed:

> ***Jesus said, "If interested people said to you, 'From where do you come?' reply to them, 'We come from the light, from the place where the light created itself, founded itself, and appears in its own image.' If they ask further, "Are you the light?' reply to them, "We are its children, and we are the elect of the living Father.' If they ask you for proof the Father dwells in you, answer them in this way, 'It is motion and rest'."***

THE MYTH OF SOPHIA

How did this become an evil world? From where did the demiurge come? Why are we stuck in this false, material world? These answers can be found in the **Gnostic** myth of Sophia. Within the Jewish tradition, Sophia (which is also the Greek word for "wisdom") was the personification of God's wisdom and His consort. Sophia appears in the "wisdom books" of King Solomon in the Hebrew Bible: ***Ecclesiastes, Proverbs***, and the ***Song of Songs***. Sophia is also referenced by use of the plural form in the story of the creation, "Let ***us*** make man in ***our*** own image, according to ***our*** likeness" (***Genesis*** 1:26). The plurals can be construed as a reference to God and his consort, Sofia (Wisdom). In **Gnostic** traditions, Sophia was one of many divine beings (like angels and archangels) that were created and emanated from God.

The difference comes **in the Gnostic creation story. Sophia took it upon herself and created this world without God's approval. Sophia's creation was a failure which she attempted to hide.** She had a bastard son who she left in charge of this world; not knowing any better he considered himself the Supreme Being but really was a demiurge, a false god. He was a mean and wrathful god who enjoyed destroying his slaves. Luckily, because of Sophia, the human beings had the "divine spark" inside of them. Our only redemption would be through that link to the divine realm.

Sophia's failed creation was a disturbance in the harmony of the divine realm, the ***Pleroma.*** In Greek, ***Pleromai*** means the fullness, suggesting perfection. In **Gnostic** cosmology, there are eight planetary spheres with the earth in the center and the ninth sphere being the divine realm where

God and all the divine beings are. Sophia fell from grace. The **Gnostics** were ascending toward divine realm. The **Gnostics** knew once they reached the divine world there would be no more births, suffering, or deaths. The material world is constantly changing and will eventually go away. The divine realm is constantly regenerating and renewing.

Clement of Alexandria was a leading orthodox Christian teacher in Alexandria, Egypt. He preserved the sayings of one a **Gnostic teacher** named Theodotus. This is his passage (78:2) that explains the basic tenets of **Gnosticism**:

> ***Baptism alone does not save us. We are saved by the knowledge of who we are and where we began, where we have been, and what we have become, where we are going, and what has liberated us, what constitutes [real] birth, and what constitutes [real] rebirth.***

THE APOSTLES' CREED

The Christian Creed is believed to have been passed down from Jesus' Twelve Disciples and it was required to be recited entirely and accurately from memory to be baptized a Christian. After some additions, it became known as ***The Apostles' Creed*** and was widely used as the Profession of Faith in Christian Churches.

Legend has it that this Creed was composed by the Apostles on the day of the Pentecost and that each of them contributed one of the twelve sections. The original Creed seems to have had three uses: First, as a profession of the Christian faith for those about to be baptized; Secondly, as a catechism of instruction for new Christians in the essentials of the Christian faith; and Thirdly, as a 'rule of faith' to give future continuity to the orthodox and true Christianity.

> ***I believe in God, the Father Almighty,***
> ***Creator of Heaven and Earth,***
> ***And in Jesus Christ, His only Son, Our Lord,***
> ***Who was conceived by the Holy Spirit,***
> ***Born of the Virgin Mary,***
> ***Suffered under Pontius Pilate,***
> ***Was crucified, died, and was buried;***
> ***He descended into Hell;***
> ***On the third day, he rose again from the dead;***
> ***He ascended into Heaven,***
> ***And is seated at the right hand of God the Father Almighty;***
> ***From there He will come to judge the living and the dead.***
>
> ***I believe in the Holy Spirit,***
> ***The holy, catholic Church,***
> ***The communion of saints,***
> ***The forgiveness of sins,***
> ***The resurrection of the body,***
> ***And life everlasting. Amen.***

This is the creed that makes everyone a Christian. This is the creed that must be recited at a person's baptism. When we refer to any type of Christian, including the **Gnostic Christians**, they recite this at their baptism and believe in this creed. This was updated thrice in the 4th and 5th Centuries into a more encompassing Nicene-Constantinopolitan-Athanasian Creed (more dogma was added such as the full "divinity" and full "humanity" of Jesus Christ, and that Jesus was not only begotten but was fully consubstantial with the Father and Holy Spirit from all eternity). We usually refer to it still as the Nicene Creed which is now considered to be the formal Christian Creed or statement of Christian beliefs. Anyone who does not profess this creed is not considered to be a real "Christian" according to the one, holy, catholic (universal), and apostolic Christian Church Councils of the 4th and 5th centuries. You would be surprised by the number of people in the current day who call themselves "Christians" but would not be considered "real" Christians according to the Church Councils who established the one universal Christian Church from which they broke away and established their own set of doctrines and "home-grown" brand of Christianity.

##

BIBLIOGRAPHY, REFERENCES, AND SUGGESTED READING

Brown, Peter, ***Rise of Western Christianity: Triumph and Diversity A.D. 200-1000*** © 2003 Blackwell Publishers, Malden, Massachusetts

Butz, Jeffrey J., ***Brother of Jesus and the Lost Teachings of the Ancient Mediterranean World*** © 2005 Inner Traditions, Rochester, Vermont

Grant, R.M., ***Gnosticism and Early Christianity*** © 1959 New York University Press, New York

Mack, Burton L., ***Q, the Lost Gospel: The Book of Christian Origins*** © 1993 Harper Collins, New York

Nardo, Don, ***Rise of Christianity, The*** © 2001 Lucient Books, San Diego, California

Pagels, Elaine, ***Gnostic Gospels, The: A Startling Account of the Meaning of Jesus and the Origin of Christianity Based on the Gnostic Gospels and Other Secret Texts*** © 1979, 1989 Vintage Books-Random House, New York

Roukema, Riener, ***Gnosis and Faith in Early Christianity: An Introduction to Gnosticism*** © 1999 Trinity Press International, Harrisburg, Pennsylvania

Stark, Rodney, ***Rise of Christianity, The: Obscure, Marginal Jesus Movement Became the Dominant Religious Farce in the Western World in a Few Countries*** © 1996 Princeton University Press

Author's Note: This Book and Treatise are a compilation from many sources on the same subject. See the Complete List of Bibliographies, References, and Suggested Readings in Appendix II

CHAPTER 6

THE ORTHODOX CHURCH BATTLES THE GNOSTICS

HISTORICAL BACKGROUND

As the unified Christian Church was being formed, these so-called "orthodox" Church leaders vigorously banished any "non-believers" to their version of Christianity. They actively persecuted speakers of "heresies" (which does not mean what you believe is wrong just that it does not conform). The Church leaders punished them and excommunicated them. They banned all their religious texts and ordered them to be destroyed by fire. Lucky for us, a library of **Gnostic Christian** books and texts were buried in the Egyptian desert. This was believed to have been done by a nearby ancient monastery of St. Pachomius. The area was known to be a place of **Gnostic Christian** activity.

Scholars believe that the monks living in St. Pachomius revered and treasured these sacred texts and purposely did not destroy them as they were ordered to do but instead hid them in a jar in a cave. They probably hoped that these texts sacred to them would be found by a future and more tolerant generation. One of their monks was found buried holding just a copy of ***The Gospel of Peter.*** Many of the Gospels and Epistles were written in **Coptic**, an ancient form of Egyptian. It is believed that these religious texts were originally written in Greek, which was the language of education, finance, and commerce in Asia Minor where Greece is located.

There are not only the Gospels of Peter, James, Philip, Thomas, Judas, and Mary Magdalene but also Epistles, letters to each other, and other texts by various **Gnostic** sects and their founders. What they all had in common was their spiritual and ideological differences from what the so-called "orthodox" Christian leaders were preaching.

IMPORTANT POINT: It ceases to amaze me how we are only allowed to read **FOUR** Gospels, and only **TWO** are attributed to Disciples, Matthew and John (it can be debated whom Mark and Luke are) when there are **SIX** other Gospels attributed to **SIX** other of Jesus' Disciples, His Inner Circle. Why were these kept from us?

IMPORTANT POINT: The reason Biblical scholars believe is that it contains the principles of **Gnosticism** and, more importantly, the majorly different **Gnostic** view of creation and salvation. They also expose the readers to the inner knowledge – **gnosis** – as a real means of attaining salvation. It also contains the highly controversial belief that there is a feminine aspect of God. These sacred texts expose you to the alternative beauty and vibrant view of ancient Christianity.

It is important to remember that Jesus did not establish a new religion, nor did his Disciples. It is equally important to realize that the Disciples were illiterate and did not write the Gospels that were "attributed to them."

In fact, the Gospels were "eventually written" based on memory and the oral transmission of stories they heard.

It is believed by the Biblical scholars that the ***Gospel of Mark*** was the first Gospel to be put in writing which was some thirty years after his the death of Jesus. Thirty years is a very long time to pass stories from groups of people to groups of people for decades with losing any integrity and without adding any embellishments. Coincidentally, no one is positively sure who Luke is. We do know that the other Gospels of Matthew, Mark, and John were written decades after Luke. In fact, it appears to the Biblical scholars that Matthew and Mark used Luke as their source document. So much so that the three of them are called the "synoptic Gospels" meaning that they are similar. Likewise, nobody positively knows who Mark is either. Neither Luke nor Mark were Disciples. The emerging Christian Church leaders liked the similarity of these three Gospels so much that these Gospels were selected by them for inclusion in the canonical, or sanctioned, New Testament. ***John*** was added to be Gospel number 4 even though it was different and more mystical. The reason: John had many followers in Asia Minor and if they did not include his Gospel they would have lost those followers.

IMPORTANT POINT: The word "**Christian**" did not come into being until decades after Jesus' death. The word "Christian" came from the Greek term ***"Christianai."***

The **Gnostic Gospels** were also written by Christians who were followers of other Disciples of Jesus: **James, Philip, Thomas, Peter, Judas, and Mary Magdalene.** However, these Gospels were rejected by the emerging Church leaders who banned them and eventually ordered them destroyed by fire because their parables were at odds with the synoptic Gospels. These Church leaders decided which direction their emerging Church will take and what its beliefs would be.

IMPORTANT POINT: It has always fascinated me to think that from the beginning the Christian Church has taken off in the wrong direction by adopted the wrong Gospels (not counting ***John***) and destroyed the more true Gospels. Consequently, Jesus' mission failed. His real message went up in smoke.

THE GNOSTIC CHRISTIANS

Unlike the so-called "Orthodox" Christians, the **Gnostic Christians'** beliefs and spirituality were on a larger and higher level. They drew from many sources and sacred texts not only from the Hebrews but also the Romans, the Greeks, the Egyptians, and indigenous others in Asia Minor, the Middle East, Africa, and the Far East.

The **Gnostics** believe that a person comes to know God through attaining the knowledge of your inner self. The divine is within all of us. Many refer to this as the "divine spark." Through this, we are all linked directly to God. This knowledge is the Greek word "**gnosis**" and the **Gnostics** are referred to as the "**gnostikoi"** in Greek, or the "Knowing Ones." They have a completely different philosophy about salvation. They don't believe we need the Christian Church to attain salvation because Jesus Christ came to tell us that salvation came through attaining the **gnosis** and when realize we already have the divine spark within ourselves that will merge us back into the divine. The fifty-two mostly **Gnostic** texts discovered in 1945 cast a new light not only on salvation but also on the diversity and conflicts of the early Christian communities in this regard. Early Christian Church leaders considered **Gnostic** writings as heretical and ordered them banned them and destroyed by fire. These texts were considered dangerous even to possess or have around at all. Apparently, this was strongly not the philosophy of the monks of St. Pachomius that they willfully disobeyed their superiors to whom they had taken the vow of obedience, and they hid the texts in desert caves near Nag Hammadi, Egypt.

Most Biblical scholars considered that Jesus' preaching was eschatological. "Eschatological" is derived from the Greek "***eschatos"*** meaning "the end." Many, even today, consider that to mean the "end-of-days," the "end-of-time", the "end-of-life-on-earth," or too many present-day evangelists the "day-Jesus-returns-to-judge-the-living-and-the-dead." During Jesus' lifetime, many of the people believed Jesus was the Messiah, the Anointed One, in fulfillment of the ancient prophets' predictions. To many, Jesus' words are all about the Apocalypse. But to the **Gnostics,** the Apocalypse is Good News, not a time to be feared.

Another major "unorthodox" belief that resonates in different forms with various **Gnostic** sects is the true "nature" of Jesus Christ. Some believe, like the "orthodox" Christians, that Jesus was an offspring of the Eternal Almighty, God the Father, and was incarnated, made to be a human being, and died a human death. Catholics take it a step further and believe Jesus Christ is consubstantiated with the Father, that is, He is one and the same as the Father. Behind the scenes, this was done in order to maintain that Christianity follows the Hebrew lead in that we too are a monotheistic religion, i.e. there is only One God. Some **Gnostic** sects believe the opposite. Jesus was born a human being and was "deified" or made God.

JESUS CHALLENGED JEWISH TEACHINGS

For the most part, Jesus and His Disciples were devout Jews, practicing and worshipping in the Hebrew tradition. But there were times Jesus sidestepped his Hebrew faith. Jesus accepted Mary Magdalene as one of His Disciples if not His wife when it was tradition to consider women inferior to men and the property of men. Jesus admonished what was found in the Hebrew Bible to take "***an eye for an eye***" (***Exodus*** 21:24), instead, He told His followers to "***turn the other cheek and do unto others as you would have them do unto you***" (***Luke*** 6:28-31). Jesus violated the strict Jewish purity rules regarding contact with the dead when He resurrected the dead child of Jairus and His friend Lazarus. Jesus ignored the rule of keeping holy the Sabbath when He preached and cured the sick on the Sabbath. This angered the Pharisees and probably contributed to Jesus being tried and executed on religious grounds such as blasphemy.

After Jesus' death, His Disciples and their followers still saw themselves as needing to follow the Law of Moses with its required male circumcision and strict dietary rules. In fact, anyone interested in becoming a Christian must first to Judaism. Everything was going smoothly until the gentile Roman Paul had a vision and began converting the non-Jewish gentiles to Christianity. This caused much concern among the Disciples and their followers in Jerusalem.

Following the dietary and purity laws were very difficult for the Gentiles to start following, but the deal breaker was for the adult males needing to get circumcised. This was an important ritual to follow in order to comply with God's command to Abraham.

"This is my covenant, which ye shall keep, between me and you and thy seed after thee: Every man child among you shall be circumcised. And ye shall circumcise the flesh of your foreskin, and it shall be a token of the covenant betwixt me and you" (***Genesis*** 17:10-11).

Paul's incessantly pled his case to the Disciples in Jerusalem, after much debate among them it was decided that most of these requirements could be relaxed for the Gentiles as long as they "***abstain from the worship of idols, from fornication, and from blood***" (***Acts*** 15:20). But still, Paul butted heads several times with the Disciples in Jerusalem, mainly James, Peter, and John who were considered the leaders of the Christianity Movement, which was fully documented by Paul in the ***Acts of the Apostles***.

Giving Paul credit where credit is due, he was responsible for a great breakthrough in converting Gentiles. However, a reading of the Epistles (Letters) of Paul exposes a great difference between his teachings and those of Jesus' Disciples. He was accused of misunderstanding and erroneously interpreting the teachings of Jesus' teachings, squabbling, and causing conflicts among the Christian communities and churches that were established by the Disciples. This all was met with fierce disapproval from the Disciples and Paul was reprimanded many times by them.

<u>**IMPORTANT POINT:**</u> Paul rebelled so much against Jesus' Disciples and was very forcefully vocal about it; at one point saying to his followers, ***"anyone who believes those imposters in Jerusalem deserves eternal damnation."***

THE GNOSTIC GOSPELS

The **Gnostic Christians** embraced the idea of attaining "**gnosis"** or "knowledge" about from where we came, why we are here, and to where we will return in the afterlife as the salvation Jesus was talking about. This conflicted with the emerging "orthodox" believers that Jesus died for our sins and His death ensured our salvation for those who accepted Him as their Lord and Savior. You also see a wider range of beliefs on the nature of Jesus among **Gnostic** sects. Some believed that Jesus was a mortal prophet who delivered a divine message; some felt that Jesus was fully human and that Christ was the divine spirit that dwelled in Him, and some believed that Jesus never actually died nor was He buried.

The **Gnostic Gospels** tell a different story and a different philosophy of Jesus. Salvation does not come from the death of Jesus. That was just Jesus' everlasting spirit being released from his temporal mortal body. It is more important to recognize that salvation comes from the inner enlightenment of who we are and how we were entrapped by the evil inferior god of this world who inflicts pain, suffering, and death to his subjects. They credit Jesus with being the enlightenment that came to this world to reveal to us that it is the real **gnosis** that lets us see the truth. This is explained in more detail in the **Gnostic *Gospels of the Egyptians.***

The theologies and Christologies of early Christians suggest all the different directions that Christianity was taking. Christianity as a whole was full of disagreement and dissension on many issues. Roman Emperor Constantine with the Council of Nicaea tried to unify all the different sects and form a common core of Christian beliefs. The result was the Nicene Creed which established a universal Christian Church. It had a limited effect. There were too many other influences and cultures with longstanding ancient roots, such as Roman and Greek polytheism, Palestinian Jews, Zoroastrians, The Pharisees, the Sadducees, The Zealots, Muslims, and that does not include the myriad of other religious beliefs beyond the Asia Minor.

Emperor Constantine's emerging One, Holy, Catholic (i.e. universal), and Apostolic Christian Church was anything but one universal Church. Almost immediately after the death of Jesus, the Disciples began to go off in different directions, literally and figuratively. They even could not decide who would be their leader. Some had pledged their loyalty toward Peter, the leader appointed by Jesus. Many had a preference for James the Just who was Jesus' brother. James remained in Jerusalem and technically was the first bishop there who oversaw the fledgling Christian community there. We know that Peter was originally there in Jerusalem with James, along with John. We know this because of this guy who came out of the blue called Saul, or Paul, who never knew Jesus but took it upon himself to preach "his own brand" of Christianity. Paul very well documented in his Epistles what a problem he was with James, Peter, and John. Eventually, James sent Peter to Rome and John to Asia Minor. The other Disciples scattered to other regions of the world to preach and convert people to the Good News about Jesus Christ.

The Disciples preached what Jesus taught them through using similar sayings, anecdotes, parables, and prayers. The direct Disciples of Jesus appointed their own apostles, or missionaries, to spread the Word of Jesus. On their own, they were getting more and more distant from the Disciples, other apostles, the theology, and Christology. Consequently, the interpretation of Jesus' teachings began to deviate or even conflicted with another's understanding. It becomes very evident when comparing the four Gospels horizontally that were selected to be in the New Testament. These four Gospels were committed to writing after being passed down purely by word of mouth. The discrepancies and contradictions could be seen when they were put into writing 60 to 90 years, 6 to 9 decades, almost a whole century after the death of Jesus [a whole chapter is devoted to the details of these discrepancies and contradictions in ***Alternative Christianities – Volume I***]. In the 2nd and 3rd Centuries, these differences caused major theological issues to be reckoned and resolved by the majority of Bishops at the Council of Nicaea.

Then there were the so-called **Gnostic Gospels,** the ***Gospels of Peter, James, Philip, Thomas, Judas,*** and ***Mary Magdalene*** which were written at about the turn of the 1st Century. They had a more mystical approach to Jesus' salvation and the emerging Church ordered them banned and destroyed.

IMPORTANT POINT: What makes the Gospels of ***Matthew, Mark*** (who?), ***Luke*** (who?), and ***John*** more valid and sanctimonious than the Gospels of ***Peter, James, Philip, Thomas, Judas, Mary Magdalene*** or anything written by anyone from those 1st and 2nd Centuries? Why are we being restricted to only four Gospels by our Church? Wouldn't any avid "Christian" want to be able to read any and all writings about their Lord and Savior, Jesus Christ? And, there are many, many more ancient texts than the aforementioned six additional Gospels.

The result in the early centuries was the splintering off into groups of Christians. Raymond Brown, a respected Biblical scholar, has suggested an early schism among Christians into main groups: **Apostolic Christians** (strict "orthodox" believers or those that follow the beliefs as outlined by the church leaders in Rome) and **Secessionists** (other than strict "orthodox" Apostolic Christian believers which include the **Gnostics**).

IMPORTANT POINT: Just to be clear, allow me to repeat myself. The word "orthodox" means the "true beliefs." Obviously, "true" is in the eyes of the beholder. Roman Catholics believe they practice the true or "orthodox" beliefs. The different Protestant denominations believe they each practice the true or "orthodox" beliefs, e.g. the Lutherans vs. the Roman Catholics, the Methodists vs. the Baptists, the Christians vs. the Jews vs. the Muslims. The "orthodox" believers call the followers, not in concert with them, to be "heretics" and their beliefs "heresy" or "not true." Like "orthodoxy," "heresy" is in the eyes of the beholder. Don't take the words "orthodox," "non-orthodox," "heresy," and "heretic" literally. It is confusing because of how those words were being used and by whom.

The belief held by the "orthodox" Church is that Jesus had been sent from God, the Father, to save humankind by His passion, death, and resurrection. The **Gnostics** do not agree with those so-called "orthodox" beliefs. Most of the **Gnostics** share in the dualistic belief. The Superior God is the source of light, life, wisdom and the eternal divine realm; while there is another inferior deity who is the one who created this world full of pain and suffering. The **Gnostics** believe that humans must be enlightened or gain this knowledge in order to escape their imprisonment. To the **Gnostics,** Jesus is our

Savior who brought us the Light, who was the revealer of **gnosis**, and this was how Jesus Christ saved mankind.

The "Apostolic Age" ends when the last Disciple of Jesus Christ's inner circle dies. Into the 2nd Century, the leadership of converting and maintaining "Christians" fell to early church fathers such as **Irenaeus, Hippolytus, Tertullian, Origen, and Epiphanius.** By default, the protection of the emerging Christian faith was left to these and other self-appointed leaders who shared common ground with their literalist "***interpretations***" of the teachings of Jesus that were passed down from the generations before them. Consequently, through the first centuries, these particular leaders were fiercely opposed to the more liberal and differing interpretations of Jesus' teachings. Especially targeted were the various groups of **Gnostic Christians** and others whose interpretations did not coincide with ***their understanding*** of Jesus' teachings. They were considered a threat to the "orthodox" Christianity; they were called "heretics" promoting "heresies."

THE GNOSTICS

In the early centuries there was a great expansion of Christianity not only in the regions around the Mediterranean but also past Asia Minor deep into Asia, far into India, and south into Africa. The new converts were culturally and politically different from the Jews, Christians, and gentiles that the Disciples and their missionaries had to deal with.

The teachings of Christianity were interpreted differently by the people of the various cultures. Before there was a centralized Christian Church, Christianity manifested itself in many different ways based on the same teachings.

<u>IMPORTANT POINT:</u> Some liberal Biblical scholars believe that is the way Jesus Christ intended it to be. He could have but did not establish a religion and lay down formal rules and guidelines. That was done by men centuries later who never knew Him. Maybe He did not intend for it to be so strict and damning but a religion of love and compassion.

Many **Gnostic Christian** religions also spread rapidly from the 2nd to 4th Centuries throughout Asia Minor in Greece, Palestine, Syria, and Egypt. Amazingly, the different sects of **Gnosticism** developed similar schools of thought about their Christianity. In many ways, they pre-dated the formal Christianity with their cohesion. They enhanced their Christianity with what they borrowed from Greek philosophers like Plato, Judaism, Hinduism, and Buddhism. It was ecumenical, probably just the way Jesus Christ wanted his followers to be.

<u>IMPORTANT POINT:</u> In the writings of the Disciple James (possibly Jesus' stepbrother from widower Joseph's first marriage) details the missing years of Jesus so obvious in the four canonical Gospels. James and his brother Jesus went on an extended journey through Asia to study the Eastern Asian religions. Traces of His visit could be found.

The main difference between the so-called "orthodox" Christians and the **Gnostic Christians** is that the latter were **<u>spiritual seekers</u>**. They constantly were on a mission to acquire knowledge, the ***gnosis***, to gain more and more understanding of the Supreme Deity and His Divine Realm. They believed it was only through this inner knowledge you can get to know God and be able to liberate your soul from this evil and materialistic world. This was their purpose in life.

They gathered this secret knowledge and wisdom from their own insights of the world around them.

The **Gnostics** presented their ideas and beliefs the same way as the "orthodox" Christians did through Gospels, letters, sayings, hymns, and treatises. Unfortunately, unlike the "orthodox" material, so little of the **Gnostic** literature survived. The best yielding find was the 1945 discovery of over fifty **Gnostic** writings in a cave near Nag Hammadi, Egypt. The material has since been translated and published in the book ***The Nag Hammadi Library***, edited by James M. Robinson. It also can be found on the Internet at **www.gnosis.org/naghamm/nhl.html**.

GNOSTIC BELIEFS

Before we get into the **Gnostic** beliefs we need to define some of the common terms you will encounter:

- **AEONS: Gnostics** believe that God is able to spread His essence through eternal subordinate deities.

- **ARCHON:** The **Gnostics** believe the archons are rulers that serve the Demiurge. Some call them fallen angels, demons, or evil forces. They are counterproductive to the work of the divine spark and create earthly obstacles to prevent the humans from knowing the truth about their salvation and the afterlife that awaits us.

- **DEMIURGE:** For **Gnostics**, the Demiurge is the malevolent creator god, the architect of this material, evil, and physical world. He is fundamentally flawed and imprisons human beings for his own pleasure and amusement. He, probably a fallen angel, is also known by the names Yaldabaoth which is Greek for "the Father of Chaos," Sakla meaning "the Foolish One," and several other names as well. Some even consider him to be the fallen Archangel Lucifer with his band of "devils."

- **DOCETISM:** Docetism comes from the Greek "to seem." This is an important principle for **Gnostics** who believe that neither Jesus' physical body nor his crucifixion was real; they only "seemed" to be real. The **Gnostics** believe that Jesus was an eternal spirit or deity (also known as an Avatar) who emanated from the Almighty God and as such did not possess a real human flesh body and could not really die.

- **DUALISM:** Many Dualistic ideas are found in **Gnostic** beliefs. This is when two things which are fundamentally different and opposite, such as good-evil, material-spiritual, or heaven-earth.

- **GNOSIS:** Is the all-important term of **Gnosticism. Gnosis** is Greek which means "knowing." The **gnosis** in **Gnostic Theology** has stood for having attained the inner spiritual knowledge of the mystical truths. This was the secret knowledge or truth shared by Jesus to a selected few who were able to grasp it but He did not reveal to the general public. To the latter, Jesus preached it in simple parables.

- **PLEROMA:** Pleroma is Greek for "fullness or whole" which refers to the totality of the universe and the Divine Realm. The Pleroma is what many would simplistically call Heaven. It is the real spiritual realm where the Almighty God is and His army of Gods or the Aeons.

- **<u>SOPHIA:</u>** Sophia is a figure that appears many times through **Gnostic** literature. Sophia means "wisdom" and is an Aeon who is considered the feminine side of God. Sophia is a part of our salvation because it is she who gives us the gift of **gnosis** allowing our divine sparks to return to Pleroma.

- **<u>EARTH AND HEAVEN:</u>** Now that is going to take a much longer explanation:

The Gnostics believe there are two main realms, what most people refer to as Earth and Heaven. Earth is the materialistic world we live in. It is full of evil, dark, and malevolent forces causing pain, suffering, misery, and death. It was created and ruled by the Demiurge, which is akin to what Christians, Jews, and Muslims refer to as "Satan." And it is ruled by the Demiurge's Archons, which is akin to what many of the same people refer to as "devils" or "demons."

The other realm is one of Light which is ruled over by the Almighty Supreme Good True God with His divine army of Aeons. Integral to Gnostic theology is the idea of a divine spark within all of us that connects us to the realm of the Almighty, the Pleroma. Unfortunately, this divine spark is trapped in the darkness of the material world where it subject to suffering. It is only when we attain the **gnosis** or inner knowledge that we will be free from this inferior world.

The good news is that although it is trapped in this dark, evil, and materialistic world, there are saviors. Aeons like Sophia who is the embodiment of wisdom and Jesus who is the embodiment of Our Savior bringing to us the secret teachings that allow our trapped divine sparks to find their way to the infinite good realm of Light.

The **Gnostic** conception of a creator god called Demiurge may have come from the figure Demiurgos in Plato's ***Timaeus*** and ***Republic***. Out of chaos was created the Demiurge which was an inferior and flawed copy of the divine entities. It purposely or unconsciously still had part of the divine source within it that gave it the power to create. This world that they created, maybe out of revenge to the Supreme God, would be evil and materialistic. The humans that inhabit this world are prisoners of this Demiurge, however, their bodies still contain the divine sparks of the Pleroma. Synonymous with a person's soul, the divine spark must escape from this materialistic world and work to get back to the Pleroma. For the **Christian Gnostics,** Jesus Christ is their Savior, the one who came to deliver us from this dark world.

Ironically it was centuries earlier in Greece that Plato had asserted the same premise. Plato said that the cosmos was created out of chaos by the ***Demiurgos.*** Plato in ***Timaeus*** relays how the ***Demiurgos*** was a "craftsman" who formed this world out of chaos making this world imperfect. Plato further expressed in his ***Phaedo*** the idea that our human bodies are imperfect copies of the higher eternal forms but they did contain an immortal soul.

Christianity, along with Judaism and Islam, is a monotheistic religion, i.e. the belief that there is only one God. The idea of a Demiurge was rejected by the Christian leaders. The idea was absurd to them that any other God or being created the cosmos than the one benevolent God.

Plato's advocating dualism. He considered that the human body is a different entity from the soul. The body is simply a temporal container for the soul. Plato's ideas coincided with the **Gnostics** in that the soul came from the spiritual realm and existed before it entered the body. It becomes the overseer of the human nature.

In ***Timaeus*** Plato explains his idea:

> "***Man is the soul which utilizes the body. Now God did not make the soul after the body… for having brought them together he would never have allowed the elder be ruled by the younger..,. Whereas he made the soul in origin and excellence prior to, and older than, the body, to be the ruler and mistress, of whom the body was to be the subject." – Timaeus***, 34

CREATION

The first book of the Hebrew Bible, Genesis, says that the One Supreme God alone created heaven and earth which was dark and without form. He then created light out of the darkness. God finally created Adam and Eve in "his own image, male and female."

> ***"And the Lord God formed man of the dust of the ground, and breathed into his nostrils the breath of life; and man became a living soul… And the Lord God caused a deep sleep to fall upon Adam and he slept; and he took one of his ribs, and … made him a woman, and brought her unto the man."*** (***Genesis*** 2:7-22)

The **Gnostics** did not see creation the same way the Jews and Christians did. Adam and Eve were not necessarily actual people but the personification of two opposing principles. Adam represented the soul and Eve was the spirit. Their existence had nothing to do with the famous couple who brought down humanity with their original sin. This puts a dent in the beliefs and religion of the so-called "orthodox" Christians... no original sin!

The **Gnostic** text, ***Apocryphon of John*** (the same John who authored the ***Gospel of John*** and the Apocryphon known as ***Revelations***), says that Adam was in the "***drunkenness of darkness.***" Adam was awakened by Luminous Epinoia (or Eve which means "life" in Hebrew) who "***lifted the veil which lay over his mind.***" The **Gnostics** considered Eve the "mother of all the living." Some of the early Christian and **Gnostic** sects believed in a deity they called "Luminous Epinoia" or the Divine Eve. The word "***luminous***" is synonymous with "light." Some **Gnostics** saw Eve as the "light bearer."

The **Gnostics** view Eve in stark contrast to the "orthodox" beliefs. For the latter, they tell us that Eve was a weak woman. She could not resist the temptation the serpent put in front of her. She did as he suggested and ate the fruit from the forbidden tree in the Garden of Eden. Eve "***saw that the tree was good for food... pleasant to the eyes, and a tree to be desired to make one wise***" (***Genesis*** 3:6). She wanted to be wise. She did not want to be considered inferior to Adam, nor be considered less intelligent than him. She wanted to be elevated to his level.

<u>IMPORTANT POINT:</u> Another disputed belief was the concept of the Holy Trinity – the Father, the Son, and the Holy Spirit – which was invented later by the Christian Church; it does not appear or is eluded in any Holy Scripture. They needed to do that in order to continue the Hebrew tradition in Christianity as being a monotheistic (One God) religion. The Church leaders put their **<u>NEW CONCEPT</u>** into their rewrite of ***Apostles' Creed*** (written about A.D. 215) which was greatly expanded by the Council of Nicaea in the form of the first ***Nicene Creed*** (published in A.D. 325) and subsequently was expanded further. These were the central, mandatory creeds to be adhered in order to be a "Christian."

IMPORTANT POINT: Both concepts of "Original Sin" and the "Holy Trinity" were major points of contention between the Church Leaders in Rome and the Eastern Orthodox Church Leaders in Constantinople and the 1054 schism.

SETHIAN GNOSTICS

In the 5th chapter of Genesis, we are introduced to a son of Adam, Seth. We are told that when Adam was 130 years old he had a son "***in his own likeness, and after his image; and called his name Seth***" (***Genesis*** 5:3). The Sethian **Gnostics** preferred **Sethian Gnostic**-leaning texts including:

> ***Zostrianos, The Three Steles of Seth, Apocalypse of Adam, Allogenes, The Reality of the Rulers, The Gospel of the Egyptians, The Apocryphon of John, The Threefold First Thought,* and *The Thunder, Perfect Mind.***

Sethian Gnostic did not believe that it was the so-called "original sin" by Adam and Eve which brought down humanity. It was the act of the inferior Demiurge creator who wanted to force his subjects to be enslaved to him.

IMPORTANT POINT: This was discussed at more length in ***Volume I*** how vengeful, revengeful, destructive, punitive, and mean the "God of the Jews" was to the humans. The Almighty God is supposed to be all-good, all-loving, all-merciful, and all-nurturing. The God of the Hebrew Bible (the

Old Testament) could not be the Supreme God and could not the creator of this world.

The Sethian's believed in an Aeon that was called Barbelo who was considered to be an original protégé of the Supreme God. In turn, Barbelo produced other emanations; sort of like cells divide and multiply. Some believe that this caused the universe to become unstable. This gave rise to Aeon Sophia. She decided to do some emanating of her own. As she tried to copy herself she caused a crisis in the Pleroma realm. The result was Sophia creating Yaldabaoth, the infamous Demiurge. For her illegitimate son, Sofia created a realm for him where he lived autonomously, isolated, and ignorant of the higher Pleroma realm and all its legitimate deities. Yaldabaoth got divine powers from his mother which he used to create our material world. Not knowing any better, his world was flawed and imperfect. As an inferior creator, this carried over to the humans with which he populated it. His creation did/does not reflect the reality of the all-good Pleroma realm. His humans became his subservient subjects and **he** ensnared them in his material, evil, and painful world. Yaldabaoth considered himself to be the Supreme God.

IMPORTANT POINT: Yaldabaoth could have been synonymous with Yahweh, the God of the Hebrews. Remember, when asked by what name he should be called, the response was YHWH which became Yahweh, or maybe it should have been Yaldabaoth. Being ignorant of any other Gods, he declares, "***I am a jealous God; there is no God but me.***" To the **Gnostics,** whether it is Yaldabaoth or Yahweh, they are both inferior and evil gods.

GOOD NEWS: Because human beings are a descendant of a deity from the Pleroma realm, all humans have a divine spark that links it back to the Pleroma. This is the important message of Jesus Christ and the **Gnostics:** we must know from where we came, why we are here, and to where we will return when we die. This is our salvation according to the **Gnostics.** This is the ***GNOSIS!***

GNOSTIC TEXTS

Theologians agree that for the first three centuries there were no unified set of beliefs among Christians, no unanimous creed to profess, or church dogmas. In fact, there was NO New Testament but innumerable texts. Instead, there was a great disparity in theological ideas such as the concept of original sin, the divinity of Jesus, the virgin birth, etc.

The **Gnostics** always considered themselves to be faithful Christians. They did not see the practices of their rites or religious sacraments as in defiance against other Christian communities only their interpretations were different. Until the Council of Nicaea and the establishment by Roman Emperor Constantine, there was no one catholic (i.e. universal) Christian Church. Until that time, there was no official Christian Church to challenge the **Gnostic Christians**. There were certain Christian leaders who wrote very strongly against **Gnostic Christians.** This led to persecution for heresy of many of the **Gnostic** sects. The Council of Nicaea and the establishment of the one Christian Church gave them the power to order compliance with the Church's doctrines. This only forced many of the **Gnostic** communities to go underground.

The **Gnostics** texts give us a different perspective and a new look at the earliest followers of Jesus Christ in the first few centuries beyond the familiar ***New Testament*** texts. These ancient texts including many Gospels about

Jesus' life and teachings by some of his closest Disciples and companions: Peter, James, Philip, Thomas, Mary Magdalene, and Judas Iscariot, among others. They were all banned, ordered destroyed by fire, by the late 4th Century one catholic Christian Church bishops when they decided which texts were deemed appropriate for the new church. Many Christians remained ignorant of these **Gnostic Gospels** until fifty-two ancient papyri texts were discovered in 1945 by peasants in a cave in the desert at Nag Hammadi, Egypt, including: ***The Gospel of the Egyptians, Pistis Sophia, The Dialogue of the Savior, The Book of Thomas the Contender, The Apocryphon of John, The Gospel of Philip, the Gospel of Thomas,*** and ***The Thunder, Perfect Mind.*** These Gospels and other texts can be found in the book, edited by James M. Robinson, ***The Nag Hammadi Library: The Definitive Translation of the Gnostic Scriptures Complete in One Volume.***

The Church leaders of emerging unified Christian Church had THEIR OWN INTERPRETATION of the teachings of Jesus Christ, and had a vested interest in preserving THEIR INTERPRETATION under the guise of protecting the "integrity" of Jesus' teachings and His new religion. They also needed to proactively differentiate their "true" religion from other Christian sects that were around. Their biggest targets were the ones that espoused **Gnostic** ideas. They called their religion the "**orthodox"** or "**true**" one, and they call all others "**heretics**" or "**not true."** Heresy, from the Greek ***hairein,*** literally translates as "the act of choosing" or "at variance with an accepted doctrine or teaching.

The self-appointed grand inquisitor and most notable heresiologist was IRENAEUS, who through his unyielding efforts got him promoted to Bishop of Lyons, France. Around A.D. 180 he published a five-volume treatise entitled ***On the***

Detection and Overthrow of the So-Called Gnosis; it is usually referred to by the simplified and very descriptive title ***Against Heresies***. His efforts were joined by other church leaders; most notably was Tertullian, the Bishop of Carthage, and Hippolytus, a Bishop in Rome, who published their own treatises against **Gnosticism** and **Gnostic Christians.**

IMPORTANT POINT: Irenaeus' five-volume ***Against Heresies*** turned out to be a blessing for **Gnosticism,** it gave details about all the **Gnostic Gospels** and other writings, many of which have not yet been discovered. Ironically but thankfully, it included **an abundance of quotes from the so-called heretical Gnostic Gospels, Epistles, Letters,** and apocalyptic literature. More importantly, ***Against Heresies*** substantiates that all these **Gnostic Gospels** and writing existed in the year A.D. 180 and were definitely in circulation even many more years earlier.

To ensure their success and suppress **Gnosticism**, the Church Bishops, with the backing of the Council of Nicaea and their orders to form a unified ***New Testament*** or Christian Bible, ordered all texts not included in their sanctioned or canonical Bible, to be banned and destroyed by fire. Consequently, very little of the **Gnostic Christian** movement survived to modern times, until it was revived when copies of several **Gnostic** Gospels and texts were discovered in an Egyptian desert in the last century, a little over 1500 years after they were banned.

With these discoveries, we are able to see how seeking enlightenment and the purpose of life was the main goal of the **Gnostics.** These appear to be the same goals professed by many religions. There was a great diversity among the Christian communities in the early centuries. But for all their differences, including **Gnosticism**, there would be many things that they all had in common with the "orthodox" Church.

Gnosticism resurfaced many times over the centuries, in various countries, and in innumerable groups. A big resurgence is happening in modern times thanks to Biblical scholars, theologians, educators, and modern translations of these newly discovered ancient texts.

GNOSTIC RITES

There are also **Gnostic** versions of creeds, the mass, prayers, and liturgical rites. We learn from the ***Gospel of Philip,*** these rites practiced by the **Gnostic Christian** were very similar to the "orthodox" Christian Church who would call them "sacraments." For the **Gnostics,** these rites would aid a person to liberate the divine spark that was dwelling inside them. It was meant to put their followers on the path to their personal enlightenment and help them realize that their real home was in Pleroma realm. The **Gnostic** rites listed in the ***Gospel of Philip*** are:

- Baptism (the immersion in water)
- Chrism (the anointing with olive oil)
- Bridal Chamber (Holy Matrimony)
- Holy Eucharist
- Redemption (Penitence)
- Anointing at Death (a/k/a Extreme Unction)
- Holy Orders (Priesthood ordination)

Baptism was an important part of the **Gnostic** rituals. Baptism had its ancient origins as a Jewish purification rite. For **Gnostics**, Baptism was a symbolic washing and weakening of the archons' control and power over the human's worldly life whether it was mentally, emotionally, materially, or intellectually. Also for the **Gnostics**, this was supposed to start the human on a journey to free themselves from the entrapments of this evil world. This immersion in water did not immediately give the recipient the necessary knowledge (**gnosis**) and enlightenment. The candidate would have to embark upon on a comprehensive ritual of studying, reading the **Gnostic** texts, contemplating, meditating on them, and other activities in pursuit of attaining that goal.

The **Bridal Chamber** is probably the least understood by Biblical scholars. It appears to be closely related to our sacrament of Holy Matrimony. It is mentioned in the ***Gospel of Philip*** as the sacred rite where **a couple joined in the Bridal Chamber can never be separated.** Remember in both Jewish and Christian traditions, there is no, or rarely under very scarce circumstances, divorce. It was said in the Sacred Scriptures, he who leaves his wife and marries another woman commits adultery and she who leaves her husband and marries another man commits adultery.

IMPORTANT POINT: As Fundamentalist Evangelical Protestant Christians love to quote the Bible to point out other people's sins, they completely ignore Jesus' commandment: it is adultery to divorce and marry another. Some even have more than two marriages. It is really only the "Catholic Church" that unto day forbids divorce, and with only limited circumstances grants an "annulment" of the marriage saying the marriage itself was fraudulent and was never valid.

GNOSTIC PHILOSOPHIES

There were much debate and differences of opinion on the true nature of Jesus Christ **whether He was a divine spirit, not a real flesh and blood human being but only appeared to be a man**. They include: Marcionites, Montanists, Valentinians, Basilidans, Ebionites (Jewish Christians), Arianists, Sethians, Thomasines, Mandaeans, Cainites, Carpocratians, Borborites, and Nassenes (followers of James, Jesus' brother).

IMPORTANT POINT: Irenaeus called heresy the Gospels, Epistles, and Apocrypha of Jesus' inner circle of Disciples like James (Jesus' brother, the leader in Jerusalem of the Disciples after Jesus' death, Peter (the Bishop of Rome and the first head of the Christian Church), Philip, Thomas, Judas, and Mary Magdalene. However, Irenaeus had no problem accepting the letters of Paul who never met Jesus and was told on several occasions to cease his preaching his unique version of Christianity by James, Peter, and John in Jerusalem; **which is recorded and told in Paul's Epistles**.

SIGNIFICANT PLAYERS

As previously stated, the philosophies and theologies in the early centuries were very diverse. There are several major players that should be given attention in the shaping of Christianity, or whose philosophies were dismissed.

PAUL is attributed with some of the earliest writings and interpretations found in the ***New Testament.*** Paul was a faithful Jew and Roman citizen who persecuted the Christians for 10 years after the death of Jesus until he had "a vision" and became an ardent follower of Jesus. Like many others, I do not refer to Paul as a Disciple (a direct student of Jesus like His inner circle of twelve) or an apostle (a missionary sent out by an authority figure, in this case, one of the inner circle of twelve). **Paul was neither**. He never met Jesus. He was not instructed by Jesus for three years, like the Inner circle. Actually, as I said previously, he was told by the Disciple several times to cease and desist from teaching his own version of Christianity. Regardless, Paul had a big effect on the emerging Christian Church with his Epistles. Not all of Paul's letters were put in the ***New Testament*** because the Church leaders of the 4th Century considered some of them to be forged. Ironically, Biblical and linguistic scholars of modern day do not feel all of them were forged. At the same time, there are those same scholars that feel some of his letters that were included in the ***New Testament*** are forged such as ***Titus*** and ***Timothy.*** Unfortunately, some of Paul's ideas, not Jesus' teachings, became Christian doctrine, such as:

- The doctrine of "**original sin**" was **FIRST** put forth by **PAUL** in his Letter to the Romans. It was adopted by Augustine but not adopted by all Christian sects.
- **PAUL** was the **FIRST** to say that Jesus' death and resurrection **"were to redeem us for our offenses"** and for gain forgiveness for our sins. (***Romans*** 4:25)
- **PAUL alone** tells us how **salvation comes through one's faith in Jesus.** This is a major doctrinal distinction between Protestantism and Catholicism where the latter believes in Faith and Good Works. Protestantism does not believe in the need to do good works to be saved, only faith alone is needed.
- **PAUL** was the first to claim the divine nature of Jesus Christ.

- **PAUL** gave us the concept of the Holy Spirit and the Holy Trinity.

The fact that Paul's letters (more or less) would be included by the "orthodox" Church leaders in the ***New Testament*** implies the acceptance and importance given to his views. Those same Church leaders did not take into account, as per Paul's own letters, the Disciples in Jerusalem told him repeatedly to stop preaching. Paul's response was to call the Disciples in Jerusalem frauds and heretics, and anyone who followed them should be damned.

IMPORTANT POINT: Professor Elaine Pagels in ***The Gnostic Paul*** makes a case for him being a **Gnostic.** Unquestionably, his influence on the early church was so powerful that someone wrote forged letters [allegedly] from Paul (the pastoral epistles to Timothy and Titus) to make it appear that Paul held beliefs in compliance with the orthodox interpretation rather than the **Gnostic** view.

MARCION was a very famous **Gnostic** who was from Asia Minor but went to Rome in A.D. 139. He was originally a faithful Christian but then took on the **Gnostic** beliefs. Consequently, he was excommunicated. Marcion preached that the Hebrew God of the ***Old Testament*** was an inferior and cruel God and that the God and Almighty Father of Jesus Christ was conversely all-loving, all-merciful, and all-good. Marcion was a great follower of Paul whom he felt understood Jesus' teachings. On the other hand, Marcion felt most of the other Gospels were too Jewish. He believed the human body was corrupted and evil. Marcion did have a large following who believed in his brand of **Gnosticism.** Marcion had his own canon of Scriptures; of course, they did not include any Hebrew Scriptures. He included ten of Paul's letters, and only the ***Gospel of Luke*** scrubbed of anything mention of the Hebrew God. More importantly, **Marcion preached the doctrine of Docetism, that is, he did not agree with the concept that Christ was born a flesh and blood human man. The flesh was corrupt and evil, and Jesus Christ was God and as such He was All-Good.**

TERTULLIAN was a convert to Christianity around A.D. 197. He was a faithful follower of the "orthodox" Christian Church. He produced thirty-one brilliant writings in Latin, so many that he was called the Father of the Latin Church. Tertullian coined the term "Trinity." He wrote five books against Marcionite heresies. Ironically, his books gave Biblical scholars a great source of information about **Gnosticism** at that time. It was many years later that Tertullian broke away from the "orthodox" Christian Church and became a **Montanist Gnostic**. That particular **Gnostic** sect would go into an ecstatic state in their personal experiences with the Holy Spirit and receive inspirations.

ARIUS was a theologian from North Africa who lived from 256 to 336. He tried to reconcile the Hebrew monotheism (one God) with the Christian ditheism (two Gods), God the Father and His Son who were both Gods. His approach was on the nature of the relationship between the Father and His Son, Jesus Christ. Arius reasoned that the Son, unlike the Father, was not eternal and thus subordinate to the Father. Something Paul touched upon in ***1 Corinthians*** 15:24-28. Arius philosophy had the support of many but not from the orthodox Christians who took the position that they were separate but distinct persons, but still there was only one God. When the bishops met in A.D. 325 at the Council of Nicaea, after long debates on the issue and for Arius' theory, it was ultimately voted down as heresy. This was not favored by the Christian sects that agreed with Arius.

CLEMENT OF ALEXANDRIA was an early Church leader who claimed to have seen alternative versions of the ***Gospel of Mark***. One of them was the ***Secret Gospel of Mark*** with the advanced teachings that Jesus only gave to His Disciples. Different from the teachings He gave to the general audiences, these were meant for the spiritually advanced. A letter from Clement to "Theodore" cite the "***unspeakable teachings of the Carpocratians***" containing passages from the ***Gospel of Mark*** that were more advanced in nature. Clement had his church in Alexandria keep careful guard over it, and that it was only to be shown to the spiritually enough advanced who are ready to read its great mysteries. The only references scholars had to this secret teaching of Jesus was the one mention of it in a letter attributed to Clement.

IMPORTANT POINT: It is assumed that only the shorter version of ***Luke*** was included in the ***New Testament.***

EUSEBIUS was an antiquities scholar from Caesarea. As **Gnosticism** spread in the 2nd and 3rd Centuries, and the emerging "orthodox" Christian church was laying down its precepts and distinguishing itself from the heretical **Gnostics,** Eusebius in the 4th Century wrote a ten-volume history of Christianity. This proved to be invaluable to future Christian historians. As a side benefit, it gave verification and authenticity to the existence at that time of the banned, lost, and destroyed **Gnostic Gospels** and other texts used by the **Gnostic Christians** of that period.

MAJOR VIEWS ON SALVATION:

ONE HOLY CATHOLIC CHURCH CHRISTIANS believe salvation is attained through **Faith** in our Savior Jesus Christ,

Hope that we will be worthy to enter the Kingdom of Heaven, and **Charity** though compassion towards our fellow human beings here on earth.

GNOSTIC CHRISTIANS believe that salvation comes through attaining the secret spiritual knowledge, the **gnosis**, which Our Savior Jesus Christ delivered to us in person. The **Gnostics** acknowledge that human beings were created imperfect. Salvation cannot be attained by only doing good deeds; you need to achieve self-discovery and inner knowledge about our inner Divine spark in order escape from beneath the darkness of the Demiurge over this world so we can enter the realm of Light. Jesus' passion and death have nothing to do with forgiveness of our sins and our salvation.

JEWISH CHRISTIANS believe in the divine messenger, Jesus, as **a Christian sect within Judaism.** They believe that to be saved you still have to follow Mosaic laws, abiding by the rules of purity, diet, and behavior as well as honoring the Sabbath and participating in the Jewish holy days.

PAULINE CHRISTIANS believe primarily in Epistles of Paul that, "**salvation comes from belief in the Son of God** (***2 Corinthians*** 5:10-21) **and faith in Jesus** that died in reparation for our sins. The ***Gospel of John*** stresses that salvation can be attained by **solely** having faith in our Redeemer Jesus Christ, "***Behold the Lamb of God, who taketh away the sins of the world***" (***John*** 1:29). But conversely, the ***Gospels of Matthew, Mark,*** and ***Luke*** tell us that salvation also comes from doing good deeds and kindness to others, especially the poor (***Matt*** 25:31-46 and ***Luke*** 10:25-27).

EARLY CHRISTIANITY

Early Christian communities began to develope their own Christian theology and traditions. Even within this Jesus' inner circle of Disciples that He had to clarify His teachings. Still, there were times the Disciples disagreed among themselves, sometimes contentiously. After Jesus' death, each Disciple went to different regions to preach Jesus' words. Consequently, each one had their own group of followers. Then Paul found himself having a few tense meetings with Peter and James, the de facto heads of the Christian Community in Jerusalem who wanted him to cease preaching because he was espousing his own version of Christianity. James sent Peter to re-convert those who were converted by Paul. At one point that Peter and Paul got into a fist fight in front of a congregation because Paul did not want Peter to interfere in his ministry. When Paul was summoned again to Jerusalem by James, he went back and told his followers that those Disciples of Jesus in Jerusalem are a bunch of heretics and anyone who listens to them should damned forever.

Most Biblical scholars agree that the **Gospel of Mark was committed to writing in the late 60's,** 30 to 35 years after the death of Jesus and His Disciples and after the stories were passed down by word of mouth. It strongly appears that **the Gospels of Matthew and Luke were written based on their forerunner, the Gospel of Mark,** plus extra material that was never in Mark. The **Gospel of Matthew was written around A.D. 70 to 100,** 40 to 70 years after the death of Jesus. The **Gospel of Luke was written around A.D. 80 to 100, but probably about 85,** 50 to 70 years after the death of Jesus. Also, it is worth noting that Jesus and His Disciples spoke Aramaic, an ancient form of Arabic. The earliest written manuscripts are in Greek and housed in the Vatican Library in Rome. About A.D. 375 the Vatican translated the Greek manuscripts into Latin, the **Latin Vulgate Bible** [the language of Rome]. This Latin Bible is also in the Vatican Library.

IMPORTANT POINT: The Protestant Reformers in the 17th Century, like Martin Luther or King James, obviously were not given access to the Vatican Library. Their translations were based on other translations. Consequently, there are many discrepancies and contradictions found among the four Gospels in the ***King James Version***. [I covered this subject extensively in ***Alternative Christianities – Volume I: Early Christian Sects and the Formation of the Bible.***]

In the early centuries, there were a lot of Gospels in circulation. The Gospels that were in the name of a Disciple carried the most weight among the early Christians. However, the authorship and integrity of many Gospels have consistently been questioned. There was no way to know if they had been changed or altered to foster a particular view of the real author, or false material was added, or important teachings deleted. Was a Disciple's name put on a completely fraudulent document so it would be accepted? Putting the real author's name would render it useless. The process of selecting which Gospels would be in the ***New Testament*** was a laborious, painful, and contentious task by the Bishops in the late 4th Century after the Council of Nicaea about 50 years earlier. It was the battle of the Gospels.

IMPORTANT POINT: The Bishops preparing the Christian Bible first had to delineate what the "orthodox" beliefs were going to be and then determine which texts best represented those beliefs and interpretations of Jesus' words.

In the 2nd Century, the Gospels that were very popular were the "**Infancy Gospels.**" They were about Jesus as a youth. Unfortunately, none of these Gospels were put in the Christian Bible. Some of the popular ones were the **Gospel of Pseudo-Matthew, Gospel of James, Infancy Gospel of Thomas, History of Joseph the Carpenter,** and the **Arabic Infancy Gospel.** Needless to say, these Gospels did not contribute to the theology or doctrines of the faith so they were deemed by the Bishops not to be included in the Sacred Scriptures. Many other texts were excluded for the same reason.

IMPORTANT POINT: I think as Christians we would want to read any and all texts about Jesus Christ, including about His youth and the missing years. Those texts were banned by the Bishops in the 2nd Century.

Imagine the Christian missionaries spread out around the Mediterranean, the Middle East, Asia Minor, and into Africa. Some of the congregations may have had Scriptures, albeit inherited from only one Disciple. Maybe that had a copy which could have been translated from another language, or a copy of a copy transcribed by unprofessional scribes. Consequently, the Gospels that may have been used in these congregations may have differed from their original versions. Errors could have been made by these less than professional scribes, or scribes may have accidentally skipped over whole paragraphs, or purposely took writing shortcuts, or embellished the wording, or worse inserted new material.

In some Gnostic texts, there are ideas that seem to have been borrowed from other belief systems of the 1st and 2nd Centuries, such as Isis and Osiris, Attis and Cybele, Mithraism (Mithras, the ancient god of light), and Zoroastrianism.

THE COUNCIL OF NICAEA

The first and most important crucial turning point in Christianity took place in Nicaea, a Turkish resort city, in A.D. 325. It set the tone and path for how Christianity and the Christian Church would go forward from thereafter, even to present day. Constantine became Emperor of the Roman Empire and his mother made him convert to Christianity. He made the capital of the Empire where his home was in Constantinople which is present-day Istanbul, Turkey.

As a new Christian, Constantine was disgusted over all the different Christian sects, beliefs, and Holy Scriptures. So he convened a Council of Bishops in the resort city of Nicaea to come to an agreement on one unified Christian Church, which he modeled after the Roman senate and government. With his backing, he empowered the Council to enforce their resolutions on the Christian faith. There were 1,800 Bishops who were invited but only 250-300 attended and they were the ones who decided Christian dogma. The Council succeeded and produced the One, Holy, Catholic (universal), and Apostolic Church which was all powerful over the masses for over 1,200 years until Martin Luther challenged it in 1597.

One of the major issues being debated and disputed among the Bishops was the Christology of Jesus Christ or the true nature of Jesus; was He God or Man? The Father, Son, and Holy Spirit – the Trinity – was favored as the Godhead. As previously discussed, the Bishop of Alexandria and some other Bishops believed in the full divinity of Jesus, that the Son co-existed eternally with the Father as one, i.e. they were consubstantial. However, Arius opposed the idea that Jesus was one with the Father. He felt that if the Son was "created" after the Father and therefore was not always eternal. The Bishop of Alexandria argued the Godhead arrangement could be found in the ***Gospel of John*** (10:30) when Jesus said, "***I and My Father are One.***" The council overwhelmingly voted to agree with the Bishop of Alexandria and against Arius. In fact, Arius was ultimately voted to be a heretic, immediately excommunicated, and expelled. It was considered settled: Jesus was an eternal deity one and consubstantial with His Father.

IMPORTANT POINT: Many of the **Gnostics** believe that the Jesus was our Divine Savior from birth while other **Gnostics** believed that Jesus' Divinity descended upon him at His baptism when His Father said, **"This is my Son in whom I am well please."** Many of the same **Gnostics** believed the Jesus' Divinity departed His body at the moment of His death when He said, **"It is done. Father, into Thy hands I commend My Spirit."** Others thought that Jesus bodily switched with Simon of Cyrene who carried His cross and then died on it in His place. All are good suppositions.

The Council of Nicaea resolved other conflicts and decided many issues including:

- Easter would be celebrated on the first Sunday following the first full moon after the vernal equinox,
- Young women were prohibited to enter the homes of clergy,
- Required kneeling during the practice of the liturgy,
- Recognized the Bishops of Alexandria and Rome to be the highest authority in their regions, and
- Declared invalid any baptisms done by the followers of Paul who were considered heretics.

ESTABLISH THE CHRISTIAN DOGMA AND CREED

Another extremely important result of the Council of Nicaea is the establishment of Christian Dogma, i.e. what we believe, and the Christian Creed, the verbal profession of our religion. They started with the Baptismal Creed passed down from the Disciples; the newly converted had to recite it from memory in order to be baptized. It was also known as ***The Apostles Creed***. The Council clarified parts and added more. The new Christian Creed was called the ***Nicene Creed***. More, much more, was added at Councils later in that century and it became the ***Nicene-Constantinopolitan Creed***.

IMPORTANT POINT: This is the one and only Christian Profession of the Christian Faith even up to today. As such it excluded heretics and their heretical ideas. There is only one "orthodox" Christian Faith as set up by this Council.

One of the new phrases, and as such Church dogma, was:

"***God from God, Light from Light, True God from True God; begotten, not made, of one substance with the Father.***" The Roman Catholic Church recently updated the last part to read ***"consubstantial with the Father."***

IMPORTANT POINT: Emperor Constantine stood by his edict. Any Bishop who did not sign and enforce that creed was excommunicated. So went Arius, Theonas of Marmarica in Libya, and Secundus of Ptolemais who refused.

PUTTING TOGETHER THE BIBLE

After establishing the rules, the dogma, and the Christian Creed for the new catholic (universal) Christian Church, Emperor Constantine commanded that after a recess they reconvene and agree upon which Sacred Texts would comprise the Christian Bible. That was another Herculean task with much jockeying going on among the Bishops to make sure their favorite text(s) were included. This proved to be more difficult and more combative than agreeing upon dogma and creed.

IMPORTANT POINT: Most people take it for granted that the Gospels were written by the person whose name is on them. To the consternation of today's fundamentalist evangelicals, **nothing could be further from the truth**.

Firstly, all the Disciples were illiterate; they could not read or write. At that time, less than 5-10% of people could read or write. Only those who were formally educated or who were professional scribes could read and write. The fact of the matter is, Biblical, language, and linguistic scholars all agree, no one knows who definitively wrote the Gospels but it surely was not the Disciples. Secondly, Jesus and the Disciples spoke Aramaic, an ancient form of Arabic. The most original versions of the Gospels in our possession are written in Greek. The Disciples definitely did not speak Greek. Next, the sentence structure and grammar syntax of the most original Gospels did not exist at the time of the Disciples.

It was probably sometime in the compilation of the Bible, if not already done at some point before then, the Bishops had to distinguish the Gospels apart when they were put into one book, so the Gospels were given their names. It was all on an **"educated guess"** basis or debate among the bishops. The Biblical scholars believe this was their logic:

- The ***Gospel of Mark*** is believed to be the first Gospel written. There is no Disciple named Mark, but he is believed to be an apostle of the Disciple Peter who authored the Gospel.
- Matthew is believed to have been written originally in Greek although it is the "most Jewish" of the four Gospels and probably was written for the Jews. Ironically, it is obvious most of it was copied from the ***Gospel of Mark.***
- There also was no Disciple named Luke. Like ***Matthew,*** the ***Gospel of Luke*** got most of its material from ***Mark.*** It is believed that Luke was a companion of Paul who also wrote the ***Acts of the Apostles***.
- The ***Gospel of John*** is different than the other three (called the synoptic or similar Gospels) is called the "spiritual Gospel." It is obviously different than the three that precede it. To the **Gnostics,** it is considered to be more of a **Gnostic Gospel.** This Gospel is attributed to John, son of Zebedee; however, not all Biblical scholars agree and challenge this assertion. This was probably the most disputed Gospel that ultimately was accepted for inclusion in the Bible. The Bishops thought John's Gospel was too **Gnostic** but John had too many followers in the Middle East-Africa region that they would lose in their unified Christian Church if they did not include John's Gospel.

GOSPELS NOT INCLUDED IN THE BIBLE

Thanks to the writings of the ancient heresiologists, religious scholars are aware of **more than fifty Gospels** whose list includes: ***Peter, Philip, Matthias, James, Hebrews, Egyptians, Thomas, Nicodemus, The Twelve Apostles, Basilides, Valentinus, Marcion, Eve, Truth, Judas, Teleiosis, The Writing of Genna Marias, Dialogue of the Savior, Apocalypse of Peter, Testimony of Truth,*** **and *Second Treatise of the Great Seth,*** and ***Mary*** (Magdalene).

I will introduce some of the major Gospels and cover them in more detail in subsequent chapters.

The Gospel of Thomas is attributed to Didymos Judas Thomas, the twin. He is believed to be one of Jesus' brothers. It contains just 114 sayings, prophecies, and parables of Jesus as recorded by the Disciple Thomas. There is speculation that ***The Gospel of Thomas*** was used by the mystic **Gnostic** Manichaeans. Many call it "The Fifth Gospel."

The Gospel of Mary (Magdalene) believed to have been written in the 2nd Century in Greek. When the Disciples established their leadership hierarchy they conveniently left out Mary. ***The Gospel of Mary*** related from her own personal experience of the death and resurrection of Jesus Christ. Because her interpretation of Jesus' teachings did not coincide with those of the emerging Christian Church, Mary's Gospel was considered false and was omitted. Some of the Bishops at Council of Nicaea said there was no way they were going to include a Gospel written by a prostitute.

The ***Second Treatise of the Great Seth*** relates how Jesus Christ came down to Earth, endured suffering and crucifixion, and then returned to the Pleroma. It is in between an "orthodox" and "**Gnostic**" Gospel. Although it is in agreement with some parts of the ***New Testament***, except it does **state that salvation is through Gnosis.** This refutes the main principle of the "orthodox" church who believes their Church is the only way to salvation.

The Gospel of Truth also dates to the 2nd Century. The actual author is not known but it is believed that it was Valentinus, a Gnostic teacher who lived at that time. Valentinus' teachings seem to coincide with the ***Gospel of Truth.***

The Gospel of the Egyptians was the Sacred Scripture during the 2nd and 3rd Centuries in the Egyptian churches. Seth, the son of Adam and Eve, is attributed with the authorship of this Gospel through his mystical intervention and inspiration. Seth was considered by them as Father of **Gnosticism**. This Gospel advocates celibacy

The Gospel of Philip coincides with the **Gnostic** catechisms. It contains stories about Jesus, discusses the sacramental rites, gives an interpretation of Biblical passages, and shows how Jesus' sayings are **Gnostic** in nature.

The Secret Gospel of John, or ***The Apocryphon of John,*** who says he is the brother of James, one of the sons of Zebedee, contains the secret teachings of Jesus Christ given to John. It contains revelations about creation and salvation. The focus is on the evil of this world and how to escape it in order to return to the Heavenly realm from where we came. ***The Secret Gospel of John*** was a very sacred text for the **Gnostics** in the 2nd Century. ***John*** was very similar to the ***Gnostic Gospels of Thomas*** and ***Philip***. Theological and Biblical experts have suggested that the original ***Gospel of John*** that was put in the ***New Testament*** was probably more **Gnostic** but was vigorously edited to make it more in line with the "orthodox" Christian beliefs.

As previously stated, John had too many followers that the Church need for them to join.

The Secret Gospel of John is very interesting. John tells us that after Jesus' death he sees a very bright light and Jesus speaks to him. First, Jesus asked John if he recognizes Him. Jesus tells John that ***He is the Father, Mother, and Son***. At first, John is shocked by this but then realizes that the Mother is probably the Holy Spirit. Nothing further is ever mentioned whether the third person of the Trinity, the Holy Spirit, could possibly be a female.

IMPORTANT POINT: Especially for sects like Evangelical Christians, I cannot understand why such Bible-based Christian groups would not want to read **EVERYTHING** written about their Lord and Savior, Jesus Christ. The **four** Gospels that were **arbitrarily** placed in the ***New Testament*** of the Christian Bible are no more valid, authentic, or authoritative than the numerous Apostolic ones that were **arbitrarily** left out. Christians have received a great disservice.

The prominent **Gnostic Valentinus** was a major believer in **Docetism**, that is, Jesus, the name of the man, was a separate and distinct entity from Christ, the name of the Savior or Anointed One. Valentinus was a firm believer that Jesus the man became the Christ, the deity and Anointed One, when Jesus was baptized based on the voice from Heaven proclaiming, ***"This is my son in whom I am well pleased"*** which also left Jesus' mortal body as He died on the cross based on His proclamation, ***"Father, into thy hands I commend my spirit."*** Of course, church leader Irenaeus screamed **"Heresy!"** No way could the idea exist that Jesus and Christ were separate and different entities. Irenaeus also objected to the absurd idea that humans had a divine spark inside of them and that it took some special knowledge to activate it. According to Irenaeus, all the knowledge that is needed for salvation can be found in the Gospels he sanctioned. Irenaeus stated that the only way to know Jesus is through the Church, and the only way to be saved is through the Church. Valentinus and other **Gnostic** leaders believed in Jesus' and His words; however, they just interpreted them differently.

The **Gnostics** can quote the ***Gospel of Luke*** for Jesus' own words which agree with the concept of the Divine spark.

> "***And when he was demanded of the Pharisees, when the kingdom of God should come, he answered them and said, 'The kingdom of God cometh not with observation: Neither shall they say, Lo here! Or lo there! For behold, the kingdom of God is within you."*** (Luke 17:20-21)

ORTHODOX VS. GNOSTIC BELIEFS

The "orthodox" Christian Church is firm in their belief that only by Jesus' death and resurrection salvation would be brought to humanity. However, like so many other **Gnostic** texts, the ***Second Treatise of the Great Seth*** maintains that human salvation has nothing to do with Jesus' death BUT only through attaining the **gnosis** that Jesus brought to us.

IMPORTANT POINT: Biblical scholar Elaine Pagels has pointed out in her many books in regard to the **Gnostic Gospels** while the accepted Gospels is all about **human sin and redemption**, the Gnostic Gospels is about **spirituality and enlightenment**, and Jesus **did not die to redeem humans for their sins** but to bring the knowledge about who they are and that the Divine Realm awaits them.

The emerging Church leaders had hoped that the Nicene Creed would have solidified their articles of faith. Ironically, it had quite the opposite effect. There were only more theological dissensions and a string of councils to resolve them which went on for centuries. Even though the Christian Church had the power of the Roman Emperor behind them, that did not silence those with opposing views, squash so-called heretical ideas, or deter the infighting within the Christian community.

THE SECOND COUNCIL

Emperor Theodosius convened the Eastern Bishops at **Second Council in Constantinople in A.D. 381**. His goal was to eliminate all versions of **Gnostic** beliefs which continued to be rapidly spreading. These **Gnostic** sects included **Arianism, Eunomianism, Apollinarianism,** and **Macedonianism.** Theodosius also wanted to establish the Bishop of Constantinople superior to Bishop of Rome, and Constantinople superior to Rome as the seat of the Christian Church. Theodosius dismissed the bishops who did not believe in the **equal divinity of the Father, Son, and Holy Spirit.**

Theodosius convened **two more bishop councils in A.D. 382 and A.D. 383**. He was attempting to unite the different groups of Christians to come to terms with the Nicene Creed. The Eastern Churches of **Arians** was completely rebellious towards any form of reconciliation with the "orthodox" Christian Church, including the **Eunomianism** sect. Their leader **Eunomius** was the Bishop of the Orthodox See of Cyzicus in Mysia before he was deposed and expelled.

Emperor Theodosius became more and more frustrated at his lack of success in expanding the One, Holy, Catholic (universal) Church; so much so that his benevolence turned to extreme measures and brutality. His mission took on a stronger emphasis to eradicate all forms of heresies including paganism, Arianism, Gnosticism, and any other religion or sect that he consider adversarial or thought to undermine the beliefs of the one "orthodox" Christian Church. He dispatched his soldiers throughout Egypt, Syria, and elsewhere in Asia Minor with the command to destroy all non-orthodox churches and make sure all "unorthodox" religious groups were disbanded and obliterated. Emperor Theodosius was generally successful; however, in some areas, it only managed to drive these **Alternative Christianities** underground.

IMPORTANT POINT: In the 4th Century, Athanasius was the first to suggest which twenty-seven Gospels and Epistles should be included in the ***New Testament,*** or the Christian Bible. This identical list is what is being used today. Athanasius also suggested the date of Easter in his letter of A.D. 367. Rightfully so, Athanasius was considered the Father of Orthodoxy as practiced by Western Christianity.

SUBSEQUENT CHRISTIAN SCHISMS

As hard as the "orthodox" Church leaders tried to suppress non-compliant sects, new sects kept sprouting up:

- **APOLLINARIANISM:** A 4th Century sect founded by **Apollinarius.** He was the Bishop of Laodicea, Syria. Apollinarius firmly asserted that **Christ the divine nature and Jesus the human nature could not coexist in one being.** This assertion put into question the doctrines of incarnation, death, and atonement for our sins. This **Alternative Christianity** sect was condemned by the "orthodox" Christian Church in A.D. 381.

- **NEOPLATONISM:** In the 3rd Century, **Plotius** founded an **Alternative Christianity** sect whose belief regarding the nature of Jesus was that **He was born a human man but then ascended through a series of mystical levels until He reached the level of a Deity.** Many felt this train of thinking very plausible and became a major Christian mystic spiritual movement in the 5th Century under **Dionysius.**
- **NESTORIANISM:** The Patriarch of Alexandria, **Nestorius,** took a very different approach and promoted the belief that **Jesus was actually two persons, one human and one divine**. In A.D. 432, the Council of Ephesus condemned this sect and their beliefs.
- **MONOPHYSITISM:** In the 5th Century, **Eutyches** formed a sect that believed **Jesus possessed only one nature and it was 100% Divine.** In A.D. 451, Leo the Great at the Council of Chalcedon condemned this sect.

IMPORTANT POINT: The amusing part is with all this theological jockeying, Disciples and their followers seriously expected the "**End-Of-Days**" was going to happen within their lifetime and Jesus would return to earth.

THE CANON

"**Canon**" comes from the Greek word "***kanon"*** which means "**rule**" or "**standard**." It has been expanded to mean "**the official position"** of the Catholic Church. It is commonly used to describe the accepted set of Sacred Scriptures. The twenty-seven books in the ***New Testament*** were considered to be the only ones containing the accepted teachings of Jesus and His Disciples. One of the mandates passed down from the Council of Nicaea was to weed through all the "gospels" and "epistles" in circulation, and develop an official Catholic Church "canon" of Sacred Scriptures. Unfortunately, Bishop Irenaeus of Lyons was a major influence in which texts "he" approved and which ones "he" labeled heretical.

Important Point: For many people, especially the **Gnostics**, this should have excluded Paul's Epistles because he was NOT a Disciple of Jesus in His inner circle. Paul was told by the Disciples to "cease and desist" his preaching.

The Gnostics used the same texts as in the "orthodox" canon; except with less reverence for the Epistles of Paul. They may have included other Gospels, such as those of Peter, James, Philip, Thomas, Judas, and/or Mary; along with any Epistles written by them. The difference was that they may have had interpretations of these Scriptures to reflect their "higher **Gnostic** level" of understanding of Jesus' teachings as expressed by these direct Disciples of Jesus. James was the head of Christianity in Jerusalem and Peter was the head of Christianity in Rome, but their Gospels and Epistles were omitted along with other actual Disciples of Jesus such as Philip, Thomas, and Mary Magdalene. They all must have done something right because they were revered and were all canonized Saints. However, their Gospels were banned.

The first list of Gospels was compiled in the 2nd Century by **Marcion,** a notable **Gnostic.** His list included ONLY the ***Gospel of Luke*** and ten of Paul's Epistles (Marcion excluded the first and second Epistles of Timothy and Titus, but included Paul's Epistle to the Hebrews). Marcion did not include any texts he was not in agreement.

Also believed to have been compiled at the end of the 2nd Century was another list known as the **Muratorian Canon.** The actual author was unknown. It was named after the person who discovered it in the 18th Century in Milan, **L. A. Muratori**, an Italian scholar. The **Muratorian Canon** included all the of books in the current ***New Testament*** plus ***Hebrews, James,*** the ***Second Book of Peter,*** and the ***Apocalypse of Peter***, which were all later rejected and left out.

APPROXIMATE DATES OF WHEN THE *NEW TESTAMENT* TEXTS WERE WRITTEN:

- c. A.D. 49 Paul's first Epistle to the Thessalonians

  [In Anno Domini, i.e. In the Year of Our Lord 49 is approximately 16 years after Jesus' death at age 33.]
- c. 51 Paul's Epistle to the Galatians
- c. 52 Paul's second Epistle to the Thessalonians
- c. 55-56 Paul's first and second Epistle to the Corinthians
- c.59-63 Paul's Epistle to the Philippians
- c.59-63 Paul's Epistles to Colossians and Ephesians
- c.60-63 Paul's Epistles to the Romans and Philemon
- c. 63-67 Books 1 and 2 of Timothy, Titus, and Book 1 of Peter, and Hebrews

- c. 65 — "Q" or the Gospel Q, considered the source for Matthew and Luke
- c. 70 — ***Gospel of Mark*** [The first Gospel was written approximately 37 years after Jesus' death.]
- c. 80-100 — ***Gospel of Matthew*** [***Matthew*** was written approximately 47–67 years after Jesus' death.]
- c. 85-95 — ***Gospel of Luke*** and ***Acts of the Apostles***
- c. 95 — ***Revelations***
- c. 100-125 — ***Gospel of John*** [***John*** was written approximately 67–92 years after Jesus' death.]

OTHER IMPORTANT DATES IN THE FORMATION OF THE *NEW TESTAMENT*

- c. 180 — Bishop Irenaeus of Lyons published "Against Heresy" and unilaterally decided there will be **ONLY FOUR GOSPELS IN THE OFFICIAL CHURCH CANON,** *"no more and no less"* because there are four corners to the Earth, four pillars of the church, and four directions of the wind. Rome agreed. THUS, THE PERSON AND REASON WE ONLY HAVE FOUR GOSPELS IN THE CHRISTIAN BIBLE TODAY, i.e. ***Matthew, Mark, Luke,*** and ***John***. The one man who did this and wanted to become the Bishop of Rome.

- c. 325 Emperor Constantine of Rome convenes the Council of Nicaea to decide once and for all which were to be the Christian beliefs and the Council issued the ***Nicene Creed***. Constantine then orders the Bishops to reconvene and decide which Gospels and Epistles were to be included in the Christian Bible that supported those beliefs. Thus, the formation of the One, Holy, Catholic (universal), and Apostolic Christian Church.
- c. 367 In his Easter Letter, Bishop Athanasius publishes the official list (canon) of Gospels and Epistles that will comprise the ***New Testament*** of the Christian Bible is still in use today.

IMPORTANT POINT: Of course, not every Christian sect agreed with this list. Many did not like to see the Gospels of their founding Disciple omitted, like James, Peter, Philip, and Thomas. John was included after fierce debates in Nicaea because John was too "**gnostic**" but he had too many followers in Africa and the Middle East that the new Catholic Church did not want to lose. The Bishops were made to agree to ban and order destroyed by fire all other works that were not in the official canon. This did cause all those texts to disappear despite consistent rumors of their existence. Then in the Egyptian desert at Nag Hammadi in the 20th Century was discovered a preserved collection of these texts.

THE CATHOLIC CHURCH'S EFFORT TO EXTINGUISH GNOSTICISM

The Christian Church had one set of common beliefs: There was only one God who created heaven and earth; His Son Jesus was both human and divine, and Jesus' death and resurrection redeemed us from "original sin" and brought us salvation. It is the fervent belief held by many Evangelical Christians that God Himself inspired both the ***Old Testament*** and ***New Testament***. Every word in the Bible is the true word of God and is infallible. All other texts are false documents. Yet no original manuscripts of any Gospels exist nor is there any proof the illiterate Disciple wrote or dictated them. As far as Biblical scholars can tell, the Gospels were written several generations after the authors whose names they bear died.

The "orthodox" Christian Church waged a full outright religious war against the **Gnostic Christians.** Besides, ordering the destruction of any and all **Gnostic** texts, they forced the **Gnostic Christians** out of their "orthodox" Christian congregations and Church services, which the **Gnostics** were always a part. Not only did they do everything in their power to disperse and disband the **Gnostic** sects, but also to vilify their **Gnostic Christian** brothers. The Church leaders used their sermons and dissertations to destroy any **Gnostic** interpretation of the Gospels, theology, or Christology.

Irenaeus of Lyons wrote five volumes (its title shortened and translated) ***Against Heresies.***

Heresiologist **Origen** wrote an extensive point-by-point refutation of **Gnostic** beliefs.

Tertullian wrote five volumes ***Against Marcion*** and more volume against other heretics with whom he disagreed.

Church leader **Hippolytus** of Rome wrote a ten-volume ***Refutation of All Heresies*** to expose how he felt that **Gnosticism** had its roots in Greek mythology and philosophy.

Origen wrote eight volumes to counter **Celsus**, the 2nd Century author of ***The True Word*** and a fierce opponent of the new "orthodox" Christianity.

These heresiologists must have been very intimidated by their **Gnostic Christian** counterparts. It particularly bothered them when **Gnostics** like Marcion stated that the God of the ***Old Testament***, the God of the Jews, was an inferior and phony God who created an evil world of suffering and pain for his own ego. The Christian Church praised Him as the God of the ***New Testament*** as the True God and Son of the Almighty Father. They used every approach including sarcasm, ridicule, and outrageous accusations such as that the **Gnostic** beliefs were counterintuitive to the true message of Jesus.

Unfortunately, sometimes only a few pages or small fragments of **Gnostic** texts survived this mass extermination. There are complete manuscripts of the ***Gospel of Peter, Secret Gospel of Mark, Dialogue of the Savior,*** and ***Egerton Gospel.*** There are only fragments of the ***Gospel of Mary*** that survived in both the Coptic and Greek; although neither is a complete version. There is a complete Coptic (an ancient form of today's Egyptian language) version of the ***Gospel of Thomas*** and three fragments in Greek. Probably, the Coptic version was translated from the Greek.

But still, neither the Greek or Coptic versions would be the original language of the Gospels. Jesus and His Disciples spoke Aramaic, an ancient version of Arabic (they were Palestinians who lived in Palestine, an Arab country). Hebrew scholars think it was most likely they spoke Hebrew while in the synagogue. Either way, the original stories of Jesus' life and ministry had to be passed along in Aramaic. Next, they were probably translated into Greek which was the language of the educated. From there translated into local languages like Latin and Coptic. The English Bible is **many generations** later with several iterations of ancient and obsolete forms of English, Latin, Greek, and Egyptian.

I went much deeper into this in ***Volume I.*** Jesus' words and teachings were passed down by word of mouth for generations and decades before they were committed to writing on papyrus. Then our Sacred Scriptures were translated and retranslated, copied and recopied, and circulated and changed through the generations. Human errors, either done purposely or accidentally in dark and dank ancient and medieval scriptoriums under candlelight, account for unknown innumerable mistranslations, misspellings, indecipherable abbreviations, omissions due to skipped over sentences, or just poor hearing. The Biblical scholars claim there are many forgeries called pseudepigrapha ("false writings") abound in the ancient world. Famously forged were the Epistles of Paul, such as the first and second Epistles of Timothy and Titus supposedly written by Paul, however, historians and Biblical scholars are certainly they were written after Paul's death. The Biblical scholars and linguistic experts today claim that some of Paul's Epistles in the ***New Testament*** are forged; and ones that the ancient Church leaders thought were forged and were left out, are real.

The ***Gospel of Peter*** was widely popular among many but was not included in the official Bible. This Gospel too was the subject of intense debates. A hint was given by a 2nd Century Church leader, Seraphim of Antioch, who said he and other orthodox bishops felt it contained too many accusations against the Jews for the murder of Jesus. Peter did not place enough emphasis on Pontius Pilate's role in Jesus' crucifixion. This would anger the Jews and forestall their conversions. Peter, from the visions he was given by Jesus, had Docetic inferences which cast doubt on Jesus' pain, suffering, and death. This was a major contention of belief for our redemption for the "orthodox" Christian Church.

GNOSTIC SCHOOLS OF THOUGHT

Some dogma is basic to all **Gnostics** with only sometimes minor differences among the schools:

- God is a transcendent deity, all-good, all-merciful, all-loving, and all-powerful,
- The realms of matter and spirit are separate and distinct, however, there is a linkage between them,
- The Fullness of the Almighty God exists in the Divine Pleroma realm,
- The Demiurge is the inferior god who is the creator of this evil and material world,
- There is a Divine Spark embedded at birth within each human being, and
- There needs to be an awakening of inner self-knowledge to merge our consciousness with the Divine.

Gnosticism was born and took root in Judeo-Christian society simultaneously with the birth of Christianity. It incorporated ideas and philosophies from their existing cultures whether it be Rome, Syria, Greece, or Egypt. **Gnosticism** grew and flourished from the 1st Century through the 4th Century until the Councils of Nicaea.

Gnosticism differed from the emerging Christian Church in that:

- Gnosticism stressed individual enlightenment and liberation by attaining the secret knowledge,
- Refused to align their beliefs with the God of the Hebrew Scriptures, Yahweh, or Jehovah.
- Interpreted Jesus' teachings and the Gospels radically different from "orthodox" Christianity.
- They believed that Christ was a divine spirit sent to earth and inhabited the body of Jesus.
- His divine nature, Christ, did not die when His human nature died when Jesus was crucified and died on the cross. The body of Jesus died but his spirit returned to the Divine Realm.
- The **Gnostics** do not subscribe to the idea that through the death of Christ we were redeemed.
- They do not believe in the literal interpretation of the Gospels but seek the deeper meanings of Jesus.

The Gnostic and "orthodox" Christian Church both considered Jesus Christ to be their Lord and Savior, and both shared many of the ***New Testament*** texts. However, there are more differences in their individual beliefs and practices. By the 2nd Century, the Christian Church followed the Roman military and established a hierarchy of bishops, priests, and deacons. The **Gnostics** had no formal organizational structure. It was a conglomeration of many different sects. This was a major hindrance to their sustainability. The very popular **Gnostic** group was **Marcionism.** Marcion was the one who developed his own set if Sacred Scriptures. Although Marcion's **Gnostic** beliefs were well thought out, he lacked missionaries to spread and perpetuate his sect. Marcionism was destined to fail while other **Gnostic** sects thrived.

Gnostics may have had different Scriptures to guide their beliefs, with or without differing interpretations of them. Religious historians found the different sects fell into a hierarchy of four main disciplines, all with subgroups:

1. SYRIAN DISCIPLINE

The **Syrian Discipline** is considered one of the first schools of **Gnosticism.** They firmly opposed the Jewish God, the God of the ***Old Testament.*** He was very harsh and cruel. They believed Jesus Christ was the true Son of the Good God and came from the Divine Realm, the Pleroma. The **Syrian Gnostics** also drew upon the philosophy of Plato. They consider this world to be physical and material which only leads to evil and suffering. Instead, we must strive to rise above this inferior world and rise up to a better higher realm. The subsets of this discipline included the **Naassenes, Ophites, Sethians, Peratai, Saturnilians,** and the **Cainites.**

NAASSENES

The Naassenes were converts and disciples of Jesus' brother, **James the Just.** James was the head of the Christ movement in Jerusalem and, as the brother of Jesus, the leader of Disciples. The Naassenes claimed to have received their **mystical (Gnostic) spiritual teachings from James who received it from his brother, Jesus**. A century or so later, Hippolytus, a church leader, was major heresiologist who call all their beliefs heretical and delusional. Preserved in Book Five of Hippolytus, a refutation of the Naassenes, was a secret sermon claimed to be given by Jesus at the Last Supper to his inner circle of Twelve Disciples. It can be found in Mark H. Gaffney's book ***The Gnostic Secrets of the Naassenes, the Initiatory Teachings of the Last Supper***, which Hippolytus claimed to have recorded verbatim.

INTERESTING FACTS: "**Naassene**" is a derivative from the Hebrew word for **serpent.** The serpent was the common symbol at that time for knowledge, wisdom, and power. Even today, the serpent is the symbol of the medical profession. In a more "unorthodox" interpretation of the story of the Garden of Eden, the serpent convinced Eve to eat from the Tree of Knowledge. It was the serpent who brought wisdom and knowledge to Eve. But to the "orthodox Christian Church," this act was branded as the "Original Sin" for which we were all doomed to suffer and repent. Luckily, there are Eastern Orthodox Christian Churches that do not believe the same as the Western Roman Church in this regard.

A common idea also for the Naassenes is flowing water as a symbol of the spirit world. It was shown flowing upward instead of downward symbolizing energy and enlightenment towards making humans more god-like. The premise of the upward flow of water symbolizing enlightenment is found in both Buddhism and Hinduism. The writings of James tell us how he and his brother, Jesus, (during those missing years) spent time touring the Far East to study the Eastern religions, notably Buddhism and Hinduism, from which He preached about the vast knowledge that He had learned there.

OPHITES

The Ophites lived about A.D. 100 around Egypt and Syria. Like the Naassenes, the Ophites refused to acknowledge the God of the Jews as the legitimate Almighty God. They particularly despised him because he forbade Adam and Eve to eat from the tree of knowledge in the Garden of Eden. The Ophites more worshipped the serpent as the giver of wisdom and knowledge. Hippolytus, Irenaeus, Origen, and Epiphanius all wrote condemning the Ophites as heretics. Ophite sects included **Sethians, Peratai, Borborites, Naassenes,** and **Mandaeans.** Some sects still exist today in those regions.

SETHIANS

The **Sethians** was an early and popular **Gnostic** sect. They were followers and revered Seth, the third son of Adam as their spiritual leader to take them out of this material world. They worshipped the serpent and considered it the redeemer of Eve delivering her from this material world. They believed the world had three parts: light, darkness, and the spirit realm that lies in between them. Many **Gnostic** Sethian writings were discovered at Nag Hammadi, Egypt.

PERTAI

The **Peratai** was founded by Euphrates, Celbes, and Ademes. They were a **Gnostic** sect which like their sister sects, the Sethians and Naassenes, revered the serpent. The serpent symbol was used in their rituals and practices, so much so that sometimes they are referred to as the "**Serpent Gnostic**" sect. Same as with other **Gnostic** communities, they considered themselves as just pilgrims visiting this material world on their way to their final home in the Divine realm. They believed that the number three was powerful and their symbol was a triangle in the circle. The Euphrates believed in astrology, an individual's karma, a person's horoscope, and the placement of the sun, planets, and moon at the time of a person's birth.

SATURNILLIANS

Saturinus was from Antioch and the founder of the **Gnostic** sect that was called **Saturnillians**. They believed that the Good God was at one end and Satan, the creator and ruler of the material world, was at the other end. Saturninus shunned marriage and the eating of meat. Saturninus believed that humans were created by divine angels. A savior (in a male form) rescued those with divine sparks and destroyed the archons or those with evil powers.

IMPORTANT POINT: Somewhere between A.D. 150-160, Justin Martyr, one of the Church leaders at the time, in his writings mentioned **Saturninus** as well as other **Gnostic** leaders like **Basilides, Marcion, and Valentinus**. It is proof through writings like his and others that these people did exist and documented their beliefs.

MANDAEANS

Mandaeans were **Gnostic Christians** whose main emphasize revolved around baptism and fertility. The sect not only owed its basics to Judaism and Christianity but also had **Islamic** influences. The **Mandaean** sect continues to exist in Iran between Tigris and Euphrates rivers. This is the region fabled to be where the Garden of Eden was.

CAINITES

In the 2nd Century, the **Gnostic** sect, the **Cainities**, revered Adam's son Cain. Cain was considered a superior power just like his brother, Abel. Cain was the victim of the evil Demiurge. Heresiologists **Irenaeus, Epiphanius, Hippolytus, and Tertullian** included the Cainites in their writings.

2. GREEK DISCIPLINE

The Greek Discipline, a **Gnostic** school of beliefs, was more philosophical than the Syrian Disciplines. The two most notable leaders within the **Hellenistic (Greek) Gnostic** sects were **Basilides** and **Valentinus**.

BASILIDIANS

Basilides was believed to have been born in Antioch but migrated to Alexandria, Egypt about A.D. 130 where he preached his beliefs. He had a son named Isidore who continued with his father's work. Not much of their writings have survived. The Basilidians became a major **Gnostic** sect in Egypt. Interestingly, the Basilidians considered their major holy day was the day on which Jesus was baptized. The sacred number for them was 365. They believed there were 365 heavens. The word "***Abrasax***" was inscribed on their talismans. Hebrew meanings for that acronym dissected were **AB** (Father), **BEN** (Son), and **RUAH** (Spirit in the feminine). Obviously, the acronym stood for the Holy Trinity.

VALENTINIANS

Valentinus founded one of the most popular **Gnostic** sects and had very many followers. He initially was an adherent to the "orthodox" Christian Church but then started adopting Plato and other Greek's scientific philosophies. He became a more cosmologically-leaning **Gnostic**. This caused him to be excommunicated from the Christian Church. His preaching began in Alexandria, Egypt; then he migrated to Rome around A.D. 160. **Valentinians** believed in the one unknowable Almighty God. Aeons, Sophia, and Christ all were prominent figures who served the Almighty God.

Valentinians believed that the humans living in this material world needed to free themselves from all this evil; only then could their inner divine ascend to the spiritual realm. Christ and the Holy Spirit were sent to Earth to be our Saviors. They believe that Jesus Christ did not really have a human body, He only appeared that way, and as such, He did not suffer nor did He die on the cross. The "**Bridal Chamber**" was a rite made famous by the Valentinians. The **Gnostic** sect

Valentinianism was popular in Syria, Egypt, Italy, and southern France.

Two disciples of Valentinus, **Ptolemy,** and **Heracleon,** were the subject of writings by heresiologists. Tertullian attacked Ptolemy and Origen attacked Heracleon. Both Origen and Heracleon wrote commentaries on the ***Gospel of John*** claiming it had shades of Valentinianism in its references to light, darkness, and mysteries.

3. THE DUALISTIC DISCIPLINE

MARCION

Marcion was born in A.D. 85, the son of a bishop in Asia Minor. He was a successful and very rich merchant. It is interesting to note: Marcion was born while some of Jesus' Disciples were still alive. He was a major architect in the almost universal **Gnostic** belief that there were two Gods. Marcion was accused of defiling a virgin, excommunicated, forced to leave his home, and he headed to Rome. The Church leaders there took many exceptions to Marcion's views that countered their "orthodox" Christian beliefs. In A.D. 144, Marcion was branded a heretic and expelled from the Christian Church in Rome. Determined not to be defeated in his beliefs, Marcion decided instead to take on the task of establishing his Church in Rome, Syria, Carthage, Smyrna, Nicomedia, Antioch, and elsewhere.

Marcionites completely rejected the God of the Jews as the Almighty Good God or the Father of Jesus. They considered the Hebrew God to be the root of evil and arch-enemy of the True God, without specifically naming him the Devil or "Satan." Needless to say, Marcion did not include any of the Hebrew Scriptures in his version of the Biblical canon. The "orthodox" Christians were very dependent on the Hebrew Scriptures and included it in their Bible as the ***Old Testament*** because it contained the prophecy of the coming of Jesus as the Messiah. Marcionites believed in the eternal struggle between good and evil. The evil and cruel god of the Jews and the Hebrew Scriptures was the Demiurge, an inferior god. The Almighty True God, the Father of Jesus, was an all-loving, all-good, and all-merciful God.

The Marcionites believed that Jesus had secret teachings that He did not preach to the general public but shared them with a chosen few. Also, there was an idea maintained by the Marcionites that made the "orthodox" leaders cringe. They claimed that Jesus Christ only appeared to be human but in reality, He was not human. Jesus was always divine. That killed the "orthodox" Church's suppositions of the Resurrection of the Flesh, a Second Coming, or a Judgment Day.

4. THE ANTINOMIAN DISCIPLINE

Antinomian Disciple (whose name comes from the Latin "***anti"*** meaning against and "***nomos"*** meaning law) espouses opposition to the rigid practices of Hebrew Mosaic Law and some of the other **Gnostic** sects. **Antinomians** believed that neither good works brought about salvation, nor did evil deeds prevent salvation. They considered that once a person is baptized a Christian, they will be saved.

CARPOCRATIANS

Carpocrates was a philosopher who preached in the first half of the 2nd Century. The **Carpocratians** were a **Gnostic** sect of Antinomians that heresiologists condemned for their lack of respect for human laws and even more for their disregard for the need for good works to attain salvation.

Like other **Gnostics,** they believed that the Good Almighty God was found within us. Humans needed to free themselves from this material world. Some believed in order to do this they must experience as many human experiences as possible. They should even practice magic and try to have sex with as many people as they wanted (Heresiologist Tertullian referred to them as fornicators). The Carpocratians believed that if they experienced everything in one lifetime, they would never be reincarnated to live life on this earth ever again. **Reincarnation was the Devil's work to keep humans under his power**. A human's actions on this earth were not as important as their individual intent. The Carpocratians believed that it was through the teachings of Jesus Christ they could find the way to their divine home.

Carpocrates rebelled against the "orthodox" Church and did not subscribe to the premise that God the Father impregnated the Virgin Mary and she had a virgin birth that gave us Jesus. They believed that **Jesus was Joseph's son**. Carpocrates saw the Divine realm and spirituality manifest itself through the Greek philosophers Plato, Aristotle, and Pythagoras. To them, Jesus was a man of purity and godliness who preached Divine wisdom. They believed that salvation was **not** attained *through* Jesus but by actually *becoming* like Jesus.

Again regarding the Carpocratians, what we know about them and their beliefs comes from the writings criticizing them by Clement of Alexandria and Irenaeus' ***Against Heresies***. It was mentioned by the critics that the Carpocratians "claimed" they possessed a copy of the ***Secret Gospel of Mark.*** A copy of the ***Secret Gospel of Mark*** was found in 1958 by scholar Morton Smith. The ***Secret Gospel of Mark***, like other "Secret Gospels," is a **Gnostic** work.

SIMONIANS

SIMON MAGUS was a Christian who was baptized by the Disciple Philip and lived at the same time as Peter and Paul. He was very familiar with the earliest roots of Christianity. Simon Magus was the founder of the **Gnostic** sect **Simonians** whose beliefs were clearly at odds with the emerging Christian movement. The Simonians believed that nothing was intrinsically good or bad. Simon and his sect presented a major challenge for the Disciples because his movement was great odds with their teachings and those of Jesus Christ. He was subsequently labeled as a heretic by several of the Church leaders including Clement, Hippolytus, Justin Martyr, and Irenaeus. Many of Simon's followers even believed he was God incarnated. That persona came about because he was a great sorcerer. The Simonian sect thrived throughout Rome, Syria, and parts of Asia Minor. There were at least two strong offshoots which had their beginnings in Simonism:

Dositheans followed Dositheus, a Samaritan disciple of Simon Magus. He believed in the Hebrew Scriptures. Dositheus said that he was sent by God and he was a great prophet.

Menandrians preached that angels were sent by Ennoia to create this material world. For them, salvation was attained through baptism.

MOST IMPORTANT POINT: This was a sampling of the numerous Early Christian sects, **Gnostic Christian** religions, and **Alternative Christianities** that existed in the early days of the Christian Movement which all flourished before Roman Emperor Constantine and his Council of Nicaea in A.D. 325 established **FOR ALL** the One, Holy, Catholic (universal), and Apostolic Church. Any other non-conforming church, congregation, preacher, or belief was **HERESY AND BANNED.** The canon of the Bible was formed to match the beliefs of the newly established Catholic Church ordering every other Gospel and Scripture banned and destroyed by fire or they would be excommunicated.

THE HOLY WAR TO FIGHT HERESY

The emerging Christ movement and the infant Church would face a rough road of trials and tribulations beginning with James, Peter, and Philip vs. Paul. Instead of the peace and harmony that Emperor Constantine wanted to achieve with the establishment of the One, Holy, Catholic, and Apostolic Christian Church in A.D. 325 instead it caused a war between factions of Christians, all claiming to be the one, true Christians. Although it was forcefully calmed down for centuries, the Protestant Reformation in the 17th Century put it went back into full swing continuing up to today.

One of the major reasons for all the dissent was the number of Sacred Scriptures that were all over the Roman Empire. **Everything would have been so much simpler if Jesus Christ's actions and words were written down verbatim in real time as they happened - but they were not.** Instead, Jesus Inner Circle of Twelve Disciples eventually scattered through the known world to spread the "Good News" of their Master. Their Gospels, or "Good News," were passed down from generation to generation before they were committed to writing. It was not put into writing until at least 60 to 100 years after the death of Jesus Christ and the Disciples to whom they were attributed. Remember, less than 10% of the population of the otherwise sophisticated and educated people were able to read or write. In fact, reading and writing was not a necessary skill until the Industrial Revolution several centuries later. So what Christianity ended up with was not four but ten Gospels by ten different Disciples, and not a few but many Epistles written by Jesus' Disciples. [As I said so many times, Paul does not count as one of Jesus' Inner Circle Disciples.] However, the One, Holy, Catholic, and Apostolic Church in its infinite wisdom has decided only four of these ten Gospels were canon, or officially authorized to be read; and the same goes for the numerous Epistles that were written. It begs the question: Were their motives theological or political? Why were we not given all ten Gospels to read, and all the Epistles written by the Disciples, such as Peter? Or letting us read all those "Secret Gospels" with Jesus' private teachings.

IMPORTANT POINT: How can we, or the millennia of believers before us, be sure we are following the actual and exact teachings of Jesus Christ? Such differences cause several schisms. It finally led to the big schism in 1054 between the Roman Catholic Church and the Eastern Orthodox Church which remains today. The next "apostate" or break (it wasn't technically a schism) from the one Catholic Church was at the end of the 16th Century and into the 17th Century with the Protestant Reformation. Today, there are tens of thousands of Protestant denominations in the world.

One of the biggest controversies was the "dogma" of The Holy Trinity. One of the main tenets of the Catholic Church (and some others) is the belief that God is three consubstantial beings, meaning in essence one entity: the Father, Son, and Holy Spirit. This means Jesus Christ was both human and divine at the same time. The Trinity is not mentioned anywhere but a matter of belief and faith without any substantiation in fact or Scripture. The "orthodox" Christian Church (and others that followed) believed that through Jesus Christ's passion and death, He was sacrificed to redeem humans from Original Sin and the other sins of humanity.

IMPORTANT POINT: Original Sin was one of the major dogmas that caused the Eastern Orthodox Church, who did not share the same belief, to split away from the Roman Catholic Church.

As the One Catholic Church grew and spread, the Church leaders vigorously fend off any purveyors of heresy. One of the main objects of cleansing was the multiple **Gnostic** sects. They had different portrayals of Jesus and interpretations of His teachings. The **Gnostics** allowed women in priestly roles. They considered the Holy Spirit as a feminine Divine form. For everyone, the **Gnostics** were the supreme heretics and had to be extinguished. The Catholic Church did everything to discredit their ideas, excommunicated their teachers, and eliminated their texts. It is unfortunate the **Gnostics** and their sects were in a "battle to the death" and ultimately lost their battle to remain a viable branch of Christianity.

Jesus instructed His Disciples and their followers "to love one another," "to make no new law," and "not to judge one another." However, many of the Church leaders were very hateful and judgmental against the **Gnostics**. For many, it was a product of their need for self-preservation. They wanted to be the only Christians; the one true Christians. To this end, 2nd century Church leader Irenaeus was one of the first to discredit the **Gnostic** beliefs. It was Irenaeus who unilaterally decided which **FOUR GOSPELS** (of the ten known Gospels) as the only ones which were divinely inspired; and the only ones that were descendant from Jesus' Disciples (including Luke and Mark whoever they are and from which Disciples they received their narratives). The early Church leaders also did not like the mystical and inner spiritual beliefs of the **Gnostics** as opposed to the Catholic Church's literal interpretations of the four canonical Gospels.

IMPORTANT POINT: Jesus is quoted in the ***Gospel of Thomas*** that He will reveal the mysteries of the universe to those who are truly worthy to receive them, and instructed His Disciples to do the same.

The ***Gospel of Thomas*** which Biblical scholars believe is older than the Church-accepted ***Gospels of Matthew, Mark, Luke,*** and ***John.*** It may even be the source for those four Gospels. The ***Gospel of Thomas*** contains 114 sayings of Jesus stated to be recorded by the Disciple Thomas, with no narratives. In Thomas, Jesus tells us that there is hidden knowledge and that we can become like him by drinking from his mouth (i.e. listening to His teachings).

The following is a list of some Gnostic beliefs that the "orthodox" Church leaders considered "heretical":

- **Gnosticism:** There were numerous **Gnostics** sects from the 1st century and the earliest beginnings of Christianity right through the Middle Ages. Many of the sects fell under the umbrella of **"Gnostic Christians"** who believed they were just, if not more, "**Christian**" than the emerging unified Christian Church. Different sects had diverse beliefs; however, a common belief was that attaining **gnosis,** or the special secret knowledge, was the real means to salvation. Below are some of the variations of beliefs about the nature of Jesus Christ (there is no definitive answer). But anyone claiming to have **Gnostic** beliefs was the main enemy of the emerging Christian Church's leaders whose mission was to eliminate any and all forms of **Gnosticism** for they alone were the "true" (or "orthodox") Christian Church.

- **Adoptionism:** Followers believed that God the Father "adopted" Jesus at His conception or at His baptism, i.e. the point was when Jesus became divine and became Jesus the Christ.

- **Apollinarianism:** Followers believed that Jesus was neither divine nor human.

- **Arianism:** Followers believed that Jesus Christ was "created" to be the savior of humanity. He was never consubstantial with the Father. He was created only at that time and never existed previously.

- **Docetism:** Followers believed that Jesus Christ was always divine and He only appeared to be human. His crucifixion also was only an illusion because He was a divine spirit and could not die.

- **Monophysitism:** Followers believed that Jesus Christ was actually two separate beings, human and divine, fused together in one body for the time He was on this Earth.

- **Pelagianism:** A 5th Century Irish priest, Pelagius, preached that Baptism was not necessary because people were capable of saving themselves through their own effort. He also did not believe that Adam and Eve eating the apple in the Garden of Eden generated any such thing as "Original Sin."

- **Sabellianism:** Followers of Sabellius believed that God the Father, Jesus Christ, and the Holy Spirit were three facets of One Being. They believed Jesus Christ was never human but always divine.

- **Manichaeanism:** They blended "orthodox" Christian ideas with **Gnosticism,** Mithraism, neo-Platonism, and possibly Buddhism. Saint Augustine investigated Manichaeanism but then ultimately rejected it.

The various sects of **Gnosticism** flourished in the early centuries. They even could have been considered mainstream Christian religions. **Valentinus** was an exceptionally effective **Gnostic** teacher. He faithfully served the Christian Church and at one point was considered a candidate to become the Bishop of Rome. He grew in his **Gnostic** thinking and consequently distanced him from the emerging Christian Church. Valentinus mission ended in A.D. 150 when, like Basilides and Marcion before him, was excommunicated and all his writings ordered destroyed.

Roman Emperor Constantine allowed freedom of religion in his empire. Constantine also designated Christianity as the official religion of the Roman Empire but not the exclusive religion. The Christian Church leaders took it upon themselves to make Christianity the only sanctioned religion. They excommunicated and banished anyone who did not follow their religion, calling them heretics. These Church Leaders ordered any unsanctioned Gospel, Epistle, or text banned and immediately destroyed by fire. This included the possible source document for the canonical Gospels, the ***Gospel of Thomas,*** which they also condemned and ordered destroyed.

Irenaeus in his famous treatise, abbreviated ***Against Heresies,*** circa A.D. 180, especially mentioned the ***Gospel of Truth***, believed to have been written by Valentinus. To counter these "heresies," the Church Leaders updated wording in the traditional passed-down **baptismal creed** into a statement of Christian beliefs. It was called the ***Apostles Creed.***

THE CATHARS

In the 12th Century in Southern France emerged a religious movement called **Catharism.** It had distinctive Gnostic elements in it and its followers were called Cathars, or the "pure ones." They mainly criticized the excesses of the Roman Catholic clergy. Several priests agreed with the beliefs of Catharism and joined the Cathars.

BELIEFS OF THE CATHARS

The Cathars followed the beliefs of the **Gnostic Christians** that came so many centuries before them:

- A divine spark was imprisoned in the human body.
- The human spirit was contained in the soul.
- This spirit was pure by nature and needed to be kept that way in order to enter the realm of light.
- This world was an inferior, material and physical realm created by an evil god, the Demiurge, possibly Satan.
- The God of the Jews was not the true good God but was an imposter.
- The Christian Church with its origins in the Hebrew God was an invalid religion only worshipping that same inferior God.
- They worshipped the Good God of Love.
- Mankind had to use their efforts in order to free themselves from this evil god and their material existence.
- They needed to attain the **gnosis,** the special knowledge, to reach an enlightened existence.
- If they did not attain the **gnosis**, they would be destined to repeat this material life through reincarnations.
- The Cathars completely rejected the Hebrew Scriptures.
- They did not believe in the Holy Trinity.
- The Sacrament of the Eucharist was not practiced by them.
- They did not believe in purgatory or hell. It was the entrapment of the divine spark in the human body which makes this world hell.
- The Cathars were pacifists and their nonviolent beliefs were also shown in their treatment of animals. This led them not to eat meat or dairy.

- They venerated Mary Magdalene. This may have had to do with mainly being around Southern France where it was believed Mary migrated after Jesus' death.

The Cathars had a two-tier hierarchy: The clergy was called the ***Perfecti,*** the elders or perfect ones; and the ***Credentes*** were the believers. The clergy could be men or women. The ***Perfecti*** wore black robes and tried to live like Jesus depending upon alms, doing prayer and penance, and living of life of serving and teaching. The ***Perfecti*** underwent the ***consolamentum*** ritual, the baptism and ordination by the Holy Spirit. The ***Credentes*** led a more worldly life, they could marry, but they had to take an oath not to take a life or kill an animal. If death was approaching, the Cathars would stop eating and drinking to hasten their death.

In A.D. 1208, Pope Eugene III issued an edict against the Cathars and demanded the Church put an end to Catharism. Pope Eugene III commissioned a crusade to eradicate them. That crusade lasted over forty years. Thousands of people were slaughtered. Scholars believe the number of people who died could be as high as 20,000 including women and children. But still Catharism itself did not die. Pope Innocent took over in the middle of the 13th century and called his bishops together to deal again with the Cather "problem." The Pope commissioned another inquisition to exterminate them permanently. They scattered and hid. The last ***Perfecti*** finally was killed in A.D. 1321.

THE EASTERN ORTHODOX CHURCHES

The initial chapters of ***Alternative Christianities – Volume I*** explain that **dogmatically** there are three major hierarchical branches of Christianity: Catholic, Orthodox, and Protestant. There are many subsets of branches and/or denominations underneath each of the three. For the final section of this Chapter, I want to talk about the Eastern Orthodox Churches which were the fertile breeding grounds for **Gnosticism.**

Mark, the author of the ***Gospel of Mark*** which is believed to be the first written Gospel from which the others were copied, traveled to the city of Alexandria, Egypt where he preached about Jesus' ministry, death, and resurrection. Mark's followers gave rise to the **Coptic Christian Church** which flourished in Egypt and throughout the region.

The **Egyptian Coptic Churches** initially were important as defenders of the faith against Gnostic heresies in the early centuries. Their Bishop Athanasius who was Bishop of Alexandria from A.D. 327 to 373 was very instrumental in forming the Christian Creed at the Council of Nicaea. Bishop Athanasius was even called "the Father of Orthodoxy."

In the first three centuries after Christ, many Christian sects developed. Many had their own sacred or "secret" texts. As the "orthodox" or "sanctioned" Christian Church grew and became more powerful, they more they suppressed any and all "unorthodox" factions; along with the destruction of their texts containing any alternative early Christianities' "unorthodox" beliefs. They would have been forever lost if it was not for modern theological scholars that knew these texts existed because they were mentioned and criticized by the heresiologist writings of orthodox fathers, like Irenaeus and others. They even mention some of the banned texts contained "secret teachings" imparted by Jesus Christ to a few.

IMPORTANT POINT: These Eastern Orthodox and Coptic Churches (Coptic can be Catholic or Orthodox) have the remnants to varying degrees of the **Gnosis** beliefs. In many ways, the Orthodox Churches at the time of the Great Schism in 1054 appear to have stuck to Christianity as it was meant to be versus the dogmatic direction of the Church of Rome.

##

BIBLIOGRAPHY, REFERENCE, AND SUGGESTED READING

Barnstone, Willis and Marvin Meyer, ***The Gnostic Bible*** © 2009 Shambhala, Boston © 2003 Harper, San Francisco, CA

Beal, Timothy, ***Rise and Fall of the Bible, The: The Unexpected History of an Accidental Book*** © 2011 Houghton Miffin Harcourt, New York

Ehrman, Bart D., ***Jesus, Interrupted: Revealing the Hidden Contradictions in the Bible (And Why We Don't Know About Them)*** © 2009 HaperOne, HarperCollins Publishers, New York

Ehrman, Bart D., ***Lost Christianities: the Battles for Scripture and the Faiths We Never Knew*** © 2003 Oxford University Press, New York

Ehrman, Bart D., ***Lost Scriptures: Books That Did Not Make It into the New Testament*** © 2006 Oxford University Press

Gibson, David, and Michael McKinley, ***Finding Jesus: Faith, Fact, Forgery: Six Holy Objects That Tell The Remarkable Story Of The Gospels*** © 2015 St. Martin Press, New York

Lester, Meera, ***The Everything ® Gnostic Gospels Book: A Complete Guide to the Secret Gospels*** © 2007 Adams Media, an F-W Publications, Inc.

Mack, Burton L., ***Who Wrote the New Testament: The Making of the Christian Myth*** ©1995 Harper, San Francisco, California

Pelikan, Jaroslav, ***Whose Bible Is It? A History of the Scriptures Through the Ages*** © 2005 Viking Press (Penguin Group), New York

Author's Note: This Book and Treatise are a compilation from many sources on the same subject. See the Complete List of Bibliographies, References, and Suggested Readings in Appendix II

CHAPTER 7

THE HISTORY OF GNOSTICISM

WHAT IS GNOSTICISM?

The **Gnostics** were around from the earliest days of Christianity; in the days of Jesus' Twelve Disciples. Were they heretics? Or did they possess the deepest secrets of Christianity? Who were their leaders? Could they be one or more of The Twelve? Have their beliefs survived these two millennia? Why were their beliefs suppressed by the emerging Christian Church? Could their Sacred Scriptures containing their beliefs, also contain the true teachings of Jesus Christ? Then why were these Gnostic texts ordered banned from circulation? Why do these banned texts keep reappearing? Has this secretive society of **Gnostics** survived despite their constant suppression?

By way of definition, the word "***gnosis***" is the Greek word for "knowledge." (***Gnosis*** is pronounced with the ***g*** silent and the ***o*** long.) The common English forms of the word are **Gnostics** (i.e. people), **Gnosticism** (the movement or religion) and **Gnostic Christians** (the **Gnostics** profess to be Christians). The **Gnostic** movement dates from the very early days of Christianity. Most of the **Gnostic Christian** sects attribute their existence to one of Jesus' Disciples, or at least to the Gospels, Epistles, and other works descending from one of Jesus' Inner Circle. Many of those texts that were banned and destroyed by the state-established central Christian Church in the Roman Empire survived.

Many times you hear from religious persons that **Gnosticism** was pure heresy – ***teachings that distorted Christ's message*** – which died out in over time. This is what they have been taught to say by the mainstream, state-established, Christian Church. When you step out of their world into a bigger sphere of knowledge, you learn differently.

G. R. S. Meed, a British scholar published in 1900 a study of **Gnosticism** called ***Fragments of a Faith Forgotten.*** He claims that **Gnosticism** is not as forgotten as has been thought in the previous hundred years. There was also a current day ***Time*** magazine which said: "***Thousands of Americans follow Gnosticism avidly in New Age publications and actually recreate full-dress spiritual practices from the early texts and other lore.***" There is Harold Bloom who claimed that Gnosticism is very much "American religion."

The roots of **Gnosticism** can be traced all the way back to the ***Gospel of Thomas.*** A copy of this ancient Gospel was discovered in Egypt in an early 2nd Century **Gnostic** community. It was also discovered in the area where the

Manicheans lived in Central Asia. The Disciple Thomas was thought to go and preach in Central Asia. The teachings of Jesus' Disciple Thomas were found throughout the Far Eastern regions. Such teachings were not isolated only to the Disciple Thomas but also found in banned writings of other Jesus' Disciples.

The **Gnostic** influence might have been suppressed by the emerging Christian Church but it did survive underground in other forms of Christianity. There was a major resurgence in the Middle Ages with the Christian religious group called the Cathars. The Inquisition was commanded to exterminate this group of "heretics," or "non-orthodox believers."

In the 18th Century, **Gnosticism** was found prevalent among the Freemasons to which many of our American Founding Fathers belonged; and our principles, buildings, and ceremonies were founded. As many times the conservative fundamentalists like to preach that the United States was founded as a "Christian" nation, which we know that it was not from Chapter 17 in ***Alternative Christianities, Volume I***. It was more so founded as a Freemason and Gnostic nation – just read their writings with that thought in mind. They were followed in the 19th Century by the writings of American Theosophists. In modern days, **Gnostic** beliefs again arose with the Jewish Kabbalists. The basic **Gnostics** principles can be found in the works of Philip K. Dick and popular Hollywood films like ***The Matrix*** series and Dan Brown's ***The Da Vinci Code*** and ***Angels and Demons.***

Gnosticism sure has held a long-lasting fascination throughout the history of Christianity. Maybe it was because **Gnosticism** was considered the **"forbidden faith"** condemned and banned by the official Christian Church. Despite that, **Gnosticism** still has long-lasting appeal. It offered logical solutions to apparent illogical situations. Their solutions were shunned by the mainstream religions whose explanations are only described as "**divine mysteries to be taken on pure faith**". **Gnosticism** offered logical answers to those mysteries but they undermined the mysteries and faith of those mainstream Christianities. However, to the **Gnostics** they were just another form of Christianity with Jesus Christ as their savior but for different reasons. They are an **Alternative Christianity**. There are **Gnostic Christians** and non-Christian **Gnostics** like **Kabbala** practiced in Judaism or other religions in the Middle and the Far East.

Unfortunately, Gnosticism was forbidden and stricken from the lives of Christians. To the newly established Christian Church, the Gnostics were not only heretics but the highest level of arch-heretics. At times throughout the centuries, there has been a resurge of interest in **Gnosticism.** Such has happened today with new philosophies, intellectualism, individualism, and a revolt against "the establishment." The interest in **Gnostic Christianity** is different than other various schisms and sects that were popular for a brief time but then just completely vanished. Most of the time they were all labeled as heretics by the all-powerful Christian Church. Likewise, this Christian Church was very accomplished at eradicating any schism, sect, group, or individuals who did NOT accept their "official teachings." Of all these schisms in the Christian family tree, the **Gnostics** have an usually powerful fascination by many. Maybe it is because the **Gnostics** offer practical solutions to mysteries taken on faith by the mainstream Christian Church. **Gnosticism** looks at religion through a wider lens, the bigger picture not only of life on Earth but also the Divine Realm.

IMPORTANT POINT: The term "Christian Church," at least the first 1000 years can be interchangeable with the

"Catholic Church" until the 1066 Eastern Orthodox schism. The Catholic Church became the Roman Catholic Church. Then at the end of the 15th Century, Martin Luther spurred the Protestant Reformation. Subsequently, the Protestant Reformation promulgated the innumerable denominations of Protestantism that we have today. On the highest level, it collectively falls under the major genus of Christianity.

Taking a step back, philosophically religion has two main purposes in human existence. First, religion enables people to connect with God, the divine realm, and the afterlife. Second, it is a pillar of society to provide decent moral values for the common good. "***Religion***" comes from the Latin ***religare*** that loosely means "***to bind together***." Religion binds people to God, the divine realm, and to each another. Of course, sometimes the two purposes conflict and clash with each other. In **Gnosticism,** a person who is in contact with their spiritual insight has the ***"gnosis,"*** and does not need any religion or an organized church like ordinary people. These people are a threat to the church's existence.

Gnosticism is not reserved for Western civilization and Christianity. Its philosophies extend to the Far East and come from the Far East. Many teachings have come from the Far East. There it is not challenged by overpowering religions like Christianity. In the Far East, it is believed that different religions can coexist. You can be a Christian and a Buddhist, or any other combination. Far East philosophies have introduced and included Asian-originated terms such as ***Zen, karma, yang*** and ***yin,*** etc.; which also have worked their way into our English vocabulary**.** Eastern philosophies always have stressed the need for spiritual experience or for a person to look within themselves for the truths that they have been told. This probably accounts for how Hinduism and Buddhism have such a popular base also outside the Far East in Europe and the Americas.

Gnosticism is along those same lines. There is more meaning about the Greek word "***gnosis"*** which translates on the surface to "knowledge." But in reality "***gnosis"*** is a very specific kind of knowledge. It is the knowledge that there is a direct link to the divine which is usually referred to as the "***divine spark***." An equivalent in Hinduism and Buddhism is when they refer to "***enlightenment."*** Through the centuries since Jesus Christ walked on this earth, many people are excited and relieved to hear that this quest for knowledge or enlightenment is really embedded in the origins of Christianity. There has always been **Gnostic Christians.** These **Gnostics** have never been deterred by the mistreatment of them by the official Christian Church's hierarchy. Their attitude, maybe their deeper understanding of Jesus' teachings, is what gives them the durability to surpass that hierarchy with the knowledge that they know they are on the right road to the Divine and His Realm.

Gnosticism also has a lot to do with our view of this material world. The **Gnostics** of the ancient world regarded this world as being defective. It is a creation of an inferior fallen deity they called the ***demiurge*** which translated to mean "craftsman." This world and the humans in it were not created by the All-Good, All-Loving, All-Merciful, and Almighty Supreme God.

The **Gnostic** beliefs peaked and were as strong as the Roman Empire in the 2nd century A.D. Remember that during that period, most of the known civilized world fell under the rule of the Roman Empire. The Roman citizens of that period lived in a society that had the highest level of culture, materialism, sophistication, and intelligence ever known to mankind. **Gnosticism** was a perfect fit in Roman Society. It feeds their intellectual status. In fact, it complemented their system of Roman deities. The **Gnostics** taught that this is a world of delusion ruled by inferior gods. The **Christian Gnostics** claimed that their True and Good God was far above these inferiorities. He had sent His divine messengers, including Jesus Christ, to restore the lost knowledge and reclaim all goodness He intended for humanity.

Even though today we are not ruled by one monopolistic political system but still in many modern civilizations it seems nothing has changed from the days of the Roman Empire. Even in nations that claim to have a Democratic political system of a government "Of the People, By the People, and For the People," many people still feel the oppression of having little say as individuals in their government. As has happened in the monarchs and oligopolies of the past centuries, most of the government is controlled by the rich supporters, corporate donors, and nepotistic bureaucracies. The democratic experiment has failed or forced by money and power to revert to government "Of the Few, By the Few, and For the Few" causing a paranoid and cynical view of government over which the people have little to no control. This may be why **Gnosticism** has been gaining widespread acceptance again; an escape from this flawed and materialistic world ruled by modern-day ***demiurges***. If not run by the master ***demiurge*** himself, surely by his well-trained sons.

The **Gnostics** have no problem accepting that they are humans imprisoned by the ***demiurge*** in this world of delusion, hate, pain, and suffering. The difference is that in ancient days these obstacles were caused by evil or vengeful gods. Today, they are caused by evil and vengeful political leaders. This was the theme of a well-known 1999 film called

The Matrix in which practically every person was kept in a collective state of sleep by evil machine-like creations. Those creations coincidentally resemblance the evil archons spoke of by the **Gnostics.**

IMPORTANT POINT: Jews and Christians have no problem believing as true in the Biblical story of Lucifer, the fallen archangel from Heaven, or Satan, the generic representation of devils roaming the earth. However, when you mention the evil fallen ***demiurge*** causing the hate and suffering in the world, they look at your crazy and consider YOUR story to be an unbelievable and impossible "fairy tale" whereas, in reality, it is the same exact scenario.

Another reason for **Gnosticism's** revival through the centuries and in modern day is an intellectual sense that ***something(s) is missing within Christianity.*** David Hawkins, a well-known author, suggests that between the time of Jesus Christ Himself preaching on this Earth and the Christian churches that exist today, something was lost. He blamed the decline in creditability of Christianity since A.D. 325 due to the misinterpretations of Christian dogma coming out of the Council of Nicaea." He is not alone in his view which has been reiterated in dozens of other books and articles. Case in point: the Great Christian Schism of 1054 into the Eastern Orthodox Church and the Roman Catholic Church. Ultimately the split was due to dogmas proclaimed by the Council of Nicaea and subsequent councils. Although this was the biggest and most publicized split of the Catholic (universal Christian) Church up to that time. There were many more schisms and clean-cut splits, including **Gnostic** ones, that occurred before 1054 because of the "official dogma" being shoved down everyone's throats as a result of the Council of Nicaea and the newly established state-sanctioned Catholic (universal Christian) Church. The Council that intended to unite all the Christian Churches really did the complete opposite. But then remember this was orchestrated by new Emperor Constantine to "politically" unite the Roman Empire which was his real purpose and priority.

Traditional Christianity is not without flaws (a dedicated chapter in Volume I). Many important elements are missing from Christianity: There are NO accounts written by an eyewitness in their native or known languages giving first-hand accounts of the life and teachings of Jesus Christ. He is a man who became revered as being God Himself incarnate. However, in His lifetime He was never considered to be God, nor was it ever written that He was God by His Inner Circle, His Twelve Disciples, in any of the accounts supposedly passed down from them. You could be sure that if Jesus ever claimed He was God (or the Son of God, not as He repeatedly said the "Son of Man") this would appear in all the Gospels of the New Testament which is it does NOT. Luke admits he was not an eyewitness because he says in his Gospel that they were relayed to him by those "***which from the beginning were eyewitnesses***" (***Luke*** 1:2, KJV). John says "***testifieth of things, and wrote these things, and we know that his testimony is true***" (***John*** 21:24). Obviously, John would not have said, "***We know that his testimony is true***" if the author of John himself had been the eyewitness. **In NONE of the Gospels ANYWHERE does ANYONE claim that THEY personally saw or hear ANY of these things with THEIR own eyes and ears. It was all passed down to them by word of mouth from generations past.**

Most Biblical scholars agree that the traditional ending of the recognized oldest of the Gospels, the ***Gospel of Mark,*** at ***Mark*** 16:8 say, "***And they went out quickly, and fled from the sepulcher, for they trembled and were amazed, neither said they anything to any man, for they were***

afraid. " Notice it says "they" not "we." In fact, in the Greek version, it ends with a conjunction. <u>There are endings that no one knows from where they came that exist in many editions of the Bible.</u> Were there more verses or pages in the Gospel of Mark that were lost, removed, or suppressed? ...So much for the true and inerrant word of God in the Gospels.

Today's Christianity, especially with the Evangelical and Fundamentalist Protestant ministers, likes to stress unequivocally that the events and words said by Jesus in the Gospels are factually true; however, an eyewitness or first-hand account is crucially missing which brings into question their "factually true" claim. Do you think it is really possible that none of Christ's Disciples ever thought to write down anything their Lord and Master said? Well, if not all, they were illiterate, but still there were educated scribes all around Judea. Is it possible that what the Disciples wrote down in their native language and handwriting were destroyed? Why would any good Christian do that? Maybe they were suppressed? Well, we do know that over 50 works were found including Gospels, Epistles, and Apocrypha that were claimed to be written by some of the same and other Disciples **WERE SUPPRESSED, BANNED, AND ORDERED DESTROYED**. Just coincidentally, they are referred to as "**<u>THE GNOSTIC GOSPELS."</u>**

Many books have been written on these Gnostic Gospels, especially by Marvin Meyers, Bart Ehrman, and Elaine Pagels. It was appropriately put by Ms. Pagels in her book ***The Gnostic Gospels*** [New York: Vintage, 1989, p.150]:

> "***The concerns of Gnostic Christians survived.... as a suppressed current, like a river driven underground. Such currents resurfaced throughout the Middle Ages in various forms***

of heresy; then with the Reformation, Christian tradition again took new and diverse forms... " [Like the Protestant Reformers, Gnosticism is just one of many] ***"interpretations of religious experience."***

GNOSTIC CHRISTIANS

When you study the origins of Christianity, the story is pretty much the same. Jesus Christ came down from Heaven as the Son of God. He was born of a virgin in Bethlehem but otherwise not much is known about Him until He was approximately 30 years old and began His ministry. He had 12 Disciples in His "inner circle" who He instructed on His mission here on earth and then dispatched them to preach His word to all the nations of the world. His legacy is Christianity to whom He entrusted to His Disciples as its leaders. Roman Emperor Constantine in A.D. 325 invited all the bishops from around the Empire to attend the Council of Nicaea with the mission to form ONE **universal** Christian church with a common set of beliefs. This Church became known as the "Catholic Church" derived from the Greek word "***katholikos"*** meaning "universal." Every Christian church in the world today, and their basic beliefs, has roots in the Roman Catholic Church and its predecessors for almost 1300 years from its inception at the Council of Nicaea.

As neat and clean that sounds, it is a lot more disjointed. There were several groups of Christians before and after the Council of Nicaea who had their own versions of Jesus Christ's Christianity. One major faction of Christians believed Jesus and Christianity were meant as an extension of Judaism, not as a separate religion. They had a valid case: Jesus lived His whole life as Jew, His Disciples lived their whole lives as Jews, Jesus studied and preached the Hebrew

Bible, He attended synagogue, and He faithfully observed Jewish law. Others, like Paul, firmly believed that Christianity is a new religion and should shun all remnants of Judaism. Some Christians never believed that Jesus was God or the Son of God but just a religious man, another in a long line of prophets, or even an anti-Rome zealot. Another group never believed that Jesus was ever human but was all divine just appearing to be a human. The Catholic Church claimed they were "***aided by the power of the Holy Spirit"*** to face down all these heretics. In the final version of the Nicene Creed, they tried to encompass both latter factions by stating that "***Jesus was fully God and fully man***." As much as that seemed like a good compromise, it is really a dichotomy or mutually exclusive contradictory terms. You cannot be "**fully God**" and at the same time be "**fully Man**" or vice versa. The Church called this "***a mystery of faith***." This did not help the Catholic Church but only caused more splits and schisms with groups retreating into their own camp of beliefs. After the Protestant Reformation some 1300 years later, the number of iterations of Christianity multiplied exponentially.

<u>**IMPORTANT POINT:**</u> Neither Jesus nor the authors of the Gospels answer any of these questions. Jesus never called Himself God or the Son of God, nor did He or His Disciples abandoned Judaism.

Biblical scholars are quick to agree that Jesus Christ did NOT talk very much at all about theology. He mainly did talk about the Afterlife and the Kingdom of His Father. Jesus seemed to have talked a lot about morals and ethics. When He was asked about His greatest commandment He replied, "***Love thy neighbors as thyself***." He talks about being sincere in the eyes of His Father. He does argue passionately with the Scribes and Pharisees the real meaning of the Jewish Law. At times He even argues with them about the true nature of their God; while at no time does He reveal who He is. Although His Disciples and others repeatedly kept asking Him if He is God, He never responds with a clear definitive answer. Why? If you God wouldn't you want to admit it? Wouldn't you be a little more revealing? And wouldn't you appear to as many as you could after you rose from the dead and not make yourself scare for 40 days?

Jesus Christ's teachings might be able to be summarized in a quote He may have said at some time from the prophet Micah: ***"What doth the Lord require of thee, but to do justly, and to love mercy, and to walk humbly with thy God?"*** (***Micah*** 6:8). It is basically the same as what He said with His greatest commandment, ***"What you do to the least of My brethren, you do unto Me***." These messages seem always to be at the heart of Christ's teachings. Maybe He had a good reason for stressing these things. What else could be misinterpreted by "***be good to each other***"? Ironically, many of the Church leaders were the worst offenders of His Greatest Commandment and **turned Jesus Christ's religion into a merciless persecutor** to anyone who was non-compliant to their human interpretation. Unfortunately, this same persecution continues into the modern era by the most conservative Christian denominations and sects for non-compliance with their **new** interpretation of beliefs and teachings. The **Gnostics** and **Gnosticism** seemed to be very much out of favor.

THE FIRST GOSPEL

One of the most interesting books among the **Gnostic Gospels** discovered at Nag Hammadi, Egypt was ***The Gospel of Thomas*** believed to be written by the Disciple Thomas. It is extremely short, only twelve pages, but was a very important discovery. It received much more attention than the other **Gnostic Gospels** that it has been referred to as ***The Fifth Gospel.*** In fact, it probably should be referred to as ***The First Gospel***. It is considered older than all the other Gospels. It is believed to have been written as early as A.D. 50; whereas the Gospels assigned to Matthew, Mark, Luke, and John are usually dated to be written between A.D. 70 and 100 (definitely many years after those four men had died). It amazes the Biblical scholars that it never was placed in the ***New Testament***. The best thing about this Gospel is that it contains no narratives. The opening statement says it is just a collection of sayings and parables **"that the living Jesus spoke."** The first time it sounds possible that it was actually written by one of the Inner Circle Disciples, Thomas.

Many Biblical scholars consider ***The Gospel of Thomas*** to be the source on which the authors of the other Gospels in the New Testament were based. ***New Testament*** scholars have compared the similarities and differences in content and wording between ***The Gospel of Thomas*** and the four canonical Gospels. Although its existence was known since the 2nd century, until it was re-discovered, the scholars always thought there was source document which they used to call **"Q"** (from the German ***Quelle***, or "source"). No other texts similar to this Gospel have ever been discovered. Scholars infer that there had to be a source document like **"Q"** because of the word for word similarities between Matthew and Luke, both of whom appear to have drawn from it. It is believed by many scholars that ***The Gospel of Thomas*** is not what is referred to as **"Q"** even though it is believed to be just a collection of sayings. It is definitely dated as older and the narratives of the four Gospels in the ***New Testament***. It sure does look like ***The Gospel of Thomas*** is one source document from which the canonical Gospels were written. A good amount of the wording in ***The Gospel of Thomas*** is found verbatim in the Gospels. ***The Gospel of Thomas*** appears to be the most original Gospel, but why would the Church Leaders ban it and order all copies destroyed? Maybe as noticed by anyone who reads it, and I do suggest to everyone to do so, some of the sayings of Jesus are very **Gnostic** in nature and we know the Church Leaders had to eradicate all traces of "heretical" **Gnosticism** even if it meant destroying SEVERAL Gospels written by five other Disciples because they contained **Gnostic ideas.** The new Catholic Church would NOT tolerate any **Gnosticism. Why?**

There are other reasons that the Church Leaders found no need to keep ***The Gospel of Thomas*** around. It did not concur with what they were preaching, if not contradicted it. ***Thomas*** never presents Jesus as God or even the Son of God made man; or someone who came here to redeem humans either from their sins or as the Second Person of a Divine Trinity. Within all the sayings in it, Jesus never claimed to God or having any divine authority. When Jesus asked His Disciples who they thought He was: Peter said He was like a righteous angel; Matthew called Him a wise philosopher, and Thomas referred to Him just as a teacher. Moreover, ***Thomas*** never called Jesus "**Christ**" which is the Greek equivalent word for the Hebrew word "***Messiah***" meaning "the anointed one."

IMPORTANT POINT: Is this all not strange that His own Disciples when Jesus asked them never considered Him to be God, nor even Divine.

It seems that the image of loved famous persons grows in stature and importance after their death than when they were alive or in reality. This accelerates as everyone with the first-hand experiences and memories die and the stories are passed down and embellished. This issue was raised years later as to the divinity of Jesus. **<u>Finally, the question of Jesus' divinity was settled when it was declared to be so by the Council of Nicaea in A.D. 325.</u>** This caused dissension, schisms, and splits from the new universal Catholic Church by sects and groups who did not agree with the Council of Nicaea. It is a fact that many did not believe that the Christianity which Jesus taught was the same that was being preached by either the Catholic, Orthodox, or Protestant denominations. Readers of the **Gnostic Gospels** and other works wonder why were they were rejected and banned. They claim to have been passed down from six of Jesus' Disciples: Peter, James, Philip, Thomas, Judas, and Mary Magdalene. They can be authenticated the same as, if not better than, the Disciples Matthew and John, and whoever Luke and Mark are which are pure guesses and assumptions.

There is an apocryphal Gospel called ***The Protenangelion of James*** that was one of the 50+ texts banned and ordered destroyed. It contains otherwise unheard of narratives about Jesus' birth and His young years. It contains more of the story of Jesus' birth than appears in either ***Matthew*** or ***Luke.*** There are other details in ***James*** that would indicate that ***Matthew*** and ***Luke*** were based on ***James.*** This would mean that ***James*** also is older than ***Matthew*** <u>and</u> ***Luke.*** In fact, ***James*** is believed to be the origin of the doctrine that Mary had an Immaculate Conception. Again **WHY** was this Gospel not included in the ***New Testament*** when obviously it was the source of the books that were included? Unless of course there was a reason that the Bishops who composed the Bible exercised censorship in what they wanted us to believe.

The most prominent thing about ***The Gospel of Thomas*** is the statement at the beginning of this Gospel: ***"Whoever***

finds the meaning of these sayings will not taste death." This was characteristic of the sayings in ***Thomas.*** Sayings like this lead Biblical scholars to believe that Thomas leaned toward **Gnosticism.** It is the central difference between the teachings of the emerging Christianity and ***Gnosticism.*** Christianity, especially evangelical Protestant Christianity of today, heavily concentrates on sin, repentance, and redemption. None of these are found in the sayings found in ***The Gospel of Thomas*** but instead encrypted mystical messages usually found in the **Gnostic** writings. In fact, many scholars feel that Jesus' sayings in ***Thomas*** are like "**koans"** which are familiar to many as those cryptic riddles usually given by Zen masters to their students to decipher. It is used to awaken and stimulate the mind. **Thus the goal of Gnosticism is to provide enlightenment to find the Divine realm whereas the goal of the traditional Christian Churches is to provide redemption and salvation.** This is the reason for the never-ending rivalry between traditional Christianity and **Gnosticism.** For some, it is much easier to follow a religion focused on sin, atonement, redemption, and appeasing an angry and wrathful God who hangs "eternal damnation" over your head. For some in ancient times, this aligns more with the worship, fear, and redemption from their pagan deities; so it was easier to convert to the emerging Christianity whereas **Gnosticism** was much too cerebral for common uneducated people.

The famous story in John's Gospel (***John*** 20:24-29) of "Doubting Thomas" when he publically announces he had not believed that Christ had risen from the dead and would only believe it when he sees it for himself, etc. Some scholars doubt the veracity of this story that a faithful Disciple who has seen Jesus perform so many miracles now doubts this miracle. Some scholars believe this story was placed in the ***New Testament*** to stick it to the **Gnostics** saying the followers of Thomas did not believe that Jesus Christ was really God but a flesh and blood man who died.

It is believed that the Disciple Thomas preached and converted in Syria. He was venerated for centuries by the Christians in Syria. That is where his Gospels probably were written and passed down. It is also believed the Disciple Thomas preached Jesus' message as far east as India where to this day can be found Christian communities that trace their roots back to their ancient origin of Thomas' preaching. Thomas surely left his mark in the East which was an area that was more receptive to his preaching than the Greeks or Romans, both who had long histories of worshipping pagan deities. So why wasn't the Disciple Thomas' Gospel or Book of Jesus' sayings not included in the ***New Testament***? You would think it is a perfect candidate; a book of Jesus' sayings without narratives? Again, it is probably because of Thomas' Gospels and the sayings of Jesus were entirely too **Gnostic** for the "teachings" of the emerging Church.

THE ANCIENT ROOTS OF GNOSTICISM

Gnosticism appears in similar forms from the Middle East to the Far East religions. There are Christian **Gnostics,** non-Christian **Gnostics**, and Jewish **Gnosticism** known as **Kabbalah.** We are only discussing the history of **Christian Gnosticism.** The history of **Christian Gnosticism** has the same beginning as Christianity with the birth of Jesus. Its roots are in the teachings of Jesus, His Disciples, and the Gospels and other writings attributed to them. The road splits at the canon, the official authorized books included, of the ***New Testament.*** The canon included just four Gospels and selected Epistles, many but not all attributed to Paul some of which are considered forgeries. The pure **Christian**

Gnostics have Gospels and Epistles which they revere that were not included by the Church attributed to one of Jesus' Disciples, such as James, Peter, Philip, Thomas, Judas, and Mary Magdalene. The exclusion of these Gospels and Epistles played a role in the schism of the Eastern Orthodox Churches. One of the most notable is the Coptic Orthodox Church out of Egypt.

To understand the History of **Gnosticism** it is necessary to explore the religions and cultures from which it arose.

The best place to start is with the renowned Roman Empire whose culture and history had a distinct effect on all the different versions of Christianity. The Roman world as vast and far-flung it was, it was remarkably unified and organized. The first two centuries of Christianity under the Roman Empire was an era of peace; for the most part the citizens, according to historian Edward Gibbon, the empire's inhabitants "***enjoyed and abused the advantages of wealth and luxury***." The Romans were doing well with their trade and commerce, and consequently there was plenty of goods and money to go around. They were also rich in philosophies and religions. They were tolerant of different cultures and religions. The Christians were persecuted not because they believed in a different God but because they refused to respect the gods of others. The pagans were in fear that the Christians would bring divine wrath upon them by their gods.

Also, obviously Judaism had the majority of influence on Christianity. Let's face it, Judaism was the mother faith and it was the Jewish Messiah from which Christianity was born. Christianity even adopted the Hebrew Bible as the base set of Sacred Scriptures, mainly to prove that Jesus was truly the Messiah, the anointed one, the Christ. Christianity also hesitantly adopted the Jewish belief in a single, monotheistic

God. They had a problem with the notion of the Trinity, three persons in one God: Father-Son-Holy Spirit. But nonetheless, Christianity had problems with Judaism from its outset. Of course, the main problem always had to do with the nature of Jesus Christ. They were in conflict with the impression of God the Father. The God of the Hebrews has many times shown wrath and vengeance to punish the bad humans, even taking out innocent good humans in the process. Technically, the Hebrew God was the first "mass murderer" and totally unapologetic about it, "***I form the light and create darkness: I make peace and create evil; I the Lord do all these things***" (***Isa***. 49:7). Christians could not reconcile the Hebrew God with the Good and Loving God preached about by Jesus.

Judaism was not the only conflict with which the Christians had to deal. In and before the time Christianity came onto the scene, there were many schools of philosophical thought. Now they had something new to add to their thought process, the nature of God. As centuries progress, also the nature of the sun, stars, and universe. Of course, this was very contentious with Christianity and today's scientists reflecting on how wrong Christianity was and how horrendously they handled it, i.e. the Sun revolves around the Earth controversy. Anyone saying anything to the contrary was a heretic! One of the main purposes of the philosophical schools is they make sense of it all and teach the students how to live in harmony with the world and universe around them.

One of the biggest challenges for emerging Christianity was **Gnosticism** and the school of thought inspired by Plato. Plato lived four centuries before Christianity was born. His legacy was the Academy in Athens, an institution of higher learning where his philosophical principles were taught. They have evolved and continued to be required reading over 2,000 years later. It is would be hard to overestimate the influence Plato and his peers have had on us.

Plato also had great influence on Gnosticism. An important work of Plato is ***Timaeus*** which is very esoteric about the creation of the world and the universe. Plato believes that God is good and says, "***God wanted everything to be good, and nothing bad, as far as it was possible***." So God tried to create a perfect world, or as perfect as it could be. Then, in accordance with Greek myth, God created a lesser realm of the gods who were charged with making the human beings.

But because humans ultimately are creations of God, they have the seed of divine in them. There is a part of them that is immortal. In ***Timaeus*** Plato speak of one true God above all and who created humans. Plato metaphorically refers to this God as the "craftsman." The Greek word for craftsman is "***demiourgos"*** which has been anglicized into "demiurge." This has become the term the **Gnostics** use for the creator of this world. However, they considered the demiurge to be an inferior deity and the one, true, and good God is not responsible for this inferior "cosmic disaster."

There were other mystical religions and cults that were around before Christianity other than **Gnosticism** which taught their followers how to get to a higher state of perception. They had rituals devoted to such gods as Dionysus, Demeter, and Isis. The latter was the beloved Great Mother of the Egyptians from whom Mary, the Mother of Jesus, would be modeled. Themes of virgin births, deaths, and resurrections were common among the pagan deities. Another common theme was about the wonderful afterlife and people should no longer have a fear to die.

Plato also discussed the true nature of God. Was God good or evil? If He is good, then why is the world such a bad place? Why is there so much hate, pain, and suffering? Plato hypothesized that this world may not be real and that is the reason there so much evil in it. What does this world say about the God who created it? Maybe instead this world wasn't created by the one, true, and good God but by some inferior, second-rate, or fallen god?

IMPORTANT POINT: The **Gnostic** beliefs seem to run concurrently with the beliefs of Plato and other ancient Greek philosophers pre-dating by at least four centuries the birth of Jesus Christ and founding of Christianity.

GNOSTIC TEACHERS

PETER, PAUL, AND THE DISCIPLES

Peter and his Church preached doctrines laced with sin and sacrifice that were already prevalent in the ancient religions which would help to get converts to Christianity. However, on the other hand, the **Gnostic** teachers have a long history of initiating powerful and compelling schools of thought about this world, the meaning of life, the divine realm, and the afterlife that awaits us. Although it is not always easy to understand, it does have a recurring allure for centuries of past generations as well as modern minds. What is the secret? It has always spoken to the emptiness inside ourselves and that nagging feeling that something is missing with the theology of the current day, whether it be today or thousands of years ago. We welcome the need for an awakening, one of the endless possibilities on a higher intellectual level. This may be why the **Gnostic Christians** have been slyly called the "elite" Christians (meaning more cerebral).

The height of **Gnostic** teachers and philosophers had to be in the 2nd and 3rd centuries A.D. before the Council of Nicaea in 325 and the changes that and subsequent councils initiated up to and including finalizing the canon of the ***New Testament*** which included only four of the ten Gospels that were in circulation, and a mere number of Epistles and other works descended down from Jesus' Twelve Disciples (Paul was not a Disciple or student of Jesus nor did he ever meet Jesus). Until they were banned and excommunicated, the **Gnostic** teachers were prolific in the doctrines of **Gnosticism** they taught in private sessions, public lectures, and written manuscripts (many of which were banned and destroyed, some of which we only have fragments, and some of them yet we don't who are the authors). The mission of the post-Nicaea Church leaders was to eradicate any and all different or dissenting alternative Christianities from what was decided by the group of bishops as "orthodox" or "true teachings," defaulting everything else as "false" or "heresy."

SIMON MAGUS

Simon Magus was a **Gnostic** teacher who appears in the ***New Testament*** in the Book of ***Acts.*** **Simon Magus** supposedly "***used sorcery, and bewitched the people of Samaria, making out that he was some great one***" (***Acts*** 8:9). **Simon Magus** did eventually convert to Christianity. When he saw Peter and John heal by the power of the Holy Spirit, he offered to buy this healing power from them for which Peter rebuked him. The Catholic Church enshrined him in perpetuity and coined a sin after him called "simony" which is the buying or selling spirituality for money. The

New Testament mentions no more about Simon probably because later Church leaders credited him with persistent **Gnostic** schools of thought and considered him to be the father of all **Gnostic** heresy. **Simon Magus** lived in the 1st century probably about the same time as Jesus and His Disciples. It did not help that he was one of innumerable "pseudo-messiahs" which were around Palestine during period all claiming to be a divine entity. As stated in ***Acts,*** Simon was "***making out that he was some great one.***"

MARCION

One of the most famous and influential **Gnostic** teachers was **Marcion**. He was a wealthy man from Asia Minor who was probably born somewhere towards the end of the 1st century. Marcion went to Rome about A.D. 140 to articulate his **Gnostic** views. He tried to gain acceptance from the Roman Church around A.D. 144 but wasn't successful.

So he started his own church which he promoted until his death around A.D. 160. His **Christian Gnostic** philosophy was very popular and spread throughout Asia Minor. There were major communities in and around Syria that continued to follow his version of Christianity, **Christian Gnosticism,** as late as the 5th century. Remnants still exist today.

Marcion was a major contributor to the schism of Eastern Orthodox branch of Christianity almost 900 years later. Marcion strongly believed that there were two gods: the True and Good Almighty God who sent His Son Jesus Christ as the savior to this world, and an evil and inferior deity who is the creator and ruler over this world known by many as the angry and vengeful God of the Hebrew Bible (the ***Old Testament***). The Eastern Churches never bought into the

Nicene bishops doctrines that Jesus was fully God and fully Man, and that He was part of a divine Trinity comprising One God. Marcion had a hostile view of the Hebrew Bible and did not include any part of in his "Christian" Scriptures. Marcion's New Testament consisted only of the ***Gospel of Luke*** (without its Jewish references) and nine of Paul's Epistles. As a direct follow up to the Council of Nicaea, and in reaction to Marcion's New Testament, in the latter part of the 4th century the newly formed Catholic Church drew up its own expanded version of the ***New Testament*** and included the whole Hebrew Bible as part of their "Christian Bible" referring to it as the ***Old Testament.***

Marcion seemed to favor the Epistles of Paul. Paul was favored by the Church leaders in the founding of the universal Catholic Church. They loved Paul's sin and repentance theme needed for salvation. However, from Marcion's view, he found Paul's writings to have more of a **Gnostic** undertone. It also has to be taken into consideration that some of Paul's writings are forgeries in his name [see Volume I]. Paul being a Roman did not have any respect for Jewish Law or the ***Old Testament*** which he considered not to be inspired by God but written by an intermediary. Paul's view would be adopted by Marcion. However, others left Paul's Epistles and the whole ***Old Testament*** out of their compilations of Sacred Scriptures. Most Biblical scholars and linguistic experts do not believe that it was Paul himself who wrote ***Ephesians***. They believe it was written in the late 1st century, at least thirty or forty years after the death of Paul. Marcion included it as part of his bible probably because he considered it to contain Gnostic themes. Marcion believed in **archons** which were divine rulers in the heavenly realm that were placed between God and humans. In the esoteric view, it was believed, as alluded to in ***Ephesians***, there were divine "**principalities**" that did the work of the Supreme God above them and the world below. The orthodox Christians and **Gnostics** pretty much agreed to the existence of divine intermediaries such as Angels and Archangels but not whether they all were good or some were evil (fallen angels).

VALENTINUS

Valentinus was another very popular **Gnostic** teacher who was a follower of Paul. Valentinus was Egyptian born toward the end of the First Century, educated in Alexandria, and it was there that Valentinus converted to Christianity. Theudas was the one who taught Valentinus the doctrines of **Gnosticism.** Theudas was believed to be a direct disciple of Paul. In this regard, Valentinus was able to claim that his spiritual lineage can be traced directly back to Paul. Valentinus, like Marcion, went to Rome and taught there. He was very popular in the Christian church that it is said by some he was a contender to be elected to be the Bishop of Rome (the forerunner position of the Pope today) and lost by a few votes. He continued to teach until he died around 160 A.D.

In his hymn "***Summer Harvest***" Valentinus speaks of some elements of **Gnosticism** in the three levels of being: "air" as the realm of the human spirit; the "soul" or psyche; and the "flesh" as the physical form. Above everyone is the divine realm. These levels of existence appear in numerous schools of esoteric thought. It was not exclusive to **Gnosticism** but to other mystical religions, Eastern philosophies, and the Jewish tradition of Kabbalah. This uniform philosophy remained consistent over a very long period. These elements of existence make it easy to explain what the **Gnostics** believe about life on earth and in the afterlife. There was a big distinction made by **Gnostic** between a person's spirit and their soul. For many, it was very obscure but to the **Gnostics** it was very clear. This distinction was very crucial in separating **Gnostic** and Christian philosophical thought. For Christians, the soul encompassed both a person's mental and emotional inner life. In psychology, this concept was called the "***psyche.***" They consider the "soul" and the "spirit" to be one in the same.

However, for the **Gnostics**, the distinction between the "soul" and the "spirit" was taught to be different by Valentinus and most **Gnostic** teacher. Most of them all separated the human existence into three distinct parts.

First, on the lowest fundamental level is the mortal "***carnal***" or "***flesh and blood***" temporal body. On a more educated level, this part of the human existence is referred to as "***hylic***" derived from the Greek for matter, "***hyle.***" It is the part of the human existence whose major concern is to secure and keep material things. This part contains the physical facets on which human life depends such as food, sex, and the survival instinct.

Second, on the next level up is the "***psychic***" that is wedged between the carnal and the spirit. Christian believers tend to live by faith; whereas **Gnostics** live by knowledge, or "***gnosis***," and are considered to be "psychic" individuals (not the same "psychic" as reading other people's minds). To some this "***psychic***" is also called being "***cerebral.***"

Finally, the highest level is "***spiritual.***" On a more educated level it is referred to as "***pneumatic***" derived from the Greek word "***pneuma***" meaning "***the spirit.***" The Spirit transcends the human body and its material ties to this world.

Once the Spirit is completely free from its earthly needs it can rise up to a higher level of consciousness.

You have control over your life and you can consciously choose on which level you prefer to live. Guess that falls under your inalienable right to "life, liberty, and the pursuit of happiness." Coincidentally this scenario is also conveniently mentioned in the ***Gospel of Matthew*** (6:21), "***Where your treasure is, there your heart will be also***." We are all well aware of persons who are completely preoccupied with the physicality and sexuality of their bodies. At the same time, there are persons, regardless of how well-educated they may be, who are preoccupied with the mysterious, the unseen, or the divine. They are leaning more toward the ***pneumatic*** or spiritual level; the favored level for **Gnostics**.

One famous work by Valentinus has survived called "***On the Three Natures.***" What makes it famous and important is that it is the first known document containing the discussion of the Holy Trinity: the Father, Son, and Holy Spirit as three persons in one divine being. The doctrine of the Trinity was a basic "orthodox" belief of the unified Christianity. It is not rooted in Scriptures and which was not favored by Eastern Christian Churches. Christianity had to follow the doctrine of monotheism of Judaism; there is only One God and no other Gods. Then how do they explain who Jesus is (was Jesus the long expected "messiah" but was not "divine") and who the Holy Spirit is? Christianity was in imminent danger of imploding if Jesus was not Divine Himself and the True only Son of God. It sounds like it was Valentinus, a condemned heretic by the unified Christian Church, was the one that proposed the Holy Trinity theory.

BASILIDES

Along the lines of Marcion and Valentinus, another famous **Gnostic** teacher was **Basilides.** Like them, Basilides lived in the early 2nd Century; however, he never went to Rome but confined his teaching to Alexandria in Egypt. He was famous for his intricate theory of the universe: the earth was surrounded by 365 heavens which is the reason there are 365 days in the year. The two rulers of these heavens were **Abraxas** or **Abrasax.** Angels were the more insignificant figures in the heavens found only in the lower hierarchies. They were credited with creating the Earth and the humans in it. Basilides considered the ruler of the Angels was the God of the ***Old Testament***.

Basilides, like other **Gnostic** teachers, believed that Christ was sent down by His Father to this earth to save us human beings from the bondage of this evil and wrathful God of the ***Old Testament*** and this suffering and pain he has inflicted upon us. Basilides also subscribed to the belief that Christ as God could not, and did not, suffer and die on the cross. Instead, Jesus switched places with Simon de Cyrene who bore the cross for him, was crucified, and died for him (so many keep forgetting Jesus Christ was supposedly God and he could pull off any illusion or miracle). It is in the banned "**Gnostic Gospel,**" the ***Gospel of Peter,*** that Jesus showed Peter how He remained above the cross laughing at the foolishness of those people who believed they just killed God. In case you missed the point, you cannot torture and kill God; maybe it was just an illusion that He wants you to see (no different than all the "taking things on faith alone" pushed by many traditional Christian religions). Basilides went as far as condemning anyone who pledged allegiance to a crucified and killed Jesus Christ as still being under the hypnotic control and bondage of the lowly divine rulers and the God of the ***Old Testament***. **Gnostics** like Basilides disliked this material world. They preach another banned "**Gnostic Gospel,**" the ***Gospel of Thomas,*** in which Jesus is quoted as saying, "***Wretched is the body that depends on a body. And wretched is the soul that depends upon these two"*** (*Thomas*, 87). **Gnostics** believe this world is an inferior creation.

Some **Gnostics** went to the extreme and treat their bodies with contempt. Basilides was one that did not consider the temporal human body to be worth very much. He really did not care what you did with your body. Basilides probably knew and was concurrent the ancient philosophical school known as the **Stoics.** They taught their adherents to have a philosophical detachment from their bodies. Some Gnostics even took it to the extreme and promoted "**antinomianism.**" They believed that we are living in a world of illusion created by a fallen God so we can do anything we want while here.

MARY MAGDALENE

The most famous **Gnostic** who is mentioned very often in **Gnostic** texts is Mary Magdalene. Mary Magdalene was a Disciple of Jesus. She was with Him for almost His entire ministry. She was considered by many to be Jesus' consort, if not His wife which some claim that the Marriage at Cana was Jesus' and Mary's wedding. His mother, Mary, and his closest companion, Mary Magdalene, were among the few female "relatives" to stand by Jesus at His crucifixion and helplessly watched Him die. Meanwhile, ALL of Jesus' Disciples immediately fled and went into hiding for fear for their own lives or imminent arrests when Jesus was arrested (yet all those Disciples are considered saints, not traitors). Mary Magdalene was an adulterous whore of mass proportions who repented and anointed Jesus' feet with oils and clean them with her hair. It was Mary Magdalene, either alone or with other women depending on which Gospel you are reading, that went to Jesus' tomb on "Easter morning" and was the first to discover that Jesus had risen, or really was the first to discover the **empty tomb** where Jesus was placed two days prior. However, it should be stated that in reality there is no direct connection that Mary Magdalene was the same "***woman taken in adultery***" as stated in ***John*** 8:3-12. The woman in ***John*** was never called by any specific name nor was ever connected with Mary Magdalene in any subsequent passage. The connection between the two women was completely arbitrary by Pope Gregory the Great in the 6th Century. The fact remains that Mary Magdalene eventually in later years was canonized a Saint. It is well-known that Mary Magdalene preached that Jesus' private teachings to her were very **Gnostic.** Very interesting reading is the banned "**Gnostic Gospels**," the ***Gospel of Mary,*** or also known as the ***Gospel of Mary Magdalene***.

Another great and famous "**Gnostic Gospel"** called ***Dialogue of the Savior*** describes Mary Magdalene as "***a woman who knew the All***." Many of the apocryphal works, especially the **Gnostic** ones, all tell a completely different story about Mary Magdalene. She is deemed to be a Disciple in Jesus' "inner circle" equal to His twelve male Disciples. Another famous **Gnostic** text called the ***Pistis Sophia,*** or translated as "***Faith Wisdom,***" in which Jesus tells Mary Magdalene: "***Thou art she whose heart is more directed to the Kingdom of Heaven than all thy brothers***."

The best passage about the high status of Mary Magdalene with Jesus Christ is found in the mutilated and banned so-called "**Gnostic Gospel,"** the ***Gospel of Philip*** says:

> "***The companion of the*** **[Savior is]** ***Mary Magdalene.*** **[But Christ loved]** ***more than*** **[all]** ***the Disciples*** **[and used to]** ***kiss her*** **[often]** ***on her*** **[mouth.]** ***The rest of*** **[the Disciples were offended]** ***by it*** **[and expressed disapproval.]** ***They said to Him, 'Why do you love her more than all of us?' The Savior answered and said to them, 'Why do I not love you like her?"*** For many the answer is obvious!

Elsewhere in the ***Gospel of Philip*** it says:

> ***"...there were three who always walked with the Lord: Mary His mother and her sister [sic] and Magdalene, the one who was called His companion. His sister and His mother and His companion were each a Mary."***

For many referring to Mary Magdalene as Jesus' "***companion***" implies they had a sexual relationship. Why not? Jesus is supposed to be a normal human being with sexual desires. He never condemned sex; heterosexual or homosexual. Adult Jewish men were expected to get married; why not Jesus? His Disciples and others called Him, "***rabbi.***" To be a rabbi, the Jewish faith in those ancient times required their "rabbis" to be married. It should NOT be out of the question that Jesus was having sex or was a married man. Of course, there are other factions that firmly believe Jesus was a life-long bachelor because He really was a homosexual... and they have the Biblical passages to support their claims.

The **Gnostic** texts have a very favorable view of their heroine Mary Magdalene who is looked at with such esteem and the opposite of the penitent adulteress and whore. The **Gnostics** regard her as a saint on equal par to the male

Disciples. As previously stated, she had a spirituality that even surpassed the male Disciples. There are many stories how she was more receptive and intelligent than her male counterparts. One prominent story is her role in getting the Disciples who were hiding in fear to pull themselves together and get out into the world to proclaim the Messiah, the Savior of us all, has risen from the dead, and to preach the "good news." Believe it or not, up to that point most of the Disciples did not even consider that Jesus had risen from the dead; more or less He was dead and missing from His tomb. It was Mary Magdalene's talk that got the Disciples moving. Could you imagine where Christianity would (not) be today if it wasn't for Mary Magdalene? When she spoke to them, some of the Disciples said, "***why should we listen to this mere woman***?"

IMPORTANT POINT: There are many prolific authors who have written several books about Mary Magdalene worth reading. I want to give a shout out to **Elaine Pagels.** In her ***The Gnostic Gospels*** Elaine Pagels suggests that Mary Magdalene was demoted as the Catholic Church was cutting into the status of women in their Church not allowing them any power over men or especially allowing a woman to serve as clergy in the Church.

IMPORTANT POINT: Luckily, modern generations have more respect and inclusion for a woman not only in religion but in all walks of life. Along with this wave, we have seen a great revival of interest in Mary Magdalene. There two popular work I highly recommend: 1) ***Holy Blood, Holy Grail*** by Henry Lincoln, Michael Baigent, and Richard Leigh; and Dan Brown's ***The Da Vinci Code*** which is also a movie starring Tom Hanks.

The rediscovery and rejuvenation of this wonderful **Gnostic** figure, Mary Magdalene, prompted a shift in the theology and spirituality of modern day. Many will credit Mary Magdalene with being a model from ancient times when Jesus Christ considered women socially equal. He always respected women in his dealings and miracles. It is a shame that the Catholic and Orthodox Church shunned the women into the background. In many **Gnostic** texts, it was apparent that it was Mary Magdalene who best understood the deepest mysteries of the universe and divine realm that Jesus was trying to impart to everyone. She really was the premier **Gnostic** and understood Jesus was here to save us and to help us escape this dysfunctional world. She should have had a bigger following instead of being suppressed by the Church.

THE RESURGENCE OF GNOSTICISM THROUGH THE MIDDLE AGES

We cannot be remiss and not acknowledge the great resurgence of **Gnosticism** during the Middles Ages to the disdain of the Medieval Church. It was major. Both the Catholic and Orthodox Churches continued to have no tolerance for **Gnostic** ideas. Any deviation from the Roman Catholic and Eastern Orthodox teachings was the pure definition of "heresy," i.e. a non-acceptance of the "true" and "accepted" teachings of the Catholic Church. Especially prickly was teaching that the God of the ***Old Testament*** was a fallen inferior deity and this world was a "cosmic mistake" of his doing. Yet these basic **Gnostic** themes persisted maybe because they seem to be more logical than to believe that One True Good Loving and Merciful Father God of Jesus was the same Mean Wrathful Mass-Murderer God of the Jews. But it still seemed that the whole latter scenario is easier to swallow for traditional Christian believers than what the **Gnostic** believed. Ironically, they have no problem in believing Lucifer is a fallen angel, along with the generic "Satan."

Another point of friction was the **Gnostic** idea of a divine realm consisting of a hierarchy of lesser deities that are between mankind and the ultimate Almighty God Himself. Although Jews, Christians, and Muslims (all descendants of the "God of Abraham") have no problem believing that angels and archangels exist and are messengers from God. In the ***First Book of Enoch*** tells us of "***the sons of God***" who married "***the daughters of men***" (***Gen.*** 6:2). ***1 Enoch*** is not clear whether these "***sons of God***" were "***angels.***" **Gnostics** recognized that there were archons who were "**dark angels.**" The Catholic and Orthodox Churches have been very ambiguous as to the existence of archons who have mutated into evil angels and archangels, like the Archangel Lucifer, who once was an active part of the esteemed divine Heavenly realm.

DIONYSIUS

A very interesting theory of heavenly hierarchy was described in the ***Celestial Hierarchy*** attributed to Dionysius the Areopagite. Dionysius was thought to be a convert of Paul (***Acts*** 17:34); although it is not believed that Dionysius wrote this actual treatise himself. It probably was written by an unknown 6th-century Greek theologian. It is not known how or from whom Dionysius developed this system of the heavenly hierarchy.

His work was widely popular in the medieval Christian world. Dionysius places divine entities into two main categories, **Principalities** and **Powers**. Dionysius' theory is found in ***Ephesians*** 6:22: "***For we wrestle not against flesh and blood, but against principalities, against powers, against the rulers of the darkness of this world, against spiritual wickedness in high places***" (cf. ***Rom***. 8:38; ***Eph.*** 3:30; ***Col.*** 1:16, 2:15). It is always debatable whether **Principalities** and **Powers** are good or bad entities.

For Dionysius, they were more positive entities. He considered being a heavenly Principality made them God-like princes having some authority in the Royal, or Holy, Order. The Powers are even higher deities and exist right below the Supreme Power, the direct source of their power. For Dionysius, the lesser orders of angels facilitate man's spiritual ascent to the higher echelon.

Ephesians described the "**Principalities** and **Powers**" in a way that coincided with the **Gnostic** idea of **archons**. For Dionysius, good entities are holy and beneficial in leading a soul to the Almighty God. When it comes to this, the 'heretic' **Gnostics** may see the deeper meaning in the Sacred Scriptures than traditional Christianity. Some **Gnostics** go as far as believing that "orthodox" Christianity teaches principles that blatantly contradict the Sacred Scriptures.

Dionysius' theories or teachings of the Divine realm would be echoed through Christianity for centuries. One of the most famous is Dante's ***Paradiso*** which considers the heavens as concentric circles around the earth; each circle controlled by a planet. Associated with each circle is a power described with similarity to the works of Dionysius. Similar theories even foreshadow Dionysius in Roman and Greek mythology.

THE CELTS

Anyone who has been to the land of the ancient Celts can see how it is elusively magical; almost eerily another realm beyond our mundane world. It feeds imaginations. Celtic Christianity had its beginnings fairly divorced from the Church in Rome. This native Christianity had more of a holistic nature combining the Christianity of love with the beauty of nature. The Celtics welcomed and incorporated Christianity into their pre-Christian realm of Druids. A wonderful combination that displayed Christianity in a new and fresh light; that is until at the Synod of Whitby in 664 the Church of Rome snuffed out this home-grown brand of Christianity and forced them into compliance with Rome. Up to that point, it could be considered an ***Alternative Christianity***, or even a **Gnostic Christianity.**

While the Dark Ages engulfed Western Europe, luckily it did not extend its fatal black hand all the way to Ireland. They continued to grow and learn. They continued to savor their rich pre-Christian heritage and folklore. The monks in Ireland amassed manuscripts from all over Europe; lucky for future generations they included texts that were ordered destroyed by Rome as heresy. This included a 9th-century treatise by John Carey called ***In Tenga Bithnua*** (The Ever-New Tongue) which included the Disciple Philip's "***twelve plains beneath the edges of the world.***" This closely resembled what we know of the now-lost ***Apocalypse of Philip*** known to have been written in Egypt and was popular in the **Gnostic** religions there.

IMPORTANT POINT: Jesus' Disciples Philip and Thomas were the most Gnostic in their writings and thus probably the reason they were banned by the emerging "Christian" Church of Rome. It still befuddles me why ANY Gospel, Epistle,

Apocrypha, or text descending from or attributed to ANY Disciple would be banned by the Christians?

THE MODERN GNOSTIC REVIVAL

A British doctor, A. Askew, in 1772 purchased a set of old manuscripts written in the ancient language of Egypt, Coptic. When a scholar named C.G. Woide was asked to examine it, he referred to the Greek "***Pistis Sophia***" as "Faith-Wisdom." After his death, his estate sold the copy he made for himself to the British Museum. It remains there today. It is believed to be dated to the 3rd century. In 1851 these manuscripts were printed and by 1896 received widespread popularity when British scholar G.R.S. Meed published an English translation of them.

Meed's timing was perfect. In the 19th century, there was a climate of radical change. An interest in the **Gnostic** texts and what they had to say was having a re-birth. It was at this time that "critical approach" method toward the interpretation of the Sacred Scriptures was nascent which introduced the 19th century's Enlightenment Period.

The public was more educated than any time in the past. They were disgusted with the religions that had torn apart their countries and many parts of Europe over past three hundred years since the Protestant "Reformation." A "reformation," "rebellion," or "protest" against 1600 years of a unified Christian doctrine. This "Reformation" did not reform anything, if anything it "destroyed it." Many had begun to lose their faith in Christianity, especially how there were now state-established or state-sanctioned religions in many of the countries in Europe. You had to belong to the "state's religion" and if there was any deviation from it, you were persecuted.

In some countries, it was "no longer easy" to remain a Catholic. **Martin Luther's 1596 attempt to "reform" some perceived ills in the Roman Catholic Church caused him to get excommunicated** (he was a priest in violation of his vow of obedience) **and was left no alternative but to start his own religion, Lutheranism.**

The educated ones, at the behest of the university scholars, were encouraged to examine Christianity's roots with a more critical eye. Scholars came to suspect the veracity of the Gospels. For the first time, at least on a larger scale, the scholars felt that the Gospels may have been changed to suit the purposes and agenda of the Christian Church. It is possible that the "Sacred Scriptures" might have never been, or are not now, the God-inspired books like we all were always taught. Maybe some myths or legends were placed intentionally in the Gospels to embellish the stories. Cross-references between texts were encouraged and are taught today in advanced schools of Religious Studies. The results were almost expected: discrepancies, inconsistencies, and falsehoods (a whole chapter is devoted this subject in ***Alternative Christianities, Volume I*** which just touches on the subject compared to whole books written about it). Could you imagine if we still had those ancient manuscripts that were destroyed to be able to compare and cross-reference? Thank God, as it is believed by some that it is His Divine intervention, that many of these ancient Gospels and other texts such as ***Pistis Sophia*** and the ***Nag Hammadi Library,*** which have been long lost or destroyed, have been resurrected. Within them, we find that these Protestant and Reformed religions, rites, and cults profess a belief in a Christianity that definitely is not the same as is what is being portrayed in other "Sacred Scriptures."

IMPORTANT POINT; It is believed by many that these ancient manuscripts had to be destroyed to mold Christianity the way Rome had wanted it and to comply with the teachings of the non-Disciple Paul. If these **Gnostic Gospels** were allowed to exist in the official Bible, a different Christianity definitely would exist today.

##

BIBLIOGRAPHY, REFERENCE, AND SUGGESTED READING

Barnstone, Wills and Marvin Meyer, ***Gnostic Bible, The***
© 2009 Shambhala, Boston © 2003 Harper, San Francisco, CA

Block, Darrell L., ***Missing Gospels, The: Unearthing the Truth Behind Alternative Christianities*** © 2006 Nelson Books, Nashville, Tennessee

Brown, Peter, ***Rise of Western Christianity: Triumpn and Diversity A.D. 200-1000*** © 2003 Blackwell Publishers, Malden, Mass.

Butz, Jeferey, ***Brother of Jesus and the Lost Teachings of Christianities, The***
© 2005 Inner Traditions, Rochester, VT

Doresse, Jean, ***Secret Book of the Egyptian Gnostics, The***
© 1960 The Viking Press, New York

Ehrman, Bart D., ***Lost Scriptures: Books That Did Not Make It Into The New Testament***
© 2006 Oxford University Press

Eusebius, **Church History**

Grant, R. M., ***Gnosticism and Early Christianity***
© 1959 New York University Press, New York

King, Karen L., ***What is Gnosticism***
© 2003 Belknapprots

Lester, Meera, ***Everything ® Gnostic Gospel Book, The: A Complete Guide to the Secret Gospels***
© 2007 Adams Media, an F. W. Publication, Inc.

McLaren, Brian D., ***Secret Message of Jesus, The: Uncovering the Truth That Could Change Everything***
© 2006 W. Publishing, Nashville, Tennessee

Meyer, Marvin, ***Secret Teachings of Jesus: Four Gnostic Gospels***
© 1986, 1984 Vintage Books-Random House, New York

Roukema, Riemer, ***Gnosis and Faith in Early Christianity: An Introduction to Gnosticism***
© 1999 Trinity Press International, Harrisburg, Pennsylvania

Rudolph, Kurt, ***Gnosis: The Nature and History of Gnosticism***
© 1987 Harper and Row, San Francisco, California

Toropov, Brandon and Luke Buckles, ***Complete Idiot's Guide to World Religions, The (4th Edition)***
© 2001 Alpha, New York

Author's Note: This Book and Treatise are a compilation from many sources on the same subject. See the Complete List of Bibliographies, References, and Suggested Readings in Appendix II

CHAPTER 8

THE GNOSTIC CHRISTIANS

HISTORY

Gnosticism was rejuvenated in December 1945 in the little town of Nag Hammadi, Egypt with the discovery of 13 leather-bound ancient **Gnostic** papyrus codices (an ancient form of a book). The brothers who found them were not literate, but even if they could read, it was written in Coptic which is an ancient and now-obsolete language of ancient Egypt which was in use nineteen centuries earlier when Jesus walked on this Earth. It was so useless their mother used some of the pages to start her cooking fire. Eventually, they sold the papyrus books to an antiquities dealer in Cairo and the codices followed a circuitous route to their home in the Egyptian Coptic Museum. A Netherlands professor and distinguished historian of religion, Gilles Quispel, was startled when he read the first line of the first codex: ***"These are the***

secret words which the living Jesus spoke, and which the twin, Judas Thomas, wrote down." These are the identical words that began in the 1890's find of the ***Gospel of Thomas***.

IMPORTANT POINT: Being a historian of religion he was aware of the existence of the "***Gospel of Thomas"*** which was banned and destroyed by the Christian Church along with other Disciples' Gospels.

It was assumed by Biblical Scholars that the Coptic codices discovered at Hag Hammadi, Egypt were probably translations made from earlier manuscripts that were written in Greek, the language of the educated in ancient times. The carbon-dating of these Coptic manuscripts confirmed that they had to be written circa 350-400 A.D. The original Greek documents that were the source were not found but we do know that they DEFINITELY existed in the 2nd century, if not earlier. That fact is thanks to Irenaeus, the Bishop of present-day Lyons, France and self-proclaimed heresiologist, who wrote about them in 180 A.D. in his treatise "***Against Heresy"*** (that is how it is commonly known although it has a much longer Latin title) who ironically tried, and succeeded, to squash these texts. In this treatise Irenaeus wrote that these heretics ***"boast that they possess more gospels than there really are;"*** and he adds that **such writings already have won wide circulation from Gaul [now France] through Rome, Greece, and Asia Minor.** Professor Helmut Koester of Harvard University feels that the sayings of Jesus in the ***Gospel of Thomas*** may date as far back as 140 A.D. or possibly even older **going back as far as the 2nd half of the 1st century (50-100 A.D.).** It is believed by many that the sayings of Jesus in the ***Gospel of Thomas*** were used to compose the four Gospels in the

New Testament: Matthew, Mark, Luke, and ***John.*** So many verbatim or variations can be found in those four Gospels.

Biblical scholars, educators, theologians, and so many more shudder to think how many whole or part of these ancient manuscripts were used by Muhammad Ali's mother in the hearth fires or just discarded while in their possession. What remained were 52 out of who knows how many texts including Gospels known as: ***The Gospel of Thomas, The Gospel of Philip, The Gospel of Truth,*** and ***The Gospel to the Egyptians.*** There were also other sacred books such as: ***The Secret Book of James, The Apocalypse of Peter, The Letter of Peter to Philip,*** and so many more.

IMPORTANT POINT: What is the most unusual claim made by these texts about their content is that many of them specifically identify the work as a "***secret*** Gospel" or the "***secret*** teachings" of Jesus Christ, unlike the four Gospels that currently appear in the ***New Testament***. This implies that these teachings of Jesus were not meant for the general public at large. As described by someone, it is the difference between the religion you learn in Sunday school once a week as a child compared to a Religious Studies class in the Master and Doctorate Programs at the most prestigious universities.

This discovery made by Egyptian peasants in 1945 really stood modern-day Christianity on its ear. What seemed to be just some useless papyrus ended up being a most important discovery in modern times, a collection the Sacred Scriptures that were read and revered by the early Christians in the 1st centuries of a pure Christianity. Most Biblical scholars call these long-forgotten texts as the "**Gnostic Gospels"** because most contain a **Gnostic** approach to Christianity. All of sudden the modern world was introduced to a completely different ancient Christianity.

Gnostic Christians are so different than today's traditional Christians. There was a whole new way of looking at Jesus Christ, His Almighty Father, and Divine Realm. These texts instill doubt in your minds as to whether Christianity, as it is practiced today, is completely wrong. It makes you wonder whether Jesus literally died and then "bodily" rose from the dead three days later. Makes you see God in a completely different light: He is not a wrathful mass-murder but all good, all loving, and so welcoming into His Heavenly Home.

This **Gnostic** version of Christianity for many was brilliant, so provocative, and absolutely stunning in its teaching. The ***Gnostic Gospels*** was a major departure from the traditional Christian teachings. It instilled a new interest in returning to the origins of the Christian faith and the "***secret***" teachings of Jesus' and His **<u>Gnostic-Christian</u>** philosophy:

> ***Jesus said, "If you bring forth what is within you, what you bring forth will save you.***
>
> ***If you do not bring forth what is within you, what you do not bring forth will destroy you."***

This quote is in ***The Gospel of Thomas.*** Within the same bound volume was ***The Gospel of Philip*** which tells another a very interesting story which is not found in the four Gospels presently in the ***New Testament***:

> ***"... the companion of the Savior is Mary Magdalene. But Christ loved her more than all the Disciples, and***

> ***used to kiss her often on her mouth. The rest of the disciples were offended....***
>
> ***They said to Him, "Why do you love her more than all of us?"***

There are many other stories found in these ***Gnostic Gospels*** that are in complete disagreement with some long-standing traditional Christian beliefs, such as, that Jesus resurrected bodily from the dead. Also bound together with ***The Gospel of Thomas*** and ***The Gospel of Philip*** was the ***Apocryphon of John,*** a book of "secret mysteries and the things" which Jesus taught to His Disciple John only in private.

IMPORTANT POINT: This is why it is important to make ALL the ancient Sacred Scriptures available to all people, not just FOUR Gospels. All should be important and complete to Biblical scholars and theologians.

Some of the texts found at Nag Hammadi tell a different story than the classical version of Adam and Eve in Genesis. One of the more fascinating versions is found in the ***Testimony of Truth*** which relays the story as told by the serpent! In ancient literature, the serpent is not depicted as an evil but in a good light. The serpent in ancient times stood for wisdom. After all, it is the symbol of the medical profession. Yes, the serpent convinces Adam and Eve to eat from the "tree of knowledge" although the Lord told them they would die if they ate from it. They ate from the tree and they did not die; however, the Lord expelled them from the Garden of Eden. Hippolytus detailed this scenario in his ***Refutationis Omnium Haeresium.*** The texts banned and prohibited for Christians maybe because there may have been no original sin.

IMPORTANT POINT: In an apparent act of rebellion by the devoted monks at the monastery of St. Pachomius near Nag Hammadi who buried these texts they considered to be Holy Scriptures in an obvious attempt to preserve them.

IMPORTANT POINT: This **Gnostic** branch of Christianity still exists ***today*** as the **Coptic Catholic Church** or the **Coptic Orthodox Church** found mainly in Egypt and Asia Minor but also have many Churches in the United States.

The greatest voice against **Gnosticism** was Irenaeus in Lyons (who was bucking for a promotion from Rome). His five volumes written in A.D. 180 called, ***"The Destruction and Overthrow of Falsely So-Called Knowledge,"*** began:

> "...***set forth the views of those who are now teaching heresy... to show how absurd and inconsistent with the truths are their statements... I do this so that... you may urge all of those with whom you are connected to avoid such an abyss of madness and blasphemy against Christ"***

Then fifty years later Hippolytus in Rome agreed with Irenaeus and issued his massive volumes on the same subject, ***"Refutation of All Heresy"*** in which he promised to ***"expose and refute the wicked blasphemy of the heretics."***

The problem with the **Gnostic Gospels** and texts is that they contradicted the teachings being put forth by the Catholic Church. The **Gnostic Gospels** talk of a "living Jesus" who spoke "enlightenment." Jesus did NOT speak "sin and repentance." They firmly believed that Jesus did not come to this earth to save us from humans' sins but He came here to be a guide and give us a higher spiritual and esoteric understanding of this world. It is through the spiritual lessons of Jesus that a person can achieve the "gnosis" or enlightenment of the higher divine realm.

In the exchange between Thomas and Jesus as relayed in the ***Gospel of Thomas*** has the following revealing **Gnostic** lesson from the mouth of Jesus, Himself:

> ***Jesus said, "I am not your Master.... He who will drink from my mouth will become as I am: I myself shall be he, and the things that are hidden shall be revealed to him"*** (35:4-7, 50:28-30, NHL 119-129).

These words seem to echo the Eastern religions, so much so, that you could interchange the "living Jesus" with the "living Buddha." It was not surprising to Biblical scholars that the ***Gospel of Thomas*** had Buddhist or Hindu philosophies, especially versed with other **Gnostic Gospels** which tell how Jesus spent the "lost years" before His public ministry with His brother James touring the Asian continent learning the indigenous philosophies of Buddhism and Hinduism. Of course, as ecumenical as that sounds, to the traditional Christians, it is called "blasphemy"!

But the truth was told by Edward Conze, a scholar of Buddhism, who verified that Christian followers of Jesus' Disciple Thomas were found among Hindu's and Buddhists in India and Far Eastern countries. These followers came with their copies of the ***Gospel of Thomas*** in hand. Trade routes between the Roman, Greek, and Middle Eastern empires and the Far East empires always existed to some extent and continued to grow. This was also the same region where **Christian Gnosticism** flourished not with mutual exclusivity but with a comradery of philosophies

At the same time, Buddhist missionaries were coming west and preaching in Africa and the Middle East. Hippolytus's writings attest to Buddhist activities in and around Alexandria, Egypt. Scholars are pretty certain that the Disciple Thomas preached and convert the people of India to Christianity. The ***Gospel of Thomas*** shows the blending of Christianity with the Eastern religions and philosophies. The East and the West were not as distinct and exclusive of each other 2,000 years ago; or as we think of them being so different today. The ***Gospel of Thomas*** shows the overlaps.

Christianity has always been diverse from its very beginnings. At the end of the 16th century, the Protestant Reformation broke Christianity into innumerable pieces. New religions, denominations, sects, and cults came into being all of whom claim to be "Christians." And since then there has been a continuous stream of Protestant reformations and schisms which have spawned an unbelievable array of denominations, sects, and cults that are too numerous to count. There are some with even the most minuscule differences in beliefs, dogmas, and attention to Scriptures. The spectrum runs from Roman Catholic Church headquartered in Rome, to the Orthodox Churches through Eastern Europe, to the state-sanctioned Lutheran Churches in the Baltics, or the Methodist-Episcopal communities in Africa, or the Mormon preachers around the world, to the Fundamentalist Evangelical preachers in a "Bible-belt" of the United States. As evidenced by the newly discovered "**Gnostic** Scriptures" in Egypt, **today's Christianity appears to be just as diverse as it was in the beginning.** The difference was that in ancient times it was **a more simple and pure Christianity**. In ancient times, although there were different communities of Christians, they more or less believed in the same basic dogma; they were able to celebrate their Christianity as one. They all happily coexisted, until the one unifying self-proclaimed "orthodox" Christian Church came into power, sanctioned by the Roman Empire, then everyone else was a "heretic."

By A.D. 200 the Christian Church was well on its way to establishing itself as a formidable institution. It had a three-level hierarchy of bishops, priests, and deacons. They were the self-appointed guardians of the true faith. It was imperative for the Church of Rome to reject all different beliefs and viewpoints as "heresy" mainly for their own self-preservation.

To this end, with his own personal goals to gain favor with the Church leaders in Rome, Irenaeus took it upon himself to make sure there is only one church, a "***catholic***" or "universal" church. Irenaeus went as far as saying that anyone who is not part of this "catholic" church would not be saved and would be damned to Hell. Everyone who challenged them, or privately had a different set of beliefs, would be considered a heretic and excommunicated from being a real Christian. Irenaeus wrote a multi-volume treatise called (abbreviated) "***Against Heresy"*** which documents all the various Christianities that he was against. Irenaeus impressed Rome and was promoted to Bishop. It culminated when Constantine became the Roman Emperor in the 4th century. He disliked the differing beliefs of the various Christian Churches and called all the Bishops to Nicaea to come to a consensus and establish the one, catholic (universal) Church. Then with the full backing of Roman Emperor Constantine, the universal Catholic Church became the "official" state religion of the Roman Empire. Of course, this gave the "orthodox" Church unlimited power to declare "heretics" and persecute them. Next, the "orthodox" Bishops were commissioned to decide which texts would comprise the ***New Testament.*** They did that and then ordered any and all other Gospels, Epistles, and texts banned and destroyed.

It was ironic, or possibly through "divine intervention," some 1500 years later, in 1945 that 52 of these banned Gospels and texts were discovered at Nag Hammadi, Egypt. This was the most major archeological find for Biblical scholars and theologians. It gave new insight into the diverse beliefs of ancient Christianity. In reality, it made what we know today as "***Christianity***" and "***Christian Dogma***" was just one branch of a multi-faceted Christianity that was around following the death of Jesus Christ and preached by His Disciples. ***So who decided which would be the ONE true, orthodox, Christian faith? How did they come about their dogma selection? How did they decide which Scriptures were authentic and to comprise the New Testament; and which Scriptures were truly false and be left out? Did they make the right decisions for all future generations of Christians? Or has Christianity been sent in the wrong direction by the power-hungry Bishops? Maybe, the true Christianity was discovered in the texts found at Nag Hammadi?***

The group that was on the top of Irenaeus' list of groups that had to be eradicated was the **Gnostic Christians.** He was very vocal and literally hated their "heretical" beliefs and ideas. **Gnostics** blame the suffering and misery on this earth on an evil god whereas the "orthodox" blame it on original and human sin. **Gnostics** biggest blasphemy was to question Jesus' resurrection. Did He literally bodily resurrect or was it spiritual and symbolic? The Orthodox Christians are the ones who are the heretics according to the **"Gnostics"** because they do not have the "gnosis" or special knowledge so they can understand Jesus' mission here on earth and from what He was here to save us. The **Gnostics** did not consider themselves the "heretics" – quite the contrary – the **Gnostics** feel they have the "orthodox" or knowledge of the true beliefs.

The **Gnostics** always seemed to raise the ire of the "orthodox" Church leaders. Notably, they objected to the Council of Nicaea's ***Nicene Creed*** issued in A.D. 325 which expanded upon and at the same time implicitly contradicted the ***Apostles' Creed*** which was thought to be handed down from Jesus' Twelve Disciples themselves to be recited from memory to be baptized a "Christian." The ***Apostles' Creed*** was the sole and universal "Christian Creed" for almost 300 years until the Bishops three centuries later decided to "improve" upon it and at the same time add in some new dogmas for "real" Christians to be required to believe going forward. The ***Nicene Creed*** was not bought into by all the Christian sects at the time and schisms resulted. The **<u>NEW</u>** "orthodox" Christian creed makes all Christians now profess that Jesus Christ is God made man; and His Almighty Father is the One True God who is all-good, all-loving, and all-merciful who is the creator of Heaven and Earth. Contradictory, He is also responsible for creating a world that is full of suffering, misery, and injustice. He is vengeful and responsible for inflicting all those wrathful punishments and mass murders in the ***Old Testament***. It just doesn't seem to make sense to many people that this all-good, all-loving, and all-merciful God would create such an evil and painful world. Not only does it not make any sense but it is also very hard to reconcile!

<u>IMPORTANT POINT:</u> The True and Good God, the Father of Jesus Christ, could NOT be the same God of the Hebrew Bible and the Jewish faith. But somehow the Christians had to adopt the God of the Jews to legitimatize them.

Then Jesus of Nazareth who came on the scene whose followers (never Himself) claimed, born of a virgin, was God made man. However, although He was God, that did not prevent Him from being arrested, tortured, and crucified by the Roman procurator, Pontius Pilate. But I thought He was God? Could He not have prevented this humiliation from discrediting him in front of His faithful Disciples and followers? Wasn't that all anticlimactic to His years of preaching? But then it was further claimed by His Disciples and followers that Jesus bodily rose from the dead "***on the third day***" following His death on the cross. The only proof they had was that "on the third day" there was an "empty grave" with the stone rolled back. Many thought that His body was purposely taken by His Disciples or stolen, thus the "empty grave;" however, His Disciples and followers went with the supposition that Jesus had bodily resurrected from the grave. Although they say He remained on this earth for forty days, very few people actually saw Him during that time.

Through the ***Nicene Creed***, Christians were told to take these uncertain "beliefs" on "pure faith." The **Gnostics** seem to have explanations to these "mysteries" but they were shunned as "heretics" by the "orthodox" Church.

IMPORTANT POINT: The acceptance of all these newly added dogma that contributed to the ultimate schism in 1054 of the universal Catholic Church into the "Roman Catholic Church" which subscribed fully to the ***Nicene Creed*** and all its subsequent amendments, and the "Orthodox Catholic Church" which did not fully subscribe to all the changes to ***Apostles' Creed*** or original ***Nicene Creed.*** You are probably more familiar with the names: Greek Orthodox Church, Russian Orthodox Church, etc. mainly around Greece, the Dalmatian Coast, and the Middle East. It is also worth noting that practically all of the Protestant religions around Europe were direct schisms from the Roman Catholic Church. Since their schisms, or what they call "reformations," they too have spawned numerous further schisms from themselves.

WAS JESUS' RESURRECTION REAL OR SYMBOLIC?

The universal Christian Church was hinged upon one arguable claim: "***Jesus Christ bodily raised Himself from the dead***." This was to be taken literally as the foundation for the Christian believers; **this literal means that Jesus resurrected Himself, that is, He brought His body and spirit back to life.** Several of Jesus' followers claimed that they had actually "seen" a living the Jesus in His full personhood after his death; not a ghost, not a vision, not hallucinations but **they saw an actual human being who they identified as Jesus Christ!** In the sacred and accepted ***Gospel of Luke,*** Jesus' Disciples assumed that what they saw was in fact just the ghost of their Master, Jesus. Begs the question, how can the Disciples mistake a living human being as a "ghost" or "spirit"? As the story goes, it was not until Jesus challenged them and said, "***Handle me and see, for a spirit does not have flesh and bones, as you see that I have."*** Afterward, Jesus asked for something to eat and they watched Him as He ate a piece of fish just like any living being.

IMPORTANT POINT: Where does the truth actually lie? Did the Disciples really feel the appearance of Jesus was a "ghost"? Were the words of proof by Jesus added later by the "orthodox" Church leaders to further their cause?

Then circa A.D. 190, the anti-heretical Tertullian speaking for the emerging Christian Church declared irrefutably that

Jesus Christ did rise bodily from the grave, all the faithful Christians must believe so, and every believer should also anticipate their own resurrection in the flesh. Tertullian is clear that he is not talking about the immortality of the soul but a bodily resurrection of the body with all its flesh, blood, nerves, bones, hair, etc. very undoubtedly human. There was no debate! Any dissenting Christian was called a "heretic" and excommunicated from receiving the sacraments.

The **Gnostic Christians** had different interpretations of Jesus' resurrection. Most insist that there is no physical resurrection and one will not meet Jesus physically but rather we will encounter Christ on a spiritual level. The universal Christian Church condemns any such interpretation. Tertullian declared anyone that does not accept the Jesus' and their ultimate "resurrection of the flesh" is NOT a true "Christian" but a practicing "heretic."

Why would the universal Christian Church leaders proclaim irrefutably that Jesus "resurrected," or brought His dead body back to life, especially since this was never told to us by His Disciples? The ***Gospel of Luke*** and the ***Gospel of John*** explicitly state that the Jesus they saw was in the same body that they had always known Him. He continued to eat and drink with them, He allowed them to touch Him; He definitely was not a "ghost." The Disciple Thomas doubted what the other Disciples had seen and he wanted to see and touch Jesus for himself. Thus the famous story of "Doubting Thomas" that Jesus appeared to him and commanded him, "***Put your finger here, and see my hands; put out your hand and place it in my side, do not be faithless, but believing***" (***John*** 20:27).

However, the *Gospel of Luke* (16:12) and the *Gospel of Mark* (24:13-22) relate a completely different scenario

about Jesus' appearances. It is stated in those Gospels that Jesus' appearance to His Disciples was "***in another form***" different than the one they previous knew Him. Such is beyond doubt in the story of two Disciples walking along the road to Emmaus while **talking with a "stranger" as they walked for hours.** It was not until they sat down to have dinner they recognized the familiar way that "stranger" blessed the bread. ***"Suddenly they recognized him as Jesus...***[and] ***he vanished out of their sight***" (***Luke*** 24:31). How could His Disciples not recognize the bodily resurrected Jesus and then have Jesus just disappeared from their sight?

More confounding is the story in the ***Gospel of John*** (20:11-17): **Mary Magdalene near Jesus' grave and sees someone who she assumes is a gardener.** It was only when this "gardener" calls her by name when **she suddenly recognizes him as Jesus.** Unlike His appearance to Thomas, Jesus instructed her NOT to touch him.

IMPORTANT POINT: The Gospels of ***New Testament*** tell different stories about Jesus' resurrection; some say He did bodily rose from the grave, while others say Jesus did not appear, at least at first, in His earthly form. This is a major cornerstone of Christianity and the details of such an important event should at least be more consistent.

The same major discrepancies exist about Paul's conversion to Christianity. In ***Acts,*** it is said that Paul while traveling on the road to Damascus persecuting Christians when:

1.) "***Suddenly a light from heaven flashed above him. And he fell to the ground.***" Jesus spoke to Paul and admonished him for his persecution of Christians (***Acts*** 9:3-4); or

2.) "***The men who were traveling with him stood speechless, hearing the voice, but seeing no one***" (***Acts*** 9:7); or,
3.) "***Those who were with me saw the light but did not hear the voice of the one who was speaking to me***" (***Acts*** 22:9).

Three completely different versions but which one of them is really the true story. Again, isn't this an important enough event+ that there should be only one story? How can you believe anything that follows it?

Although Paul's followers were very instrumental in getting Paul's teachings accepted by the Church leaders in Rome, Paul did have some different versions of Jesus' bodily resurrection, such as Paul says, "***I tell you this, brethren: flesh and blood CANNOT inherit the kingdom of God, nor does the perishable*** (the mortal body) ***inherit the imperishable***" (***I Corinthians*** 15:50). Then 15:51-53 continues that Paul says: **Jesus' resurrection is a "mystery;" He actually transformed Himself from a human being into a spiritual existence.** Completely different than what the Christian Church is teaching.

Why is the "orthodox" teaching in the 2nd century only the belief of Jesus' bodily resurrection while considering any questioning or opposing view as "heresy?" Elaine Pagels in her books suggests a political reason for this: **it gives legitimacy to the Church leaders and their authority as the direct successors of the Disciple Peter**. This specific chain of command past down from His Twelve Disciples has lasted unabridged for the past 2,000 years. Only Jesus' Disciples had the authority and power to ordain their future successors; and so on down the line. Thus all future leaders of Jesus' Church would derive their power and authority in a direct line from Jesus and His "Inner Circle" of twelve. The ordination of Bishops can be traced directly back through 20 centuries of Apostolic succession from the Disciples. Only those Bishops can ordain priests and confirm Catholics, an extension of their Apostolic powers. The Pope can trace his power, authority, and mission directly back to the Disciple Peter, the head of His Church appointed directly by Jesus Christ Himself.

As has been discussed many times already, there have been so many iterations of Christianity that existed in the years immediately following Jesus' death. Hundreds of preachers compete with each other in their diverse interpretations of the teachings of the "true Christ" while denouncing all their competitors as heretical frauds. Paul's teachings were at extreme odds with the Twelve Disciples of Jesus; so much so the Paul told his followers that anyone who even listens to The Twelve deserves to be damned and loses their salvation. Multiple diverse Christian Churches or denominations stretched from Central Europe to Greece to Asia Minor to Jerusalem and beyond. Not only did they disagree on dogma but they were also sharply divided over the form the church's leadership and hierarchy should take. Putting all that aside, each "church" claimed it held and taught "the authentic Christianity" from Jesus Christ.

During His three years of public ministry, Jesus traveled with His Disciples and followers around Palestine, no one dared to challenge Him. It was only after His execution that His followers were shaken, feared for their own lives, and scattered in different directions. This caused many to think that the "Jesus Movement" and His Disciples were arrested and had died alongside Him. It was the astonishing miracle that Jesus had resurrected from the grave that brought life back into Jesus' ministry. Luke proclaimed, "***the Lord has***

risen indeed, and has appeared to Simon [Peter]*!*" (***Luke*** 24:34). Luke announced that Jesus had named Peter to be His successor and the head of His Church. The ***Gospel of Matthew*** says the same thing but while Jesus was still alive. Jesus proclaimed Peter to be the "rock" on which He would build His "church" and who would be His successor (***Matthew*** 16:13-19). The ***Gospel of John*** likewise is in agreement with Matthew and Luke that the risen Christ explicitly wanted Peter to be the leader of His flock (***John*** 21:15-19).

IMPORTANT POINT: Like with so many other conflicting accounts between Gospels, we will never know which is really true or false "historically" speaking. We are just reminded that we only have at minimum second-hand and third-hand related accounts of what happened.

The Gospels are consistent that Jesus remained on earth for forty days in His human form after His resurrection giving further instruction to His Twelve Disciples. Very few others saw Him in the flesh during that period. After which, Jesus withdrew and bodily ascended into heaven as they all watched in amazement (***Acts*** I: 6-11). From then after NO ONE, **including Paul,** ever saw Jesus again in the flesh after those forty days.

IMPORTANT POINT: It confounds Biblical scholars and theologians alike why Jesus would have spent ALL his time in those forty days with His Disciples that He just spent three years traveling, eating, and preaching. Why would He not go outside His "inner circle" and accomplish SO MUCH MORE by showing His resurrected self to further His creditability and teachings? This could have been the most effective part of His earthly ministry.

The **Gnostic Christians** did not concur with this line of thinking. The **Gnostics** even were quoted as calling the view of literally believing that Jesus bodily resurrected from His grave as the "**faith of fools**" (documented by Irenaeus in his ***Against Heresy*** 1.30.13). The **Gnostics** insisted that Jesus' resurrection was really just a symbolic event to show that a person's life continues on forever in the hereafter on a spiritual level. A bodily resurrection is minor and insignificant, not nearly as important as a spirit living on forever. The Disciples had misunderstood that Jesus' resurrection was bodily whereas it was a spiritual event. It was probably only Paul who realized he had seen Jesus as a spirit in his vision.

The Gospel of Philip, a Disciple, **ridiculed any Christian who was "ignorant" and believed that Jesus' resurrection was "bodily."** Philip says, "***Those who say they will die first and then rise are in error***" but instead they should "***receive the resurrection while they live***" (73:1-3). The **Gnostic Christian** teachers went beyond the mediocre Church teachings offered to the general congregations and provided the "spiritually mature" the exoteric teachings of Jesus. These "***secret teachings***" were only available to their selected few. The **Gnostic** Valentinus (c. 140) realized that during Jesus' lifetime He instructed only the Disciples in His Inner Circle with the mysteries and secrets of the universe and the hereafter which He did not share with the general public. This is found in the ***Gospel of Mark*** when Jesus said:

> "***To you have been given the secret of the Kingdom of God, but for those outside everything is in parables; so that they may indeed see but not perceive, and may indeed hear but not understand; lest they should turn again, and be forgiven."*** (***Mark*** 4:11)

The ***Gospel of Matthew*** confirms this fact that when Jesus spoke to the public He only spoke in parables or generalized stories. Jesus replied when the Disciples asked Him about this: "***To you it has been given the secrets and mysteries of the Kingdom of Heaven, but to them it is not given***" (***Matthew*** 13:11). The Disciples maintained Jesus' philosophy and kept these esoteric teachings secret; except to those in private who exhibited sufficient "spiritually maturity" to understand and accept a higher level of "***gnosis***" or secret knowledge.

It was in all the **Gnostic Gospels** that were revered by Valentinians in which he claimed to disclose the private teachings of Jesus Christ. The stories in the **Gnostic Gospels** about the risen Christ seem to be consistent that it was a spiritual event; and that it was the spirit of Jesus which appeared to people. Of course, this put the **Gnostic Gospels** out of favor with the Church because they were in direct contradict the **four** Gospels that they selected to be put in the ***New Testament***; on which they based their "Christianity." The difference between the **four** canonical Gospels and the **Gnostic Gospels** is that the latter does not tell the story of Jesus life biographically from His birth to death; the **Gnostic Gospels, more importantly, begin where the four *New Testament* Gospels end with Jesus' higher teachings during the 40 days with His Disciples post-resurrection.**

> ***The Apocryphon of John*** is the only "Gospel" that tells us what happened at Jesus' crucifixion and death: ***"Immediately… the heavens were opened, and the whole creation under heaven shone and the world was shaken. I was afraid, and I saw in the light a child… while I looked he became like an old man, and he changed his form again, becoming like a***

servant... I saw an image with multiple forms of light" (1.30–2.7).

John went on to tell us he was spoken to: ***"John, why do you doubt, and why are you afraid? <u>You are not familiar with this form, are you?</u> Do not be afraid! I am the one who is with you always...I have come to teach you what is and what was, and what will come to be...."*** (2.9-13)

The ***Letter of Peter to Philip*** which was also discovered at Nag Hammadi relates that after Jesus' death He appeared to His Disciples while they were praying at the Mount of Olives:

> ***"...<u>a great light appeared</u>, so that the mountain shone from the sight of Him who had appeared. And a great voice called out to them saying 'Listen... I am Jesus Christ, who is with you forever.'"***

In the ***Wisdom of Jesus Christ*** also found at Nag Hammadi also tells what happened to the Disciples when they were gathered after Jesus' death on a mountain:

> ***"...when then there appeared to them the Redeemer, <u>not in His original form but in the invisible spirit.</u> But His appearance was the <u>appearance of a great angel of light</u>."***

Jesus then continued to teach them the "**<u>secrets" of the plan of the universe and its destiny</u>**.

<u>IMPORTANT POINT</u>: The **Gnostic Gospels** contrasts the accepted "orthodox" version and consistently claimed that Jesus did NOT appear in His easily recognizable human form to His Disciples. Jesus appeared as a spirit or otherwise luminous presence speaking out of the light, and He transforms himself and appeared in different forms.

> ***The Gospel of Philip*** describes, ***"Jesus took them all by stealth, for he did not reveal himself in the manner in which he was, but in the manner in which they would be able to see him. He revealed himself to them all. He revealed himself to the great as great.... And to the small as small.*** (***Gospel of Philip*** 57.28-35)

Instead of embracing the Gospels of these other Disciples, Irenaeus and other "orthodox" Church leaders accused the **Gnostic Christians** of being frauds and spreading heresy. At the prompting of the self-appointed heresiologist Irenaeus, the emerging Church's leaders condemned all such "**gnostic"** texts; "**gnostic"** was turned into an evil word. But Irenaeus did us a favor by his multi-volume "***Against Heresy"*** where he wrote in detail about the Gospels and other texts that should be banned. He made it known that all these rediscovered texts at Nag Hammadi, Egypt in 1945 **existed in the year A.D. 180!** We know that such treasured and informative works like the ***Gospel of Thomas,*** the ***Gospel of Philip,*** the ***Letter of Peter to Philip,*** and the ***Apocryphon*** (Secret Book) ***of John*** existed in the 2nd Century and gives credence to their existence and validity. Irenaeus accused the ***Gnostics*** of passing off these "***heretical***" writings as being legitimately the works of "**Apostles.**"

IMPORTANT POINT: In his publication to Rome in A.D. 180, Irenaeus **U-N-I-L-A-T-E-R-A-L-L-Y** considered **O-N-L-Y** the **FOUR GOSPELS** which he chose because, *in his words*, "***they actually were written by Jesus' own disciples and their followers, who personally witnessed the events they described.***" Irenaeus claims that **FOUR** was the "holy" number because there are "FOUR corner to the Earth, and FOUR directions to the wind, and FOUR pillars of the Church." Contrary to Irenaeus' "legitimacy" claim, **most of the Biblical scholars today firmly challenge Irenaeus; very few believe that any of the contemporaries of Jesus or His Disciples actually wrote any of the New Testament Gospels**. **No one really knows who actually wrote the Gospels that are entitled Matthew, Mark, Luke, and John**. AT BEST the ***Gospels of Matthew*** and ***John*** ***are attributed to be stories passed down*** from those Disciples (who were illiterate and could not have "written" them) and the ***Gospels of Mark*** and ***Luke*** ***were attributed to being stories passed down*** from the **FOLLOWERS** of those Disciples. The more plausible theory is that the "original authors" of the Gospels were assigned as a "best guess" from the Bishops compiling the ***New Testament*** in the 4th Century in order to distinguish them apart.

A very telling quote can be found in the ***Apocalypse of Peter*** discovered at Nag Hammadi in which the Disciple Peter tells us that many "***will fall erroneously***" and "***will be ruled heretically***" (74:16-21). Peter claims that the risen Christ told him that those who "***name themselves bishop, and also deacon, as if they received their authority from God,***" are, in reality, "***waterless canals***" (79:24-30). They "***do not understand the mystery,***" while they "***boast that the mystery of truth belongs to them alone.***" They misinterpreted the Apostles' teachings and thus have set up an "***imitation church***" in the place of a true Christian "***brotherhood***" (78.31 - 79.10).

Valentinus and other **Gnostics** never challenged a bishop, priest, or deacons' preaching the traditional Gospels passed down from the Disciples. But they still felt that the teachings of these church leaders lacked the special ***gnosis*** and enlightenment. The **Gnostic** beliefs go beyond the commonplace teachings of the church. The forefront is the difference in beliefs over whether Jesus' resurrection was bodily or spiritually. Physical resurrection was the Catholic focal dogma.

IMPORTANT POINT: **Gnostics** held close to the traditional Greek philosophy, akin to Hindu and Buddhist philosophies, that **the human spirit is residing "inside" the body and only uses the body as a temporal instrument.** This implies there is no need for a church hierarchy, **Gnosticism offers everyone direct personal access to God.**

MONOTHEISTIC CHRISTIANITY

The Catholic Church had another "heresy" that they believed the Alternative Christianities needed to be squashed. The Nicene Creed defined "Christianity" as monotheistic, that is, having one God and began with: ***"I believe in One God, Father Almighty, Maker of Heaven and Earth."*** Church historians and theologians are sure this introductory statement in the Nicene Creed was explicitly placed there to ban **Gnostic** and their leaders like Marcion (c. 140) from being part of the one, true, Christian Church. The followers of Marcion and other **Gnostic Christianities** always considered themselves to be "true" Christians. They considered themselves to be a full part of the Christian Community and Christian Church. They worshipped alongside other Christians in their churches; they may have had private meetings afterward to discuss Christianity on a different level or from a different perspective **but** they always considered themselves as full-fledged Christians and were always accepted as such by other Christians in their communities.

However, the Catholic Church could not let these "heretics" to exist or coexist. The **Gnostics** believed there was a definite difference between the mean and wrathful God of the ***Old Testament***, the God of the Jews, the God who is credited with creating this earth and human beings, who demanded obedience from His human beings and violently punished them at will, who filled this world with pain, suffering, hatred, war, and killing of innocent men, woman, children, and babies. And now this God was the Father of Jesus Christ, the God of the ***New Testament***, and the God of the new and everlasting covenant, someone who is considered to be all-loving, all-forgiving, and all-merciful. The two Gods cannot possibly be the same God. It does not make sense. Jesus could not be describing His Father as the same one who is in the ***Old Testament***. Marcion and other **Gnostic** teachers gave the benefit of doubt to the God described by Jesus, His Father, by saying there just had to be two different Gods. There can be no other logical explanation. However, the Christian leaders at the time had to fully condemn a "dualistic" view. This was accomplished by requiring "authentic" Christians to publically profess without reservation to believe in only one God who is the "creator of heaven and earth" and the same God of Jesus. The Marcionites and other **Gnostics** and their beliefs were considered officially "heretical." Irenaeus, the self-proclaimed heresiologist, of course, was a very vocal critic of Marcionites and any **Gnostic** view that there could be another God besides the one who created this world.

There is another reason for their actions as pointed out by scholars and theologians: the heritage religion and base for Christianity was Judaism which was a monotheistic religion. To give validity to Jesus being the Messiah, Christianity had to believe in the same God, Scriptures, and prophecies as the Jewish religion otherwise Jesus would not be able to attain credence or support among the Jews. They could <u>not</u> now claim that there really are two Gods.

Many of the texts that were found at Nag Hammadi supported their beliefs that there was an evil creator God different than the good God told to us by Jesus Christ:

In ***Hypostasis of the Archons*** you hear the story of the "creator" God's false claim to be the sole supreme deity: [he] ***"is blind....because of his power, and his ignorance, and his arrogance. He said... 'It is I who am God; there is none other apart from me.' When he said this a voice came forth from above saying, 'You are mistaken'."***

Similarly in ***On the Origin of the World*** tells the same story: ***"... he boasted continually, saying 'I am god, and no other one exists except me.' But when he said these things,*** [he was told from above] ***'You err'."***

Another text ***The Secret Book of John*** tells us: ***"In his madness... he said, 'I am god, and there is no other god besides me,' for he is ignorant of... the place from which had come.... And when he saw the creation which surrounds him and the multitudes of angels around him which had come forth from him, he said to them, 'I am a jealous God, and there is no other god besides me.' But by announcing this he indicated to the angels that another God does exist; for if there were no other one, of whom would he be jealous."***

Similar sources relate a completely different story than ***Genesis*** of what happened in the Garden of Eden where the creator god is seen as an overbearing and jealous master. Also, the serpent is a beneficial creature in their narratives. It was common in ancient times that the serpent was a symbol of divine wisdom. Even today, it is the symbol used by physicians and the medical profession. The serpent was a friend to Adam and Eve, he taught them that they needed to rebel against the tyrannical god who was really imprisoning them and using them for his amusement. He proves to them that this phony god was lying to them about the "forbidden fruit":

"…[the creator] ***God gave a command to Adam, 'From every tree you may eat, but from the tree which is in the midst of Paradise do not eat, for on the day that you eat from it you will surely die.' But the serpent was wiser than all the animals that were in Paradise, and he persuaded Eve, saying, 'On the day when you eat from the tree which is in the midst of Paradise, the eyes of your mind will be opened.' And Eve obeyed… she ate, she also gave to her husband." Observing that the serpent's promise came true – their eyes were opened – but that God's threat of immediate death did not*** [occur], ***the Gnostic author goes on to quote God's words from Genesis 3:22, adding an editorial comment: "… 'Behold, Adam has become like one of us, knowing evil and good.' Then he said, 'Let us cast him out of Paradise, lest he take from the tree of life, and live forever.' But what sort of God is this? First, he envied Adam that he should eat from the tree of knowledge…. Surely he has shown himself to be a malicious envier."***

Of course, Irenaeus denounced all these texts as false, blasphemous, and heretical. He claimed Christians must adhere to the fundamental teachings of the Hebrew Scriptures that ***"the Lord your God is one God."***

However, there were Christian and **Gnostic** sects that completely forsake the Hebrew Bible and the ***"Old" Testament*** as out-of-date and replaced by the new covenant and the ***New Testament.*** <u>**Valentinus**</u> was one of those **Gnostic** teachers who rediscovered a third text, ***The Interpretation of Knowledge,*** that is emphatic Jesus Christ was Our Savior from the mean and wrathful God of the Hebrew Bible when Jesus taught us to pray: "***Our Father, who art in heaven, hallowed by Thy name. Thy Kingdom come, Thy will be done, On Earth as it is in Heaven..."*** It is <u>the God and Father of Jesus Christ who is the One and Only True God.</u> Jesus' God is all-good, all-loving, and all-merciful completely unlike the so-called, self-proclaimed "god" of the Jews and ***Old Testament***. Irenaeus may have been successful in banning the Marcionites from his Christian Church and their claim that there were two Gods, but he was not as effective in banning the Valentinians. The Valentinians publically recited the Christian Creed in the churches they attended; however, in Irenaeus' mind he knew that even though they said they believed in "one God" deep in their private thoughts and meetings they say one thing while believing another in their hearts." <u>**It irked Irenaeus further that many of their fellow Christians with whom they worshipped alongside never considered the Valentinians as heretics**</u> to the point that he wrote it in his five-volume treatise called, "<u>***Refutation and Overthrow of Falsely So-called Gnosis.***</u>" The purpose was to "help" people to distinguish the "orthodox" teachings of Christianity which will save them as opposed to the false teachings of the **Gnostics** which, in Irenaeus' words, will lead them in "***an abyss of madness and blasphemy***."

According to the Valentinians (***A Valentinian Exposition*** 22.19-23), they do profess that they believe in ONE God. However, the Valentinians conscientiously do not confuse God and Father of Jesus as the one and only Lord and Master who is the ultimate source of all, visible and invisible, comprehensible and incomprehensible, and is the One who is absolutely indescribable and "shall remain nameless" (***Interpretation of Knowledge*** 9.29). Valentinians complain that the "orthodox" Christian leaders insist on portraying God with "human images and emotions" in order for people to better relate to Him. This is not consistent with the reality. This is leftover from the ***Old Testament*** where there were constant descriptions of God in terms of an "emotional" human being; an all-powerful tyrant, a demanding master, a wrathful enforcer, or as a King who ruthlessly rules over serfs from His heavenly throne. But under the new covenant, Jesus never uses these same unfavorable human traits when He described His Father in more esoteric terms like "Truth" or "Love." This was "Christianity" presented on a higher intellectual level which is confusing to those of a lower intellect, and the people of those times rarely received any formal education other than basic survival skills. To most of the commoners, these complicated concepts sound to be untrue and blasphemous; and the ones espousing such falsehoods to be heretics. Of course, this played right into the hands of the Church leaders to corral the masses into their flock. To the ones that are able to acknowledge Christianity on a more "esoteric" perspective, they would refer to the **Gnostics** as the "***Elite Christians,"*** the ones who possess "***mature or advanced spirituality***" because of their ***"gnosis"*** or ***"special knowledge."***

The Gospel of Philip puts it another way, ***"names can be very deceptive, for they divert our thoughts from what is accurate to what is inaccurate."*** He could mean when we try to use "human-invented" words to describe non-humans like God. There really is no "human" way to describe God, "***He who shall remain nameless!***"

Irenaeus considered even the slightest deviation from monotheism to be "unChristian" and unforgivably reprehensible. As such, he demanded the Christian Church leaders all immediately excommunicate all the followers of Valentinus for being "heretics." Irenaeus proclaimed about the **Gnostics**, "***They asked…how is it that when they confess the same things, and hold the same doctrines, we call them heretics!"***(Irenaeus ***Against Heresy.*** 3.15.2).

IMPORTANT POINT: The theistic tenets of **Gnosticism** and the **Gnostic** writings actually may make more sense than the strict but irrational and unexplainable monotheistic stance of the "orthodox" Christian Church.

Valentinus claimed to be a student of Theudas who was a disciple of Paul. It was from him that Valentinus learned the "***secret gnosis***" or "special knowledge. Theudas claimed that Paul did not share this "special knowledge" with everyone but only to those he considered to be "spiritually mature." Likewise, Valentinus only taught this "special knowledge" to those who were "spiritually mature" and able to understand and accept it (Irenaeus ***A.H.*** 3.2.1-3.1).

One of the most controversial parts of this "secret knowledge" is that most Christians, like the Jews before them, ***are naive and worship, as their Almighty God and the creator of heaven and earth, one who is NOT the true Father God***. Valentinus is known to be one of the leading accusers of the emerging Church leaders who mistakenly worship the Hebrew "***creator***" (Greek "demiurgos") God who is really a lesser divine being who is NOT "the" Father

Almighty but an inferior God. This inferior divine being is the one that the Jews worshipped as the "**God of Israel,**" the "**God of Hebrew Bible,**" the "**God of the Old Testament,**" who claims to reign as the lord over this world and the one who gave Jews the law to strictly follow. He is the one who will judge and punish anyone who does not follow it (Irenaeus ***A.H.***1.7.4).

Valentinus taught his followers to reject this inferior God and ignore his laws because this "God" made the false claim that: "***I am God, and there is other.***" This was because of his own ignorance of the higher power, the Almighty Father. In ***Volume I***, his origin and ignorance are discussed. Valentinus preaches that when a person achieves the "**gnosis"** along with it they will recognize the real true, almighty, and all-powerful Supreme creator of the universe. The next step will lead to the discovery of one's true self, origin, destiny, and the True Heavenly Father.

In **Gnostic Christianity** when this "**gnosis"** or knowledge is attained, one then is ready to receive the **Gnostic** sacrament of **Redemption (*apolytrosis*** in Greek) which means "**release.**" A person who has reached this **Gnostic** level realizes that these other Christians are worshipping the false demiurge thinking he is the One True God. Through the sacrament of Redemption, a person is able to release themselves from the earthly power of the false demiurge. It is in this sacrament that a person directly addresses the demiurge, declares himself independent from him, tells the demiurge that he will no longer acknowledge that the demiurge has any authority, and he has transcended him (Irenaeus *A.H.* 1.21.1-4):

> ***"I am a son from the Father – the Father who is pre-existent.... I derive from Him who is,***

> ***pre-existent, and I come again to my own place whence I came forth"*** (Irenaeus *A.H.* 1.21.5)

Of course, all this talk about the demiurge put Valentinus and his followers at fatal odds with the bishops in Rome and the emerging Christian Church. In effect, Valentinus was telling the bishops and the Church that they claimed to represent and worship the True God but in reality they were worshipping the demiurge, an inferior divine being. The **Gnostic Valentinians** had attained "superior knowledge" and therefore surpassed the misguided authority of the bishops of the Church of Rome; whereas their bishops derive their false authority from the demiurge – not the Almighty. Irenaeus took personal offense especially now that he was a bishop realizing that the Valentinians' belief in the demiurge completely undermined the authority of all the bishops in the Church. Irenaeus accused the **Gnostics** of invoking their so-called "special knowledge" as their reason for not obeying the bishops and the Church.

In Irenaeus' book he describes how the bishops took offense to the "beliefs" of the Valentinus and his followers:

> ***"They*** [meaning the Valentinians] ***maintain that they have attained to a height beyond every power, and that therefore they are free in every respect to act as they please, having no one to fear in anything. For they claim that because of "Redemption"... they cannot be apprehended, or even perceived, by the judge"*** (Irenaeus ***A.H.***1.7.4)

The **Valentinians** and **Gnostics** countered the admonishments from the bishops that they should "***fear God,***" or that "***God will judge them as sinners***" by reiterating the absence of authority they derive from the false demiurge who they consider to be the Almighty God.

Tertullian, another heresiologist and condemner of **Gnostics,** criticizes Valentinus and attributes his arrogance and dislike for the authority of the Church of Rome because he was passed over for a promotion to bishop. Valentinus, in an act of rebellion, cut himself off from the church and started his own religion. Historians do not think Tertullian's reasoning is true because church leaders always considered Valentinus a heretic. He never considered that he or his followers to be heretics. Valentinians considered them to be members of the Church while others rejected them. (***A.H.*** 3.15.2).

IMPORTANT POINT: According to Valentinus, this treatment by the Church leaders and rejected these people as heretics proves that it was the Church who initiated their break by excommunicating them.

While some groups were being outright "excommunicated" from the "orthodox" Christian Church, there were other **Alternative Christianities** who caved on their differing beliefs and were forced to be incorporated into the beliefs of the dominant church. Once completely independent Christian communities were now blurred into ranks of the laity, deacons, priests, and bishops all under the auspicious of the Church of Rome. The transition was not easy for some. Some congregations were given a bishop, especially if they never had a bishop before, that was authorized by the powers in Rome to be the judge and disciplinarian over his new flock of subordinating the clergy and laity, making them conform to the ways and teachings of Rome. Most of the Gnostic communities were against having a formal church hierarchy. Such is a statement found in the ***Apocalypse of Peter*** which was found at Nag Hammadi, Egypt:

> ***"Others… outside our number… call themselves bishops and also deacons, as if they received their authority from God…. Those people are waterless canals"*** (***Ap. Peter*** 79:22-30).

Irenaeus demanded that the human authority is respected in the Church because it was derived from the divine authority given to Peter by Jesus. Irenaeus was firm in his belief that there is only One True God, so likewise there is only One True Church, and in turn, there is only One True representative of God on earth in that Church. Irenaeus insisted the Jesus Christ who represented His Father, the creator and judge of all human beings, established the One, Holy, Catholic, and Apostolic Christian Church. In his eyes, there can be no other Christian Churches or representatives of Jesus Christ.

Many **Gnostic** groups gave up arguing theology and Christology with Irenaeus and placated the Church by just agreeing with them and whatever they said; however, they never did give up their deep-rooted beliefs. Behind their backs, they just humored Irenaeus and his Church as people who lacked the "**gnosis.**" This is reflected in how Irenaeus ended his treatise:

> ***"Let those persons who blaspheme the Creator… as do the Valentinians and all the falsely so-called 'Gnostics,' be recognized as agents of Satan by all who worship God. Through their agent Satan even now… has been seen to speak against that God who has prepared eternal fire for apostasy"*** (5.26.1).

Irenaeus also went after any clergy that seemed to allow **Gnostic** teachings to infiltrate their congregations without being discouraged. Of course, Irenaeus was also after those priests who could be purveyors of these heresies. Irenaeus warned Victor, a Bishop of Rome, that **Gnostic** writings were found in circulation among the congregation of one priest, Florius. Irenaeus believed he was secretly a **Gnostic** and was not doing his duty of "***placing the fear of God***" in his congregation. Self-proclaimed heresiologist Irenaeus was on a mission to rid the "orthodox" Church of any clergy who were secretly allowing **Gnostics** believers and beliefs within their private inner circles.

Valentinus like many of the **Gnostic** communities believed that One True Almighty God would never favor watching His people being subservient to anyone, especially the priests and bishops continuing on the mission of Jesus Christ in the emerging universal (Catholic) Church. Irenaeus was very much in favor of the structure and hierarchy of the Christian Church that was emerging and would go to any lengths to defend his Church. Even Martin Luther almost 1300 years later took to challenging the hierarchy of the Catholic Church rejected having a Pope, bishops, and priests. Ironically, Martin Luther's views were very similar to the views of the **Gnostics** on this subject.

<u>IMPORTANT POINT:</u> Many historians and scholars feel that Irenaeus actions had a very personal motive behind them. He sent this multi-volume treatise ***Against Heresy*** to the Pope and the hierarchy in Rome. He did manage to get their attention and with that he got himself promoted to Bishop. But it is really believed by some that his main ambition was to become Pope. That was the position for which he was passed over which just made him more bitter.

THE PASSION AND DEATH OF JESUS CHRIST

The **Gnostics** and traditional Christian Church agreed on **most** of the facts surrounding the passion and death of Jesus Christ. However, it is when you read the newly discovered **Gnostic Gospels,** the **Gnostics** part ways on what happens when Jesus dies. The **Gnostic Gospels** show how "Jesus" the human is separated from "Christ" the God.

We are ***fairly*** certain that the execution of Jesus Christ happened circa A.D. 30-33. We do know that Pontius Pilate who was the Roman Perfect at that time in Jerusalem was the one who condemned Jesus Christ and ordered Him to be crucified. Tacitus (c. 55-115), who was a renowned Roman historian, wrote this about Jesus' execution:

> ***"... substituted as culprits and punished with the utmost refinements of cruelty, a class of persons hated for their vices, whom the crowd call Christians. Christus, the founder of the name, had undergone the death penalty in the reign of Tiberius, by sentence of the procurator Pontius Pilate..."***

The Jewish historian, Josephus writes about the troubled relationship between the Jews and the Roman Empire when Pontius Pilate was Prefect over Judea circa A.D. 16-36:

> ***"Pilate, having heard him accused by men of the highest standing among us...condemned him to be crucified."***

The ***Gospel of Mark*** believed to be written circa A.D. 70-80 relays how Jesus was charged with sedition against the Roman Emperor by Pontius Pilate, condemning Him to death by crucifixion. Jesus was arrested in the Garden of Gethsemane by Roman soldiers as His Disciples denied knowing Him, fled like cowards in fear of their own lives, and went into hiding.

IMPORTANT POINT: Everyone condemns Judas forever as being the "traitor" but on the other hand canonizes all the rest of the Disciples as "Saints." Seems like all twelve of them were "traitors." They all abandoned Jesus in His time of need. Saint Peter did as Jesus predicted and denied Him three times as the cock crowed. But he was forgiven.

The ***Gospels of Luke*** and ***John*** were written circa 90-110 reveal that Jesus forgave his persecutors.

IMPORTANT POINT: Would the all-good, all-merciful Jesus NOT have forgiven Judas first for "handing Him over" [the correct translation of the word, not "betrayed"], or as the story goes, for doing what Jesus asked him to do?

All four Gospels give accounts (although they don't agree with each other) of His passion, death, and burial; however, the reasons they give for Jesus' arrest and execution are **completely different:**

- The ***Gospel of Mark*** says it was Jewish high priests in Jerusalem who demanded that Jesus be arrested and executed for heresy and blasphemy because He questioned their teachings.

- The ***Gospel of John*** gives completely different reasons. ***John*** says that Jesus was arrest and executed because of His popularity. He was attracting larger and larger crowds. The Jewish High Priests were worried that the crowds would break out in riots. The followers of Jesus were claiming that He was the expected Messiah and He is the long-awaited king who came to free the Jews from Roman rule. These crowds were getting more and more aroused hearing that this Jesus was claimed to be the Messiah and the perfect time has come to start their revolution against Rome rule. The High Priests amicably worked with the Roman magistrates to keep the peace in Judea. Together they did not know whether if they arrested Jesus it would defuse any potential revolution or it would do the opposite and cause a revolution. Finally, Caiaphas who was the chief Jewish High Priest convinced Pontius Pilate that Jesus needed to be arrested and executed. He went as far as convincing Pilate that besides blasphemy, Jesus was guilty of inciting sedition and riots against the Roman Empire and deserves to be crucified.

Also in the ***Gospel of John,*** which obviously was written after the death of John, includes the Jewish insurrection of 66-70, the Temple was burned down, the town of Jerusalem was destroyed, and the Jews decimated even more.

- The **Gnostic *Apocalypse of Peter*** was a banned text that came back to light when it was found at Nag Hammadi. Peter gives a very interesting version of Jesus' crucifixion:

> ***"...Who*** [is] ***this one above the cross, who is glad and laughing?"*** The Savior said to Peter, ***"He whom you saw being glad and laughing above the cross is the Living Jesus. But he into whose hands and feet they are***

> ***driving the nails is his fleshy parts, which is the substitute. They put no shame which remained in his likeness."*** (***Peter*** 81:4-24)

<u>IMPORTANT POINT:</u> The ***<u>Apocalypse of Peter</u>*** is one of the sources from where the **Gnostic** beliefs arise that Jesus was the human man who died on the cross and His divine spirit, Christ, left and ascended to His Father in Heaven.

- In ***<u>The Second Treatise of the Great Seth,</u>*** another text rediscovered at Nag Hammadi relays a similar version to the one as told by Peter but this one claims to be Christ speaking:

> ***"It was another... who drank the gall and vinegar; it was not I. They struck me with the reed; it was another, Simon, who bore the cross on his shoulder. It was another upon whom they placed the crown of thorns. But I was rejoicing in the height over... their error... And I was laughing at their ignorance."*** (56:6-19)

> ***<u>The Second Treatise of the Great Seth</u>*** validates the belief by some of the **Gnostic** sects that believe it was Simon who took it upon himself to carry the cross for Jesus; the two of them were miraculously switched likenesses. It was Simon looking like Jesus who was the one who suffered and died.

<u>IMPORTANT POINT:</u> Both these scenarios show how Jesus was really God and no one can kill God.

- The ***Acts of John*** is a **Gnostic** text supposedly relayed by the Disciple John that was also considered fraudulent and heretical by the Christian Church. This text, however, was discovered before the others at Nag Hammadi. This text was banned because it claimed that Jesus was NEVER a real human being but was always a divine spirit who made Himself appear to be a human. The ***Acts of John*** tells us how Jesus would appear in different forms: a child, a young man, or an old man. John says:

> ***"I will tell you another glory, brethren; sometimes when I meant to touch him I encountered a material, solid body; but at other times again when I felt him, his substance was immaterial and incorporeal... as if it did not exist at all"*** (93).

John further tells us that when he checked for footprints, Jesus never left any, nor did Jesus ever blink his eyes.

IMPORTANT POINT: The ***Acts of John*** reinforced the **Gnostics** that believed Jesus' real nature was spiritual, not human.

- Also, the ***Acts of John*** relates how when John was in Gethsemane he had seen a vision of Jesus holding a cross of light. Jesus says to John:

> ***"I have suffered none of the things which they will say of me; even that suffering which I showed to you and the rest in my dance, that it be called a mystery"*** (101).

- The ***Treatise on Resurrection,*** another text rediscovered at Nag Hammadi, relates that if Jesus was the "**Son of Man**" then He was a human who would suffer and died just like every other human; however, if Jesus was also the "**Son of God**" then He would be a deity who could not die but transcended any suffering and death.

IMPORTANT POINT: So was Jesus really a human being like us or a divine being like His Father, the Almighty? The universal Christian Church insisted that Jesus was a human being and considers His suffering, crucifixion, and death as a literal and historically accurate event. They placed it prominently and without ambiguity in the Nicene Creed, the creed of the Christian faith, with the words: ***"Jesus Christ suffered under Pontius Pilate, was crucified, died, and was buried."*** But they contradict themselves within the same Creed saying that Jesus was "***fully human and fully divine***." That is the same as saying Jesus was 100% human and 100% divine which is a 100% oxymoron! Pick one.

Pope Leo (c. 447) condemned the ***Acts of John*** as "***perverse***" which ***"should not only be forbidden but entirely destroyed and burned with fire."*** Some of the **Gnostic** sects, especially the ones that were said to be started by John and his disciples, revered and treasured these texts of John so much that they ignored Pope Leo and continued to copy these texts. The Second Nicene Council, about 300 years later, reinforce what was proclaimed in the Nicene Creed, issued an edict forbidding anyone to copy this book, and ordered all copies of John's text to be destroyed by fire.

The Christian Church's Traditional View of the Passion and Death of Christ

The emerging Christian Church in the 1st and 2nd centuries were the closest to the event and legacies of Jesus Christ, Peter, Philip, Thomas, James, and all of the Disciples. Many saw the persecution and execution of their beloved mentors. They also saw the persecution and execution of so many others with their own eyes because they were Christian believers and followers of Jesus and His Disciples. The Church Leaders needed to keep their flocks from deserting the Christian Church that was placing them in the same dangerous path as Jesus and His Disciples. One step to counteract those fears, the Church leaders proclaimed that anyone who died as a martyr for Jesus and their Christian faith would surely be taken directly into Heaven and would have their own sainthood guaranteed.

After Jesus' death and throughout the 1st, 2nd, and 3rd centuries the Roman Emperors always considered Christianity as a seditious movement against the Roman Empire. Nero felt the Christians were merely a group of people given to fantasy and superstition. Emperor Augustus wanted to suppress these Christian dissidents who were believers in the supernatural and magicians. They followed a man who performed magic before crowds small and large; He was a blasphemer before the Jewish High Priests in Jerusalem; executed for sedition against Roman Emperor; His followers claimed to convert bread and wine into His flesh and blood which they eat and drank as a sacred ritual. The Christians further aggravated the Romans by calling them "pagans" who worshipped multiple "false gods" to bring about good fortune to them. The Romans were justified in persecuting the Christians on so many levels. It was not until the 4th century when the newly-converted

Christian Constantine became the Roman Emperor that he made Christianity the officially accepted state religion in the Roman Empire. Up to that moment, the Christian leaders took much convincing to get converts and retain the previously converted, in such dire and fatal politically charged environment.

The Nag Hammadi text, ***The Testimony of Truth*** (31.22-32.8), criticizes the Christian leaders' proclamation that martyrdom for Christianity's sake ensures a persons' salvation. If it were that simple then everyone would declare Jesus Christ was also their savior to be saved! However, it is an illusion these martyrs have if they deliver themselves to be killed for the sake of their faith in Him so that they will be saved (33.25 – 34.26). Does a martyr's death gain forgiveness for his life of sin? Is martyrdom a human offering to God? Does God want "human sacrifice"? Then that would relegate God to being a heartless cannibal.

The Testimony of Truth leads the readers to believe that **Christians are only "destroying themselves."** They are forced to believe that Jesus Christ was a human and thus as mortal as they are. Whereas, Jesus was really a Deity with divine power and He could never suffer or die. It says: "***The Son of Man came forth from imperishability, being alien to defilement. He went down to Hades and performed mighty works; He raised the dead therein.... and the lame, the blind, the paralytic, the dumb, and the demon-possessed were granted healing.... For this reason, he destroyed his flesh from the cross which he bore***" (30.18-0; 32.22 -33.11)

In ***The Apocalypse of Peter,*** it is stated that only the body of human flesh and blood, which is "***the substitute***," can die. The Lord told Peter when the **"*primal part*"** or the

"intelligent spirit," is released to join **"the perfect light with My Holy Spirit"** (83.12-15).

Valentinus is very consistent in his writings that Jesus Christ was not capable of suffering and dying. ***The Gospel of Truth*** **completely contradicts** the "traditional" Christian teachings that Christ's passion, crucifixion, and death were a "human sacrifice" which He had to do in order to redeem human beings from our sins (20.10-32).

Valentinus' ***The Tripartite Tractate*** says: "***that which He was before, and what He is eternally, and unbegotten, impassible Word, who came into being in flesh***" (113.35-38). Valentinus was one of the first theologians to seriously challenge a matter of faith central to Christianity: **How could Christ be simultaneously fully human and fully divine?**

From the very beginning, the early Christian Churches in the Asia Minor, Africa, and Middle to Eastern Asia were very much aware of the theological differences they had with the Christian Churches in the West. There was always resistant to be folded into "**One Holy Catholic Church of Rome**." Irenaeus in the 2nd century acting as the Great Unifier insisted that all the Christian Churches around the world become one and agree on all Christian doctrines. Victor, who was the Bishop of Rome in A.D. 190 (equivalent to the Pope today, who still is considered to be the "Bishop of Rome") pushed for this uniformity among all the Christian Churches. He demanded that Churches in Eastern Europe and Asia Minor stop celebrating Easter after Passover and to move it to the beginning of Passover as celebrated by the Church of Rome and the Western Churches; otherwise cease to refer to themselves "Catholic Christians."

The Church of Rome also compiled the "canon" or list of sacred texts that were to be accepted by all Christian churches, forsaking all others. The Church of Rome issued orders to consolidate many communities into the centralized Church of Rome hierarchy. Irenaeus was the Great Unifier for the "***the catholic church dispersed throughout the whole world, even to the ends of the earth***" all with the same doctrines, rituals, Scriptures, and hierarchical structure.

The Catholic Church defined the official story of Christ's life. They rejected any differing views that do not portray Jesus as a human being like us, including all **Gnostic** teachings that considered Jesus was a spiritual being. They insisted that Jesus was born, worked, ate, drank, grew weary, suffered, and died. They persisted that Jesus ***bodily*** "resurrected" Himself from the dead after three days "in accordance with the prophecies" to prove He really was God.

Many of the Eastern Orthodox had no problem with Jesus' ***bodily*** experiences; although some did consider Him as always being a divine spirit. However, the **Gnostics** did believe completely different. For them the main essence of a person is their **"inner spirit,"** all physical experiences are temporal while they are on this earth, it is a person's "**inner spirit**" that will live on for all eternity spirituality, and the body will die and rot. It was difficult for some people to comprehend the "bodiless spirit" of the **Gnostics** than the more tangible Catholic Church's view.

IMPORTANT POINT: The idea of a person's "inner spirit" living on forever was not in the Jewish tradition.

THE SECRET GNOSIS IS IN THE GOSPELS

The ***Gospel of John*** contains a very popular saying of Jesus that Catholics, Protestants, Evangelicals, and **Gnostic Christians** all interpret **VERY** differently. But then according to Irenaeus himself, the ***Gospel of John*** was considered by many in the Western Churches to be a **Gnostic Gospel**, or at least too **Gnostic**, to be included in the ***New Testament*** (Irenaeus, ***A.H.*** 3.11.7). But John had too many followers around Asia Minor that the Catholic Church could not afford to lose.

> ***"... Thomas said to him, 'Lord, we do not know where you are going, how can we know the way?' Jesus said to him, 'I am the way, the truth, and the life; no one comes to the Father, but by me.' "*** (***John*** 14:5-6)

***John* clearly states that no one can get to the Almighty Father except through Jesus.** It can be interpreted many different ways. The **Gnostics** feel that in order to understand the Almighty Father one must first understand the mission of His Son, Jesus Christ, here on earth and fully understand Jesus' secret message to us. For the Catholic Church, this statement means that it is only through Christianity that people can find Jesus and His Almighty Father. This then supports the need for having an institutional church and one set of "orthodox" teachings. Many Protestant denominations, especially the 20th-century evangelists, believe in a stricter interpretation, i.e. Jesus is the sole mediator to the Father, only Jesus can deliver you to the Father, and you cannot talk to the Father directly.

IMPORTANT POINT: The ***Gospel of John*** is found to be very similar to the ***Gospel of Thomas*** or ***Dialogue of the Savior***

The Church leaders accepted the ***Gospel of John*** but had serious problems accepting similar Gospels and texts. Probably they automatically rejected anything the **Gnostics** embraced. The ***Gospel of John*** contained the same different perspective on Jesus' mission and message. Similar to what is found in ***The Gospel of John,*** when asked the same question in the ***Gospel of Thomas*** Jesus is said to reply: ***"There is light within a man of light, and it lights up the whole world. If he does not shine, he is darkness"*** (38.4-10). ***The Dialogue of a Savior*** shares the very same perspective in that one's inner capacity is to find the "***light within***."

Valentinus and the Valentinians were major fans of the ***Gospel of John*** which they considered to be an authentic **Gnostic Gospel**. They were not the only ones, there were many "orthodox" Christians, including Irenaeus, who accepted the ***Gospel of John*** to be a companion to the Gospels of ***Matthew, Mark,*** and ***Luke.*** But then we do not really know how much the large following of people who revered the ***Gospel of John*** that the Church did not want to lose played into it being included in the ***New Testament*** considering it was so different than the Gospels of ***Matthew, Mark,*** and ***Luke.***

The ***Gospel of Thomas*** was also responsible for another phenomenon. Faithful Christians in the 3rd and 4th centuries began to take monastic lives of solitude, self-disciple and constant prayer to reach a higher level of religious insight. The terms "**monk**" and "**monastery**" come from the Greek word "***monachos"*** meaning to be "solitary." This term was commonly found in the ***Gospel of Thomas*** in relation to attaining **Gnostic** or Secret Knowledge. By the 4th century the Catholic Church embraced monks and monastic life and found a place for it within its institution.

Christianity According to the "Gnostic" Gospels and Texts

First, **Gnostic Christian** sects consider themselves to be full-fledged "Christians" just with a different perspective and interpretation of Jesus' mission and message. NOT any different than the different perspective and interpretation between Catholics and Protestants, or between different factions of Protestant denominations.

This difference can be found in the variety of texts found in 1945 at Nag Hammadi, Egypt. As far as the most denominations in the Catholic, Orthodox, and Protestant branches of the Christian Church is concerned, the **Gnostic Christians** have a very different viewpoint on which they totally disagree on many issues. Each side feels the other side has the completely wrong take on Jesus' ministry and Christianity. And there are beliefs everyone agrees upon too.

Some of the greatest differences between the beliefs of the **Gnostic Christian** denominations in relation to the **Catholic Church** are: the true nature of Jesus Christ, the institutionalize Romanesque military-style organization of the Catholic Church, the proclamation of immediate sainthood for anyone martyred for their faith, and their total different paths to attaining salvation in the afterlife. The Catholic Church declared that human beings needed their "divine" leadership in order to be saved. The Catholic Church went as far as saying: "***Outside the Church there is no salvation***."

Gnostic Christianity believed that God created man and His divine presence or spirit is in each human being, referenced by some as the "divine spark." This belief can be found in ***The Gospel of Philip:***

> ***"... God created humanity, but now human beings create God.***
>
> ***That is the way it is in the world – human beings make gods, and worship their creation.***
>
> ***It would be appropriate for the gods to worship human beings!"*** (71.35 – 72.4)

Valentinus taught his followers that a spark of the divine is found in all human lives because all human beings were created by a divine being. The **Gnostics** believe that God created everything so He is everywhere. The **Gnostics** felt that the structured religious institutions were really a constraint to a person's normal spiritual development. Despite their differences, the Valentinians and many other **Gnostic** groups attended and prayed alongside their neighbors in the local Catholic Churches; or at least until those Churches forbade their attendance and participation, and kicked them out.

Gnostic Christians and the "mainstream" Catholic Church had very different or opposite views of the relationship of God to human beings. The Catholic Church believed along the same lines as the Jews that man was not connected to God but in fact subservient to God. This was all due to humans being sinners. This is also why main-line Christians feel Jesus came to this earth especially to die for the sins of humans. **Gnostic Christians** do not feel the same. Then to say Jesus died to release us from the "original sin" of Adam and Eve is more incomprehensible. Some even go to the extreme of saying humans suffer both mentally and physically because we are sinners. It all doesn't make any sense, especially if the Almighty is all-good, all-powerful and merciful. Ironically in the original Greek versions of the ***New Testament*** the term that appears for sin is "***hamartia;***" which coincidentally was used in the **sport of archery** to mean "***to miss the mark***." Let's face it; we were made to be fragile and fallible human beings who will fall short of the mark in our moral characters. As it says in ***Romans*** "***all have sinned, and all fall short of the glory of God***" (3:23).

The ***Gospel of Mark*** also relays that Jesus was sent to this earth to reconcile humanity with the Almighty: "***The time is fulfilled, and the kingdom of God is at hand; repent, and believe in the gospel***" (***Mark*** 1:15). Mark believed that only Jesus forgives our sins; of course to be forgiven people would have to accept His message in their hearts.

The ***Gospel of John*** tells us that we are estranged from our God:

> ***"For God sent the Son into the world... that the world might be saved through Him. He who believes in Him is not condemned; he who does not believe is condemned already because he has not believed..."*** (***John*** 3:17-19)

<u>**IMPORTANT POINT:**</u> The **Gnostics** believe the complete opposite: it is human ignorance not human sin that causes humans to suffer.

The **Gnostic *Gospel of Truth*** which was written either by Valentinus or one of his followers says:

> ***"... Ignorance ...brought about anguish and terror. And the anguish grew solid like a fog, so that no one was able to see..."*** (***Gospel of Truth*** 17:10-16).

Valentinus is telling us that most people are oblivious or otherwise completely unaware of the origins and nature of this world. The ***Gospel of Truth*** considers this ignorance to be the nightmare for people causing them to live in "***terror and confusion and instability and doubt and division***" with "***many illusions.***" Consequently, people remain ignorant and a "***creature of*** [their] ***oblivion***" never experiencing total fulfillment. (***Gospel of Truth*** 29:2-6).

Gnostics consider that many people "***dwell in deficiency***" ["deficiency" is the **Gnostic** opposite of fulfillment]:

> "... ***As with someone's ignorance, when he comes to have knowledge, his ignorance vanishes by itself; as the darkness vanishes when light appears, so also the deficiency vanishes in the fulfillment"*** (***Gospel of Truth*** 24.32 – 25.3).

The Dialogue of the Savior considers many people ignorant of their nature and the universe around them which is detrimental to their wellbeing.

> ***"... If one does not understand how the fire came to be, he will burn in it, because he does not know his root. If one does not first understand the water, he does not know anything.... If one does not understand how the wind that blows came to be, he will run with it. If one does not understand how the body that he wears came to be, he will perish with it.... Whoever does not understand***

> ***how he came will not understand how he will go..."*** (***Dialogue of the Savior*** 134.1-22).

Gnostics believe that contained within every person is a **<u>psyche that has the potential for self-liberation or self-destruction</u>**. The ***Gospel of Thomas*** quotes Jesus as saying:

> ***"If you bring forth what is within you, what you bring forth will save you.***
>
> ***If you do not bring forth what is within you, what you do not bring forth will destroy you"*** (45.30-33).
>
> ***... "Recognize what is before your eyes, and what is hidden will be revealed to you"*** (33.11-13).

Gnostics believe that in order to attain the "**gnosis"** one must go through a personal and solitary reflection process which includes an internal struggle of resistance. Jesus did say:

> "***I am the knowledge of truth***."

The ***<u>Gospel of Truth</u>*** concurs in fuller terms:

> ***"Whoever is to have knowledge in this way knows where he comes from, and where he is going."*** and
>
> ***"... in you dwells the light that does not fail... Be concerned with yourselves, do not be concerned with other things which you have rejected from yourselves*** (22.15) and (33.14).

In The ***<u>Gospel of Thomas</u>***, Jesus ridicules those who misinterpret the "<u>Kingdom of God:</u>"

> ***"… Rather, the Kingdom is inside of you, and it is outside of you. When you come to know yourselves, then you will be known, and you will realize that you are the sons of the living Father. But if you will not know yourselves, then you dwell in poverty, and it is you who are that poverty"*** (32.19 – 35.7).

IMPORTANT POINT: The Disciples and many people, even today, **believe that "the Kingdom of God" is going to be a future event.** That is not what Jesus ever said.

> ***"When will the new Kingdom come,"*** the Disciples asked.
>
> Jesus replied, ***"What you look forward to has already come, but you do not recognize it."***
>
> Another time Jesus' reply to Disciples, ***"It will not come by waiting for it. It will not be a matter of saying 'Here it is.' Rather, the Kingdom of the Father is spread out upon the earth, and men do not see it"*** (***Thomas*** 42.7 – 51.18).

Unlike the three synoptic Gospels in the New Testament all claiming to contain the teachings of Jesus Christ, the ***Gospel of Thomas*** states that the "**Kingdom of God is an actual historical event.**" The ***Gospel of Mark*** implies that the Disciples were expecting the Kingdom of God to arrive as **a cataclysmic event in their own lifetime** interpreting Jesus' words as they would see the "***Kingdom of God***" (***Mark*** 9:1). **All three synoptic Gospels** implied to different extents that the Kingdom of God will come soon ***– and that was 2,000 years ago!***

It is only found in the ***Gospel of Luke*** where Jesus said, ***"The Kingdom of God is within you."*** (***Luke*** 17:21)

The ***Gospel of Philip*** says of a person's inner spirit:

> ***"… You saw the spirit, you became spirit. You say Christ, you became Christ. You saw the Father, you shall become the Father… You see yourself, and what you see you shall become."*** (61.21-35)

The ***Gospel of Philip*** says "***gnosis***" is achieved when you are ***"no longer a Christian, but a Christ"*** (67.26-27)

Gnosticism has a completely different theological perspective from mainstream Christian Churches. The **Gnostics** felt that those who wanted to learn the "special knowledge" to "become a Christ" would not be able within the current overpowering Christian Church.

The ***Book of Thomas the Contender*** says: ***"whoever has not known himself has known nothing, but he who has known himself has at the same time already achieved knowledge about the depths of all things."*** (138.16-18)

Hippolytus writes that Simon Magnus speaks of the infinite power being in each human:

> ***"That in him dwells an infinite power… the root of the universe,"*** [which] ***"exists in a latent condition in everyone."***

SUMMARY

"***To the Victor go the Spoils!***" That is exactly what happens when history is written; history is written by the winners – or at least their version of the events that happened. Rarely do the losers write their version of the events and put out their failures and embarrassments for all future generations to see. Well, we do know who won the "Battle of the Christianities" – the so-called "orthodox" Church. To be clear, this "orthodox" (small "o") Church became the Catholic Church. The "Orthodox" (capital "O") Church is the moniker for many of the Eastern Orthodox Churches (or for some, Orthodox Catholic Church) mainly in the Eastern part of what was the Roman Empire after they broke away from Rome for a final time in 1054. The Catholic Church based in Rome under the Pope became the Roman Catholic Church. The mainline Protestant religions split from the Roman Catholic Church in the late 16th Century. That is an important fact, Catholicism is the "heritage" religion the Protestants broke away from, or as they put it, reformed it. Then there are numerous additional splits or reformations from the original Protestant denominational split or reformation, ad infinitum. For clarity, we call them collectively "traditional Christianities" with many of the same dogmatic beliefs as their forerunner, the Roman Catholic Church; but at the same time, some vastly different as the centuries continued on.

Of course, the Roman Catholic and Eastern Orthodox Churches consider themselves to be sole holders of the "**orthodox**" or "**true**" teachings of Jesus Christ on which they were "***guided by the Holy Spirit.***" Anyone with differing beliefs would be labeled as "**heretics.**" That would technically make all Protestants "**heretics**" who have differing beliefs.

It is not as bad as it sounds. The term "**heretic**" has always had a bad connotation to it but its real meaning originally was "***an opinion or belief deviating from the accepted or dominant opinion or belief.***"

The 1945 discoveries at Nag Hammadi changed history and dogma as the winner, the Catholic Church, wrote it. Begs the fundamental questions: is the "traditional" Christianity practiced today by the Catholic and Protestant Churches the right Christianity? Were the ancient **Gnostics** texts discovered at Nag Hammadi the real "orthodox" or true Gospels?

Were the **Gnostics** erroneously labeled as "heretics" (dissenters) by the emerging Christian Church? Or was it the other way around? In reality are the "orthodox" really the "heretics" and the "heretics" really the "orthodox"?

If the texts discovered at Nag Hammadi were not destroyed but instead were accepted with the other Gospels and Epistles, included in the ***New Testament***, would Christianity have developed completely differently? Would we be practicing a completely different type of Christianity? Or if there was no strong centralized Church but scattered autonomous Churches, would Christianity have survived for 2000 years up to present day? Would it survive with so many multifaceted and multicultural communities? Would its diversity really be a strength? Or would most of the people of the world be converted to and swallowed up by the massive presence of Islamism?

Renowned author and professor of Religious Studies, Elaine Pagels, and many others scholars and theologians believe that **we owe the survival of Christianity to the organizational and theological structure that became**

the Roman Catholic Church. I wholeheartedly agree. Regardless of your personal or religious feelings towards Catholics, it was a major achievement of the Catholic Church to carry Christianity through the many turbulent times over 20 centuries. We all should be grateful. The Catholic Church's framework and hierarchy modeled after the successful Roman Empire may have been what was needed through those centuries to give people stability and moral direction. Very similar to how the Law of Moses provided stability and moral direction for the Jewish faith.

The Roman Catholic Church had the organizational strengths to dedicate tireless resources to distributing the Sacred Scripture of Jesus Christ's life and teachings for 16 centuries. We can thank thousands of monks who sat in dark and damp candle-light scriptoriums who tirelessly made more copies of these Sacred Scriptures **by hand** before the printing press was invented. Without them, we would not have a Christian Bible today. Of course, that was until Martin Luther and King James decided to make adjustments to it with new translations of ancient obsolete languages, deleting Chapters and whole Books from it, and publishing a new revised Christian Bible.

The biggest boost for Catholicism was in the 4th century when the newly converted Emperor Constantine through the Council of Nicaea established the One, Holy, Catholic, and Apostolic Christian Church and designated it as the official state religion of the Roman Empire. With this, the Catholic Church began to take on a flourishing growth as a major religion. Unfortunately, the same could not be said for those Christians whose perspective was more **Gnostic.** They were no match for the emerging Catholic Church back by the vast Roman Empire whose power seemed to be limitless.

Although it survived the test of time, it was much more difficult for **Gnosticism** at the hands of the Catholic Church trying century after century to have them permanently eliminated. Miraculously, **Gnostic Christianity** survived in many underground circles; it just could not be suppressed. There were several resurgents of **Gnosticism** during the Middle Ages. Every time it surfaced, it was attacked by the Catholic Church with their familiar accusations of heresy.

Gnosticism had a very different perspective on the origin of evil and sin. **Gnostics'** notion of the **origin of evil** is not to be interpreted the same as **moral evil**. When you investigate the original meaning of the Greek "***kakia"*** it is interpreted as "**what is bad.**" This gives it a much large spectrum to consider. It could mean when a person avoids or hope something would not happen, such as misfortune, misery, suffering, sickness, or death. To the Valentinians, there was another dimension to "***kakia"*** by going past just the physiological to also include psychological **"emotional harms"** such as fear, hatred, melancholy, grief, confusion, etc. **Gnostics** believe that **Gnosticism** is a better way than traditional Christianity in overcoming suffering by placing it in perspective with attaining the **"gnosis"** about human being's purpose and place on this earth, and their ultimate destiny in the universe. Many of these answers can be found within all of us.

The **Gnostics** take joy finding their solace in the ***Gospel of Truth***:

> ***"The Gospel of Truth is a joy for those who have received from the Father of Truth the grace of knowing Him... For He discovered them in Himself, and they discovered Him in themselves,***

the inconceivable one, the Father, the perfect one, the one who made all things" (***Truth*** 16.1 - 18.34)

IMPORTANT POINT: Then in 1945 a miracle of miracles happened, if not by pure Divine intervention, the discovery of 50+ texts banned by the dominant Catholic Church in Nag Hammadi, Egypt. It may have been 1500 years late but it is what has always been feared by the Catholic Church and "tradition" Christianity – its validity was brought into serious question according to the Gospels and Epistles of six other of Jesus' Disciples.

These discoveries were the biggest archeological find for Biblical scholars, theologians, and educators. For the first, it gave them a new and expansive perspective on the early and diverse Christian beliefs that could have been wrongly banned and should be revisited.

Today the scholars and theologians are much more educated and open-minded than the ancient Christians. They are able to question the "traditional" Christian religions and can freely ask questions about the mission, teachings, and meanings intended by Jesus Christ.

BIBLIOGRAPHY, REFERENCE, AND SUGGESTED READING

Brown, Peter, ***Rise Of Western Christianity: Triumph and Diversity A.D. 200-1000***
© 2003 Blackwell Publishers, Malden, Mass.

King, Karen L., ***What is Gnosticism***
© 2003 Belknapprots

McLaren, Brian D. ***Secret Message of Jesus, The: Uncovering the Truth That Could Change Everything***
© 2006 W. Publishing, Nashville, Tennessee

Meyers, Marvin and Willis Barnstone, ***Gnostic Bible, The***
© 2003 Harper, San Francisco, CA © 2009 Shambhala, Boston, MA

This Book and Treatise are a compilation from many sources on the same subject.
See the Complete List of Bibliographies, References, and Suggested Readings in Appendix II

PART III – THE GNOSTIC GOSPELS

CHAPTER 9

THE GOSPEL OF THOMAS: THE SECRET SAYINGS OF JESUS

HISTORICAL BACKGROUND

The ***Gospel of Thomas*** is one of the most famous codices that were discovered in 1945 at Nag Hammadi in Upper Egypt in the area where the ancient monastery founded by St. Pachomius had once stood. The codices that were found there were probably buried in the desert because they were very important to the monks from that monastery. The collection had fifty-three manuscripts written in **Sahidic Coptic**, an extinct ancient Egyptian language. That fact alone attests to the age of the manuscripts. This Gospel is said to contain phases uttered by our Lord and Master, the "Living Jesus Christ," which were written down by **Didymus Judas Thomas**, who we know more popularly as the Disciple Thomas, one of the twelve.

What makes it unique from the Gospels found in the ***New Testament*** is that it **does not contain any narratives** about the life and works of Jesus Christ; instead, **it is a collection of 114 sayings of Jesus.** They were compiled by one of Jesus' closest Disciples, Thomas, When it was unearthed it was not welcomed with the glorious fanfare you would expect, but instead met with a new round of skeptical criticism. Some of these teachings of Jesus Christ were in conflict with the interpretations immortalized in the Gospels that were placed in the ***New Testament***. For many who read these 114 sayings, they believe the ***Gospel of Thomas*** could be the source document from which the other Gospel drew their narratives. So many sayings appeared in the four canonical Gospels, so there has to be a connection between them. For many, the connection is so strong that some refer to the ***Gospel of Thomas*** as "**The Fifth Gospel**."

To the dismay of Biblical conservatives, the sayings in the ***Gospel of Thomas*** seem to have more in common with the **Gnostics** schools of thought. Jesus was preaching about the coming of a new type of man; a man with superior knowledge. In this Gospel, Jesus describes man taking a journey from limited to unlimited consciousness. The Jesus of ***Thomas*** invites us to drink deeply from the well of knowledge that lies within ourselves, not so that we may become good Christians, but so that we may attain the self-knowledge that will make us, too, a Christ.

Jesus Christ started the most earth-shattering religious movement for all of mankind. He spoke in very deep parables that encourage man to understand the meaning of his being, his place in the universe, and all our relationship to the infinite divine realm. As simple as His parables sounded, they really included complex ideas with very deep meanings.

Many people became disciples and followers of this simple man, the son of a carpenter, Jesus of Nazareth and His religion and ethics which we call Christianity. His movement was like the small mustard seed He described that grew into a mighty tree. But like any large tree, it has many branches. Christianity likewise had many diverse movements and patterns of thought. Trouble is the emerging Christian Church decided on only 27 texts that would compose the ***New Testament*** – the only texts that would be considered "orthodox" or "true" rejecting all other texts as "heresy" or "non-compliant." Anyone who revered any other texts, even if they included the 27 texts, was considered to be "heretics."

Half of the 114 sayings attributed to Jesus in the ***Gospel of Thomas*** are found in some fashion in the four canonical Gospel; some differ greatly. Many of these other sayings NOT found in the four canonical Gospels are known to us because they have been included in the writings of early Christian critics and heresiologists such as Clement of Alexandria, Irenaeus, Origen, Tertullian, etc. Their writings prove the ***Gospel of Thomas*** existed in the first centuries.

For many Biblical scholars, the ***Gospel of Thomas*** may be the "source document" for which they have been looking; or at least the closest thing to it, from which the four canonical Gospels drew upon. The ***Gospel of Thomas*** is a good candidate because it appears to predate them. The ***Gospel of Thomas*** could be the "proto-gospel" that contains the original and authentic words of Jesus to which the other Gospels added narratives around.

It is nearly impossible to know which if any are the "original and authentic" words of Jesus." What a fallible human "hears" may carry through to what he writes down, accidentally or purposely. The ***Gospels of Mark, Matthew,***

Luke, John, Thomas, and others can relate five different translations of the word of Jesus. This can be due to each's individual human understanding or interpretation. Also, linguistic and cultural differences come into play as words and stories are passed from language to language or from culture to culture, or both. Then there is the "telephone effect" of passing down stories verbally with each progression more detail gets added, subtracted, or changed.

THE PHILOSOPHY IN *GOSPEL OF THOMAS*

Thomas does seem to have an interest in passing down the pure sayings of his Master. Each saying Thomas recorded could be treated as a mustard seed with the potential of developing into bigger and grander concepts. They could parallel human consciousness and development. Thomas and his followers interpreted Jesus, or who they referred to in their Hebrew writings as Yeshua (sometimes Yeshiva or other spellings) to be fully **Gnostic** in nature and in His message.

Yeshua asked His Disciples, **"*Who am I to you?*"** Thomas replied, ***"Master, my mouth could never utter what you are like."*** This was a **Gnostic** practice of not specifically saying ***"Jesus is this"*** or ***"Jesus is that."*** This has its roots from the ancient Hebrews when ***Yhwh*** represented "the one who has no name" or "He who shall remain nameless," (sometimes spelled out as Yahweh). The **Gnostics** and other theologians do not concern themselves with finding names for the unnamable, but "**remain silent**." To them, Yeshua ***"Is What He Is."*** No one human has ever possessed a complete vision of Him. Yeshua is complete power and love. He describes himself just simple as, "**I Am.**" This is what places the ***Gospel of Thomas*** in the **"Gnostic"** realm of Gospels; not to be confused with other forms of ***Gnosticism*** whose main concern is the dualism or non-dualism of Jesus.

Jesus appears in Thomas' Gospel as one who wants to awaken the higher state of consciousness within each one of us. Thomas is on par with a similar passage in the ***Gospel of John***, ***"Where I am, I also wish you to be... the Spirit given me by my Father, I also have given to you...I am in you, and you are in me...."*** Jesus wants us to become more cognizant of our origins and in turn our future of boundless freedom.

He reminds us that we come from dust and to dust we shall return. In the ***Gospel of Mary Magdalene,*** we are reminded "***All that is composed shall be decomposed***." Another work tells us, "***We are light, and return to light***." But we are assured that within us is a sun that never sets. Reality is that we are neither male nor female, but that we are fully both. **Gnostics** claim that it is the integration of our masculinity and femininity that we are able to attain fullness.

It is important to cross from limited to unlimited consciousness. The ***Gospel of Thomas*** commands us, "***Be passersby!***" The main way to raise consciousness comes from attaining knowledge, or **gnosis,** about ourselves and the "Living One" that is within each one of us. The ***Gospel of Thomas*** encourages us not only to be "good Christians" but to become like Christ or awakened human beings.

The mission of Jesus in the ***Gospel of Thomas*** is markedly different from the Jesus portrayed in the four canonical Gospels. The difference is not as much in the nature of Jesus Christ but in the presentation of Jesus' teachings. It is a difference in the interpretation of the words

He spoke. It is possible to interpret Jesus' words differently as they are presented in ***Matthew, Mark, Luke***, and ***John***. Leaving the **Gnostic** points out of the equation, it is arguably the feeling of many scholars that the ***Gospel of Thomas*** is a superior Gospel to the chosen canonical Gospels. It is probably the only authentic Gospel that hasn't been diluted by narratives and Thomas just presents the unadulterated sayings of Jesus Christ.

IMPORTANT POINT: Maybe we should cherish the differences in the Gospels and read ALL the Gospels and digest their different points of view and seek out the points of view that make most sense to us and is able to let us attain that higher level of intelligence – the ultimate goal. **We should learn to find and listen to the Divine Spirit within us.**

Is it possible to read a scripture such as the ***Gospel of Thomas*** without any embellishing narratives and just allow it to speak for itself, let the words make their way into our hearts and minds, transform our lives, and gain our full potential? Silent meditation of Jesus' sayings can be so beneficial.

What is great about the discovery of the ***Gospel of Thomas*** at Nag Hammadi is that it is a complete Coptic version of the 114 "sayings." It has been well-known that there existed a collection of "sayings of Jesus" from the early years. Luke had indicated that "many Gospels" had already been written by the time he had written his Gospel (***Luke*** 1:1-4). It is widely believed that the same written source was behind and was used by Matthew and Mark to write their Gospels. Paul draws from the collection of Jesus' sayings when he quotes Jesus, "***It is more blessed to give than to receive***" (***Acts*** 20:35) which is found in none of the canonical

Gospels. Paul frequent drew from other texts that were already in circulation.

Origen quotes in his homily on ***Jeremiah*** 3:3 something we found from where it came, Logion [Saying] 82 in ***The Gospel of Thomas, "He who is near me is near the fire. He who is far from me is far from the Kingdom."***

Origen said he had "***read somewhere***" Jesus said, and Augustine quoted, what we now find is ***Gospel of Thomas'*** Logion 52: ***"His Disciples said to Him, 'Twenty-four prophets spoke in Israel and they all spoke about You.' He said to them, 'You have dismissed the Living One who is before you and spoken about the dead'."*** Augustine admitted ignorance of the source but was sure it came from a "non-canonical" source.

It has always amazed Biblical scholars that there are **272 verses that can be found in common between the *Gospels of Matthew* and *Luke* but completely absent from the *Gospel of Mark*.** This led to the assumption that there had to be an earlier collection of "logia" or, as the Germans believe it to be the "***Quelle***" (translated as the "source") or simply referred to "***Q***" by the scholars. To take it a step further, there are some scholars who believe that the collection of sayings believed to be "***Q***" could very well be the ***Gospel of Thomas.*** In all fairness, there is another group of scholars who maintain an opposite view about the ***Gospel of Thomas.***

Most of the 114 logia in the ***Gospel of Thomas*** are just mere isolated "sayings" out of their context. We don't know whether they are taken out of a dialogue between Jesus and Thomas or some other person. Or whether they are answers given by Jesus to specific questions asked of Him. Are they one person's interpretation of Jesus' parables? Could they be just one person's personal theology? But let us assume the best scenario and consider it the verbatim sayings of Jesus Christ written down by one of His trusted Disciples, Thomas.

For the **Gnostics** there is another important angle, all 114 logia have a **Gnostic** flavor that runs through them. While some of the sayings are blatantly not "**Gnostic**" they do seem to parallel the historic **Gnostic** teachings. Also, take into consideration that the monastic community which hid this Gospel along with all the other similar texts at Nag Hammadi was **Gnostic** leaning. A case can be made that the inclusion of the ***Gospel of Thomas*** with this library of banned books due to their **Gnostic** proclivity can only mean that the monastic community considered the **Gospel of Thomas** to also be a **Gnostic** work. Remember that the **Gnostics** were among the earliest Christian theologians. It was only because the power of the emerging Christian Church, especially as sanctioned by Roman Emperor Constantine, the lesser organized theologies were pushed aside. In reality that is an understatement, they were regarded as downright heretical and they needed to be extinguished as dangerous rivals of "orthodox" Christian Church. It was easy for the empowered Christian Church to order their non-canonical texts banned and destroyed. Luckily, some remnants survived.

IMPORTANT POINT: In retrospect, when we look at the theology contained in the ***Gospel of Thomas,*** as **"Gnostic"** as it seems to be, it has to be admitted that the ***Gospel of Thomas*** is not all bad and has solid Christian values.

It is important to note that in both the Coptic version and the Greek version of the ***Gospel of Thomas*** claim that "these are '***secret words***' which the '***Living Jesus***' spoke that were recorded by '**Didymus Judas Thomas**'."

The expression "***secret words***" could mean in **Gnostic** terms that these words were not meant for everyone as they have deeper "secret" or "hidden" meanings. Usually, they are reserved for the ones who possess the "**gnosis**" or special knowledge. "***Living Jesus***" is how **Gnostics** refer to the post-resurrected "**Eternal Christ**" in contrast to the "**incarnate Jesus**" who was manifested to the Disciples and world.

Logion 92 supports that Jesus only gave these secret teachings after his resurrection. The **Gnostics** did not believe Jesus' post-resurrection ministry was limited to the forty days as told in ***Acts***. There is no consensus on the exact time that transpired from His resurrection to His ascension. In his ***Against Heresy***, it was documented by Irenaeus that the **Valentinian Gnostics** believed it was more like 18 months. As they were not that far away from those events, makes you wonder why they said that. ***Pistis Sophia*** claims it was more like eleven years!

The Disciple we call Thomas was formally **Didymus Judas Thomas.** "**Didymus**" is the Greek for "the twin" (***John*** 11:16, 20:24); just as "***Thom"*** is the Aramaic word for "twin" and the root of the word Thomas. The Disciple Thomas was a favorite among **Syrian Christian** converts. In some of the apocryphal books, he is known by the name of **"Judas."** For reasons unknown, he was referred to as the twin brother of Jesus, i.e. as far as we know Jesus was a singular birth. It may be that Thomas was more enlightened than the other Disciples because of the secret knowledge given to him.

The **Gnostics** believe Jesus had given Thomas the "**gnosis**" [*John* 7:38-39] because he apparently was the recorder of the revelations imparted by Jesus, some of these have "**secret words**" or teachings embedded within. In the four canonical Gospels, there are sayings of Jesus that can be found in the earlier ***Gospel of Thomas.*** This means the ***Gospel of Thomas*** was not only known to the writers of ***Matthew, Mark, Luke,*** and ***John*** but it was revered by them otherwise they would not quote it. The ***Gospel of Thomas*** really does deserve the honor of being called ***The Fifth Gospel.***

There are two other similar apocryphal Gospels that were revealed to us: **The Gospel According to the Hebrews** and **The Gospel According to the Egyptians.** References were made to these Gospels in other early Christian writings. Clement of Alexandria quotes Jesus from the ***Gospel of the Hebrews***, "***He that marvels shall reign, and he that has reigned shall rest***" (***Stromata II***, 9:45). This is also found as Logion 3 in the ***Gospel of Thomas*** which is the closest to Clement's quote but without the "***and he that has reigned shall rest.***" Regardless, the source of this statement is definitely from **The *Gospel According to the Hebrews*.**

In Logion 104 "they" [probably meaning His Disciples] urged Jesus to join them in their fasting and praying. Jesus asked what sin He committed that He should fast and pray. Jesus said there would be plenty of time for fasting when the bridegroom left the bridal chamber. This can also be found in ***The Gospel According to the Hebrews.*** Logion 104 with its reference to fasting can also be found in ***The Gospel of the Nazarenes*** which could be a form of ***The Gospel According to the Hebrews.*** Legion 22 is very similar to what appears in ***The Gospel According to the Egyptians*** about how in Kingdom all differences disappear including between the sexes, "***the male will not be male and the female will not be female...***"

IMPORTANT POINT: Any way you look at it, there is a complex relationship among these ancient texts. Was the ***Gospel of Thomas*** the earlier source document for many other writings including the four canonical Gospels? Or was it the other way around? Or did everyone copy from each other?

IMPORTANT NOTE: It was at the Council of Carthage in A.D. 397 that the Bishops, as ordered from the Council of Nicaea in 325 and Constantine, published the sole "authentic," "authoritative," and "authorized" (a/k/a canonized) list of Christian texts which formed the "New Testament" of the Christian Church. Any and all other texts were banned and ordered destroyed. This included the ***Gospel of Thomas, the Gospel of Peter, the Gospel of Philip, the Gospel of James*** and dozens of other texts attributed to the Jesus' Inner Circle of Twelve Disciples. Let us hope they were truly "Divinely" inspired to do what they did and it was 100% correct; otherwise they have done a GREAT disservice to Christianity up to and including completely ruining it.

GNOSTICISM IN THE *GOSPEL OF THOMAS*

When Thomas sayings were being compiled sometime in the 2nd Century, Christian "theology" was not yet formed. In fact, it has been noted that the Gnostics were more systematic in coalescing their common theology. In reality, Christian theology was highly fragmented throughout the developed world until Constantine called the Council of Nicaea in 325 for the specific purpose of forming the One, Catholic (universal), and Apostolic Christian Church.

As of this result of this Council, the "theology" of the Disciple Thomas was "Gnostic theology" which was rejected by the universal Christian Church, although the theology of Thomas was the mildest expression of Gnosticism.

In ***The Gnostic Problem*** (p. 106) the author Wilson puts **Gnosticism** in perspective, "***Gnosticism is not simply a depraved form of Christianity. It has deep roots in the Hellenistic world. It weaves into Christianity threads of Greek philosophy uniting the Christian concept of redemption with the Greek concept of deliverance from the world and its controlling powers."***

But why wasn't the ***Gospel of Thomas,*** a Gospel purportedly by one of Jesus' Disciples, included with the accepted (a/k/a orthodox) Scriptures at the Council of Carthage in A.D. 397? The Church leaders during the 2nd and 3rd centuries (e.g. Irenaeus, Clement, Origen, Tertullian) thought it was too **Gnostic.** But that is the same reason they did not include the Gospels and Epistles of other Disciples like Peter, James, Philip, Judas, and Mary Magdalene. They were too **Gnostic** so therefore they must be fraudulent. A lot more is discussed about this in ***Alternative Christianities: Volume I.*** It is highly possible that these Church Leaders were the ones who were wrong. Bottom line: because of them we all may be following the wrong Christian path that Jesus Christ really intended for us. Remember, ***Matthew, Mark, Luke,*** and ***John*** were not written by any Disciple, who were illiterate, and also are purportedly attributed to them. Looking at some of the theology and philosophy in the ***Gospel of Thomas***, and other so-called "**Gnostic"** texts, it moves **Christianity out of their historical Judaic-Hebrew roots and instead mixes it with ancient Greco-Hellenistic mystical roots.**

IMPORTANT RELATIONSHIPS

LOGIA REGARDING THE FATHER

One common factor in the study of ***world religions*** is their **concept of God**. It has to be a deity that man would like to worship and be able in whom to put his faith and hope. "Worship" comes to us from the old English meaning to "have worth." A person with "worth" is high on a man's list of priorities. Also, it has to be someone he can be put on a pedestal for him to look up to and try to emulate him/her to become "god-like."

Many **Gnostic** schools considered the "god of creation" to be an evil, malicious, and corrupt god. In ***The Apocryphon of John***, another discarded Disciple's text found at the Nag Hammadi, his name is **Yaldabaoth,** the son of Sophia who was a low level "Aeons." It was her unstable nature that led to her fall from the Supremes' divine realm and expulsion. Against the divine rules about procreation, she conceived and produced a son. He created and took command over this world and humanity. It was he who later struggled with the Supreme Being in the Garden of Eden over allowing Adam and Eve to know the truth about their creation. The Supreme Being won and Adam and Eve received the "***gnosis"*** or superior knowledge. It is a whole other story, but the serpent was one of the "good guys" who enlightened Adam and Eve with the superior knowledge.

None of this is discussed in the ***Gospel of Thomas***. Thomas more agrees with John that the Father and Son, Jesus, are one person or the son is an extension of the Father. This was also stated in Logion 15:

"When you see him who was not born of woman

> ***Fall upon your faces and worship him. He is your Father."***

It is generally considered that "***him who was not born of woman***" means He is **God**, ***he who is not a human being.*** He is also ***unseen.*** This can also reference the Son. When the Disciples realized Jesus Christ's ***true nature*** they came to believe He truly was God and as such "**One with His Father.**"

Logion 50: Another identification of Jesus the Son ("**The Light**") and God the Father ("**The Living Father**") is:

> ***"Jesus said, 'If they ask you, 'What is your origin?'***
>
> ***Answer them, 'Our origin is the Light, where the Light of itself came to be...'***
>
> ***If they ask, 'Who are you?'***
>
> ***Answer, 'We are His sons and the chosen of the Living Father....'."***

The most frequently personal expression used to describe the Supreme Being is ***"Father."*** Throughout history, the Supreme Being was always referred to as **"He who shall remain nameless"** or **"He whose name we dare not speak."** In ancient Hebrew texts when the Almighty was asked His name, they really never got an answer. They improvised. Throughout the Gospels, the Divine Realm was repeatedly referred to as ***"the Kingdom of the Father," "the Kingdom of God,"*** or ***"the Kingdom of Heaven."*** In the same tradition, true **Gnostics** would not utter the name of Jesus. Likewise, Thomas is reluctant to do so (Logion 13). Only in Logion 100 does Thomas refer to the Supreme Being generically when he says "***Give to God, God's things.***" Elsewhere Thomas refers to the deity ***"Father"*** in Logia 3, 27, 40, 44, 50, 57, 61, 64, 69, 76, 83, 96, 97, 98, 99, and 113).

LOGION REGARDING THE HOLY SPIRIT

There is only one reference to the Holy Spirit in the ***Gospel of Thomas*** in Logion 44 regarding blasphemy:

> ***"Jesus said, 'Whoever blasphemes the Father, it shall be forgiven him.***
>
> ***Whoever blasphemes the Son, it shall be forgiven him.***
>
> ***Whoever blasphemes the Holy Spirit, it shall not be forgiven him either on earth or in heaven'."***

LOGIA REGARDING JESUS

Logion 44: The ***Gospel of Thomas*** may be considered "Trinitarian" as far as Jesus Christ is definitely presented as a deity. Thomas' other references to the importance of Jesus Christ are found throughout his logia:

Logion 31: Jesus is the prophet without honor in His own village, the physician who will not be called by those who know Him.

Logion 38: He is the one who will one day be sought but not found by men (probably a reference to his death).

<u>Logion 61:</u> He reclines at the table with Salome and speaks to her of His having come from the Father to reveal light to those in darkness.

<u>Logion 78:</u> He appears to be the man unbent by the winds and living the rugged life of the open (a reference which in the Synoptic Gospels is applied to John the Baptist).

<u>Logion 99:</u> This man Jesus is sought by His anxious mother and brothers.

<u>Logion 100:</u> He is asked to settle the mundane question of paying taxes.

<u>Logion 104:</u> He is so human that He must face the question of fasting.

<u>Logion 105:</u> He is so human that enemies not knowing the identity of His father called Him the "son of a harlot."

These logia deal mainly with the human side of Jesus in the ***Gospel of Thomas.*** There are other logia that reference His ***death as being the sacrificial lamb that brings us redemption*** (Logion 60).

The thing that is noticeably different than in the synoptic Gospels is that in the ***Gospel of Thomas*** Jesus is called the "***risen Christ".*** The Gospel begins with introducing Him as "***the Living Jesus***" and the "author" of the "sayings" Thomas is about to reveal. Logion 1 tells us that the sayings mean "**life**" and it is important to find the hidden meaning within them; failure to find the meaning is "**death.**" This first Logion can also be considered referring to the "**gnosis**" or the special knowledge given by <u>**divine revelation**</u> resulting in a superior <u>**human understanding**</u> of the divine world.

Logion 37: Jesus tells His Disciples when they see Him again they will refer to Him as the "***Son of the Living***."

Logion 24: The Disciples ask Jesus to show them the "place" where He is. Jesus answers with ambiguous words that He was ***a "light" within men to dispel their darkness.***

Logion 28: Jesus speaks that He is ***present in the world*** having to come into the world to examine men. Jesus said that He found them "***drunk***" (could be interpreted as being ignorant of salvation) but yet none of them "***thirsting for water***" meaning that these **men were so "*blind*" and did not see that the world is just a temporary place**. Jesus said that **He longs for when men will throw off their "*drunkenness*" and being "*thirsting*" for the water that He offers**.

Logion 43: Jesus rebuking His disciples because they do not recognize His ***identity*** and His ***teachings.*** He tells them they are "***like the Jews who love the tree but hate the fruit, or love the fruit but hate the tree.***"

Logion 44: Is about the sin of blaspheming the Holy Spirit for which by its very nature there is no forgiveness.

Logion 46: Is about the distinction and properly recognizing the true nature of Jesus and John.

Logion 47: Interweaves putting new wine into an old wineskin, the impossibility of riding two horses in different directions, and shooting arrows at different targets. All can be taken as having faith in two different Gods.

LOGIA REGARDING THE WORLD

Even in the ***Gospel of Thomas*** the "world" is referred to as a **Gnostic** dualistic theme: the ***world below*** or the **material** world, and the ***world above*** or the **spiritual** world. One is man's ***gaol*** (jail) and the other is man's ***goal***. He can only reach his ***goal*** by escape the ***gaol,*** this material world that imprisons him, when attains the **"*gnosis*"** or the special higher knowledge.

Logion 12: Considers this material world of ours is an evil world. Throughout the Gnostic writings, this material world is considered corrupt while others go as far saying that this world was created by an inferior and corrupt god.

Logion 56: This material world is not the home for one who truly has attained the ***"gnosis"*** or secret knowledge.

Logion 21: One must be on guard against the evils of this material world.

Logia 56, 60 and 80: Say to know the true nature of this evil world is to realize that it is a corpse.

Logion 87: One must not depend upon this material and evil world.

Logia 21, 36 and 37: Says this world should be stripped off as if it was old clothes: this is very similar to what is expressed in ***Matthew*** 6 (Logion 36) on the unimportance of a person's clothes; and Paul's teaching about to put off the old and putting on the new (***Col***. 3:8-14; ***Eph***. 4:22-24).

Logia 83 and 84: Tells us that the ***world above*** should be the goal for those who have attained the ***"gnosis"*** or secret knowledge; it is a world of "light" and "images." The

Father is the "light" and His "image" is His eternal nature. For those who have attained the ***"gnosis"*** will also be able to see the ***"images"*** of the world above; seeing them will bring great joy in knowing about one's true temporary place in this material and evil world. This is one of the ***earliest*** statements about the duplicity of material and spiritual worlds, but it also indicates man's emanation from this world.

Logion 76: Tells us that the ***world above*** is an abiding treasure.

Logion 24: Says that the ***world above*** is the place where Jesus dwells in "light".

Logion 4: The ***world above*** is the "place" where there is the real Life.

LOGIA REGARDING MAN

The ***Gospel of Thomas*** tells us that man also has a **dualistic** nature. A man may be a product of this world but he originated in the ***world above*** and it is his ultimate goal is to return to the ***world above***. This could be what Jesus is trying to explain to His Disciples in Logion 18:

> ***"The disciples said to Jesus, 'Tell us what our end will be like.'***
>
> ***Jesus said, 'Have you already discovered the beginning and now you ask about the end?***
>
> ***Where the beginning is, there the end will be.***
>
> ***Blessed is the one who will stand at the beginning and will know the end and will not taste death'."***

<u>Logion 49:</u> The "elect" come from the Kingdom of the Father, to which they will return. It is important to realize that our origin is in the ***world above.*** It is our goal to leave this ***world below*** and return to the ***world above.*** This is one of the wonders when a person attains the "***gnosis***."

<u>Logion 19:</u> Continues on this theme by telling us, "***him who was before he came to be***."

<u>Logia 59 and 70:</u> Man will die in this material world. Those who have <u>not</u> attain the ***"gnosis,"*** the enlightenment, are apprehensive about dying. Conversely, those who have attained the ***"gnosis"*** dying have no such apprehension.

<u>Logia 49, 50, 61, and 75:</u> Man's destiny is to release himself from this transitory world and transcend it to be in perfect union with the Father and with the world of light.

<u>LOGIA REGARDING SIN AND SALVATION</u>

In the ***Gospel of Thomas*** sin and salvation are opposite values. Sin is the negative value and indicates a lack of salvation. Salvation is the positive value of one being free from sin. The "**Gnosticism**" in the ***Gospel of Thomas*** is portrayed as a means to salvation in a mystical way. Sin is to hold on to our material things. Salvation is to give up all our worldly things.

<u>Logion 36:</u> The true **Gnostic** would have no concern for mundane things such as clothing. It is a sin to hold on to such things.

<u>Logion 63:</u> It is also a sin for the rich man to try to nourish his ***soul*** with material things. To cling to material things such as clothes is a sin.

Logion 55: To cling to the ties of this world, even if it is within one's own family, is sin; However to hate one's father, mother, brothers, and sisters, and instead follow Jesus' way of the cross is salvation.

Logion 101: Emphasizes a human mother-child relationship is from birth to death; however, a divine mother-child relationship gives birth to life.

Logia 6 and 14: Claims that the practices of formal religions with alms-giving, praying, and fasting are sins.

Logion 53: Even circumcision, the most cherished expression of God's covenant, is unnecessary and serves no purpose when it comes to our spirituality.

Logion 101: Sex is just an impulse and expression; it must be given up. **To have sex and bring more people into the bondage of this material, evil, and suffering world is a sin.**

Logion 22: In reality, there is no difference between males and females because any worldly difference will be erased when you enter the Kingdom.

THE KINGDOM OF THE FATHER

The ***Gospel of Thomas*** considers the only men who have received the "***gnosis***" can enter the Kingdom. Thomas usually refers to the "***Kingdom of the Father***" which parallels with three synoptic Gospels which uses the terms the "***Kingdom of Heaven***" or the "***Kingdom of God***." **When you read the many Kingdom sayings in the *Gospel of Thomas* they echo multiple words and ideas from the Synoptics (the three similar Gospels).**

IMPORTANT POINT: The "***Kingdom of the Father,***" the "***Kingdom of Heaven***" or the "***Kingdom of God***" is this ***world below***; it is the ***world above***; it is the present; it is the past; it is the future; it is the visible; it is invisible; it is spiritual; it is inside you; it is outside you; and it is all very real. In the ***Gospel of Thomas***, the "***Kingdom***" is referred to as the "***world above"*** as opposed to the current place where we are living on is the ***"world below."***

Death in the ***Gospel of Thomas*** simply means being released from this evil material world for those who attain the *"**gnosis.**"* According to Logion 11, it would be the end for those who have not reached this spiritual level. There is no mention of a human resurrection in the ***Gospel of Thomas***. In the original Coptic version of the ***Gospel of Thomas,*** there are no references to human resurrection that are found in the Greek version. The Coptic Logia 5 and 6 reference that ***Death was freedom from the body.*** Also in the ***Gospel of Thomas,*** there is no "final judgment." Your judgment is happening while you are ***in this world.*** To be released from this material world is also to be released from Hell.

IMPORTANT POINT: Along the lines of the Greek philosophers, the Gnostic had no desire for their bodies to be resurrected. They are perfectly happy with spending eternity in the happy, carefree, and pleasant ***Kingdom***.

Also in the ***Gospel of Thomas,*** there is no reference to a Second Coming of Christ:

Logion 12: Has the familiar story of when His Disciples ask Jesus when He goes away, who will be their leader. There is no mention of Jesus' return by the Disciples or by Jesus Himself.

Logion 24: The Disciples ask Jesus to show them where He dwells so that they may seek Him. This indicates that they are not anticipating that Jesus will return, but they want to dwell with Him. When the Disciples asked Jesus, "***When will we see you?***" Jesus answered them; they will see Him in His true nature when they stripped of the world and all its necessities.

Logion 49: For those who have attained the "**gnosis**," eternity will be a return to the world of light, the "Kingdom" from where they have come. It is a wonderful destiny with complete freedom from this material world. The ***Gospel of Thomas*** tells us that the Kingdom is here and now.

Logion 3: Jesus tells us that the Kingdom is spiritual; it is *internal* not *external.*

EPILOGUE

This chapter contained more of an interpretation and discussion of the ***Gospel of Thomas,*** but the next chapter is the complete and full version of the ***Gospel of Thomas*** for you to make your own conclusions.

BIBLIOGRAPHY, REFERENCE, AND FURTHER READING:

Barnstone, Willis, ***Restored New Testament: A New Translation with Commentary, Including the Gnostic Gospels of Thomas, Mary, and Judas***
© 2009 Harper, San Francisco, California

Pagels, Elaine, ***Beyond Belief: The Secret Gospel of Thomas*** © 2003 Vintage Books-Random House, New York

Pagels, Elaine, ***Gnostic Gospels, The: A Startling Account of the Meaning of Jesus and the Origin of Christianity Based on the Gnostic Gospels and Other Secret Texts.***
© 1989, 1979 Vintage Books-Random House, New York

Meyers, Marvin, and Willis Barnstone, ***Gnostic Bible, The***
© 2003 Harper, San Francisco, California

Davies, Stevan, ***Gospel of Thomas: A Guidebook for Spiritual Practice.***
© 2004 Skylight Paths Publishing, Vermont

Davies, Stevan, ***Gospel of Thomas: Annotated and Explained***
© 2006, 2002 Skylight Paths Publishing, Vermont

Deloup, Jean Yves, ***Gospel of Thomas: The Gnostic Wisdon of Jesus***
© 2005, 1986

Summers, Ray ***An Interesting and Enlightening Study of the GOSPEL OF THOMAS: The Controversial 4th Century Manuscript Recently Discovered at Nag Hammadi.***
© 1968 Word Books, Waco, Texas

van Unnik, W.C., ***Newly Discovered Gnostic Writings,***
© 1960 Alec R. Allenson, Inc. Naperville, Illinois

Till, W.C. "**New Sayings of Jesus in the Recently Discovered Coptic '*Gospel of Thomas'*,"** ***Bulletin of the John Rylands Library, XLI*** © 1959

Guillaumont, A., H. C. Puech, G. Quispel, W. C. Till, and Y. A. A. Mashih, ***The Gospel According to Thomas,***
© 1959, Harper and Brothers, New York, N.Y.

Doresse, Jean, ***The Secret Book of the Egyptian Gnostics,***© 1960, The Viking Press, New York

Hennecke, Edgar, ***New Testament Apocrypha***, W. Schneemelcher ed.,
© 1963, The Westminster Press, Philadephia

Gaertner, Bertil, ***The Theology of the Gospel According to Thomas,*** ©1961, New York: Harper and Brothers

Montefiore, Hugh, and H. E. W. Turner, ***Thomas and the Evangelists,***
© 1962, Naperville, Illinois: Alex R. Allenson, Inc.

Grant, R.M.,***The Interpreter's Dictionary of the Bible***,
© 1962, New York: Abingdon Press

Grant, R.M., ***Gnosticism and Early Christianity***,
© 1959, New York: Columbia University Press

This Book and Treatise are a compilation
from many sources on the same subject.
See the Complete List of Bibliographies, References,
and Suggested Readings in Appendix II

CHAPTER 10

THE COMPLETE SECRET GOSPEL OF THOMAS

These are the secret sayings which the living Jesus spoke and which Didymos Judas Thomas wrote down.

(1) And he said, "Whoever finds the interpretation of these sayings will not experience death."

(2) Jesus said, "Let him who seeks to continue seeking until he finds. When he finds, he will become troubled. When he becomes troubled, he will be astonished, and he will rule over the all."

(3) Jesus said, "If those who lead you say to you, 'See, the Kingdom is in the sky,' then the birds of the sky will precede you. If they say to you, 'It is in the sea,'

then the fish will precede you. Rather, the Kingdom is inside of you, and it is outside of you. When you come to know yourselves, then you will become known, and you will realize that it is you who are the sons of the living Father. But if you will not know yourselves, you dwell in poverty and it is you who are that poverty."

(4) Jesus said, "The man old in days will not hesitate to ask a small child seven days old about the place of life, and he will live. For many who are first will become last, and they will become one and the same."

(5) Jesus said, "Recognize what is in your sight, and that which is hidden from you will become plain to you. For there is nothing hidden which will not become manifest."

(6) His Disciples questioned Him and said to Him, "Do you want us to fast? How shall we pray? Shall we give alms? What diet shall we observe?"

Jesus said, "Do not tell lies, and do not do what you hate, for all things are plain in the sight of Heaven. For nothing hidden will not become manifested, and nothing covered will remain without being uncovered."

(7) Jesus said, "Blessed is the lion which becomes a man when consumed by man, and cursed is the man whom the lion consumes, and the lion becomes a man."

(8) And He said, "The man is like a wise fisherman who cast his net into the sea and drew it up from the sea full of small fish. Among them, the wise fisherman found a fine large fish. He threw all the small fish back into the sea and chose the large fish without difficulty. Whoever has ears to hear, let him hear."

(9) Jesus said, "Now the sower went out, took a handful of seeds, and scattered them. Some fell on the road; the birds came and gathered them up. Others fell on rock, did not take root in the soil, and did not produce ears. And others fell on thorns; they choked the seeds and worms ate them. And others fell on the good soil and produced good fruit: it bore sixty per measure and a hundred and twenty per measure."

(10) Jesus said, "I have cast fire upon the World, and see, I am guarding it until it blazes."

(11) Jesus said, "This heaven will pass away, and the one above it will pass away. The dead are not alive, and the living will not die. In the days when you consumed what is dead, you made it what is alive. When you come to dwell in the light, what will you do? On the day when you were one, you became two. But when you become two, what will you do?"

(12) The Disciples said to Jesus, "We know that you will depart from us. Who is to be our leader?" Jesus said to them, "Wherever you are, you are to go to James the righteous, for whose sake heaven and earth come into being."

(13) Jesus said to His Disciples, "Compare me to someone and tell me whom I am like."

Simon Peter said to Him, "You are like a righteous angel."

Matthew said to Him, "You are like a wise philosopher."

Thomas said to Him, "Master, my mouth is wholly incapable of saying whom you are like."

Jesus said, "I am not your master. Because you have drunk, you have become intoxicated from the bubbling spring which I have measured out."

And He took him and withdrew and told him three things. When Thomas returned to his companions, they asked him, "What did Jesus say to you?"

Thomas said to them, "If I tell you one of the things which He told me, you will pick up stones and throw them at me; a fire will come out of the stones and burn you up."

(14) Jesus said to them, "If you fast, you will give rise to sin for yourselves; and if you pray, you will be condemned; and if you give alms, you will do harm to your spirits. When you go into any land and walk about in the districts, if they receive you, eat what they will set before you, and heal the sick among them. For what goes into your mouth will not defile you, but that which issues from your mouth-it is that which will defile you."

(15) Jesus said, "When you see one who was not born of woman, prostrate yourselves on your faces and worship him. That one is your Father."

(16) Jesus said, "Men think, perhaps, that it is peace which I have come to cast upon the World. They do not know that it is dissension which I have come to cast upon the earth: fire, sword, and war. For there will be five in a house: three will be against two, and two against three, the father against the son, and the son against the father. And they will stand solitary."

(17) Jesus said, "I shall give you what no eye has seen and what no ear has heard and what no hand has touched and what has never occurred to the human mind."

(18) The Disciples said to Jesus, "Tell us how our end will be." Jesus said, "Have you discovered, then, the beginning, that you look for the end? For where the beginning is, there will the end be. Blessed is he who will take his place in the beginning; he will know the end and will not experience death."

(19) Jesus said, "Blessed is he who came into being before he came into being. If you become my disciples and listen to my words, these stones will minister to you. For there are five trees for you in Paradise which remain undisturbed summer and winter and whose leaves do not fall. Whoever becomes acquainted with them will not experience death."

(20) The Disciples said to Jesus, "Tell us what the Kingdom of Heaven is like."

He said to them, "It is like a mustard seed, the smallest of all seeds. But when it falls on tilled soil, it produces a great plant and becomes a shelter for birds of the sky."

(21) Mary said to Jesus, "Whom are your disciples like?" **[Most scholars believe the Mary referred to is Mary Magdalene]**

He said, "They are like children who have settled in a field which is not theirs. When the owners of the field come, they will say, 'Let us have back our field.' They will undress in their presence in order to let them have back their field and to give it back to them. Therefore I say to you, if the owner of a house knows that the thief is coming, he will begin his vigil before he comes and will not let him dig through into the house of his domain to carry away his goods. You, then, be on your guard against the World. Arm yourselves with great strength lest the robbers find a way to come to you, for the difficulty which you expect will surely materialize. Let there be among you a man of understanding. When the grain ripened, he came quickly with his sickle in his hand and reaped it. Whoever has ears to hear, let him hear."

(22) Jesus saw infants being suckled. He said to his Disciples, "These infants being suckled are like those who enter the Kingdom."

They said to Him, "Shall we then, as children, enter the Kingdom?"

Jesus said to them, "When you make the two one, and when you make the inside like the outside and the outside like the inside, and the above like the below, and when you make the male and the female one and the same, so that the male not be male nor the female be female; and when you fashion eyes in place of an eye, and a hand in place of a hand, and a foot in place of a foot, and a likeness in place of a likeness; then will you enter the Kingdom."

(23) Jesus said, "I shall choose you, one out of a thousand, and two out of ten thousand, and they shall stand as a single one."

(24) His Disciples said to Him, "Show us the place where you are since it is necessary for us to seek it."

He said to them, "Whoever has ears, let him hear. There is a light within a man of light, and he lights up the whole World. If he [or: it] does not shine, he is darkness."

(25) Jesus said, "Love your brother like your soul, guard him like the pupil of your eye."

(26) Jesus said, "You see the mote in your brother's eye, but you do not see the beam in your own eye. When you cast the beam out of your own eye, then you will see clearly to cast the mote from your brother's eye."

(27) Jesus said, "If you do not fast as regards the World, you will not find the Kingdom. If you do not observe the Sabbath as a Sabbath you will not see the Father."

(28) Jesus said, "I took My place in the midst of the World, and I appeared to them in flesh. I found all of them intoxicated; I found none of them thirsty. And My soul became afflicted for the sons of men, because they are blind in their hearts and do not have sight; for empty they came into the World, and empty too they seek to leave the World. But for the moment they are intoxicated. When they shake off their wine, then they will repent."

(29) Jesus said, "If the flesh came into being because of spirit, it is a wonder. But if spirit came into being because of the body, it is a wonder of wonders. Indeed, I am amazed at how this great wealth has made its home in this poverty."

(30) Jesus said, "Where there are three gods, they are gods. Where there are two or one, I am with him."

(31) Jesus said, "No prophet is accepted in his own village; no physician heals those who know him."

(32) Jesus said, "A city being built on a high mountain and fortified cannot fall, nor can it be hidden."

(33) Jesus said, "Preach from your housetops that which you will hear in your ear and in the other ear. For no one lights a lamp and puts it under a bushel, nor does he put it in a hidden place, but rather he sets it on a lampstand so that everyone who enters and leaves will see its light."

(34) Jesus said, "If a blind man leads a blind man, they will both fall into a pit."

(35) Jesus said, "It is not possible for anyone to enter the house of a strong man and take it by force unless he binds his hands; then he will be able to ransack his house."

(36) Jesus said, "Do not be concerned from morning until evening and from evening until morning about what you will wear."

(37) His Disciples said, "When will You become revealed to us and when shall we see You?" Jesus said, "When you disrobe without being ashamed and take up your garments and place them under your feet like little children and tread on them, then will you see the Son of the Living One, and you will not be afraid."

(38) Jesus said, "Many times have you desired to hear these words which I am saying to you, and you have no one else to hear them from. There will be days when you will look for Me and will not find Me."

(39) Jesus said, "The Pharisees and the scribes have taken the keys of knowledge and hidden them. They themselves have not entered nor have they allowed to enter those who wish to. You, however, be as wise as serpents and as innocent as doves."

(40) Jesus said, "A grapevine has been planted outside of the Father, but being unsound, it will be pulled up by its roots and destroyed."

(41) Jesus said, "Whoever has something in his hand will receive more, and whoever has nothing will be deprived of even the little he has."

(42) Jesus, "Become passers-by."

(43) His Disciples said to Him, "Who are You, that You should say these things to us?"

Jesus said to them, "You do not realize who I am from what I say to you, but you have become like the Jews, for they either love the tree and hate its fruit (or) love the fruit and hate the tree."

(44) Jesus said, "Whoever blasphemes against the Father will be forgiven, and whoever blasphemes against the Son will be forgiven, but whoever blasphemes against the Holy Spirit will not be forgiven either on earth or in Heaven."

(45) Jesus said, "Grapes are not harvested from thorns, nor are figs gathered from thistles, for they do not produce fruit. A good man brings forth good from his storehouse; an evil man brings forth evil things from his evil storehouse, which is in his heart and says evil things. For out of the abundance of the heart he brings forth evil things."

(46) Jesus said, "Among those born of women, from Adam until John the Baptist, there is no one so superior to John the Baptist that his eyes should not be lowered before him. Yet I have said, whichever one of you comes to be a child will be acquainted with the Kingdom and will become superior to John."

(47) Jesus said, "It is impossible for a man to mount two horses or to stretch two bows. And it is impossible for a servant to serve two masters; otherwise, he will honor the one and treat the other contemptuously. No man drinks old wine and immediately desires to drink new wine. And new wine is not put into old wineskins, lest they burst; nor is old wine put into a new wineskin, lest it spoils it. An old patch is not sewn onto a new garment, because a tear would result."

(48) Jesus said, "If two make peace with each other in this one house, they will say to the mountain, 'Move away,' and it will move away."

(49) Jesus said, "Blessed are the solitary and elect, for you will find the Kingdom. For you are from it, and to it you will return."

(50) Jesus said, "If they say to you, 'Where did you come from?' say to them, 'We came from the light, the place where the light came into being on its own accord and established itself and became manifest through their image.' If they say to you, 'Is it you?' say, 'We are its children, and we are the elect of the Living Father.' If they ask you, 'What is the sign of your Father in you?' Say to them, 'It is movement and repose.'"

(51) His Disciples said to Him, "When will the repose of the dead come about and when will the new World come?"

He said to them, "What you look forward to has already come, but you do not recognize it."

(52) His Disciples said to Him, “Twenty-four prophets spoke in Israel, and all of them spoke to you.”

He said to them, “You have omitted the One living in your presence and have spoken only of the dead.”

(53) His Disciples said to Him, “Is circumcision beneficial or not?”

He said to them, “If it were beneficial, their father would beget them already circumcised from their mother. Rather, the true circumcision in spirit has become completely profitable.”

(54) Jesus said, “Blessed are the poor, for yours is the Kingdom of Heaven.”

(55) Jesus said, “Whoever does not hate his father and his mother cannot become a disciple to Me. And whoever does not hate his brothers and sisters and take up his cross in My way will not be worthy of Me.”

(56) Jesus said, “Whoever has come to understand the World has found only a corpse, and whoever has found a corpse is superior to the World.”

(57) Jesus said, “The Kingdom of the Father is like a man who had a good seed. His enemy came by night and sowed weeds among the good seed. The man did not allow them to pull up the weeds; he said to them, ‘I am afraid that you will go intending to pull up the weeds and pull up the wheat along with them.’ For on the day of the harvest, the weeds will be plainly visible, and they will be pulled up and burned.”

(58) Jesus said, "Blessed is the man who has suffered and found life."

(59) Jesus said, "Take heed of the Living One while you are alive, lest you die and seek to see Him and be unable to do so."

(60) They saw a Samaritan carrying a lamb on his way to Judea.

He said to His Disciples, "Why does that man carry the lamb around?"

They said to Him, "So that he may kill it and eat it."

He said to them, "While it is alive, he will not eat it, but only when he has killed it and it has become a corpse."

They said to Him, "He cannot do so otherwise."

He said to them, "You too, look for a place for yourselves within Repose, lest you become a corpse and be eaten."

(61) Jesus said, "Two will rest on a bed: the one will die, and other will live."

Salome said, "Who are you, man, that you, as though from the One, (or: as whose son), that you have come up on my couch and eaten from my table?"

Jesus said to her, "I am He who exists from the Undivided. I was given some of the things of My Father."

Salome said, "I am your disciple."

Jesus said to her, "Therefore I say, if he is undivided, he will be filled with light, but if he is divided, he will be filled with darkness."

(62) Jesus said, "It is to those who are worthy of My mysteries that I tell My mysteries. Do not let your left hand know what your right hand is doing."

(63) Jesus said, "There was a rich man who had much money. He said, 'I shall put my money to use so that I may sow, reap, plant, and fill my storehouse with produce, with the result that I shall lack nothing.' Such were his intentions, but that same night he died. Let him who has ears hear."

(64) Jesus said, "A man had received visitors. And when he had prepared the dinner, he sent his servant to invite the guests. He went to the first one and said to him, 'My master invites you.' He said, 'I have claims against some merchants, They are coming to me this evening. I must go and give them my orders. I ask to be excused from the dinner. 'He went to another and said to him, 'My master has invited you.' He said to him, 'I have just bought a house and am required for the day. I shall not have any spare time.'

He went to another and said to him, 'My master invites you.' He said to him, 'My friend is going to get married, and I am to prepare the banquet. I shall not be able to come. I ask to be excused from the dinner.' He went to another and said to him, 'My master invites you.' He said to him, 'I have just bought a farm, and I am on my way to collect the rent. I shall not be able to come. I ask to be excused.' The servant returned and said to his master, 'Those whom you invited to the dinner have asked to be excused.' The master said to his servant, 'Go outside to the streets and bring back those whom you happen to meet, so that they may dine.' Businessmen and merchants will not enter the Places of my Father."

(65) He said, "There was a good man who owned a vineyard. He leased it to tenant farmers so that they might work it and he might collect the produce from them. He sent his servant so that the tenants might give him the produce of the vineyard. They seized his servant and beat him, all but killing him. The servant went back and told his master. The master said, 'Perhaps they did not recognize him.' He sent another servant. The tenants beat this one as well. Then the owner sent his son and said, 'Perhaps they will show respect to my son.' Because the tenants knew that it was he who was the heir to the vineyard, they seized him and killed him. Let him who has ears hear."

(66) Jesus said, "Show me the stone which the builders have rejected. That one is the cornerstone."

(67) Jesus said, "Whoever believes that the All itself is deficient is himself completely deficient."

(68) Jesus said, "Blessed are you when you are hated and persecuted. Wherever you have been persecuted they will find no Place."

(69) Jesus said, "Blessed are they who have been persecuted within themselves. It is they who have truly come to know the Father. Blessed are the hungry, for the belly of him who desires will be filled."

(70) Jesus said, "That which you have will save you if you bring it forth from yourselves. That which you do not have within you will kill you if you do not have it within you."

(71) Jesus said, "I shall destroy this house, and no one will be able to rebuild it."

(72) A man said to Him, "Tell my brothers to divide my father's possessions with me."

He said to him, "O man, who has made me a divider?"

He turned to his Disciples and said to them, "I am not a divider, am I?"

(73) Jesus said, "The harvest is great but the laborers are few. Beseech the Lord, therefore, to send out laborers to the harvest."

(74) He said, "O Lord, there are many around the drinking trough, but there is nothing in the cistern."

(75) Jesus said, "Many are standing at the door, but it is the solitary who will enter the bridal chamber."

(76) Jesus said, "The Kingdom of the Father is like a merchant who had a consignment of merchandise and who discovered a pearl. That merchant was shrewd. He sold the merchandise and bought the pearl alone for himself. You too, seek his unfailing and enduring treasure where no moth comes near to devour and no worm destroys."

(77) Jesus said, "It is I who am the light which is above them all. It is I who am the All. From Me did the All come forth, and unto Me did the All extend. Split a piece of wood, and I am there. Lift up the stone, and you will find Me there."

(78) Jesus said, "Why have you come out into the desert? To see a reed shaken by the wind? And to see a man clothed in fine garments like your kings and your great men? Upon them are the fine garments, and they are unable to discern the truth."

(79) A woman from the crowd said to Him, "Blessed is the womb which bore You and the breasts which nourished You."

He said to her, "Blessed are those who have heard the word of the Father and have truly kept it. For there will be days when you will say, 'Blessed are the womb which has not conceived and the breasts which have not given milk.'"

(80) Jesus said, "He who has recognized the World has found the body, but he who has found the body is superior to the World."

(81) Jesus said, "Let him who has grown rich be king, and let him who possesses power renounce it."

(82) Jesus said, "He who is near Me is near the fire, and he who is far from Me is far from the Kingdom."

(83) Jesus said, "The images are manifest to man, but the light in them remains concealed in the image of the light of the Father. He will become manifest, but his image will remain concealed by his light."

(84) Jesus said, "When you see your likeness, you rejoice. But when you see your images which came into being before you, and which neither die nor become manifest, how much you will have to bear!"

(85) Jesus said, "Adam came into being from a great power and a great wealth, but he did not become worthy of you. For had he been worthy he would not have experienced death."

(86) Jesus said, "The foxes have their holes and the birds have their nests, but the Son of Man has no place to lay his head and rest."

(87) Jesus said, "Wretched is the body that is dependent upon a body, and wretched is the soul that is dependent on these two."

(88) Jesus said, "The angels and the prophets will come to you and give to you those things you already have. And you too, give them those things which you have, and say to yourselves, 'When will they come and take what is theirs?'"

(89) Jesus said, "Why do you wash the outside of the cup? Do you not realize that he who made the inside is the same one who made the outside?"

(90) Jesus said, "Come unto Me, for My yoke is easy and My lordship is mild, and you will find repose for yourselves."

(91) They said to Him, "Tell us who You are so that we may believe in You."

He said to them, "You read the face of the sky and of the earth, but you have not recognized the One who is before you, and you do not know how to read this moment."

(92) Jesus said, "Seek and you will find. Yet, what you asked Me about in former times and which I did not tell you then, now I do desire to tell, but you do not inquire after it."

(93) Jesus said, "Do not give what is holy to dogs, lest they throw them on the dung-heap. Do not throw the pearls to swine, lest they grind it to bits."

(94) Jesus said, "He who seeks will find, and he who knocks will be let in."

(95) Jesus said, "If you have money, do not lend it at interest, but give it to one from whom you will not get it back."

(96) Jesus said, "The Kingdom of the Father is like a certain woman. She took a little leaven, concealed it in some dough, and made it into large loaves. Let him who has ears hear."

(97) Jesus said, "The Kingdom of the Father is like a certain woman who was carrying a jar full of meal. While she was walking on a road, still some distance from home, the handle of the jar broke and the meal emptied out behind her on the road. She did not realize it; she had noticed no accident. When she reached her house, she set the jar down and found it empty."

(98) Jesus said, "The Kingdom of the Father is like a certain man who wanted to kill a powerful man. In his own house, he drew his sword and stuck it into the wall in order to find out whether his hand could carry through. Then, he slew the powerful man."

(99) The Disciples said to Him, "Your brothers and Your mother are standing outside." He said to them, "Those here who do the will of My Father are My brothers and My mother. It is they who will enter the Kingdom of My Father."

(100) They showed Jesus a gold coin and said to Him, "Caesar's men demand taxes from us."

He said to them, "Give Caesar what belongs to Caesar, give God what belongs to God, and give Me what is Mine."

(101) Jesus said, "Whoever does not hate his father and his mother as I do cannot become a disciple to Me. And whoever does not love his father and his mother as I do cannot become a disciple to Me. For My mother gave Me falsehood, but My true mother gave Me life."

(102) Jesus said, "Woe to the Pharisees, for they are like a dog sleeping in the manger of oxen, for neither does he eat nor does he let the oxen eat."

(103) Jesus said, "Fortunate is the man who knows where the brigands will enter, so that he may get up, muster his domain, and arm himself before they invade."

(104) They said to Jesus, "Come, let us pray today and let us fast." Jesus said, "What is the sin that I have committed, or wherein have I been defeated? But when the bridegroom leaves the bridal chamber, then let them fast and pray."

(105) Jesus said, "He who knows the father and the mother will be called the son of a harlot."

(106) Jesus said, "When you make the two one, you will become the sons of man, and when you say, 'Mountain, move away,' it will move away."

(107) Jesus said, "The Kingdom is like a shepherd who had a hundred sheep. One of them, the largest, went astray. He left the ninety-nine and looked for that one until he found it. When he had gone to such trouble, he said to the sheep, 'I care for you more than the ninety-nine.'"

(108) Jesus said, "He who will drink from My mouth will become like Me. I Myself shall become he, and the things that are hidden will be revealed to him."

(109) Jesus said, "The Kingdom is like a man who had a hidden treasure in his field without knowing it. And after he died, he left it to his son. The son did not know about the treasure. He inherited the field and sold it. And the one who bought it went plowing and found the treasure. He began to lend money at interest to whomever he wished."

(110) Jesus said, "Whoever finds the World and becomes rich, let him renounce the World."

(111) Jesus said, "The heavens and the earth will be rolled up in your presence. And the one who lives from the Living One will not see death." Does not Jesus say, "Whoever finds himself is superior to the World?"

(112) Jesus said, "Woe to the flesh that depends on the soul; woe to the soul that depends on the flesh."

(113) His Disciples said to Him, "When will the Kingdom come?"

Jesus said, "It will not come by waiting for it. It will not be a matter of saying 'Here it is' or 'There it is.' Rather, the Kingdom of the Father is spread out upon the earth, and men do not see it."

(114) Simon Peter said to them, "Let Mary leave us, for women are not worthy of Life." Jesus said, "I Myself shall lead her in order to make her male, so that she too may become a living spirit resembling you males. For every woman who will make herself male will enter the Kingdom of Heaven."

FINAL THOUGHTS:

Congratulations to everyone who made it through all 114 sayings. That was difficult and so abstract.

It makes many Biblical scholars, educators, theologians, priests, ministers, and the faithful lay Christians wonder if the ***Gospel of Thomas*** along with the ***Gospel of Peter***, the ***Gospel of Philip***, the ***Gospel of James,*** the ***Gospel of Mary*** and other **GNOSTIC** texts that had been banned and ordered destroyed were instead included in the final ***New Testament*** canon by the Council of Carthage in A.D. 397, many historical events would not have taken place and today's world would be substantially different. Maybe, as a result, the world would be living in peace and harmony.

In such a potential Christian World under a Christian Church hierarchy that strictly taught salvation was attained through the Greatest Commandment: **"Love Your Neighbor As Yourself"** Some of the following horrific events may not have happened:

- The Dark Ages
- The Crusades
- The Inquisition
- The need for an alternative path to the same God via Islam
- Protestantism and its many offshoots (religions and cults) that exist today
- Many Holy Wars raged in the name of God or a specific religion to gain dominance
- The innumerable number of "Christian" denominations throughout the world

- The vast wealth and materialism of the ministers of some churches today
- The division among nations, cultures, and people

<u>**CHALLENGE:**</u> Read the **Gnostic** Gospels, Epistles, Apocrypha, and other texts that have been banned for dubious reasons and think about how the history of the Christian World would have been and what our world would be like today!

BIBLIOGRAPHY, REFERENCE, AND FURTHER READING:

Barnstone, Willis, ***Restored New Testament: A New Translation with Commentary, Including the Gnostic Gospels of Thomas, Mary, and Judas*** © 2009 Harper, San Francisco, California

Pagels, Elaine, ***Beyond Belief: The Secret Gospel of Thomas*** © 2003 Vintage Books-Random House, New York

Pagels, Elaine, ***Gnostic Gospels, The: A Startling Account of the Meaning of Jesus and the Origin of Christianity Based on the Gnostic Gospels and Other Secret Texts,*** © 1989, 1979 Vintage Books-Random House, New York

Meyers, Marvin, and Willis Barnstone, ***Gnostic Bible, The*** © 2003 Harper, San Francisco, California

Davies, Stevan, ***Gospel of Thomas: A Guidebook for Spiritual Practice,*** © 2004 Skylight Paths Publishing, Vermont

Davies, Stevan, ***Gospel of Thomas: Annotated and Explained*** © 2006, 2002 Skylight Paths Publishing, Vermont

Dart, John and Ray Riegert, ***Unearthing the Lost Words of Jesus: The Discovery of "The Gospel of Thomas"*** © 1998 Ulysses Press, Berkley California/Oxford University Press

Summers, Ray, ***Interesting and Enlightening Study of The Gospel of Thomas: The Controversial 4th Century Manuscript Recently Discovered at Nag Hammadi*** © 1968 Word Books, Waco, Texas

Till, W.C., ***New Sayings of Jesus Recently Discovered Coptic "Gospel of Thomas"*** © 1959 Bulletin of the John Rylands Library

This Book and Treatise are a compilation from many sources on the same subject. See the Complete List of Bibliographies, References, and Suggested Readings in Appendix II

CHAPTER 11

THE LEGEND OF JUDAS ISCARIOT

HISTORICAL BACKGROUND

A hand-written codex of ***The Gospel of Judas*** was found. ***The Gospel of Judas*** was written in **Coptic** and appears to be the work of a professional scribe or scriptorium highly trained in Greek to Coptic translations.

Besides ***The Gospel of Judas,*** the bound Codex contained other texts:

- ***The Letter of Peter to Philip,***
- A letter written by James the Just,
- A letter from Peter to James in which he says: "***He rose from the dead, my Brother! Jesus is a stranger to death....***"

- The ***First Apocalypse of James the Just*** which tells us "***He is from the Father who exists from the beginning***."

Everyone knows the forefront story about Jesus' Disciple, Judas Iscariot. After Jesus' crucifixion, Judas has been hated and despised by all future generations as the betrayer of Jesus Christ's who was bought for 30 pieces of silver. The stories of Judas Iscariot differ severely from Gospel to Gospel. In some Gospels, Judas' actions are not mentioned at all.

The Gospel of Judas was immediately dismissed as any such "Gospel" written by Jesus' betrayer is ludicrous. One such blistering reference to this absurd idea was written in A.D. 180 an influential Church leader named Irenaeus. He strongly protested against ***The Gospel of Judas*** which depicted the last days of Jesus according to Judas Iscariot. But when you read ***The Gospel of Judas,*** it is entirely plausible. It also changes the whole scenario and you are told Judas is not the traitor as everyone has been lead to believe, but he is a hero. He only did what Jesus commanded him to do. The story behind Judas' actions is well depicted in the popular operatic musical ***Jesus Christ, Superstar.***

In fact, Judas' story makes much more sense than the opposite story that has been passed down through the ages. However, once it was denounced by Irenaeus as being a fraud and complete heresy, ***The Gospel of Judas*** vanished from sight among others that were so demonized unilaterally by Irenaeus.

Irenaeus adamantly opposed ***The Gospel of Judas,*** but then we are not sure if Irenaeus ever bothered to read ***The Gospel of Judas.*** In Irenaeus's writings, there is no indication that he did ever read it. He had no reason to read it in order to condemn it. The title is enough to condemn it! For Irenaeus, the title in itself was "blasphemous." How could Judas Iscariot, the one who betrayed Jesus, write a Gospel? He committed suicide, at least as stated by only one Gospel.

The Church leaders in Rome were easily convinced by Irenaeus of his personal convictions. They were tainted by what Irenaeus believed Christianity should believe. Like the other texts that did not meet Irenaeus' approval, it was all but forgotten; even as far as when the Bishops were compiling the list of books that would be included in the ***New Testament***. Almost two millennia later this maligned Gospel was found in its original Coptic script and like many others is getting a well-deserved second look. In 1995, a collection of **Gnostic** writings was uncovered near the town of Nag Hammadi, Egypt including many lost gospels – ***The Gospel of Philip, The Gospel of Thomas, and The Gospel of Judas.***

In A.D. 180 Irenaeus wrote his five-volume "***Against Heresy***" (which had a much longer Latin title) condemning any "Christian" sect who he considered to be "heretics" or those who held the "wrong beliefs." He especially hated the **Gnostics** sects who preached that the way to salvation and the afterlife was not through the death and resurrection of Jesus Christ for our sins, but through learning the "secret knowledge" or **Gnosis** (Greek for "knowledge). Jesus preached to throngs of His followers; however, to His Disciples He gave much more in-depth insights. This "secret knowledge" explained to the people that they must escape the prison of this evil world and their material bodies; instead, they need to focus on returning to His Kingdom which is the spiritual realm from whence we all came. The **Gnostic** sects were on a higher spiritual level and had a very different perspective on this world.

Irenaeus unilaterally also made the fateful decision that there could not be numerous Gospels; there should only be **four** Gospels. He announced that only ***Matthew, Mark, Luke,*** and ***John*** were really "***divinely inspired.***" Irenaeus considered everything else was heresy and fraudulent. He was able to document in his five-volume "***Against Heresy***" how dozens of texts, including other Disciples' Gospels and Epistles, were heresy according to his definition, although no one ever knew what the definition was in **his mind**.

However, we can thank Irenaeus for documenting some facts that would have been lost forever. He tells us that ***The Gospel of Judas*** was being used primarily by a group of **Gnostics** called "Cainites." These people very much believed in the **Gnostic** doctrine that this material and evil world full of suffering was not created by the One True God but a lesser and inferior deity - the Hebrew God of the Old Testament.

The One True God could never be as mean and revengeful as the God revered by the Jews. ***The Gospel of Judas*** supported the Cainites' belief. Besides, ***The Gospel of Judas*** dispelled the persistence throughout Christian History that Judas was the traitor of Jesus. Though the stories vary in the synoptic (similar) Gospels, Judas was the Disciple who turned evil and betrayed his Master for thirty pieces of silver. But according to ***The Gospel of Judas***, Judas was a close friend to Jesus and he alone understood Jesus' mission; what Jesus had to do; what Jesus begged him to do; what Jesus persuaded him to do; and ultimately what Jesus commanded him to do. This was shown as one of the main plots in ***Jesus Christ, Superstar,*** especially in the dramatic song lyrics that were sung by Judas.

Athanasius was one of the attendees at the Council of Nicaea in A.D. 325. He became a bishop in A.D. 328 and took on the vigorous holy crusade to establish the orthodox Christian faith. He was a very vocal critic of the "Arian Heresy" which was favored by the new Emperor, the son of Constantine, Constantius. The Arian Heresy was the belief that when Jesus Christ was born He was separated from the Almighty God and became a man. Although He was the Son of God, He was not God Himself, or a God. This doctrine had many adherents but was bitterly contested within the Church so **they added** to the Nicene Creed that Jesus Christ was "***consubstantial***" with the Father, i.e. one and the same being.

Following an edict from the Council of Nicaea, the final canon of the Christian ***New Testament*** was being coalesced between A.D. 330 and 380 so that there would be only one single book of Sacred Scriptures that would be allowed to be read by all Christians. In 367, Bishop Athanasius basically unilaterally, following Irenaeus' lead, forced his will upon the other delegates on what would be and would not be accepted. Athanasius made sure he gave HIS approval on the "final" version of the New Testament. Any and all other Gospels and texts were to be destroyed by fire.

It then became natural that the alternative Gospels, Epistles, and other text were forgotten. The scribes had stopped copying them which was done by hand. They had no reason to copy the banned books. When a person who could afford to pay for it requested a copy of the ***New Testament***, obviously they would not pay for books that were banned. In addition, many times the scribes were monks and they would not be disobedient to their Church and refuse to provide the banned books. In those times to find quality scribes was difficult and thus not cheap. It can be seen when there was no demand, a book would just disappear. It was not until recent centuries that the general public needed to be educated in reading and writing. Many important texts were lost this way, including ***The Gospel of Judas***. We assume very few copies survived. Luckily in the 1970's a preserved Coptic copy of ***The Gospel of Judas*** was found in Egypt. Some theologians and Biblical scholars firmly believe this find might be an Act of God to correct a misguided Christianity.

The Gospel of Judas gives us a completely different scenario than we all have been taught. Judas did not do anything evil or corrupt; instead, Judas did a good and compassionate act that needed to be done. Judas allowed Jesus' corporal body to be destroyed so that His inner spirit could be set free. ***The Gospel of Judas*** changes everything we were taught in traditional Christianity and the ***New Testament*** Gospels. No wonder Irenaeus banned ***The Gospel of Judas.***

HIGHLIGHTS OF THE *GOSPEL OF JUDAS*

The Gospel of Judas is unlike any other Gospel. Judas tells us that he was not a traitor but a faithful and trusted friend to Jesus. He was asked by Jesus to hand Him over to His enemies. A whole copy miraculously survived.

The Gospel of Judas was obviously written by someone who adored Jesus Christ. Jesus does not seem to have suffered or been tormented but was actually happier and more joyful than He is portrayed in the four canonical Gospels. ***The Gospel of Judas*** brims over with love and affection.

Judas tells us in his ***Gospel of Judas*** that Jesus said to him: "***Come that I may teach you about the secrets no person has ever seen. There is a great and boundless realm....which no eye of an angel has ever seen, no thought of the heart has ever comprehended, and it was never called by any name.***"

In ***The Gospel of Judas,*** Jesus is a friendly teacher that radiates divine wisdom. It tells the story of a great master and teacher who came to Earth to save not only the people who have been waiting for Him but also for all humanity. He was not accepted by "the powers that be" and was eventually arrested by the authorities, put to death, and transcended death to eternal life in the Heavenly afterworld. It was not meant to alienate the four canonical Gospels but to complement them. Let us not forget this is one of the six Disciples' Gospels that were not included in the ***New Testament*** to which ***The Gospel of Judas*** has more in common. Judas teaches us the same as the Disciple Peter, the Disciple Thomas, the Disciple Philip, the Disciple James, and considered by some to be the greatest Disciple of all, Mary Magdalene. [Excellent books have been written about the Disciple Mary Magdalene by Professor Elaine Pagels.] Professor Pagels says it perfectly, "***People who are interested would want to read all the Gospels.***"

The Gospel of Judas gives us a new and fresh insight into early Christianity and its varied beliefs. It is an alternative narrative that does not challenge the Christian faith but provides a different view of the personality of Jesus. ***The Gospel of Judas*** stands as an independent story. It is not illogical or contradictory. Jesus came to save humanity, He predicted His own death, Jesus had to sacrifice Himself in order to fulfill His mission, and Judas was only an instrument Jesus used to achieve His goal. The twist on the narrative gives us a different perspective on those fateful events that became the basis for the Christian faith. Irenaeus condemned ***The Gospel of Judas*** if for no other reason than solely based on its title. For Irenaeus, it was simply outrageous to have a ***Gospel of Judas,*** the man who had betrayed Jesus.

Plato in his work ***Timaeus*** says that each person has his own soul and his own star. Jesus told the same to Judas, "***Lift up your eyes and look at the cloud and the light within it and the stars surrounding it. The star that leads the way is your star***." Judas apparently understood and believed.

It was Judas that Jesus asked, "***Step away from the others and I will tell you about the mysteries of the Kingdom. It is possible for you to reach the Kingdom but you will grieve a great deal***."

Jesus forewarns Judas and future generations about those who ***"make use of My name... plant trees without fruit, in My name, in a shameful manner.***" However, He warned them, "***The Lord who commands, the Lord of All, will judge them on the last day.***"

Jesus explicitly told Judas, "***People of this world have a divine spark trapped within them that needs to be set free."*** Jesus even rephrased it, "***When people have completed their time... the spirit leaves them, their body dies, but their souls will stay alive and will be taken up***." Jesus had a spirit and divine spark within Himself that had to be freed.

The close relationship between Jesus and Judas is mentioned very often in ***The Gospel of Judas.*** It is very clear in this Gospel that Judas is Jesus' favorite disciple who was the most trusted one for Jesus to ask to **"*sacrifice the man that clothes Me*"**

The ***Gospel of Judas*** is considered to be a **Gnostic** Gospel because it goes into much detail how this world we live in is really an evil material world. Judas explains how it became this way and how we all trapped in it. It is based on his understanding of the teachings of Jesus. Judas tells us in his account that he was a trusted member of Jesus' "inner circle" to whom Jesus gave "secret revelations" or "secret knowledge." We do know that Judas was entrusted by Jesus and the other Disciples as the keeper of their purse. Judas says he was a very devoted Disciple that Jesus shared much as he really understood Jesus' deep meaning in His message about who will be saved. Many of the other Disciples did not get Jesus' deeper message and the religions of their followers are rooted in ignorance.

The perceived problem that enraged Irenaeus was that this ***Gospel of Judas*** does not conform to emerging Christianity, or more precisely, the "Christianity" that Irenaeus wanted to emerge. What Judas was espousing was an "Alternative Vision of Christianity" according to a different interpretation of Jesus' parables and hidden messages.

We do know that Judas was one of Jesus' Twelve Disciple, he was their treasurer and, by some accounts, Judas was Jesus' most trusted friend. The ***Gospel of Judas*** narrates the relationship between Jesus and Judas. But the most important part of the ***Gospel of Judas*** is when Judas describes how he was so trusted by Jesus, that he never did betray Jesus but only did what Jesus wanted him to do. Judas finally agreed because he understood the real truth about this world and about the afterlife that he learned from Jesus.

IMPORTANT POINT: If Jesus Christ was really God, why would He take someone into His "inner circle" of Disciples and instruct him for three years if, as an all-knowing God, He knew this person was going to "betray" Him and "hand Him over" to His enemies to be made to suffer, being publically humiliated, crucified, and killed? It just doesn't make sense. Whereas, Judas' version makes more sense and is really not disputed by the Disciples, who, by the way, all ran away while Jesus was being arrested and went into hiding.

THE "BETRAYAL" OF JESUS

Jesus said to Judas, "***You will exceed all of them, for you will sacrifice the man that clothes Me.***" Judas had superior knowledge given to him by Jesus Himself; Judas knew human bodies are only temporary housing for the spirit and soul. Judas, therefore, did what his Master commanded him to do. He did what was needed and necessary to be done.

MOST IMPORTANT POINT! The translations from the most-original Greek manuscripts, the Greek word **"PARADIDOMI"** does not mean literally "***to betray***" but rather means "***to hand over***" or "***to surrender.***" It makes a big difference between "***to hand over***" or "***to surrender***" versus the stronger usual English translation of "***to betray.***" There is also a big difference between when you say "***Judas betrayed Jesus to the Romans***" and "***Judas handed over Jesus to the Romans.***" The latter more lends itself to Judas doing what Jesus asked him to do because it was His time to be sacrificed.

The betrayal narrative is an integral part to the validity of Christianity. The "betrayal" was the first step followed by Jesus' arrest, trial, conviction, crucifixion, death, and of course, His bodily resurrection. It is pointed out by one of the best authorities on the subject of the "***betrayal***" of Jesus: the Garden of Gethsemane where the "***kiss of betrayal***" supposedly took place is on the eastern side of Temple Mount. The hill above it from the Mount of Olives has a commanding view of Jerusalem. Being nighttime, it was dark. Roman soldiers marching towards Gethsemane would have been very obvious to Jesus and His Disciples. It is claimed that Jesus was God. As God, He had to know what was happening. He alluded to it being His last night with them at supper. Jesus could have left Gethsemane at any time. Even in His arrest, passion, and execution, Jesus, if He was God, could have changed the circumstances. But He did NOT. Why? Because He had to fulfill the prophecies, He had a mission to accomplish, and He needed an accomplice. That was Judas.

<u>**IMPORTANT POINT:**</u> To quote Religious Studies Professor and author Bart Ehrman, "***If Judas did NOT betray Him that would change the whole Christian relationship. What if it turns out that Judas did NOT betray Jesus, but simply did what Jesus wanted him to?***"

Jesus says in ***Matthew*** 26:2, "***You know that in two days time it will be Passover, and the Son of Man is to be handed over for crucifixion.***" Again, if Jesus was really God, and He knew His fate, why did He do nothing to avoid it?

In the Garden of Gethsemane, "***…Judas went up to Jesus and said 'Greetings, Rabbi' and kissed Him and Jesus replied to him, 'Friend, do what you have to do'.***"

What an unusual exchange between a supposed "betrayer" and his supposed "prey." Then Jesus was led to His passion, crucifixion, and death; or was it on the path to His destiny? Again without Judas help, Jesus would not have been able to complete His mission.

The Gospel in the name of the Disciple Matthew goes succinctly on the record as to Judas' terrible and immediate fate. It tells us that by morning, Judas was overcome with guilt at what he had done. As a sign of remorse, he brought back the 30 pieces of silver to the chief priests admitting, "***I have sinned by betraying innocent blood.***" To his dismay, they replied, "***What is that to us?***" Out of frustration, Judas threw the 30 pieces of silver on the floor of the temple, left, and proceeded to commit suicide by hanging himself (***Matthew*** 27:3-5).

Matthew 14:21 tells us that Jesus said: "***The Son of Man goes as it is written of Him, but woe to that one by whom the Son of Man is betrayed! It would have been better for that one not to have been born.***" But what does that really mean? Whether God and Jesus (who did nothing to prevent his arrest, etc.) would be angry with "**the one who handed him over**" or would it only be all future generations that would be angry with him, albeit unjustly for doing what he was asked to do, what he had to do.

Luke has a completely different version of the story behind Judas' deed. In Acts, which is believed to also have been written by the same person who wrote Luke, it has a theological explanation: "***Then Satan entered into Judas Iscariot, who was one of the twelve, he went away and conferred with the chief priests and officers of the temple police about how he might betray Him to them.***

They were greatly pleased and agreed to give him money" (***Luke*** 22: 3-5).

The ***Gospel of John*** appears to be written independently of the first three synoptic (i.e. similar) Gospels, tells us that at the Passover feast (i.e. the Last Supper): "***the devil had already put it into the heart of Judas, Son of Simon Iscariot, to betray Him (John*** 13:2***). After dipping the bread and giving it to Judas, Satan entered into Judas and Jesus said, "Do quickly what you are going to do***" (***John*** 13:24-27). Furthermore, according to John, when Judas left dinner, Jesus said, "***Now the Son of Man has been glorified, and God has glorified Him"*** (***John*** 13:28-31).

IMPORTANT POINT: Maybe John did not mean it that way, but it sure seems like he is telling us **Jesus was fully aware of what Judas was doing and was absolutely fine with it! He did nothing to stop Judas, which He could.**

In Acts, believed to have been descended from Luke, we are told a completely different story. Judas did not return the thirty pieces of silver nor did he commit suicide. Judas was "***the guide for those who arrested Jesus;***" a very interesting choice of words. Again it can be the difference between "**betraying**" Jesus and "**handing over**" Jesus. ***Acts*** tell us further that Judas bought a plot of land with his ill-gotten reward, but in an ironic twist falls head first into a pit on that land, his guts are gorged, and he dies (***Acts*** 1:16-20). This is not uncommon. To anyone who has read my Volume I, or other works on the same subject, the story of Judas is completely different depending on which book you read about it in the ***New Testament***.

There is a wide range of differing opinions and scenarios; not just the one as we have been led to believe. Judas was a Palestinian and a Jew just like Jesus. Judas likewise was very popular in the Middle East where he was one of them. Many people believe that the actions taken by Judas, regardless of his reasons or motivation, were foretold by Jesus. All along, Jesus foretold that He was would be handed over (He also foretold that Peter would deny Him before the cock crowed thrice, and by all His Disciples who disappeared into hiding….. but they were all declared Saints), going to die, but will rise from the dead to a new life in His Father's Kingdom. Remember Jesus' prayers in the Garden of Gethsemane asking His Father to take this cup from Him. He keeps waking up His Disciples asking them to sit with Him on the last night that He was going to be with them. Jesus well knew what was imminently going to happen and that it was the will of His Father that He sacrificed Himself. Judas was just as unwilling to do what Jesus needed for him to do.

The way ***The Gospel of Judas*** ends is very abrupt without any narratives of the trial, crucifixion, and resurrection of Jesus Christ. To him they were really irrelevant:

> ***"The High Priests murmured because Jesus had gone into the guest room to pray.***
>
> ***The Scribes were working to arrest Him during His prayers, for they were afraid of the people, since Jesus was regarded by all as a prophet"***

According to ***The Gospel of Judas,*** when the High Priests saw Judas they asked, "***What are you doing here? You are Jesus' Disciple.***" Nothing was said about Judas coming to them requesting money for him to "hand over" Jesus. There was no betrayal, there was no conspiracy.

Judas already accepted to do this for Jesus. There are no second thoughts, no agonizing pangs of conscience, no weeping, and no suicide looming in the future. The deed was done, Judas acted on Jesus' behalf, sacrificing Him, and freeing His spirit and soul to ascend to the Kingdom of His Father.

IMPORTANT POINT: Judas ends his Gospel there which may be the proper and real ending to the story.

According to renowned authorities on the subject, Professor Bart Ehrman, and other **Gnostic** authors, ***Judas*** makes more sense than the resurrection of His body in ***Matthew, Mark, Luke,*** and ***John*** where He appeared to His Disciples, who did not immediately recognize Him. According to ***The Gospel of Judas,*** there is no bodily resurrection.

What ***The Gospel of Judas*** does NOT say may be as important as what it does say:

- It does not criticize or contradict the four canonical Gospels, or take any direct issues with them, but still was not acceptable for inclusion in the ***New Testament***.
- ***The Gospel of Judas*** does not mention the ***"handing over"*** or the ***"betrayal"*** because Judas did NOT ***"betray"*** his Master. Instead, he fulfilled Jesus' wishes. He was above the other Disciples who faded into the background. Judas was Jesus' instrument of fulfillment.
- ***The Gospel of Judas***' account of the final days of Jesus gives no indication of guilt. As the favored Disciple, he obeys his Master's wishes. Judas liberated Jesus from ***"the man that clothes me"*** so

that He can achieve His rightful place in the Heavenly Realm for all of eternity.

To reiterate some important points found in the variety of books written by different authors, all Biblical scholars, whereas they claim ***The Gospel of Judas*** makes more sense than the scenario put forth by the four canonical Gospels:

- Jesus was God, at any time He could have changed future or present events.
- His death was foretold by the prophets for centuries prior to His birth.
- He was very aware of these prophecies in Hebrew Scripture as a devout Jew and a rabbi.
- Jesus on many occasions acknowledged His forthcoming death.
- Jesus spoke in accurate detail at the Last Supper about the events to unfold that night.
- He went to pray that night after the Last Supper and begged His Father to let this cup pass.
- From the Mount of Olives, He could see the approaching soldiers and He did nothing.
- When the soldiers arrived He TWICE said that He was the one who they were seeking, not exactly something someone would say if they were being "betrayed."
- The Disciples slept, and none of them tried to stop the soldiers, much worse, they denied Him.
- He went with the soldiers without resistance, and even cured a soldier's severed ear.
- Jesus did not put up any resistance, verbally or physically or miraculously, to His arrest, torture, crucifixion, and death. As God and a miracle worker,

at any time He could have changed any of the events as they were happening.

- The biggest evidence comes from what He said on the cross: "Today you will join me in Paradise," "Father, forgive them for they know not what they do," "Women, do not cry for me," and "Father, into Thy hands I commend My spirit."

IMPORTANT POINT: Just think about all these points! Do the canonical Gospels make sense? Do the Church's teachings still make sense? Or does the ***Gospel of Judas*** make more sense?

BIBLIOGRAPHY, REFERENCE, AND SUGGESTED READING

Barnstone, Willis, ***Restored New Testament: A New Translation With Commentary, Including the Gnostic Gospels of Thomas, Mary, and Judas*** © 2009 Harper, San Francisco, California

Ehrman. Bart D. ***Lost Gospel of Judas Iscariot, The: A New Look at Betrayer and Betrayed*** © 2006 University Press

Ehrman, Bart D., ***Lost Scriptures: Books that Did Not Make It into the New Testament***, © 2006, Oxford University Press

Iscariot, Benjamin, ***Gospel According to Judas, The*** © 2007, St. Martin Press

Gubar, Susan, ***Judas: A Biography*** © 2009 W.W. Norton & Co., New York

Kasser, Rodolphe, Marvin Meyer and Gregor Wurst ***Gospel of Judas, The Second Edition*** © 2008, National Geographic Society

Krosney, Herbert, ***Lost Gospel The:The Quest for the Gospel of Judas Iscariot,*** © 2006, National Geographic Society

Lester, Meera, ***The Everything®, The – Gnostic Gospels Book***, © 2007 F+W Publications

Meyers, Marvin, ***Judas: The Definitive Collection of Gospels and Legends About Infamous Apostle of Jesus*** © 2007 Random House, New York

Meyers, Marvin, ***Secret Teaching of Jesus: Four Gnostic Gospel*** © 1986, 1984 Vintage Books-Random House, New York

Pagels, Elaine, ***Gnostic Gospels, The*** © 1979, Random House; ©1989, Vintage Books

Pagels, Elaine, and King, Karen L., ***Reading Judas: The Gospel of Judas and the Shaping of Christianity***, © 2007 Viking Penguin

This Book and Treatise are a compilation from many sources on the same subject. See the Complete List of Bibliographies, References, and Suggested Readings in Appendix II

CHAPTER 12

THE GOSPEL OF JUDAS AND OTHER GNOSTIC TEXTS

INTRODUCTION

As discussed in the previous chapter, discoveries in the sands of Egypt have preserved the shocking ***Gospel of Judas*** which has not been seen by anyone since the early Christians. It is a story that completely changes everything we have been taught by the Christian Church. The four Gospels in the ***New Testament*** say little to nothing about the fate of Judas who they claim was the one who betrayed Jesus Christ and sold Him to His enemies to be put to death. The emerging Church in the early centuries categorically banned the ***Gospel of Judas*** as just being preposterous. The four Gospels in ***New Testament*** contradict each other when it comes to discussing Judas' fate, if they even mention it at all.

The ***Gospel of Judas*** shades a new and more plausible light when it portrays Judas not as a traitor but as a hero. It tells us that, over Judas' protests, Judas did what his master commanded him to do, what had to be done. Jesus had to be "handed over" and persecuted to be our Savior. Without Judas Iscariot action, there would be no Christianity today.

We know that the ***Gospel of Judas*** existed in antiquity because Irenaeus severely criticized it in his ***Against Heresy*** which was published in A.D. 180. Many modern authors and Biblical scholars have written works on Judas Iscariot (see **Bibliography** section in the previous chapter) all giving similar perspectives on the character and motivation of Judas. This Chapter will contain select passages from the ***Gospel of Judas.*** We owe a large debt of gratitude to Rodolphe Kasser, Marvin Meyer, George Wurst and Francois Gaubard for their years of ardent labor translating the fragile manuscripts from their original Coptic into legible English prose in ***The Gospel of Judas,*** Second Edition, 2008. In brackets, is included their alternate translations of a specific word for modern usage and clarification. The ***Gospel of Judas*** is not in contradiction to the teachings of Jesus found in the other Gospels; however, it is definitely **Gnostic** and at times more uplifting and positive.

HIGHLIGHTS FROM *THE GOSPEL OF JUDAS*

This is the secret words which Jesus spoke in conversation with Judas Iscariot during the eight days before He celebrated Passover.

When He appeared on earth, He performed miracles and great wonders for the salvation of humanity. And since some in the way of righteousness while others walked in their transgressions, the twelve were called. He began to speak to them about the mysteries beyond the world and what would take place at the end. But often He does not appear to His Disciples but you will find Him among them.

...anyone of you among human beings [can] bring out the perfect human and stand before My face... But their spirits could not find the courage to stand before [Him], except for Judas Iscariot. He was able to stand before Him but could not look at Him in the eyes, and he turned his face away Judas said to Him, "***I know who You are and where You have come from. You have come from the immortal Aeon*** [i.e. the eternal realm] ***of Barbelo. And I am not worthy to utter the name of the One who sent You***.

<u>IMPORTANT POINT:</u> In Jewish tradition, the name of God was unspeakable. They called Him "Yahweh."

Knowing that he [Judas] was reflecting upon the rest [of things] that are exalted, Jesus said to him, ***"Step away from the others and I shall tell you the mysteries of the Kingdom, not so that you will go there but you will grieve a great deal.***

Now, the next morning, after this happened, He appeared to His Disciples. And they said to Him, ***"Master, where did You go and what did You do when you left us?"*** Jesus said to them, ***"I went to another great and holy generation"*** [another world].

Another day Jesus came up to them. They said to Him, ***"Master, we have seen You in a*** [vision] ***for we have had great*** [dreams this] ***night that has passed.*** [We have] ***seen a great house, large altar, twelve men – they are the priests... and a crowd of people is waiting at that altar,***

the priests [presenting] ***the offerings… the men who stand*** [before] ***the altar invoke your*** [name]***."*** After they said this, they were quiet, for they were troubled. Jesus said to them, ***"Why are you troubled?"*** I say to you, "***All the priests who stand before that altar invoke my name. And again I say to you, My name has been written on… of the generations of the stars by the human generations. They have planted trees without fruit, in My name, in a shameful manner."***

IMPORTANT POINT: Jesus metaphorically references the planting trees that do not bear fruit as an indictment of those who preach in the name of Jesus but what they proclaim is fruitless.

Jesus said to them, ***"It is you who are presenting the offerings on the altar you have seen. That one is the God you serve, and you are the twelve men you have seen."***

Jesus said, ***"The souls of every human generation will die. When these people, however, have completed the time of the Kingdom and the spirit leaves them, their bodies will die, but their souls will be alive, and they will be taken up."***

Judas said, ***"Master, could it be that my seed*** [the spirit, the divine spark of the divine] ***is under the control of the rulers*** [the archons, the evil rulers of the world, and the demiurge]***."*** Jesus answered***, "You will be cursed by the other generations, and you will come to rule over them."***

Jesus said, "[Come] ***that I may teach you about the*** [things] ***that*** [no] ***human will*** [ever] ***see. For there exists a great and boundless aeon, whose extent no generation of angels could see,*** [in] ***which is the great invisible***

Spirit... which no eye of an [angel] ***has ever seen, no thought of the heart has ever comprehended, and it was never called by any name."***

__**IMPORTANT POINT:**__ Such references can also be found in the ***Secret Book of John*** and the ***Holy Book of the Great Invisible Spirit***. There are many similarities found in other texts to the ***Gospel of Judas***.

"***And a luminous cloud appeared there."*** And He said, "***Let an angel come into being as my attendant. And a great angel, the Self-Generated, the God of the light emerged from the cloud. And because of him, four other angels came into being from another cloud, and they became attendants....***"

"He made 72 luminaries appear...in accordance with the will of the Spirit. And the 72 luminaries themselves made 360 luminaries appear..." "And the twelve Aeons of the twelve luminaries constitute their Father, with six heavens for each Aeon, so that there are 72 heavens for the 72 luminaries and for each [of the five] ***firmaments*** [for a total of] ***360*** [firmaments]. [They] ***were given authority and a*** [great] ***host of angels without number, for glory and adoration, and also virgin spirits for glory and*** [adoration] ***of all the Aeons and the Heavens and their firmaments."***

Then He said, ***"Let twelve angels come into being*** [to] ***rule over chaos and the*** [underworld]." From the cloud, there appeared an angel whose face flashed with fire and whose appearance was defiled with blood. His name was Nebro [who also appears in the ***Holy Book of the Great Invisible Spirit***]. Nebruel is a great demoness who produces twelve Aeons. In the ***Holy Book of the Great Invisible***

Spirit, Nebro is Nebruel whose name is shown with the honorary suffix of "-el" which means God in Hebrew. "***A cloud*** [named] ***Sofia of matter appeared, surveyed the regions*** [of chaos]." Nebro created twelve angels in the heavens with each one receiving a portion in the heavens. Nebro, meaning "rebel," has been also called Yaldabaoth which is a common name for the demiurge in Sethian texts. Yaldabaoth can mean "child of Chaos" in Aramaic. Sakla in the ***Gospel of Judas*** is referred to as Saklas, a common name for the demiurge in Sethian texts, which can mean "fool" in Aramaic.

"Then Saklas said to his angels, 'Let us create a human being after the likeness and after the image'." (Similar accounts of the creation of a human being are found in other Sethian texts. They fashioned Adam and his wife Eve, but she is called 'Zoe." Zoe is Greek for "life" and is the name of Eve in the Septuagint.)

Judas said to Jesus, ***"***[What] ***is the advantage of human life?"*** Jesus said, ***"Why are you wondering about this, that Adam, with his generation, has received his span of life in such a number in the place where he has received his Kingdom in such a number with his ruler?"***

Judas said to Jesus, ***"Does the human spirit die?"*** Jesus said, ***"In this way, God ordered Michael to give the spirits of people to them as a gift on a loan so that they might offer services. But the Great one ordered Gabriel to grant spirits to the great generation with no ruler over it – the spirit and the soul.*** [The] ***spirit within you*** [which] ***you let dwell in this*** [flesh] ***from the generations of angels. But God caused knowledge*** [gnosis] ***to be*** [given] ***to Adam and those with him so that the kings of chaos and the underworld might not lord over them."***

Jesus said to Judas, ***"But you will exceed all of them, for you will sacrifice the man who bears me***." (This means that the earthly flesh which houses the spirit and soul of Jesus, and the inner spirit of a person, Jesus, will never actually die but instead will be liberated.)

Jesus said, ***"Look, you have been told everything. Lift up your eyes and look at the cloud and the light within it and the stars surrounding it. And the star that leads the way to your star."*** So Judas lifted up his eyes and saw the luminous cloud, and he entered it. (This passage may be describing the transfiguration of Judas. Judas appears to be vindicated and glorified by being accepted into the luminous cloud. This cloud of light may be the home of the Great Invisible Spirit.)

IMPORTANT POINT: So ends the ***Gospel of Judas,*** very abruptly. There is no account of the passion, crucifixion, death, or resurrection of Jesus; because, according to Judas, Jesus' mission here on earth ended with His death. Jesus was trying to explain to everyone that "Death" is the end of your life here on earth and really is "Your Birth into your new everlasting life of peace and happiness."

COMMENTS REGARDING *THE GOSPEL OF JUDAS*

It is important to note that the title is ***Gospel of Judas,*** unlike the other Gospels whose titles are the ***Gospel According to..."*** This may mean ***The Gospel of Judas*** was more a direct recording of the words than the other Gospels.

IMPORTANT NOTE: It should be noted before, that by saying "the Gospel According to..." which is definitely used by the Catholic Church, it sort of lets us know that the Gospels may not be in agreement with each other in relaying the events about Jesus Christ.

Unlike the Gospels that were included in the ***New Testament,*** the ***Gospel of Judas*** was not considered as being written by one of Jesus' faithful Disciples but by His betrayer; and maybe in a more direct line from Judas to paper than the other Gospels. However, to the shock of the world, by reading the ***Gospel of Judas*** you find out it was written by one of Jesus' closest companions and friends, Judas Iscariot. Judas was not evil, or corrupted, or taken over by the Devil, but a close enough Disciple that he would be asked "to hand over" his Master to His death so that the prophecies could be fulfilled, His mission on Earth could be consummated, and His spirit could return to the Divine Realm of His Father. Judas only did what His Master convinced him to do. Judas understood Jesus and His mission better than all the other Disciples. Jesus wanted to leave this imperfect world and return to His Heavenly realm. Judas was an important part to complete Jesus' mission on this earth.

The ***Gospel of Judas*** gives us a completely different perspective on the teachings of Jesus. What was Jesus really saving us from? What is the real purpose of our human existence? In light of this Gospel, how accurate are the Christian Church's creeds? Did the established Christian Church go completely off in the wrong direction for the past two millennia? Has Judas given us new insight into the teachings of Jesus Christ and what the religion that established Jesus Christ as its figurehead should have been like? Maybe for all these reasons, the ***Gospel of Judas*** was purposely and intentionally left out of the ***New Testament.*** The early Church leaders did not want anyone to read this and then claim that the stories in the other four Disciples'

Gospels, which they selected to be in the ***New Testament,*** were false.

I have brought this point up before, Judas "betraying" Jesus just does not make any sense. First off, the translation of the Greek word is more accurate as "handed over" but has been "lost in the translation" to be "betrayed." There is a big difference between the meanings of those two words in English usage. Secondly, Jesus spoke of departure from this earth and even when it was imminently about to happen. Next, Jesus was God (or we considered Him to be God) and at any time He could have altered His surroundings and His fate, but He did not. He never defended Himself, even when asked He kept silent. This all makes you think that there is something more realistic about the ***Gospel of Judas*** compared to the story being told in the four canonical Gospels that made it into the ***New Testament*** whose stories are all not in agreement with each other. This means we don't know the real truth.

"***It would have been better for that man never to have been born"*** it was said in the ***Gospel of Mark*** 14:21. "It would have been better"? Really? It would have been better if Jesus did not die and be resurrected for our salvation? How? Mark's Gospel doesn't give any reason or motive for Judas' betrayal just that he went to the Jewish leaders and freely volunteered to "hand him over." In return, the leaders gave him some money.

The ***Gospel of Matthew,*** considered to have been written after the ***Gospel of Mark,*** it is possible that the writer of the ***Gospel of Matthew*** used ***Gospel of Mark*** as the source for that Gospel. However, ***Gospel of Matthew*** changes the story slightly. Judas went to the Jewish leaders to see how much they would pay him to "hand Jesus over." They agreed on thirty pieces of silver. The ***Gospel of Matthew*** insinuates that Judas' motive was monetary greed. (Reference ***Matthew*** 26:14-16)

The ***Gospel of Luke*** is thought to have been written about the same time as ***Gospel of Matthew,*** it is possible that the writer of the ***Gospel of Luke*** used the ***Gospel of Matthew*** or the ***Gospel of Mark*** as his source. However, the ***Gospel of Luke*** adds another wrinkle. Satan <u>entered</u> Judas, took over Judas, and used Judas to do this dastardly betrayal. (Reference ***Luke*** 22:3)

The ***Gospel of John,*** which is believed to be the last Gospel written, embellished the story of Judas even more by claiming Judas was the devil all along. "***Jesus said, 'one of you is a devil.'"*** (***John*** 12:4-6) John even goes further by claiming that as the treasurer of the group Judas would steal from their funds for himself. The ***Gospel of John,*** the last of the Gospels written, takes into account the prior versions. The writer of the ***Gospel of John*** portrayed Judas as being motivated to "hand over" Jesus due to his own evil nature, his greed, and by demonic possession.

<u>**IMPORTANT POINT:**</u> In modern day law, if Judas was being tried for the murder of Jesus Christ, the prosecuting attorney (or in this case, Pontius Pilate) would have to prove that he committed the crime "beyond a reasonable doubt." These Disciples as witnesses alone would cause "reasonable doubt." In fact, we know that Pontius Pilate had "reasonable doubt" about the guilt of Jesus Christ that He committed any crimes sufficient enough to warrant Him to be put to death.

Then comes all the inconsistencies and contradictions about Judas' fate <u>after</u> the demise of Jesus: ***Luke, Mark,*** and ***John*** say nothing about his fate at all in their Gospels.

Guess, according to them there were no significant events worth noting.

The ***Gospel of Matthew*** tells us the Judas was filled with remorse, returned the thirty pieces of silver, and hung himself.

The ***Acts of the Apostles,*** considered to have been written by the same person who wrote the ***Gospel of Luke,*** tells a completely different story. Judas does not hang himself; instead, he purchased a field near Jerusalem. He falls into a pit onto a pitchfork, rips open his stomach, his intestines are spilled on the ground, and he died. It was not considered an act of suicide but an Act of God who made Judas have a gory death in retribution for His betrayal.

IMPORTANT POINT: Again, what is the truth? What really happened? For all we know, as evidenced by the wording in some Gospels, Judas never died. The Disciples never persecuted him for what he did; they realized what had to be done. Judas was one of the Twelve who went forth to evangelize the world and his followers wrote down the teachings he learned directly from Jesus.

THE STORY ACCORDING TO JUDAS

The ***Gospel of Judas*** tells a completely different story in stark contrast to the four Gospels that were placed in the ***New Testament.*** Judas did a GOOD deed, not an evil one. Judas was a hero, not a villain. He did what he was commanded to do by Jesus, which was the will of the Father. Jesus had to die. Jesus had to resurrect himself from the dead. The Divine Spark inside Jesus had to be released from being trapped in His human body and He would be able to return to His Heavenly home. Otherwise, His teachings would not have been worth any more than other religious zealots, preachers, or philosophers.

Judas tells us from the beginning that his Gospel will be something different than the Gospels of the other Disciples when he says, "***the secret word of the declaration of which Jesus spoke in conversation with Judas Iscariot."*** The secret word means that which was not revealed to everyone but to a select few. Other Disciples had "secret" Gospels too which were also not placed in the ***New Testament.*** Disallowing Judas' Gospel is one thing, but to accept one Gospel for inclusion in the ***New Testament*** but not another from the same Disciple, such as Mark and John is strange. How is one better than the other? Or is it the only one that the bishops wanted to hear and the other one was not. Why would they not include the Gospels of other Disciples, such as Peter, James, Philip, and Thomas? Maybe, they too were not what the bishops wanted to hear.

The **Gnostics** claim that those excluded Gospels were too mystical. Like Judas, these other Gospels convey "secret" teachings made to those Disciples by Jesus Christ. One thing Judas must have realized was the Jesus was NOT of this world but comes from the divine realm above. Judas had said, "***You have come from the immortal Aeon of Barbello."*** Barbello was thought to be one of the primary divine beings in the realm of the true God from where Jesus came. It may be because of Judas' understanding that Jesus took him aside to impart to him "the mysteries of the Kingdom." Judas received the secret knowledge about salvation. Jesus did tell him that he will be saved, although he will first grieve, and be rejected by many. He will be cursed by generations of mortals, but they will not attain salvation. Judas will eventually come to rule over them for he will be superior to everyone in this material world based on his secret knowledge.

Much of Judas' Gospel is about Jesus' revelations to him. He talks about the great and boundless Aeons in the eternal heavenly realm of truly divine beings beyond this world and superior to the deities created by the human beings. These inferior deities created this material world and the human beings in it. Humans were made to worship them. The superior divine beings were long in existence before these inferior deities. These inferior deities are depicted in the ***Old Testament.*** The deity in charge of this world is the god in the ***Old Testament.*** The mean, angry, and wrathful god, the deity in the ***Old Testament*** who is NOT The Supreme Being, the Father Almighty, He Who-Shall-Remain-Nameless, who is all-good, all-loving, and all-merciful. He could never do the things the god of the ***Old Testament*** did or threatened to do!

It is believed that the god, or deity, **Salkas** is in charge of the deities that possess this world. **Salkas** is really the god of the ***Old Testament*** who was a bloody rebel, a fool. **Salkas** is believed be the one who created human beings in his own image. This revelation to Judas prompted Judas to ask of Jesus whether humans can transcend this world into the divine realm. Jesus' answer is an unqualified Yes. Many humans have the divine spark inside of them, the connection to the Almighty. They will survive and transcend this world to the divine realm.

IMPORTANT POINT: This is a very important message from Jesus about the real salvation that He is preaching.

Jesus assures Judas that he will be accepted into the divine realm. Jesus did show Judas his star in the heavens. Jesus adds that Judas' star will be superior to all the others and his star "leads the way." It does that through his understanding of all the things Jesus had taught him. Salvation does not come from worshipping the inferior God of this world; however, it comes by rejecting this material world and throwing off their flawed humanity. This is why the deed that Judas was convinced to do was right and a good deed. Judas allowed Jesus to escape His mortal flesh and return to His Divine Home. His act did not damn Judas but gave him instant entry into the divine realm. He was not the villain but was the one who excelled beyond all the others. Jesus said to Judas, "You will exceed all of them; for you will only be sacrificing the man who bears me." Jesus was praising Judas and what he was doing.

Needless to say, Judas in his Gospel tells a completely different narrative about him "handing over" Jesus than relayed in the other Gospels in the ***New Testament.*** Jesus was not outside praying but was in the "great room" which could be interpreted as the "dining room" where they were having their Seder dinner or their Last Supper. Also, it was the Jewish leaders which Judas refers to as the "scribes" (Pharisees) who wanted Jesus arrested and wanted it to be done privately "***for they were afraid of the people, for he was regarded by all as a prophet."*** Several of the Jewish leaders considered Jesus to be a troublemaker and really did not need to have him "preaching" throughout crowded Jerusalem during the Passover holy days. Judas said the "scribes" were surprised to see Judas there and said to him, ***"What are you doing here? You are Jesus' Disciple?"*** [58] They too were not aware of Judas' need to be there to make sure his Master was "handed over" to the authorities so that He could be put to death and fulfill His mission. Judas says he gave them the response they wanted to hear; they gave him money for his deed. And that is where the ***Gospel of Judas*** ends. For Judas, that is the end of the story of

Jesus' life and mission on earth. Jesus' death, resurrection, and appearances were a natural progression expected as He transformed back to a heavenly Spirit.

IMPORTANT POINT: There have been different and conflicting accounts of Jesus' arrest and resurrection. The story of whom had Jesus arrested and condemned have gone back and forth between the Romans and the Jews. In those days, the Gospels would never say the Romans had Jesus killed while they were already being oppressed by the Roman Empire. Then in later days, it was OK to blame the Romans. At different points of history, it was convenient to blame and persecute the Jews for putting Jesus to death. Each seemed to have perfectly justified scenarios, so much so, we may not ever know the real truth.

THE THEOLOGY ACCORDING TO JUDAS

It is not surprising that the ***Gospel of Judas*** has a different perspective on the mission of Jesus than the four Gospels that were put in the ***New Testament.*** However, at this point, it should not be surprising that the perspective of Judas is not much different than the Gospels of the other Disciples which also did not make it into the ***New Testament.***

Many agree that the creator of this world is not the True God and Supreme Being, thus making it an evil place which needs to be escaped. Jesus Christ is not the Son of this inferior creator god. Our salvation does not come through the death and resurrection of Jesus Christ. Our salvation is in Jesus' revelation of secret knowledge, the **gnosis,** about from where we came and to where we will return. All this was suppressed by the early and current Christian Church who in the early centuries developed and cemented a completely different line of beliefs, doctrines, and creeds. Their views were considered correct, or "orthodox," and any differing views were wrong, or "heresy." Such is just an **opinion of men.**

Over the centuries, the opposing viewpoints kept coming to light and have been quickly debunked by the Catholic Church. The ***Gospel of Judas*** gives us a good narrative of a conflicting viewpoint. All these "conflicting viewpoints" also did have their "Sacred Apostolic Scriptures" passed down from one of Jesus' Disciples to back up their viewpoint; at least, until those books were banned by the Catholic Church. The favored faction powered by the Roman Empire under Emperor Constantine won the skirmish and got to establish the One, Holy, Catholic, and Apostolic Church as a result of the Council of Nicaea in A.D. 325. A major part of this success, they got to formulate the "One, Holy, Catholic, and Apostolic" Christian Creed which begins with:

> ***"I believe in one God, the Father Almighty,***
> ***the Maker of Heaven and Earth,***
> ***and of all things visible and invisible."***

IMPORTANT POINT: The Gospels of Judas and other Disciples who did not support this fact, albeit a fact that was established after those Gospels had long been in circulation, had to be extinguished, banned, and destroyed by fire.

Also important to note: Christianity in order to be the successor to Judaism, and pliable to the Jews they wanted to convert, had to ALSO be a monotheistic religion meaning that there is only one God who obviously was the only one who could be the maker of Heaven and Earth, and of all things visible and invisible.

The ***Gospel of Judas*** from its beginning makes it clear that the God and Father of Jesus was NOT the God of the Jews.

In one of the opening narratives, when the Disciples were having a meal and giving thanks to God for the food they were about to eat, Jesus began to laugh. When the Disciples asked Jesus why He was laughing, He told them in an ambiguous way that they were giving praise to their God who was NOT the God of Jesus. Jesus tells them again how "***God is within you.***"

The ***Gospel of Judas*** shows how the Disciples did not realize who Jesus really was; who was the God that Jesus was worshipping; who was Jesus' Father; who sent Jesus to Earth; who was the Supreme Being; and what was Jesus' real mission on Earth. Judas credits himself with being the only one that really understands. Judas makes that clear when he tells Jesus he knows He came from ***"the immortal aeon of Barbelo,"*** or the realm of the true immortal divine beings.

It was early Church patriarch Irenaeus who in A.D. 180 who began preaching that there is only one God who was the maker of Heaven and Earth, and all things that exist. Judas tells us that Jesus tried to explain to him that there were enormous numbers of divine beings: 72 Aeons, each with a luminary, and each with five firmaments of the Heavens (or 360 firmaments), along with countless throngs of angels. Not that all these divine beings were good, in fact, many belonged to a realm of corruption [50]. The humans that inhabited this world were not a creation of the one, true, good God. This was the existence from which the God of the Jews, the God of the ***Old Testament,*** came into being. They included the rebel Yaldabaoth and the fool, Saklas. It was these two latter beings that created the world and inhabited it with human beings to serve and worship them. These were the inferior gods that Jesus was referring to that the Disciples were worshipping, and giving thanks and praise.

On the positive side, in contrast to the mean and vengeful God of the Jews, the God portrayed in the ***Old Testament*** (a/k/a the Hebrew Bible), we are told by Judas and others: the God of Jesus is a total spirit who is Supreme, Almighty, above-all, all-good, all-powerful, all-knowing, all-loving, and all-merciful. He is far removed from this material and evil world of hatred, war, sin, pain, and suffering. He could never sanction what goes on in this world. Likewise, Jesus wants to return to the perfect Heavenly realm of His Father. After His death, he "appeared" at various times, in a different place, sometimes as a discernible form to several people or, sometimes, only selected people in a crowd could see Him. This proves He transitioned back to being a Spirit. He could easily alter His appearance. This becomes another bone-of-contention when the **Gnostic Gospels** profess Jesus did NOT have a bodily resurrection.

As found in the **Gnostic Gospels,** Jesus spent a lot of time discussing the "secret mysteries" about the immortal realm where the true God reigns. He tells us that this is the realm from which we came. He often appears to His Disciples (usually as Himself), but He also was found in their midst as a young child [33]. Some Biblical scholars believe that Jesus was always Docetic (from the Greek ***dokeo*** meaning "seem" or "appear"), that is, through His whole time on Earth He only appeared and looked like a human. At any time, Jesus could take any form or person that He wanted. He would do this often according to the non-canonical book, the ***Acts of John.*** Of course, this was one of the books that was banned and ordered destroyed. [Why would you include the ***Gospel of John*** and ***Revelations*** but order the ***Acts of John*** banned?]

The secret knowledge is found throughout the ***Gospel of Judas;*** the secret knowledge (**gnosis**) that Jesus imparted to Judas. Why was Judas the only one worthy to be told this secret knowledge? Maybe it had to do with Judas admitting to Jesus that he realized He was from the "**Aeons of Barbelo.**" Judas knew Jesus' destiny was to return to that divine realm; a realm that Judas believed Jesus visited even during this time on earth. At one point when the Disciples asked Jesus where He had been, Jesus replied, "***I went to another great and holy generation.***" Jesus merely laughed them off as part of their ignorance. They would not understand that it was realm beyond this world, a realm of perfection and truth, and the ultimate destination of those that possess the divine spark and can escape this material and evil world. Judas alone understood what Jesus had explained to him. Judas knew Jesus came from that realm and it will be to where He will return. It was Judas that was more of an intimate follower of Jesus in this regard and as such the only one worthy enough to receive the secret knowledge about this eternal divine realm that exists beyond this earth. Likewise, it was Judas that realized it was through Jesus' arrest and death that He would be released from His earthly body and could permanently return to His divine Heavenly home. This is why the ***Gospel of Judas*** ends where it does at the "hand-off" of Jesus.

<u>IMPORTANT POINT:</u> Remember that in the time of Jesus and His Disciples, the Jewish faith did not believe there was eternal life after death. Some people believe that was the whole purpose of Jesus coming to this Earth, dying and re-appearing after His death. Judas apparently grasped and accepted the controversial concept of "life after death."

IMPORTANT POINT: Irenaeus and other proto-orthodox Church leaders had interpreted the Gospels and the Epistles of Paul [Paul, the loose cannon Paul who never met Jesus] that Jesus' death was to atone for the sins of humans against God in order to secure their salvation and regain their acceptance into Heaven. Jesus never said any of this!

IMPORTANT POINT: The ***Gospel of Judas*** offends the aforementioned people even more by not talking about "resurrections" whether it is Jesus' body or ours. That is because resurrections will not happen. There will be no "bodies coming back to life;" not then, not now, not in the future, and not at the end of the world. Life after death is on a "spirit" basis. The whole point of Jesus' salvation is to escape this mortal body and this material world. Resurrection will bring the person back into this world of the evil creator. That is the very last thing Jesus would want to happen.

As Jesus said in the ***Gospel of Judas:***

> ***"The souls of every human generation will die. When these people*** [those that came from the divine realm], ***however, have completed the time of the kingdom and the spirit leaves them, their bodies will die, but their souls will be alive, and they will be taken up."*** [43]

As many of Judas' peers believe, the human is made up of 3 distinct parts: a body, a spirit, and a soul. The body is the material and mortal part that contains the soul. The spirit is the force that animates the body and gives it life. When the spirit leaves the body, the body dies and the person ceases to exist. For those that lack the divine spark, their soul dies too.

Jesus famously said: "***It is impossible to sow seed on*** [rock] ***and harvest is fruit."*** [43-44] This means unless a human contains the divine spark inside themselves, there will be no life after death; there will be no return to the Heavenly Kingdom. But doesn't everyone have a divine spark? Not necessarily. Persons who are born as "dark entities" will never see the divine realm and some believed to be cursed to forever to dwell in this evil world where they will belong until the end of days, constantly being born here, again and again, to live lifetime after lifetime. This is their hell.

An explanation can be found in the ***Gospel of Judas.*** Judas asked, ***"Does the human spirit die?"*** [53] Jesus explains to Judas that there are two forms of humans: one whose body has been given a temporary spirit by the Archangel Michael and serves a purpose to others; and those who have been granted an eternal spirit by the Archangel Gabriel. It is the latter group who has the divine spark inside of them which will allow them to return to the divine realm after their death. [53] Jesus does assure Judas that he is in the latter group, but Jesus does not mention into which group the other Disciples fall. Does this imply they fall into the former group and the other eleven Disciples do not exist in the afterlife?

Along those lines, it is constantly implied in the ***Gospel of Judas*** that the other eleven do not understand the truth about this world and the afterlife the same way Judas does. This would mean they are outside of the ones that will be saved. Ironically, they were the first to criticize and persecute Judas; however, it was Judas that Jesus entrusted with the "mysteries of the universe." Judas grasped what Jesus was telling him. Jesus even referred to Judas as "the thirteenth" which can be implied that Judas is above all the other Disciples. Repeatedly, the eleven continued ignorantly to worship the inferior creator-God. This is why Judas was chosen by Jesus to be a hero – Judas was definitely not a traitor.

The emerging Christian Church and its leaders did and did not break away from Judaism. Yes, they got away from strict adherence to the Law of Moses and worshipping in Synagogues. However, they did adopt the Hebrew Bible (calling it the ***Old Testament***) as an integral part of their Christian Bible (calling it the ***New Testament***); and worse, they continued to worship the monotheistic God of the Jews, the God of the Hebrew Bible, the Messiah in fulfillment of the Hebrew prophecies (some exaggerating to make that fulfillment), who is the mean and vengeful God which is a slap in the face to the True, Almighty, All-Good, All-Loving, All-Powerful, and All-Merciful Supreme God.

The ***Gospel of Judas*** is among other **Gnostic Gospels** that were banned and ordered destroyed because they would show how the emerging Christian Church had totally misleading their followers. The Church Leaders in the early stages firmly installed the God of the Jews as the One, True God. They perpetuated our miserable lives. This world is material and evil full of pain and suffering to the muse of this inferior creator-God who demands to be feared and worshipped. This gave the Church Leaders power over their flocks. The real Supreme God would never have allowed this world to go so awry. That is why He sent His Son to enlighten us and save us from this miserable world. Any **Alternative Christianities** that were taught by Peter, Thomas, Philip, and James was completely extinguished by these self-proclaimed leaders. The ***Gospel of Judas***, along with the other banned Gospels, probably contains the real Christianity as it was taught by Jesus. Ironically, they relied heavily on the Christianity according to one-vision-wonder Paul.

JUDAS AS A GNOSTIC

It has been mentioned in previous narratives that the ***Gospel of Judas*** is considered a **Gnostic Gospel.** The truth is that the beliefs and narratives which appear in the ***Gospel of Judas*** are strikingly compatible with similar texts and Gospels that were revered by the other **Gnostic** communities of the day. Along with all the so-called **Gnostic Gospels,** the ***Gospel of Judas*** was discredited by Irenaeus and eventually banned and ordered destroyed. Irenaeus probably never even read the ***Gospel of Judas*** because he was quoted as saying it was preposterous that the betrayer of Jesus would write a Gospel; besides Judas (supposedly by ONE canonical account) immediately killed himself.

Gnostics believe they possess a higher knowledge (the Greek word ***gnostikoi*** means the knowers or the people of knowledge). They interpret Jesus' teachings as more mystical, not about the material world found in the four canonical Gospels, but it transcends this earth. They teach salvation is attained through this advanced knowledge. ***Gnosis*** is found twice in the ***Gospel of Judas*** [50 and 54]. For example in 54 he says, "…***knowledge given to Adam and those with him so that the kings of chaos and the underworld might not lord over them."*** This suggests that this special knowledge or ***gnosis***, i.e. the divine connection within them, was given to Adam and his descendants to protect them and learn how to save themselves from the evil powers that created this world.

In fact, the ***Gospel of Judas*** follows the **Sethian Gnostic** tradition's school of thought. The other Disciples never understood who Jesus was; they claimed He was the Son of their God, the God of the Jews, the God of the Hebrew Bible (the ***Old Testament***), and the creator and ruler over this evil world. But Judas realized who Jesus was and said, ***"I know who you are and where you have come from. You have come from the immortal Aeon of Barbelo. And I am not worthy to utter the name of the One who has sent you."*** (***Gospel of Judas*** 35) The eternal realm of Barbelo is mentioned many times in Sethian texts as the exalted divine realm beyond this world. Many times the prominent divine figure Barbelo in Sethian texts is assumed to be our Divine Mother in Heaven.

It is uncertain about the origin of Barbelo. Possibly it derives from the four-letter name attached to God from when He was asked what He shall be called: **YHWH.** This was pronounced **YAHWEH,** which became **JEHOVAH** in Jewish Scriptures and in English. The Hebrew word for "four" is "***arba***" which could substitute for YHWH, and the word for "God" is "***El.***" Put together it becomes BARBELO or the realm of the Almighty Divine God.

The **Sethian Texts** put down the world in which we live. They consider the creator of this world a mega-maniac demiurge that humans mistakenly worship and serve. But Sethians believe that humans need to realize that there is a divine spark inside of them that connects them to the Almighty life giver. When they realize their true selves are really also divine, they will be able to overcome the evil powers of this world and realize the peace that comes with enlightenment. The ***Gospel of Judas*** tells us that Jesus taught Judas that humans need to get a proper understanding about life in this world and what lies in the afterlife. This parallels the Sethian teachings.

The ***Gospel of Judas*** also identifies the Father of All as the "Great Invisible Spirit" [47], or "the Great One" [53]. It is implied that referring to the Great One as "God" or "Divine" should be used only to identify the lower powers of the Divine universe which includes the creator of this world [48]. The Great One transcends the finite term of "God."

The ***Secret Book of John***, which was also banned, concurs with the ***Gospel of Judas***:

> ***"The One is a sovereign that has nothing over it. It is God and Parent, Father of All, the Invisible One that is over All, that is incorruptible, that is pure light at which no eye can gaze. The One is the invisible Spirit. We should not think of it as a God or like a God. For it is greater than a God because it has nothing over it and no lord above it...."***

This phraseology and facts appear when Jesus gave private instruction to Judas:

> ***"[Come], that I may teach you about the [things...] that [no] human will [ever] see. For there exists a great and boundless Aeon, which is the Great Invisible Spirit, which no eye of an angel has ever seen, no thought of the heart has ever comprehended, and it was never called by any name."*** [47]

The ***Secret Book of John*** and ***Allogenes the Stranger*** expand upon the above description:

> ***"The One is illimitable...unfathomable... immeasurable...invisible...eternal...unutterable... unnamable...."***
>
> ***"The One is the immeasurable light, pure, holy, immaculate. It is unutterable and is perfect***

> ***in incorruptibility. Not just perfection, or blessedness, or divinity: It is much greater."***
>
> ***"The One is not corporal and it not incorporal.***
> ***The One is not large and it is not small.***
> ***It is impossible to say, 'How much is it?' 'What [kind is it]?'***
> ***For no one can understand it."*** [II: 3]

This reinforces the words of Judas to Jesus at the beginning of the ***Gospel of Judas:***

> ***"I am not worthy to utter the name of the one who has sent you."*** [35]

In the ***Gospel of Judas*** [47-50], Jesus tells us about the glorious manner in which the Divine extends itself. The Great One, the Great Invisible Spirit, transcends all aspects of this world of mortality here below, so some manifestation of the divine must bring about the creation and salvation of the world.

The Great One expands through Aeons and countless entities to the fullness of its Divine glory. It was because of a tragic mistake in the divine realm, a lapse of wisdom, a fallen and inferior God that corrupted this world to his own Glory and made its inhabitants his fearful slaves. The story of Adam and Eve in ***Genesis*** had a different meaning to the **Sethian Gnostics.** When Adam and Eve yielded to the serpent [known to be the symbol of wisdom] and ate from the tree of knowledge against the command given them by their God, they were able to distinguish between good and evil. They may have realized their God was evil and not the real God but were floundering to get out from under his control.

Adam and Eve may have also realized they were the prodigy of the fallen Aeon Sophia. The ***Secret Book of John*** (which was banned by the powers-that-be) describes the fall of Sophia in some great detail:

> ***"Now Sophia, who is the Wisdom of Insight and who constitutes an Aeon, conceived of a thought from herself, with the conception of the invisible Spirit for Foreknowledge. She wanted to bring forth something like herself, without the consent of the Spirit, who had not given approval, without her partner and without his consideration. The male did not give approval. She did not find her partner, and she considered this without the Spirit's consent and without the knowledge of her partner. Nonetheless, she gave birth. And because of the invincible power within her, her thought was not an idle thought. Something came out of her that was imperfect and different in appearance from her, for she had produced it without her partner. It did not resemble its mother, and was misshapen."*** [II: 9-10]

In the ***Letter of Peter to Philip*** there is further detail about the fall of Mother Sophia:

> ***"To begin with,*** **[concerning]** ***the deficiency of the Aeon, what is deficient is disobedience. The Mother, showing your judgment, came to expression without the command of the Great One.... when the Arrogant One appeared. A body part from within her was left behind and the Arrogant One grabbed it, and deficiency came to be. This then is the deficiency of the Aeons."*** [3-4]

The word "deficiency" is a keyword used in Sethian and other **Gnostic** texts and can be found in the ***Gospel of Judas*** 39. The deficiency or diminution referred to is the divine spark or divine light due to a bad conception. This can also be found in the ***Secret Gospel of John.***

The interpretation is very clear to Biblical Scholars. Fallen Sophia created Adam and Eve and used Adam and Eve to create the human race. Because of her misdeed and misconception, she created a race of people but not proper children of the Great One; however, because of her deity status, the race has the divine spark and connection to the Great One.

In the ***Letter of Peter to Philip,*** the Mother that is referenced could be either Sofia or Eve. Many **Gnostics** believe there is an ambiguous connection between Sophia and Eve. The divine spirit in either was passed on to their offsprings.

The ***Gospel of Judas*** agrees with the aforementioned and other texts on this subject. The deficiency of this world comes from the lapse of Wisdom (Sophia) and the divine spark with the human beings needs to be restored to the Divine Supreme Being again. They must realize that this will happen when they leave their mortal bodies and this world. The ***Gospel of Judas*** clearly states that Jesus said that when the people die, their mortal bodies will die, but their souls will be liberated, remain alive and return to their Heavenly home [43]. Jesus told Judas that "***their souls go up to the Aeons on high."*** [44]

<u>**IMPORTANT POINT:**</u> In retrospect, it is possible that Jesus' message was simply telling us that when we die our soul and spirit will live on forever in His Father's Heavenly

Home. It is possible to read the parables and teachings of Jesus and draw this message. Remember, Judaism at that time did not believe in life after death.

IMPORTANT POINT: The ***Gospel of Judas,*** like the **Gnostic** Gospels attributed to other Disciples, is on a higher ***mystical*** level. The Divine Light of God flowing into this world is reminiscent of the Hebrew mystical tradition of Kabbalah and the Divine Energy emanating from the infinite God. The **Gnostic** Gospels may be the link and natural progression from Judaism to **Gnostic Christianity.**

In the Valentinian **Gnostic** traditions, they go a step further in their discussions about Sofia and claim there is a higher Wisdom and a lower Wisdom. This may have been done to account for a basically good Higher Power and a much more evil Lower Power responsible for this evil and this inferior world. The Valentinians favored the ***Gospel of Philip.*** The Higher Wisdom, the more divine, is called Sophia and the Lower Wisdom, the wisdom of evil, is called Echmoth.

There is also a reference to "corruptible wisdom." This could be alluding to the offspring of Sophia, the product of her mistake, the child described in the ***Secret Book of John.*** Known from the Sethian texts, he is one who has been labeled "the Arrogant One" in the ***Letter of Peter to Philip*** described as the creator and ruler of this mortal world. He is not a kind or gentle figure but a demiurge responsible for imprisoning the divine spark inside our mortal bodies. He is sometimes called Yaldabaoth which can be translated to mean "child of chaos." The ***Gospel of Judas*** refers to him as Nebro (an abbreviated form of Nebroel found in the ***Holy Book of the Great Invisible Spirit)***. The ***Holy Book*** goes further to say he had sex with Salda and produces 12 Aeons. It was with these lower deities that the creator made this world. This account is paralleled, with very little variation, in different texts describing the bureaucracy of rulers over this world.

The ***Secret Book of John*** tells us that there are seven deities that are placed over the seven spheres of the heavens (the Sun, the moon, Mercury, Venus, Mars, Jupiter, and Saturn). John also tells us there are five deities over the abyss.

SETHIAN GNOSTICS

One major branch of **Gnosticism** is **Sethian Gnosticism**, which is also mentioned in the ***Gospel of Judas*** and the ***Secret Book of John.*** Judas portrays Adam and Eve, and their sons Cain and Abel, as a very dysfunctional family. Honestly, that is not a stretch from the Biblical narrative in Genesis. First, Adam and Eve were disobedient to God and thus were evicted from the Garden of Eden. Both Cain and Abel came to tragic ends. But we know, according to Genesis 4-5, Adam and Eve had a third son named Seth. Seth was the good descendant of Adam who was a creation of God. Seth carried on the family of Adam. Seth became known by the Greek "***Allogenes***" which means "one of another kind" or "the stranger." Seth himself had a son called Enoch. Part of the discovery at Nag Hammadi was also a text called "***Allogenes***" or by the combined translation "***Allogenes the Stranger."*** In the Codex Tchacos, it is the fourth tractate and immediately follows the ***Gospel of Judas.*** Sometimes it is referred to as the ***Book of Allogenes*** alluding to Seth.

The story told of the creation of Adam and Eve and their children in the ***Gospel of Judas:*** "***Then Saklas said to his***

angels, 'Let us create a human being after the likeness and after the image'." (52) Similarly, in Genesis tells us that the creator fashioned human beings after his likeness and image of the divine (***Gen***. 1:26). The divine probably being the same "Arrogant One" described in the ***Letter of Peter to Philip***.

One unique characteristic of the ***Gospel of Judas*** was its references to the astronomical and astrological roles of the planets and stars in the life of humans. Judas says humans have souls which are ruled by the stars that make their souls immortal. When the body dies, the spirit will leave them, their souls remain alive, and they will be taken up. (43) How those powers of the sky rule over humans can be found in other Sethian texts.

It is defined in many texts that the spirit is the breath of life and the soul is the inner person, which comes from the divine, and upon the death of the body, the soul will return to the divine. In the ***Gospel of Judas,*** Jesus told Judas and the other Disciples, "***Each of you has his own star."***

At the end of the ***Gospel of Judas,*** Jesus tells Judas that he is unique. Judas will have a fate full of grief; he will be ousted by the Circle of Twelve Disciples; he will be replaced in the Circle of Twelve by another; he will be cursed by many generations. But in the end, Judas will become "***the thirteenth one"*** and his star will lead the way for the others. (***Judas*** 35-36; ***Acts*** 1:15-26) One day his star will rule over the "***thirteenth Aeon***." The "***thirteenth Aeon***" is found more than forty times in the ***Pistis Sophia*** where it is a righteous place located above the twelve Aeons and twenty-four Luminaries. The "***thirteenth Aeon***" is the home of Sophia.

IMPORTANT POINT: This is interpreted to mean that when the others realize what Judas did was what had to be done, and what he was commanded by Jesus to do, he will become the brightest star among the Circle of Twelve.

SUMMARY

Judas in the ***Gospel of Judas*** is portrayed as the main recipient of the special knowledge about God and the universe taught to him by Jesus Himself.

We know that the ***Gospel of Judas*** existed in the 2nd Century thanks to Irenaeus, he wrote about it in his ***Against Heresies*** which was published in A.D. 180. We also are told that there were many followers who revered the ***Gospel of Judas*** and its revelations about salvation. It was a story of hope about the wonderful afterlife that awaits us and how it can be realized through **gnosis** and insight of the divine and the Godly spark within us. The thing that made it controversial with the emerging Christian Church, Judas claims that he knows the real road to salvation and it is not through the sacrifice on the cross. The ***Gospel of Judas*** was the principal text used by the Sethian Christians. They looked upon Jesus Christ as a spiritual being who was sent to us from above, a deity, with the mission to inform the world that within us is a divine spark, a perfect human being, who is destined to also be divine. We just need to tap into the strength of our inner self because at the end of our mortal lives we will leave this material world. This was all explained to Judas by Jesus when He shared the secrets of the universe and cosmos (***Gospel of Judas*** 47-53). Obviously, this has been a major contention between the Catholic Church and the various **Gnostic** sects all of whom shared common or core beliefs.

The ***Gospel of John*** espouses similar philosophies but with a very ironic twist. It seems to have transformed Jewish Sethian **Gnostic** teachings from the famous Eugnostos the Blessed, a Jewish **Gnostic**, into Christian Sethian **Gnostic** teachings. Jesus was considered to be the Son of the Divine Barbelo (II: 6-7). There remains a Jewish **Gnostic** sect known as Kabbalah still being practiced today.

IMPORTANT POINT: The early Church Leaders did not want the ***Gospel of John*** to be included alongside the synoptic (similar) Gospels of ***Matthew, Mark,*** and ***Luke*** because it was too **gnostic.** It is clear that the ***Gospel of John*** and ***Revelations*** (believed to have also been from John) are completely different, such as Jesus is considered to be more Divine by John than portrayed in Gospels of ***Matthew, Mark,*** and ***Luke.*** But the Disciple John had a very big following and without including John's Gospel in the Bible the emerging Christian Church would have lost a large chunk of people who were followers and a part of the world. They were forced to include the ***Gospel of John.***

CONCLUSION

The ***Gospel of Judas*** leaves some people with many questions and some people with an abundance of hope. In the ***Gospel of Judas*** Jesus gives Judas an enlightening message of hope for all humanity of liberation and salvation. Some believe that Jesus did provide the same revelations to all the Disciples but it fell on deaf ears; they still walked away ignorant about what He was trying to tell them. Interesting is the timeline laid out by Judas in his Gospel of when this famous discussion took place, "***during eight days, three days before His passion.***" This can be construed to mean eleven days before His arrest. Jesus must have considered

Judas more receptive to this information. This may have also included the discussion when Jesus asked Judas to "hand over" Him to the Jewish high priests so that His destiny could be fulfilled. Judas reluctantly understood and performed this greatest service to his master by liberating Him from His mortal body.

BIBLIOGRAPHY, REFERENCES, AND SUGGESTED READING

Barnstone, Willis, and Marvin Meyer, ***The Gnostic Bible,*** © 2003 Shambhala, Boston

Barnstone, Willis, ***Restored New Testament: A New Translation With Commentary, Including the Gnostic Gospels of Thomas, Mary, and Judas*** © 2009

Ehrman, Bart D., ***The Gospel of Judas Iscariot: A New Look at Betrayer and Betrayed*** © 2006 Oxford University Press, New York

Ehrman, Bart D., ***Lost Christianities: The Battle for Scriptures and The Faiths We Never Knew*** © 2003 Oxford University Press, New York

Ehrman, Bart D., ***Lost Scriptures: Books That Did Not Make It Into The New Testament*** © 2003 Oxford University Press, New York

Klassen, William, ***Judas: Betrayer or Friend of Jesus?*** © 1996 Fortress, Minneapolis

Kasser, Richard, Marvin Meyer, and Gregor Wurst, ***Judas: The Gospel of Judas, Second Edition*** © 2008 © 2006 National Geographic Society, Washington D.C.

Koester, Helmut, and Elaine Pagels, ***Introduction to the "Dialogue of the Savior"***

Krosney, Herbert, ***The Lost Gospel: The Quest for The Gospel of Judas Iscariot*** © 2006 National Geographic Society, Washington D.C.

Meyers, Marvin, ***The Gnostic Gospels of Jesus: The Definitive Collection of Mystical Gospels and Secret Books about Jesus of Nazareth*** © 2005 Harper, San Francisco

Meyers, Marvin, ***Judas: The Definitive Collection of Gospels and Legends About The Infamous Apostle of Jesus,*** © 2007 HarperOne, San Francisco

Pagels, Elaine and Karen L. King ***Reading Judas: The Gospel of Judas and The Shaping of Christianity*** © 2007 Viking Press, New York, N.Y.

Robinson, James M. ***The Secrets of Judas: The Story of The Misunderstood Disciple and His Lost Gospel*** © 2006 Harper, San Francisco

Wright, N. T. ***Judas and The Gospel of Jesus: Have We Missed the Truth About Christianity?*** © 2006 Baker, Grand Rapids, MI

This Book and Treatise are a compilation from many sources on the same subject. See the Complete List of Bibliographies, References, and Suggested Readings in Appendix II

CHAPTER 13

THE GOSPEL OF MARY

INTRODUCTION

The ***Gospel of Mary*** is considered to be a **Gnostic Gospel** found written in Coptic (the ancient Egyptian language) and written in Greek (the language of the educated). The best-educated deduction by historians is that this Gospel was written in the late First Century or early Second Century, probably in Syria or Egypt. The ***Gospel of Mary*** is mainly a dialogue between Jesus and His Disciples which included Mary Magdalene.

The ***Gospel of Mary*** is another uplifting story that was banned. We know that Mary Magdalene was a constant companion and always by the side of Jesus Christ. She was a part of His Inner Circle and an integral of His mission. In many ways, she was one of the better Disciples of Jesus.

When all the other Disciples ran and hid, and denied being one of Jesus' Disciples, Mary Magdalene stood by His side through His passion, crucifixion, death, and resurrection. She was the first to see He had risen from His tomb. But in the eyes of the early Christian Church, she was a woman, a former prostitute, and did not socially or religiously merit being on the same level as His male Disciples.

Mary Magdalene was a strong and independent woman who adored Jesus Christ. Many believe that Jesus and Mary were married, and the Wedding at Cana was really their wedding. Many references can be found to suggest their relationship was more than just platonic. Mary played a leading role in the life, crucifixion, death, and resurrection of Jesus Christ. She was the first to see the risen Christ. She ran to the Disciples to tell them that their Master had risen. This is attested to in the Gospels of Matthew, Mark, Luke, John, Thomas, Philip, and other texts; even though it may have been downplayed. As Peter assumed the role of leader of the Christian Church in Rome, he continued with his hostile relationship with Mary Magdalene. Jesus pronounced "***You are Peter and on this rock I shall build My Church....***" This made Peter the leader of the twelve male Disciples. For Peter, this did not include Mary, in large part due to the fact that she was a woman. A woman at that time was not on equal footing with any male. Women never had a leadership role in any capacity. It was a male-superior culture even though Jesus had many female followers. ***First Apocalypse of James*** says Jesus had twelve male Disciples and seven female Disciples including Mary.

Mary Magdalene, although instrumental, did not have a place in the emerging Church. Ironically, it was Mary Magdalene that strongly argued with the Disciples that they should come out of their 40-day hiding and preach about the Messiah to the world. In a way, if it wasn't for Mary, the Disciples may have never left their hiding place and Christianity just would have withered and died with the Twelve. A lot has been written about Mary Magdalene. Great fans of her were Elaine Pagels and Karen L. King who have written books about her, her life with Jesus, and her importance in jump-starting Christianity. Nikos Kazantzakis in his ***The Last Temptation of Christ*** does much speculation about the sexual and marital relationship between Jesus and Mary. Mary Magdalene has prominent storylines in books such as Dan Brown's ***The Da Vinci Code***, in which she is referred to as being the Holy Grail. Dan Brown's assertion was that Mary Magdalene was impregnated by Jesus and she was carrying His offspring, His bloodline, and His future descendants.

MARY MAGDALENE IN ANCIENT LITERATURE

All the accounts of Mary Magdalene seem to be consistent in their description of her. Besides being the repentant prostitute who washed Jesus' feet with her hair, she immediately became a close and beloved Disciple of Him. She was an ardent preacher of His gospels. According to the ***Gospel of Mary***, while the other Disciples were in hiding and mourning the departure of Jesus from this earth, it was Mary who was the strong one and got them moving. She lifted their spirits and assured them that Jesus was still with them and will guide them. She gave them a mission and goals.

The ***Dialogue of the Savior*** goes as far as to portray Mary Magdalene many times as the lead Disciple in conversations with Jesus Christ. She was described as the one that understood everything that Jesus was teaching.

In ***Pistis Sophia,*** Mary was the considered the most prominent of all the Disciples. She was very insightful in what Jesus was conveying. She understood the nature and real meaning of Jesus' salvation. Jesus says to Mary, "***You are one whose heart is set on Heaven's Kingdom more than all your brothers."*** And, ***"You are more blessed than all women on Earth...***[because you are a] ***pure, spiritual woman."***

In the ***Manichaean Psalms of Heracleides,*** Mary is the one that casts the net to gather up followers for Jesus because she is "***the spirit of wisdom."***

Karen L. King has written much about Mary Magdalene. She gives an excellent description of Mary Magdalene in her essay, <u>***Why All the Controversy? Mary in the Gospel of Mary?***</u>

"Although she, too knew the historical Jesus, was a witness to the resurrection and received instruction from the Savior, these experiences are not what set her apart from the others. Mary is clearly portrayed throughout the Gospel as an exemplary disciple. She does not falter when the Savior departs. She steps into His place after His departure, comforting, strengthening, and instructing the others. Her spiritual comprehension and spiritual maturity are demonstrated in her calm behavior and especially in her visionary experience.... She does not teach in her own name but passes on the words of the Savior, calming the Disciples, and turning their hearts toward the Good." (73-74)

In the ***Acts of Philip,*** there appears a woman named Mary who was referred to as the "sister" of the Disciple Philip. Biblical scholars believe this person is the one and the same

Mary Magdalene. She was a leading figure in this text. Her saliva has healing qualities, she taught, and she administered the sacraments. Philip would baptize the men while Mary baptized the women. Mary was ultimately arrested for her beliefs and practices.

Epiphanius of Salamis, a mean-spirited heresiologist, questioned a text known as ***Great Questions of Mary*** which Jesus made certain revelations to a Mary, probably who we know as Mary Magdalene. One such revelation Epiphanius criticized centers on the Genesis story of Adam and Eve and when Jesus took Eve from the side of Adam.

There are other tales and legends about Mary Magdalene that have become popular in Modern Times such as ***The Da Vinci Code; Holy Blood, Holy Grail;*** and ***The Woman and the Alabaster Jar.*** These texts strongly suggest that Jesus and Mary Magdalene were married and had children. The Holy Grail was actually the royal bloodline of Jesus and it is Mary Magdalene who is the Holy Grail, i.e. the holder of the blood and semen of Jesus. The descendants of Jesus have had a powerful impact on history and probably existent today. There is a feasible school of thought that Jesus did NOT die on the cross; especially in **Gnostic** and **Islamic** circles. Instead, Jesus, Mary Magdalene, and their children moved to the Marseilles area of France and could have migrated from there. The bloodline could have had a connection to, or at least influence on, the royal families of Europe.

It is told by Mary Magdalene in the ***Gospel of Mary*** how the Disciples hid in fear for their lives after the "departure" of their Master. Mary says she was the one who assured them by recounting all of the Master's visions and all that He had taught them. Mary Magdalene not only knew Jesus intimately but often spoke on His behalf. His wisdom was recorded and immortalized in the ***Gospel of Mary***, such as:

> ***"Do not weep or grieve or be in doubt, for His grace will be with you all and will protect you. Rather, let us praise His greatness, for He has prepared us and made us truly human."***

The ***Gospel of Mary*** begins with the discussion of our nature and destiny. The Savior tells us that all creation will return back to their roots. We see this in many of the **Gnostic** texts where we are told that we all come from the Heavenly cosmos and we all will return to the Heavenly cosmos from which we came. He advised His Disciples not to be distracted but rather to look within that our salvation comes from inside ourselves.

Jesus: ***"All natures, all formed things, all creatures exist in and with each other, and they will dissolve into their own root."***

Peter said to him, ***"Tell us… what is the sin of the world?***

Jesus replied, ***"There is no such thing as sin, but you create sin when you mingle as in adultery*** [i.e. improper dealing with the world] ***and this is called sin…. That is why you become sick and die…. Be of good courage. And if you are discouraged, be encouraged in the presence of the diversity of forms of nature."***

Jesus greeted the Disciples with, ***"Peace be with you. Receive My peace, Be careful that no one leads you astray by saying 'Look here' or 'Look there.' The child of humanity is within you. Follow that. Those who***

seek it will find it. Go and preach the good news of the Kingdom. Do not lay down any rules other than what I have given you, and do not establish law, as the lawgiver did, or you will be bound by it." He then left them.

Peter said to Mary, "***Sister, we know the Savior loved you more than any other woman. Tell us the words of the Savior that you remember, which you know but we do not because we have not heard them."*** She began to speak to them.

Mary tells them that she had seen the Master in a vision. She said she asked Him, ***"Master, how does a person see a vision, with the soul or with the spirit?"*** She then relays to them how the Savior answered her, ***"A person sees neither with the soul nor with the spirit. The mind, which is between the two, sees the vision."***

The Disciples Peter and Andrew never would give any credence to Mary. Andrew said to the other Disciples, ***"Say what you think about what she said, but I do not believe the Savior said this. These teachings certainly are strange ideas."*** Peter said something similar, if not more damning, ***"Did He really speak with a woman in private without our knowledge? Should we all turn and listen to her? Did He prefer her to us?"*** Mary cried and replied to Peter, ***"My brother Peter, what do you think? Do you think that I made this up by myself or that I am lying about the Savior?"***

To this exchange, Levi, a disciple and friend of Matthew, said the Peter, ***"Peter, you always are angry. Now I see you arguing against this woman like an adversary. If the Savior made her worthy, who are you to reject her? Surely the Savior knows her well. That is why He has***

loved her more than us." Levi continued giving the same advice as Mary had done, ***"... as He commanded us, and preach the good news, not making any rule or law other than what the Savior indicated."*** It was with this, the Disciples began to leave to teach and preach.

Mary Magdalene was referenced consistently throughout the various Gospels. Similar stories can be found in the ***Gospel of Mary.*** We know that all the Gospels were not written at the same time by the same people (that is, other than the synoptic Gospels which we know two were copied from an earlier one). Having the same stories in it just gives more credence to the ***Gospel of Mary.***

MARY IN THE *GOSPEL OF THOMAS*

Two references to Mary are found in the ***Gospel of Thomas*** and the Mary within the context that can be considered to be Mary Magdalene. This is especially true in Saying 114 knowing the hostility that Peter had for Mary Magdalene.

Saying 21: "***Mary said to Jesus, 'What are your Disciples like?' He said, 'They are like servants entrusted with a field that is not theirs. When the owners of the field come, they will say, 'Give our field back to us.' They take off their clothes in front of them in order to give it back to them, and they return their field to them."***

Saying 114: ***"Simon Peter said to them: 'Mary should leave us for females are not worthy of life.' Jesus said, 'Look, I shall guide her to make her male, so that she too may become a living spirit resembling you males. For***

every female who makes herself male will enter Heaven's Kingdom."

This does not fare well for Mary as much as it does for Peter with Jesus telling Peter that He will guide Mary to becoming a male so that she will be able to enter the Kingdom of Heaven. This could have many interpretations. It could be purely symbolic or mean for her to have a strong masculine spirit and demeanor. Or it could have a deeper meaning telling Peter more or less than a person's gender in the Kingdom is of no importance anymore.

MARY IN THE *GOSPEL OF PHILIP*

There are also two references to Mary in the ***Gospel of Philip***

Passage 59: ***"Three women always walked with the Master: Mary, His mother, [His] sister, and Mary Magdalene, who is called His companion. For 'Mary' is the name of His sister, His mother, and His companion."***

Some Coptic translations say "her" sister. Then there are different interpretations of who the "her" is. Many think "her" is a reference to Mary, His mother's sister. In some historical texts, Jesus had a sister named "Mary" in which case "His" sister would be appropriate; but in other texts, none of His sisters were named "Mary."

In the first sentence, Mary Magdalene is referred to as "***kiononos"*** which originates from the Greek; and in the second sentence is referred to as "***hotre"*** which originates from the Egyptian; both can be translated as a "companion, partner, or consort." This could mean they were really a couple. Some just think it refers to the love Jesus had for Mary Magdalene.

Passage 63-64: ***"The companion of the [Savior] is Mary Magdalene. The [Savior loved] her more than [all] the Disciples [and He] kissed her often on her [mouth]. The other [Disciples] said to Him: 'Why do you love her more than all of us?"***

Again, the Coptic translation is less precise where He kissed her; could have been the forehead or cheeks. Many Biblical Scholars believe Jesus and Mary were married. In the ***Gospel of Philip,*** there are discussions about sexuality, marriage, and the bridal chamber. Different than the Epistles of Paul, Philip believes in sex and the institution of marriage. He believes in the sanctity of Bridal Chamber. This is aligned with other Valentinian texts that also have emphasized the physical human relationship as part of their spiritual union. Kissing plays an important part. The Bridal Chamber is considered one of the greatest sacraments. This would be the equivalent of today's sacrament of Matrimony. The ***Gospel of Philip*** says, "***the perfect conceive and give birth through a kiss."*** This could be referring to the ceremonial kiss beginning a marriage. It could also mean how life and spirit are communicated between husband and wife.

The ***Gospel of Philip*** says:

"Animals do not have a wedding chamber, nor do slaves or defiled women. The wedding chamber is for free men and virgins. No [one can] ***know when*** [a husband] ***and wife have sex except for those two, for marriage in this world is a mystery for those married."***

MARY IN *THE DIALOGUE OF THE SAVIOR*

The Dialogue of the Savior was one of the texts found at Nag Hammadi. It is believed to have been written in the early decades of the 2nd Century. Materials in it can also be found in other texts. ***The Dialogue of the Savior*** contains many of the same **Gnostic** issues and themes that are found in the ***Gospel of Thomas.*** Mainly it is a discussion by Jesus to His Disciples about **Gnostic** issues. The Disciples referenced the most are: Judas (could also be Judas Thomas of the ***Gospel of Thomas***), Matthew, and Mary (certainly was Mary Magdalene). It references a **Gnostic** apocalyptic vision by Judas, Matthew, and Mary whereas a light from God comes down from the realm of fullness and the world must be saved through the word and restored to the light above. They discussed the meaning of this vision with Jesus putting forth His wisdom. The text does say that Mary was "***as a woman who understood everything"*** [or understood completely.]

The Dialogue of the Savior says:

"He [took] ***Judas, Matthew, and Mary*** (136) [to show them the final] ***consummation of Heaven and Earth, and when He placed his [hand] on them, they hoped the might [see] it. Judas gazed up and saw a region of great height, and he saw the region of the abyss below."...***

"[His] Disciples marveled at everything He told them, and they accepted all of it in faith. And they understood that there is no need to keep wickedness before one's eyes."...

"He went on to say, 'Do your best to save what can come after [me], and seek it and speak through it, so that whenever you seek may be in harmony with you. For

I [tell] you the truth, the living God [is] in you, [as you also are] in God.' (138)

"Judas [said], 'I really want [to learn everything].'"

Mary and the Disciples ask the Master about the dead and the living:

"Matthew asked, 'Tell me, Master, how the dead die and how the living live.' " (140)

"The Master said, '...I say to you, when what moves a person slips away, that person will be called dead, and when what is living leaves what is dead, it will be called alive.'"

"Judas asked, 'So why really do some [die] and some live?'"

"The Master said, 'Whatever is from truth does not die. Whatever is from woman dies.'" (144-145)

MARY IN *PISTIS SOPHIA*

Pistis Sophia translates as "Faith" or "Wisdom" which is a reference to a female deity who may have originally fallen from the divine realm. The manuscript discovered dated to the second half of the fourth century but is believed to have been composed at least a century earlier in Egypt. It contains numerous **Gnostic** reflections and revelations which agree with similar older ancient texts including the ones discovered at Nag Hammadi in Egypt.

What is unique about this text is the special and prominent status of Mary Magdalene. Mary and John the

Virgin are considered to be the greatest of the followers of the Master. Mary is even described as a beautiful speaker. She is praised by Jesus for being more devoted to the Heavenly Kingdom than the others. In ***Pistis Sophia,*** Mary asks Jesus approximately thirty-nine of the forty-six questions.

Two of Jesus' familiar sayings are found in the ***Pistis Sophia*** that also appear in other ***New Testament*** and **Gnostic** Gospels: ***"Whoever has ears to hear should hear"*** and ***"The first will be last and the last will be first."*** This shows there is a relationship between the different texts.

Mary Magdalene is exalted by Jesus: ***"Jesus answered and said to Mary, 'Blessed Mary you whom I shall complete with all the mysteries on high, speak openly, for you are one whose heart is set on Heaven's Kingdom more than all your brothers.'"*** (18)

Receiving the wisdom of Jesus, Mary Magdalene responds, ***"Before You came, the power within the prophet Isaiah prophesied about You, that You would take away the power of the rulers of the realms and turn their sphere and their fate to that from now on they would know nothing.... You have said to us, 'Whoever has ears to hear should hear' so that you may know whose heart is directed toward Heaven's Kingdom."***

When Mary finished, Jesus said to her, ***"Well done, Mary. You are more blessed than all women on earth, because you will be the fullness of fullnesses and the completion of completions."*** This exchange between Jesus and Mary can be found across different texts: ***Pista Sophia*** 17, ***Gospel of Mary*** 10, and the ***Gospel of Philip*** 59, 63-64 which give validity to all these texts. There is no evidence that they were copied from one another.

We also find Peter's disdain for Mary Magdalene in ***Pista Sophia. "Peter stepped forward and said to Jesus, 'My Master, we cannot endure this woman who gets in our way and does not let any of us speak, though she talks all the time."*** (36) In ***Pista Sophia*** 146, Peter's rebuke is phrased differently, ***"My Master, make the women stop asking questions, so that we also may raise some questions."*** Jesus responds, ***"Give the men, your brothers, a chance to ask some questions."*** Regardless of the phraseology, Peter's dislike for Mary appears not only in ***Pista Sophia*** but also in the ***Gospel of Mary*** 17-18 and the ***Gospel of Philip*** 114.

However, in ***Pista Sophia*** Mary does confront Jesus on Peter's hostility, ***"Mary came forward and said, 'My Master, I understand in my mind that I can come forward at any time to interpret what Pista Sophia has said, but I am afraid of Peter, because he threatens me and hates our gender.'"***

Jesus marveled at Mary's questions and understanding of what He had said which prompted Him to say to her, ***"Well done, Mary, pure spiritual woman. This is the interpretation of the word."***

MARY IN *THE PSALMS OF HERACLEIDES*

Mary Magdalene is mentioned several times in ***The Psalms of Heracleides;*** she is actually listed as one of Jesus' Disciples. This is a part of a beautiful book of songs in the Manichaean Psalm Book. Manicheism was a world religion that was begun by Mani. He was a prophet who came out of the Judeo-Christianity culture of the 3rd Century. He had a vision from an angel he referred to as "the twin." Manicheism spread from Europe and Africa to Central Asia and China. It was an incorporation of Christianity, Zoroastrianism, and Buddhism, while having similar ideas as **Gnosticism.**

Mary was described as: ***"Mary is one who casts a net in an effort to catch the other eleven who were lost."*** Along with Mary, Martha (Mary's sister), Salome, and Arsinoe are mentioned in these texts as women Disciples, as well as also being mentioned in the ***Gospel of James***. In ***The Psalms of Heracleides,*** Mary Magdalene held in high regard and is given glory:

> ***"because she has listened to her Master,***
> ***[she has] carried out His instructions***
> ***with joy in her whole heart."***

Excerpts from ***The Psalms Of Heracleides:***

"Mary, Mary, know me,
But do not touch [me]
[Dry] the tears of your eyes
And know that I am your Master
Only do not touch me,
For I have not yet seen my Father's face.

Your God was not taken away
As you thought in your pettiness.
Your God did not die,
Rather, He mastered [death]
I am not the gardener.
I have given, I have received....

I did [not] appear to you
Until I saw your tears and grief... for me.

Cast this sadness away
And perform this service.
Be My messenger to these lost orphans.
Hurry with joy, go to the eleven.
You will find them gathered on the banks of the Jordan.
The traitor convinced them to fish
As they did earlier.....

Say to them, 'Arise, let us go.
Your brother calls you.'...
Use all your skill and knowledge
Until you bring the sheep to the shepherd....

Rabbi, my Master, I shall carry out your instructions
With joy in my whole heart.
I shall not let my heart rest,
I shall not let my eyes sleep,
I shall not let my feet relax
Until I bring the sheep to the fold.

Glory to Mary
Because she has listened to her Master
[She has] carried out His instructions
With joy in her heart."

MARY MAGDALENE PLACE IN CHRISTIANITY

Mary Magdalene has garnered much interest with Biblical Scholars and much has been written about her. We know that the discovery of the ***Gospel of Mary,*** believed to have been written in the 2nd Century, has had a major impact on the Christian theological community. She should take her rightful place alongside the ***Gospels of Matthew, Mark, Luke, John, Peter, Thomas, James, Philip,*** and ***Judas.*** In the opinion of many Biblical Scholars, Mary was the closest Disciple of Jesus who understood Him better than the others. She was a major force after His death to preach His Word and the Good News. Of course, many blame the emerging Christian Church for its bias against women and as such dismissed anything written by Mary. But then, remember Irenaeus who unilaterally dictated there would only be four Gospels, no more, no less, because there are four corners to the Earth, four directions of the winds, and four columns to the Church. So in light that there were ten Gospels, the ***Gospel of Mary*** did not stand a chance to be one of the four. Irenaeus who immediately dismissed the ***Gospel of Judas,*** Jesus' betrayer, probably also dismissed a Gospel by Mary Magdalene, a woman and a prostitute. The ***Gospels of Peter, Thomas, James,*** and ***Philip*** were dismissed by Irenaeus on lesser grounds, just because they were too **Gnostic.**

Consequently, the texts that were included in the ***New Testament,*** say so little about her. In fact, they seem to downplay her role in Jesus' ministry. Matthew does acknowledge that Mary Magdalene saw the open tomb, met the risen Jesus, and is eager to tell the other Disciples that "He is Risen." (***Matthew*** 28:1-10) Meanwhile, Luke claims the Mary Magdalene had been healed of her evil spirits. (***Luke*** 8:2) In ***Luke,*** Mary was not believed that Jesus' tomb was empty. Both Matthew and Luke deemphasized the important role of Mary in the resurrection of Jesus. More so it downplayed the role of a woman and emphasized the role of the male Disciples. The spreading of the word of Jesus was the work of men. John, the most ***Gnostic*** of the four canonical Gospels, shows women in a more favorable light, such as they would have dialogues with Jesus. It can be implied by all the Gospels that there were many women who followed Jesus, although they may not have engaged Jesus directly in conversation, or at least were given any credit for them.

As they had said, could the Disciples trust what Mary claims Jesus taught her? Why would He teach this woman what He did not teach his male Disciples? But the ***Gospel of Mary*** puts Mary Magdalene on the same footing as The Twelve as a real Disciple, part of His Inner Circle.

IMPORTANT POINT: A point to ponder, maybe Mary Magdalene's presence on Easter Sunday at the empty tomb, seeing the Risen Jesus, and to be the one to run and tell the Disciples what she saw… may have been for a greater than the superficial purpose than presented. That might have been the stepping stone to being the Greatest Disciple and Emissary of Jesus.

If it wasn't for Mary Magdalene's biggest fans Elaine Pagels and Karen King who wrote many books about Mary Magdalene and the **Gnostic Gospels**, her legacy would be lost. Elaine Pagel's book ***The Gnostic Gospels*** exhibit Mary Magdalene as the epitome of female leadership. We owe a lot of gratitude to them and many other **Gnostic Gospel** writers for keeping this important part of Christian history alive and at the same time showing us the vast arrays of the existence of **Alternative Christianities.**

####################################

BIBLIOGRAPHY, REFERENCES, AND SUGGESTED READING

Alberry, C.R. C., ed.: ***Manichaean Psalm-Book, A: Part II*** (translation) 1938, Kohlhammer, Stuttgart

Barnstone, Willis, ***Restored New Testament: A New Translation With Commentary, Including the Gnostic Gospels of Thomas, Mary, and Judas*** © 2009 W.W.Norton & Co., New York, NY

Barnstone, Willis and Marvin Meyer: ***Gnostic Bible, The*** © 2009 Shambhala, Boston, MA

BeDuhn, Jason: ***Manichaean Body, The*** © 2000 John Hopkins University Press, Baltimore, MD

Blatz, Beate and Einar Thornassen: ***Dialogue of the Savior, The***

Block, Darrell L., ***Missing Gospels, The: Unearthing the Truth Behind Alternative Christianities*** © 2006 Nelson Books, Nashville, TN

Burstein, Dan and Arne J. De Keijzer, ***Secrets of Mary Magdalene***. Introduction by Elaine Pagels. Contributors include: Bart Ehrman, Elaine Pagels, and Marvin Meyer © 2006 CDS Books, New York

de Boer, Ester A: ***Gospel of Mary, The*** and ***Mary Magdala: Beyond the Myth*** © 1997 Trinity Press Intl, London, England

Ehrman, Bart D., ***Lost Scriptures: Books That Did Not Make It Into The New Testament*** © 2006 Oxford University Press

Ehrman, Bart D., ***Peter, Paul, & Mary Magdalene: The Followers of Jesus in History*** © 2006 Oxford Press

Good, Deirdre: ***Pistis Sophia*** © 1987 Scholars Press, Atlanta, GA

King, Karen L.: ***Gospel of Mary of Magdala, The: Jesus and the First Woman Apostle***

Koester, Helmut and Elaine Pagels: ***Introduction to the Dialogue of the Savior***

MacRae, Wilson and George W.: ***Gospel According to Mary, The***

Meyer, Marvin, ***Gospels of Mary, The: The Secret Tradition of Mary Magdalene, the Companion of Jesus*** © 2004 HarperCollins Publishers, Inc. New York and San Francisco

Meyer, Marvin, ***Gospel of Thomas, The***

Meyer, Marvin, ***Gnostic Bible, The*** © 2009 Shambhala, Boston, MA

Meyer, Marvin, ***Secret Teaching of Jesus: Four Gnostic Gospels*** © 1986, 1984 Vintage Books-Random House, New York

Randolph, Kurt: ***Gnosis***

Schmidt, Carl and Violet MacDermot, ed.: ***Pistis Sophia*** © 2001 Lindisfarne Books, Great Barrington, MA

This Book and Treatise are a compilation from many sources on the same subject.
See the Complete List of Bibliographies, References, and Suggested Readings in Appendix II

PART IV – THE PAUL FACTOR

CHAPTER 14

PAUL WAS A FRAUD

I have disparaged Paul many times in this ***Alternative Christianities – Volume II: The Validity of Today's Christian Teachings and The Lost Gospels of The Other Disciples***. I feel I must substantiate my strong feelings against any teachings emanating from Paul, who is neither a Disciple nor an Apostle under their textbook definitions. I expressed these feeling also in ***Alternative Christianities – Volume I: Early Christian Sects and the Formation of the Bible.*** *(*2014 Author House). I want to do a summary about Paul and why his books should be stricken from the ***New Testament*** of the Christian Bible. I have spent so much time researching the Gospels, Epistles, and Apocrypha of Saints and Disciples Peter, James, Philip, Thomas, Judas and Mary Magdalene, all of which were politically banned by the Catholic Church bishops from the Christian Bible. Meanwhile, the Epistles of Paul were included by these same Catholic

Church bishops. Whereas, NOTHING attributed to Paul should be there or given any credence whatsoever. I stand with many Biblical Scholars who also feel this way.

I learned while researching for my books on ***Alternative Christianities –Volume I,*** many Biblical Scholars said to ignore anything Paul had written, or was attributed to him. He was a fraud who was a total psycho and very far from being a Saint. First off, Paul was an avid Jew who came on the scene ten years after Jesus died after he was spent those ten years killing Jews that dared to abandon Judaism and convert to Christianity. After ***claiming*** to have visitation from Jesus (there is no consistent story on that visitation), he converted to Christianity and began converting Gentiles to Christianity without any consultation or guidance from Jesus' Disciples in Jerusalem, in fact, he was belligerent towards them.

Let me give you some facts about Paul which lead me to this conclusion about him:

1. Paul was neither a "Disciple," i.e. a person trained directly by Jesus; nor was Paul an "apostle," i.e. an authorized missionary trained by Disciples. Neither term applies to Paul. He was nobody!

2. Paul ***claims*** to have been converted on the Road to Damascus about 10 years after Jesus was killed, but his story changes with his audiences. All three versions agree that a great light descended from heaven, shines around Paul, who is alone, falls to the ground, and is blinded. Jesus says to him, "***Saul, Saul, why are you persecuting me?***" and adds, "***It hurts you to kick against the goads.***" Jesus explains to him what his mission will be. In the first version, the people he is travelling with remained

speechless "***because they hear the voice but saw nothing;***" in the second version, it is the opposite, "***they see the light but they don't hear the voice;***" and in the third version, "***they see the light which knocks them to the ground along with Paul, they apparently hear the voice.***"

<u>**IMPORTANT POINT:**</u> You would think for such an important event, Paul would get his story straight? Unless, of course, it just isn't the truth.

3. Paul did not feel he had to be accepted or take direction from James, Peter, John or any of the other "Disciples" in Jerusalem. Paul was striking out on his own; after all, <u>**he had a "vision**</u>" and was given a mission. Paul not only downplayed but very vocally criticized Jesus' Disciples there.

   <u>**IMPORTANT POINT:**</u> This is a common theme. Paul had no respect for Jesus' Inner Circle of Disciples and always claimed, although he never met Jesus, he was the one, true, and the only disciple of Jesus and His teachings.

4. James, Peter, John and the other Disciples who were preaching in Jerusalem wanted nothing to do with Paul, who they considered to be "loose cannon." The Disciples called Paul to Jerusalem to tell him they did not agree with his teachings which Paul claimed to be Jesus' teachings. Paul ignored them that caused James to send Peter to Antioch to put Paul in check. There they got into several public fights over Jesus' message, even at one point getting physically between them. James, Peter, John and the other Disciples told Paul "to cease and desist preaching

his own version of Christianity"; which he refused and continued to do. At another point, James sent Peter back to Antioch to re-convert and re-baptize "Paul's Christians" in Antioch and other places where Paul had been preaching.

IMPORTANT POINT: Does that sound like you should listen to Paul over, or on equal footing with, Matthew, Mark, Luke, John, Peter, James, Philip, or Thomas?

5. Paul's view was very different than the Disciples James, Peter, and John. Paul felt THEY did not understand Jesus' message which was salvation was attained through the grace of God by having faith in Jesus Christ. This was a very crucial point of contention between James, Peter, John and the others in Jesus' Inner Circle of Disciples with whom He spent three years instructing. This is where the **"Protestant Fork"** has its roots – in the rebellious teachings of Paul.

   IMPORTANT POINT: The teachings of Paul are mutually exclusive from the teachings of the Disciples Matthew and John, and by extension, Mark and Luke. Paul preached that you only need **Faith and Believe** in Jesus Christ to be saved, whereas the Disciples preached **Faith plus** the need to do **Good Works** like Jesus preached.

6. Paul very vocally did not agree with **"Jesus Movement"** (precursor to Christian Church) that was being taken by (Paul's ***derogatory words***) **"the reputed leaders in Jerusalem" being James, Peter, and John** (and the other Disciples who were

with them in Jerusalem) but considered himself to be more and better enlightened than them and took it upon himself to teach his brand of "Christianity." In ***Galatians*** 2, Paul is very blunt about his resentment towards the Disciples when he sarcastically says, "***And from those who were supposed to be the acknowledged leaders, what they actually were made no difference to me, God shows no partiality, those leaders contributed nothing to me… James, Cephas [Peter], and John who were acknowledged pillars.***"

IMPORTANT POINT: Paul is not only overly disrespectful to Jesus' Disciples and their teachings to his congregations and thinks he is better than them with his brand of Christianity.

7. When Paul was called back to Jerusalem the second time about a decade later, around A.D. 50, the meeting was even less cordial than the first one. He had been summoned to appear before James, Peter, John and the other Disciples there again to defend his teachings and his self-appointed role of one of their missionaries (although the way Paul tells it, he was not summoned to Jerusalem, but he went of his own accord because Jesus had told him to do so).

   IMPORTANT POINT: This was another attempt by the Disciples in Jerusalem, headed by Jesus' brother James, to instill in Paul their unanimously disapproved of his teachings and told him again "to cease and desist" his brand of Christianity that he preaching and converting people.

8. Curiously, some forty or fifty years later, Luke writes about that meeting as being perfectly harmonious between Paul and the Disciples; Peter (***who disliked Paul***) supposedly defended Paul and took his side (***not true***). James, as the elected head of the Disciples, (***who was the most against the teachings of Paul***) even blessed Paul's teachings (***not true***) and welcomed the Gentiles into the fold without having to follow the Law of Moses (***Acts*** 15:1-21). Luke tries an obvious ploy to legitimize Paul's ministry. However, Paul <u>**himself**</u> contradicts Luke in the letter he wrote to the Galatians not long after that meeting. Paul claims he was ambushed at the meeting by the Disciples, or "<u>***by a group of false believers,***</u>" not hiding his outrage at "<u>***the supposedly acknowledged leaders***</u>" of the church: James, Peter, and John (***Galatians*** 2:1-10).

   <u>**IMPORTANT POINT:**</u> This calls into question the legitimacy of the account of the meeting in ***Acts.*** Were the real events in ***Acts*** fraudulently changed to show them in Paul's favor?

9. Coincidentally, after Paul left Jerusalem, James immediately sent his own missionaries to Paul's congregations including Galatia, Corinth, Philippi, and other places where Paul was preaching. James was doing this to correct "Paul's teachings" about Jesus and replace them with "Jesus' true teachings." Paul was further incensed as is reflected in his subsequent letters (his first letter to the Thessalonians written between A.D. 48 and 50, and his last letter to the Romans written around A.D. 56) where he spent much time defending his status as an apostle, his direct connection to Jesus, and he

bad-mouthed the Disciples in Jerusalem "***who are disguising themselves as Apostles of Christ***" and are "***servants of Satan who are corrupting the people he had converted***" (***Corinthians*** 11:13-15). Paul implored his followers not to listen to these missionaries sent by James and "***If anyone else preaches a gospel contrary to the gospel you received*** [from him, Paul]***, let him be damned***" (Galatians 1:9); **even if it comes "*from an angel in heaven*" they should ignore it** (***Galatians*** 1:8). They should obey Paul and only him (***1 Corinthians*** 11:1).

IMPORTANT POINT: Maybe Paul ended up losing his mind? This is the final nail in Paul's coffin for so disrespecting Jesus' Inner Circle of Disciples. Again, it gets down to you deciding whether you believe anything Paul says in this writings, or do you believe in the Gospels of Matthew, Mark, Luke, and John. The two versions of Christianity are mutually exclusive.

10. Again in A.D. 57, Paul was summoned to Jerusalem. Paul was telling everyone to forsake Moses and NOT to circumcise their children or observe the usual customs (***Acts*** 21:21), more or less thumbing his nose at the Jewish-Christians. Paul was going as far as saying that those who let themselves be circumcised will "***cut themselves off from Christ***" (***Galatians*** 5:2-4). James forces Paul to renounce what he had been preaching and to partake in a purification rite in the Temple (which Paul was opposing). To make a long story short, Paul ended up getting arrested in Jerusalem, but since he was a

Roman citizen he demanded that he be sent to Rome for a Roman trial for which he was entitled.

IMPORTANT POINT: This was the third time Paul was summoned by the Disciples to Jerusalem.

11. Uninvited Paul followed Peter when James sent Peter to Rome, the capital of the Roman Empire. Going to Rome was perfect for Paul. First, he wanted to get far away from Jerusalem and the watchful eye of James and the other Disciples. Paul was under house arrest in Rome but was able to continue his ministry, although many Jews and Gentiles there were not all very responsive to his unique interpretation of Jesus' teachings. This may have been due to the fact that Peter who knew Jesus was also preaching in Rome. Peter had been sent to Rome by James to minister to the well-established community of Greek-speaking Jews in the seat of the Roman Empire. **Peter's** "***Petrine Christianity***" was taking a firm hold in Rome, whereas **Paul's** "***Pauline Christianity***" was not faring as well there. For whatever reason, Luke ends his narrative of Paul's life with his arrival in Rome. Luke also makes no mention of Peter also being in Rome. Nor does Luke make any mention that in the year A.D. 66 when Nero began persecuting the Christians in Rome that Peter and Paul were executed.

12. Upon the execution of Peter, Paul became the heir-apparent. Paul then had free rein on interjecting his "***Pauline Christianity***" on the developing Christian Church, the forerunner to the Catholic Church and subsequent offshoot Protestant religions centuries later. When Paul was executed in Rome, he was

considered a martyr and instant saint. His followers lobbied the Church leaders to have Paul's teachings be included as Sacred Scriptures in the ***New Testament***.

IMPORTANT POINT: Paul, whose teachings were not initially welcomed in Rome, as opposed to Peter who was more successful converting the Romans to Christianity. However, upon the execution of Peter, by default, Paul became the heir-apparent and got to push his version of Christianity which became seeded in the emerging Christian Church.

13. Paul's writings are among the earliest accounts in the Bible but Jesus' teachings are missing from Paul's epistles along with anything about the Resurrection of Jesus, the "empty tomb," or Jesus' Ascension. These miracles **must have come up** in conversations with the Disciples.

    IMPORTANT POINT: The Epistles of Paul to his congregations were among the first scarce texts available to the early Christians. Consequently, they revered them as Sacred Scriptures.

14. Paul's preaching seemed to have very little to do with Jesus' teachings; they all seem to be Paul's unique interpretation of Christianity called "***Pauline Christianity***" so different than the Disciples.

    IMPORTANT POINT: Paul's teachings were the first major fork in the road for Christianity.

15. Paul's writings famously introduced the fearful fate of eternal damnation and Hell into the ***New Testament.***

Jesus definitely would not have condoned the "Hellfire and brimstone" preachers of His word today. Luke says of Jesus, "***all wondered at the gracious words from His mouth.***" Jesus taught us all about the joys of His Father and His Heavenly Kingdom never threatening us with a fiery Hell as eternal punishment for disobedience. These evangelical preachers pride themselves in instilling a fear of God and transforming an All-Loving and All-Merciful God into a rabid watchdog waiting for any misstep, no matter how small, how rare, to pounce and be able to damn you for all eternity to a place of fire, suffering, and pain. (Of course, while continually demanding Faith in Jesus while asking for donations from their TV pulpits, you can be spared from going to Hell!)

IMPORTANT POINT: Paul was the first to introduce Hell as punishment for disobedience.

16. In the 16th century, the Protestant Reformation placed more emphasis on the Epistles of Paul. **This steered Christianity more off course.** Then the evangelical movement in the 20th century preached the ***New Testament*** is irrefutably 100% the inerrant, directly inspired Word of God – willfully blind to its obvious discrepancies, contradictions, and inconsistencies – put **MORE** emphasize on the Epistles of Paul and effectively "**drove Christianity completely off the cliff**"!

    IMPORTANT POINT: The Protestant Reformation initiated by Martin Luther was a major fork in the road for Christianity in the 16th century. There were many more "reformations" to come.

17. Jesus said absolutely NOTHING about homosexuality – it must NOT have been very high on His moral agenda – but it was sure very high on Paul's agenda whose letters constantly recommended abstinence, not only homosexual but also heterosexual including inside marriage. There are some very interesting ideas floating around on why Paul and his sordid past made him so against any and all sex out of his own guilt and repentance for him violating the strict Laws of Moses.

    IMPORTANT POINT: a) Jesus never said anything about homosexuality or any sexuality; and b) There are stories about Paul's sexually sinful past that make him against anyone having sex.

18. All his epistles, many of which are doubted to have been written by Paul as they were not in the same style, structure, or vocabulary used by Paul. Biblical scholars consider some to be definitely fraud, and some that were left out are considered by these scholars to be actually authentic.

    IMPORTANT POINT: All of the writings of Paul should be deleted from the ***New Testament.*** To this day, they are doing harm to the "real and true" teachings of Jesus Christ.

19. Whereas today's Christianity has been unduly tainted by Paul's Epistles and teachings, conversely the Gospels, Epistles, and Apocrypha passed down from Jesus' personally chosen and taught Disciples (Peter the first Pope, James who was the "brother" of Jesus and the first head of the Christian Church, Thomas

the recorder of Jesus' sayings), were not included in the ***New Testament***.

IMPORTANT POINT: Bishop Irenaeus decreed there will only be four Gospels, we should be able to read anything and everything written about Jesus Christ by His Disciples.

20. Is today's "Traditional Christianity" really just another "Alternative Christianity"? Is it better or worse than all those other "Apostolic Christianities" that existed in the 1st, 2nd, and 3rd centuries, the most immediate years following Jesus Christ and founded by His direct "inner circle" Disciples? Did the "right" Christianity survive? Or has the "right" Christianity been lost because of powerful, political, and selfish early Church leaders who banned, suppressed, and destroyed it?

FINAL POINT:

Paul's writings should be taken out of the New Testament and not given the same stature as the Gospels and Epistles from one of Jesus' Disciples with whom He lived, taught, and inspired for three full years. Paul's writings and teachings could be treated as any other notable religious and pious figures, such as St. Augustine, St. Francis, St. Benedict and numerous other "God-inspired" people. More or less, you can take it or leave it, but Paul's epistles are definitely not "God Inspired" works and have had a major negative effect on the direction and philosophy of Christianity today.

##

BIBLIOGRAPHY, REFERENCES, AND SUGGESTED READINGS

Boulton, David, ***Who on Earth Was Jesus? The Quest For the Jesus of History*** © 2008 O Books-John Hunt Publishing, Hants, United Kingdom

Ehrman, Bart D., ***Peter, Paul, & Mary Magdalene: The Followers of Jesus in History*** ©2006 Oxford Press

Eusebius, ***Church History***

Nardo, Don, ***Rise of Christianity, The*** © 2001 Lucient Books, San Diego, California

Shelby, John, ***Resurrection: Myth or Reality? A Bishop's Search for the Origins of Christianity*** © 1994 HarperCollins, New York

Stark, Rodney, ***Rise of Christianity, The: Obscure, Marginal Jesus Movement Became the Dominant Religious Force in the Western World in a Few Countries*** © 1996 Princeton University Press, © 1997 First HarperCollins

This Book and Treatise are a compilation from many sources on the same subject.
See the Complete List of Bibliographies, References, and Suggested Readings in Appendix II

ALTERNATIVE CHRISTIANITIES II

TREATISE CONCLUSION

CONGRATULATIONS to everyone that have read this entire Volume!

I feel I have continued and accomplished my mission with ***Alternative Christianity - Volume II***. Again, as with ***Alternative Christianity - Volume I,*** this was done with the immense help of the writings of the many Biblical scholars and educators of Religious Studies, the experts. I still have only scratched the surface of the published texts on the subjects around Early and Alternative Christianities. It has helped their cases that many ancient Sacred Scriptures containing diverse beliefs have been discovered in modern times and their existence cannot be denied. We don't know what else still remains buried, or may never be discovered, that contain more diverse beliefs that existed in early Christianity.

Firstly, all this research, reading, and learning have rejuvenated my Christian Beliefs. Jesus Christ has spoken in much broader and deeper term than we are being taught by the established Churches. I personally feel I have gained the extra knowledge, the ***gnosis,*** to Jesus' mission and Our Heavenly Home. My preferred route to eternity is Christianity; however, I also believe Christianity is not the sole path to the heavenly hereafter. As much as "born-again" Christians think they have the monopoly of getting into Heaven, it is not at the exclusion of all other faiths. What sort of mean and egotistical god do they worship and believe in? All of us have the same goals but just go about it differently. Jesus Christ is **Our** Lord and Savior and brings us to His Heavenly Father. The same as Mohammed is the conduit for the Muslims, Abraham and Moses are conduits for the Jews, and Buddha is for the Buddhists. Most believe there is only **One Almighty** and we are **all** His children; we **all** worship Him, look to please Him, and **ALL** praise of Him is acceptable. No religion or faith has an exclusive claim on the Almighty. It is hard to believe that Christianity has the sole lock on the Almighty God and salvation. Coincidentally, most religions refer to the Almighty God as "He who shall remain nameless."

However, as there are hundreds of different religions in the world, there are thousands of denominations and sects (and cults) that all claim to be the "true" Christianity. It is probably the only major faith in the world that has so many conflicting divisions in it, all favoring their "One True Denomination." Looking from the outside, and compared to other world religions, that does not say much for Christianity as a whole for being stable, coherent, and attractive. Volume I pointed out all the flaws in Christianity. This Volume's intention was to expand upon and then look beyond the flawed Christianity we know today. This Volume took a deeper look at some of the **Alternative Christianities** which existed at the very beginning of Christianity that were suppressed, trampled upon, disenfranchised, and obliterated. Maybe it was those **Alternative Christianities** whose messages and approaches happen to be closer to Jesus' true message and mission. Maybe Christianity has been **wrong** for 2,000 years. **I think this treatise makes a good case to say YES!**

Next, I do believe the **Gnostic Christians** were on to something but were persecuted for what they believed. They were ostracized and called "heretics." However, their beliefs make more sense about the world, salvation, and Jesus Christ's message. Whereas, the mainline Christian teachings seem in perspective, especially to an outsider, to be more like a fairy-tale story, just a continuation of Greek and Roman mythology. The more you read the accounts, with all its errors and contradictions, the more incredulous it all sounds. Then this was further exacerbated by the early Church Fathers in the 4th century by dismissing and ordering the destruction of dissenting Gospels and Epistles of the same, and other, Disciples. The main reason was that they did not support what **these Church Leaders**, centuries removed from Jesus' Disciples, considered to be the "**orthodox**" message and teachings. I feel this treatise has set forth my belief that because of these men; Christianity took off in a completely wrong direction. This was compounded by Paul's completely erroneous teachings being sanctioned by the constructors of the ***New Testament.*** They chose the texts of late-comer Paul over those of Jesus' Disciples like Peter, James, Philip, and Thomas. This further contributed to Christianity barreled down the wrong path for centuries.

Christianity should have been led 100% and only by Jesus' Disciples, with the core leaders of James, Peter, and John. They spent years together with Jesus; they first-hand heard His parables and saw His miracles; they had private instruction by Him; they understood Jesus, His teachings, and His mission more than anyone else; and they were His chosen to spread His word. However, Paul followed Peter to Rome, Paul outlived Peter in Rome, and eventually, Paul's teachings overpowered Peter's sending the faith in the completely wrong direction.

The Bible should have been a "collection" of all the "available" texts. No texts should have been excluded.

Then, the Protestant Reformation leaned more towards the "**Pauline Epistles**" and teachings embraced his words. In recent centuries, Christianity took another sharp turn in the wrong direction with the Evangelical Fundamentalist Christians who revere every single word in **their** Bible as the directly inspired Word of God Himself. Their preferred Bible is the King James Version. Most Biblical Scholars consider the King James Version to be the poorest translation of the Bible. King James did not have the most-original source documents which are stored in the Vatican Library, nor the competent translators to get the most-accurate translation to English. (See **Alternative Christianities Volume I – Early Christian Sects and the Formation of the Bible** where I go much deeper into this.)

The remnants of the Disciples' teachings, called the **Petrine** teachings, named after the Disciple Peter the First Pope and Founder of the Catholic Church, can be found in the Apostolic roots of Western and Eastern Catholic, Orthodox, and Coptic rites. In fact, many **Gnostic** beliefs can be found in the Catholic Coptic and Orthodox Coptic rites.

I hope I opened your minds to what many scholars believe is the true and glorious "Christianity" of Jesus that can be found in the numerous suppressed Alternative Christianity texts and Gospels cited in this treatise. Be forewarned, the Authors, Bibliographies, and Suggested Readings listed is just the tip of a gigantic iceberg.

With Gratitude, Vince Nicolas

ALTERNATIVE CHRISTIANITIES– APPENDIX I

WELL-KNOWN AUTHORS AND THEIR BOOKS ON THIS SUBJECT

EHRMAN, BART D. (www.bartehrman.com)
Distinguished Professor of Religious Studies at the University of North Carolina at Chapel Hill
Leading authority on the Bible and the life of Jesus. Featured in Time Magazine, NBC's Dateline, CNN, The History Channel. Author of:

After the New Testament: A Reader in Early Christianity.
Apostolic Fathers, Volumes I and II, The.
Brief Introduction to the New Testament, A
Christianity in Late Antiquity 330-450 C.E.
Didymus the Blind and the Text of the Gospels.
Forged: Writing in the Name of God – Why the Bible's Authors Are Not Who We Think They Are.
From Jesus to Constantine: A History of Early Christianity. (DVD)
God's Problem: How the Bible Fails to Answer Our Most Important Question – Why We Suffer
Jesus: Apocalyptic Prophet of the New Millennium.

Jesus, Interrupted: Revealing the Hidden Contradictions in the Bible and Why We Don't Know About Them
Historical Jesus. (AB & CD)
History of the Bible, The: The Making of the New Testament Canon.(AB & CD)
Lost Christianities: The Battle for Scripture and The Faiths We Never Knew.
Lost Gospel of Judas Iscariot: Betrayer and Betrayed (Reconsidered), The.
Lost Scriptures: Books That Did Not Make it into the New Testament.
Misquoting Jesus: The Story Behind Who Changed the Bible and Why.
New Testament: A Historical Introduction to the Early Christian Writings: A Reader, The. (3rd Edition)
New Testament and Other Early Christian Writings, A Reader, The. (2nd Edition)
Orthodox Corruption of Scripture: The Effect of Early Christianity on the Text of the New Testament, The.
Peter, Paul, and Mary Magdalene: The Followers of Jesus in History and Legend.
Studies in the Textual Criticism of the New Testament.
Text of the New Testament: It's Transmission, Corruption, and Restoration, The. (4th Edition)
Truth and Fiction in the DaVinci Code: A Historian Reveals What We Can Really Know About Jesus, Mary, Con.

MEYER, MARVIN

Professor of Bible and Christian Studies at Chapman University. Expert in Gnosticism.

Ancient Christian Magic: Coptic Texts of Ritual Power.
Ancient Mysteries, A Sourcebook: Sacred Text of the Mystery Religions of the Ancient Mediterrean World.

Gnostic Bible, The.
Gnostic Discoveries, The: The Impact of the Nag Hammadi Library.
Gnostic Gospels, The.
Gnostic Gospels of Jesus, The: The Definitive Collection of Mystical Gospels and Secret Books About Jesus of N.
Gospel of Judas, The: From Codex Tchacus, The.
Gospels of Mary, The: The Secret Tradition of Mary Magdalene, the Companion of Jesus, The.
Gospel of Thomas: The Hidden Sayings of Jesus, The.
Gospel of Mary, The.
Judas: The Definitive Collection of Gospels and Legends About the Infamous Apostle of Jesus.
Magical Book of Mary and the Angels, The.
Nag Hammadi Scriptures, The.
Secret Gospels of Thomas, The.
Secret Gospels of Mark, The.
Secret Teachings of Jesus, The: The Four Gnostic Gospels.
Unknown Sayings of Jesus, The.
Jesus Then and Now: Images of Jesus in History and Christology.

PAGELS, ELAINE

Professor of Religion at Princeton University,
B.A. in History and M.A. in Classical Studies from Stanford University, Ph.D. from Harvard University, and Author of:

Adam, Eve, and the Serpent.
Beyond Belief: The Secret Gospel of Thomas (contains the complete *Gospel of Thomas).*
Gnostic Gospels, The. A Startling Account of the Meaning of Jesus and the Origin of Chrisitianity
Based on the Gnostic Gospels and Other Secret Texts.

Gnostic Paul, The: Gnostic Exegesis of the Pauline Letters.
Johannine Gospel in Gnostic Exegesis, The.
Origin of Satan, The.
Reading Judas: The Gospel of Judas and the Shaping of Christianity (written with Karen L. King).
Secrets of Mary Magdalene: The Untold Story of History's Most Misunderstood Woman

KING, KAREN L.

Professor of Ecclesiastical History at the Harvard Divinity School. Author of:

Gospel of Mary of Magdala, The: Jesus and the First Woman Apostle.
Reading Judas: The Gospel of Judas and the Shaping of Christianity (written with Elaine Pagels).
Secret Revelation of John, The.
What is Gnosticism?

MICHAEL BAIGENT

He graduated with a Bachelor of Arts degree in psychology from Canterbury University, Christchurch,
Master of Arts degree in mysticism and religious experience from the University of Kent, England,
Religious historian and leading expert in the field of arcane knowledge, he has undertaken a quest for the truth about Jesus
He is the author or the co-author of these international bestsellers

Holy Blood, Holy Grail,
From the Omens of Babylon
Ancient Traces,

The Messianic Legacy (with Henry Lincoln and Richard Leigh),
The Temple and the Lodge,
The Dead Sea Scrolls Deception,
Secret Germany,
The Exixir and the Stone, and
The Inquisition.

BARNSTONE, WILLIAM

The Restored New Testament: A Translation with Commentary, including the Gnostic Gospels of Thomas, Mary, and Judas.

BUEHRENS, JOHN A.

Graduate Harvard Divinity School and the Graduate Theological Union in Berkley, Professor of Theology
Former President of the Unitarian Universalist Association from 1993 to 2001
Minister of the First Parish in Needham, Massachusetts
Special Assistant to the Secretary General of the World Conference of Religions for Peace

Understanding the Bible: An Introduction for Skeptics, Seekers, and Religious Liberals
A Chosen Faith

BUTZ, JEFEREY J.

Ordained Luther Minister and Professor of World Religions at Penn State University, Berks-Lehigh Valley campus

Brother of Jesus and the Lost Teachings of Christianity, The.

COPAN, PAUL

Chair of Philosophy and Ethics at Palm Beach Atlantic University in Florida

> *How Do You Know You're Not Wrong? Responding to Objections That Leave Christians Speechless.*
> *That's Just Your Interpretion.*
> *True for You, But Not For Me.*

CURRIE, DAVID B.

Degree from Trinity International University, and Masters of Divinity at Trinity Evangelical Divinity School.
David was raised in a devout Christian family whose father was a fundamentalist preacher and taught at Moody Bible Institute.

> *Born Fundamentalist – Born-Again Catholic* (His reasons for conversion from Fundamentalism to Catholicism)

DAVIES, STEVAN

Professor of Religious Studies at Misercordia College.
Author of:

> *The Gospel of Thomas: A Guidebook for Spiritual Practice.* (with Ron Miller)
> *The Gnostic Gospel: Annotated and Explained*
> *The Secret Book of John*

DE BOER, ESTER P. Ph.D.

Minister of The Protestant Church in the Netherlands.

> *Mary Magdalene: Beyond The Myth*
> *The Gospel of Mary: Beyond a Gnostic and a Biblical Mary Magdalene.*

DELOUP, JEAN YVES

Professor at International College of Therapists and Institute of Other Civilizations.

The Gospel of Philip.
The Gospel of Mary Magdalene.

GUBAR, SUSAN

Professor of English at Indiana University

Judas: A Biography

KROSNEY, HERBERT

Works for BBC, PBS, The History Channel, and National Geographic Society.

The Lost Gospel: The Quest for the Gospel of Judas Iscariot.

MACK, BURTON

Who Wrote the New Testament: The Making of The Christian Myth,
The Lost Gospel: The Book of Q & Christian Origins,
The Christian Myth: Origins, Logic, and Legacy,
Patterns of Persuasion in the New Testament,

McLAREN, BRIAN D.

Author of 10 highly acclaimed books on contemporary Christianity including:

Secret Message of Jesus, The: Uncovering the Truth That Could Change Everything
New Kind a Christian, A.
Generous Orthodoxy, A.

MILLER, RON

Chairman of Religious Studies at Luke Farely College, Illinois. Author of:

The Gospel of Thomas: A Guidebook for Spiritual Practice. (with Stevans Davies)
The Hidden Gospel of Matthew.

RODOLPHE KASSER

Professor of Cultologists at University of Geneva, Switzerland

Gospel of Judas: From Codex Tchaces, The (with Marvin Meyer)

RUPRECHT, LOUIS A. JR.

Chair of Religious Studies at Georgia State University. Professor at a number of most prominent religious programs. Active member of the American Academy of Religion and the Society for Biblical Literature

This Tragic Gospel: How John Corrupted the Heart of Christianity

SHELBY, JOHN

Ressurection: Myth or Reality?
The Easter Moment.
Living in Sin? A Bishop Rethinks Human Sexuality.
Rescuing the Bible from Fundalmentalism.

SPOTO, DONALD

Has M.A. and Ph.D. degrees in Theology from Fordham University concentrating on New Testament Studies.
He taught Theology, Christian Mysticism, and Biblical literature at the university level for 20 year.

Now is a full time writer and has published 17 books since 1976, mainly biographies of Stars and Celebrities.

The Hidden Jesus: A New Life.

SUMMERS, RAY
Chair of Religion at Baylor University in Waco TX

The Secret Sayings of the Living Jesus.

ALTERNATIVE CHRISTIANITIES– APPENDIX II

BIBLIOGRAPHY, REFERENCE, AND SUGGESTED READINGS

(By Title for Ease of Reference)

ADAM, EVE, AND THE SERPENT.

By Elaine Pagels © 1998 Random House, NY

ANCIENT CHRISTIAN MAGIC, A SOURCEBOOK: SACRED TEXT OF THE MYSTERY RELIGIONS OF THE ANCIENT MEDITERRANEAN WORLD.

By Marvin Meyers © 1997, 1999 First University of Pennsylvania Press Edition

BEYOND BELIEF: THE SECRET GOSPEL OF THOMAS.

By Elaine Pagels © 2003 Vintage Books-Random House, New York

BROTHER OF JESUS AND THE LOST TEACHINGS OF CHRISTIANITY, THE. (JAMES)
By Jeferey J. Butz © 2005 Inner Traditions, Rochester VT
© 1984, 1965 Dorset Press, New York

COMPLETE IDIOT'S GUIDE TO WORLD RELIGIONS, THE (4th Edition)
By Brandon Toropov and Luke Buckles © 2011 Alpha, New York

DIALOGUE OF THE SAVIOR, THE
By Beate Blutz and Einar Thornassen © 1984 Nag Hammadi codices. III, 5

EVERYTHING ® GNOSTIC GOSPELS BOOK, THE: A COMPLETE GUIDE TO THE SECRET GOSPELS
By Meera Lester © 2007 Adams Media, an F.W. Publications, Inc.

EUSEBIUS: CHURCH HISTORY
CHURCH HISTORY: THE HISTORY OF THE CHURCH FROM CHRIST TO CONSTANTINE
Translated and Commentary by Paul L. Meier, Paperback May 2007

FALLEN ANGELS AND THE ORIGINS OF EVIL: WHY THE CHURCH FATHERS SUPPRESSED THE BOOK OF ENOCK AND ITS STARTLING REVELATIONS
By Elizabeth Clare Prophet © 2000 Summit University Press, Montana

FINDING JESUS:
FAITH, FACT, FORGERY: SIX HOLY OBJECTS THAT TELL THE REMARKABLE STORY OF THE GOSPELS
By David Gibson and Michael McKinley © 2015 St. Martin Press, New York

GNOSTIC BIBLE, THE.
By Marvin Meyer and Willis Barnstone © 2003 Harper, San Francisco CA

GNOSTIC GOSPELS, THE: A STARTLING ACCOUNT OF THE MEANING OF JESUS AND THE ORIGIN OF CHRISTIANITY BASED ON THE GNOSTIC GOSPELS AND OTHER SECRET TEXTS.
By Elaine Pagels © 1979, 1989 Vintage Books-Random House, NY

GNOSIS AND FAITH IN EARLY CHRISTIANITY: AN INTRODUCTION TO GNOSTICISM
By Riemer Roukema © 1999 Trinity Press Int'l., Harrisburg PA

GNOSIS: THE NATURE AND HISTORY OF GNOSTICISM
By Kurt Rudolph © 1987 Harper and Row, San Francisco CA

GNOSTIC BIBLE, THE
By Willis Barnstone and Marvin Meyer © 2009 Shambhala, Boston, Mass.

GNOSTIC DISCOVERIES, THE: THE IMPACT OF NAG HAMMADI LIBRARY.
By Marvin Meyer © 2005 Harper, San Francisco CA

GNOSTIC GOSPELS OF JESUS, THE: DEFINITIVE COLLECTION OF MYSTICAL GOSPELS AND SECRET BOOKS ABOUT JESUS OF NAZARETH.

By Marvin Meyer © 2005 Harper, San Francisco CA

GNOSTIC SCRIPTURES, THE: ANCIENT WISDOM FOR THE NEW AGE

By Bentley Layton © 1987 Doubleday, NY

GNOSTIC SCRIPTURES, THE: A NEW TRANSLATION WITH ANNOTATIONS

By Bentley Layton © 1995 Doubleday, NY

GNOSTICISM: NEW LIGHT ON THE ANCIENT TRADITION OF INNER KNOWING.

Stephan A. Hoeller © 2002 Quest, Theosophical Publishing, Wheaton IL

GNOSTICISM AND EARLY CHRISTIANITY

By R.M. Grant © 1959 New York University Press, New York

GOD'S PROBLEM, HOW THE BIBLE FAILS TO ANSWER OUR MOST IMPORTANT QUESTION – WHY WE SUFFER.

By Bart D. Ehrman © 2008 HarperOne, Harper Collins Publishers, NY

GOSPEL ACCORDING TO JUDAS, THE.

By Benjamin Iscariot & Jeffrey Archer & Rev. Francis J. Moloney © 2007 St. Martin Press, NY

GOSPEL ACCORDING TO MARY

By Miriam Therese Winter © 1993 Crossroad, New York, NY

GOSPEL ACCORDING TO MARY

By Clive Doucet © 1990 Black Moss Press, Windsor, Ontario

GOSPEL ACCORDING TO THOMAS, THE

By A. Guillaumont, H.C. Puech, G. Quispel, W.C. Till, and Y.A.A. Mashih © 1959 Harper and Brothers, New York

GOSPEL OF JUDAS (2nd Edition) (DVD)

By Rodolphe Kasser, Marvin Meyers, and Gregor Wurst © 2008 National Geographic Society Films

GOSPEL OF JUDAS: FROM CODEX TCHACES, THE (2nd Edition).

By Rodolphe, Marvin Meyer, and George Wurst © 2008 National Geographic Society

GOSPELS OF MARY, THE: THE SECRET TRADITION OF MARY MAGDALENE, THE COMPANION OF JESUS.

By Marvin Meyer with Esther A. deBorr © 2006 Harper Collins, NY

GOSPEL OF MARY MAGDALA, THE: JESUS AND THE FIRST WOMAN APOSTLE.

By Karen L. King © 2003 Polebridge Press, CA 95406

GOSPEL OF THOMAS

By Marvin Meyer

GOSPEL OF THOMAS: A GUIDEBOOK FOR SPIRITUAL PRACTICE.

By Ron Miller & Stevan Davies © 2004

GOSPEL OF THOMAS: ANNOTATED AND EXPLAINED.

By Stevan Davies © 2002 Skylight Paths Publishing, VT

GOSPEL OF THOMAS: THE GNOSTIC WISDOM OF JESUS.

By Jean Yves DeLoup © 2005, 1986

HIDDEN JESUS, THE: A NEW LIFE

By Donald Spoto © 1998 St. Martin Press, NY

HOW DO YOU KNOW YOU'RE NOT WRONG? RESPONDING TO OBJECTIONS THAT LEAVE CHRISTIANS SPEECHLESS.

By Paul Copan © 2005 Baker Books

HOW TO BE AN OPEN-MINDED CHRISTIAN WITHOUT LOSING YOUR FAITH

By Jan G. Linn © 2002 Chalice Press, St. Louis, MO

INTERESTING AND ENLIGHTENING STUDY OF THE GOSPEL OF THOMAS: THE CONTROVERSIAL 4TH CENTURY MANUSCRIPT RECENTLY DISCOVERED AT NAG HAMMADI

By Ray Summers © 1968 Word Books, Waco, Texas

INTERPRETER'S DICTIONARY OF THE BIBLE, THE

By R.M. Grant © 1962 Abingdon Press, New York

INTRODUCTION TO THE DIALOGUE OF THE SAVIOR

By Helmut Koester and Elaine Pagels

JESUS, INTERRUPTED: REVEALING THE HIDDEN CONTRADICTIONS IN THE BIBLE (AND WHY WE DON'T KNOW ABOUT THEM).

By Bart D. Ehrman © 2009 HarperOne, Harper Collins Publishers, New York

JESUS FAMILY TOMB, THE THE DISCOVERY, THE INVESTIGATION, AND THE EVIDENCE THAT COULD CHANGE HISTORY

By Simcha Jacobovici and Charles Pellegrino © 2003 Harper Collins Press, 10 E 53 St. NY 10022

JESUS PAPERS, THE: EXPOSING THE GREATEST COVER-UP IN HISTORY

By Michael Baigent © 2006 HarperCollins, New York

JUDAS: A BIOGRAPHY.

By Susan Gubar © 2009 W.W. Norton & Co. New York

JUDAS: THE DEFINITIVE COLLECTION OF GOSPELS AND LEGENDS ABOUT INFAMOUS APOSTLE OF JESUS.

By Marvin Meyers © 2007 HarperCollins, New York, NY

LORD OR LEGEND? WRESTLING WITH THE JESUS DILEMMA

By Gregory A. Boyd and Paul Rhodes Eddy © 2007 Baker Books, Grand Rapids MI

LOST CHRISTIANITES: THE BATTLES FOR SCRIPTURE AND THE FAITHS WE NEVER KNEW

By Bart D. Ehrman © 2003 Oxford University Press, NY

LOST GOSPEL, THE: THE BOOK OF Q AND CHRISTIAN ORIGINS.

By Burton Mack © 1993 HarperSanFrancisco, San Francisco, CA

LOST GOSPEL, THE: THE QUEST FOR THE GOSPEL OF JUDAS ISCARIOT (DVD)

By Herbert Krosney © 2006 National Geographic Society, Washington, DC

LOST GOSPEL OF JUDAS ISCARIOT, THE:A NEW LOOK AT BETRAYER AND BETRAYED

By Bart E. Ehrman © 2006 Oxford University Press, New York, NY

LOST SCRIPTURES: BOOKS THAT DID NOT MAKE IT INTO THE NEW TESTAMENT

By Bart D. Ehrman © 2006 Oxford University Press, New York, NY

MANICHAEAN PSLAM BOOK: PART II (Translation)

By C.R.C. Alberry © 1938 Kohlhammer, Stuttgart, Germany

MARK'S STORY: A NOVEL
THE JESUS CRONICLES: THE GOSPEL ACCORDING TO PETER.

By Tim F. La Haye & Jerry B Jenkins © 2007 Putnam, New York, NY

MARY MAGDALA: BEYOND THE MYTH.

By Ester Boer, Ph.D.

MISQUOTING JESUS: THE STORY BEHIND WHO CHANGED THE BIBLE AND WHY.

By Bart D. Ehrman © 2005 HarperCollins

MISSING GOSPELS, THE: UNEARTHING THE TRUTH BEHIND ALTERNATIVE CHRISTIANITIES

By Darrell L. Block © 2006 Nelson Books, Nashville, Tennessee

NEW SAYINGS OF JESUS RECEN TLY DISCOVERED COPTIC "GOSPEL OF THOMAS"

By W.C. Till © 1959 Bulletin of the John Rylands Library, XLI

NEW TESTAMENT APOCRPHA

By Edgar Hennecke © 1963 The Westminister Press, Philadelphia, PA

NEWLY DISCOVERED GNOSTIC WRITINGS

By W.C. van Unnik © 1960 Alec R. Allenson, Inc., Naperville, Illinois

ORIGINS OF SATAN, THE.

By Elaine Pagels © 1995 Random House, NY

OXFORD DICTIONARY OF POPES

By J.N.D. Kelly, Revised by Michael J. Walsh © 2010 Oxford University Press, New York

PASSOVER PLOT: NEW LIGHT ON THE HISTORY OF JESUS

By Hugh J. Schonfield © 1965 Hutchison, London

PETER, PAUL, & MARY MAGDALENE: THE FOLLOWERS OF JESUS IN HISTORY.

By Bart D. Ehrman © 2006 Oxford Press

PISTIS SOPHIA

By Deirdre Good

PISTIS SOPHIA

By Carl Schmidt and Violet MacDerment

POPULAR SURVEY OF THE NEW TESTAMENT, A.

By Norman L Geiser © 2007 Baker Books, Grand Rapids MI

PUTTING AWAY CHILDISH THINGS:THE VIRGIN BIRTH, THE EMPTY TOMB, AND OTHER FAIRY TALES YOU DON'T NEED TO BELIEVE TO HAVE A LIVING FAITH.

By Uta Ranke-Heineman © 1994 HarperSanFrancisco, San Francisco, CA

Q, THE EARLIEST GOSPEL: AN INTRODUCTION TO THE ORIGINAL STORIES AND SAYINGS OF JESUS.

By John S. Kloppenborg © 2008 Westminister Press

Q, THE LOST GOSPEL: THE BOOK OF CHRISTIAN ORIGINS.

By Burton L. Mack © 1993 Harper Collins, NY

READING JUDAS: THE GOSPEL OF JUDAS AND THE SHAPING OF CHRISTIANITY.

By Elaine Pagels & Karen L. King © 2007 Viking-Penguin Books, NY

RECOVERING JESUS: THE WITNESS OF THE NEW TESTAMENT

By Thomas R. Yoder Neufeld © 2007 Brazos Press-Baker Publishing, Grand Rapids, MI

RESCUING THE BIBLE FROM FUNDALMENTALISM: A BISHOP RETHINKS THE BIRTH OF JESUS, and ***A BISHOP RETINKS SCRIPTURE***, and ***A BISHOP RETHINKS HUMAN SEXUALITY.***

By John Shelby © 1991 Harper, San Francisco

RESPONSES TO 101 QUESTIONS ABOUT JESUS.

By Michael L. Cook, S.J. © 1993 Paulist Press, New York, NY

RESURRECTION: MYTH OR REALITY? A BISHOP'S SEARCH FOR THE ORIGINS OF CHRISTIANITY.

By John Shelby © 1994 Harper Collins, New York, NY

RESTORED NEW TESTAMENT: A NEW TRANSLATION WITH COMMENTARY, INCLUDING THE GNOSTIC GOSPELS OF THOMAS, MARY, AND JUDAS.

By Willis Barnstone © 2009 W. W. Norton & Co., New York, NY

RISE AND FALL OF THE BIBLE, THE: THE UNEXPECTED HISTORY OF AN ACCIDENTAL BOOK

By Timothy Beal © 2011 Houghton Miffin Harcourt, New York

RISE OF CHRISTIANITY, THE

By Don Nardo © 2001 Lucient Books, San Diego, California

RISE OF CHRISTIANITY, THE: OBSCURE, MARGINAL JESUS MOVEMENT BECAME THE DOMINANT RELIGIOUS FORCE IN THE WESTERN WORLD IN A FEW COUNTRIES

By Rodney Stark	© 1996	Princeton University Press, Princeton, NJ
	© 1997	First Harger Collins/ Harper One, San Francisco, CA

RISE OF WESTERN CHRISTIANITY: TRIUMPH AND DIVERSITY A.D. 200-1000

By Peter Brown	© 2003	Blackwell Publishers, Malden, Mass.

SCANDALOUS GOSPEL OF JESUS, WHAT'S SO GOOD ABOUT THE GOOD NEWS.

By Peter J. Gomes	© 2007	HarperOne, Harper Collins Publishers, New York

SECRET BOOK OF THE EGYPTIAN GNOSTICS, THE

By Jean Doresse	© 1960	The Viking Press, New York

SECRET GOSPEL, THE: THE DISCOVERY AND INTERPRETATION OF THE SECRET GOSPEL ACCORDING TO MARK, CLEMENT OF ALEXANDRIA AND A SECRET GOSPEL OF MARK

By Morton Smith	© 1973	Harvard University Press, Cambridge & Harper and Row, NY

SECRET MESSAGE OF JESUS, THE: UNCOVERING THE TRUTH THAT COULD CHANGE EVERYTHING.

By Brian D. McLaren © 2006 W. Publishing, Nashville, TN

SECRET SAYINGS OF THE LIVING JESUS.

By Ray Summers © 1968 Word Books, Waco, Texas

SECRET TEACHING OF JESUS: FOUR GNOSTIC GOSPELS.

By Marvin Meyer © 1986, 1984 Vintage Books-Random House, New York

SECRETS OF MARY MAGDALENE: THE UNTOLD STORY OF HISTORY'S MOST MISUNDERSTOOD WOMAN.

By Dan Burstein and Arne J. De Keijzer © 2006 CDS Books, New York

Introduction by Elaine Pagels. Contributors include: Bart Ehrman, Elaine Pagels, and Marvin Meyer.

THEOLOGY OF THE GOSPEL ACCORDING TO THOMAS

By Bertil Gnertner © 1961 Harper and Brothers, New York

THIRD JESUS, THE: THE CHRIST WE CANNOT IGNORE

By Deepal Chopra © 2008 Harmony/Crown Publishing/Random House, NY

THOMAS AND THE EVANGELISTS

By Hugh Montefiore and H.E.W. Turner © 1962 Alec R. Allenson, Inc., Naperville, Illinois

THREE FAITHS ONE GOD: JUDAISM, CHRISTIANITY, ISLAM: A DOCUMENTARY (DVD)

By Gerard Krell and Meyer Ovdze © 2005

UNDERSTANDING THE BIBLE: AN INTRODUCTION FOR SKEPTICS, SEEKERS, AND RELIGIOUS LIBERALS

By John A. Buehrens © 2003 Beacon Press Books, Boston, Mass.

UNEARTHING THE LOST WORDS OF JESUS: THE DISCOVERY AND TEST OF **THE GOSPEL OF THOMAS**

By John Dart and Ray Riegert © 1998 Ulysses Press, Berkley CA/Oxford University Press

WHAT IS GNOSTICISM.

By Karen L. King © 2003 Belknapprots

WHO ON EARTH WAS JESUS? THE QUEST FOR THE JESUS OF HISTORY

By David Boulton © 2008 O Books-John Hunt Publishing, Hants UK

WHO WROTE THE NEW TESTAMENT: THE MAKING OF THE CHRISTIAN MYTH.

By Burton L. Mack © 1995 Harper, San Franciso CA

WHOSE BIBLE IS IT? A HISTORY OF THE SCRIPTURES THROUGH THE AGES

By Jaroslav Pelikan © 2005 Viking Press (Penguin Group), New York

This Book and Treatise are a compilation from many sources on the same subject. See Appendix I for the Notable Authors and a list of their books on these subjects The origin of some books are from outside the United States of America

########

AUTHOR BIO

Vince Nicolas was born, raised, and educated in New York City. Being the son of Italian immigrants, he was privileged to spend many summers in Italy and Europe. He was fascinated by Rome and its ancient history. When he was in High School, Italian was not offered as one of the language electives, so he studied Latin for four years. In learning the language and culture, there were a heavy emphasize on translating Latin writings from ancient times. He spent many vacations in Italy and Rome among the antiquity of Roman culture, art, mythology, and architecture. Learning Latin paid off because he was able to adapt it to learn Italian very quickly. The history of Rome after the birth of Jesus Christ was intricately intertwined with the history of early Christianity.

Christianity struggled to survive and grow in the Roman Empire. In the 4th Century, Emperor Constantine decided to make Christianity the official state religion of the Roman Empire with the personal motive of pulling his empire together. In forming the one large universal Christian or Catholic Church, the smaller diverse Christian groups were being snuffed out. Many shows about this period of time, especially about the "lost" or "banned" Gospels, can be seen on major networks especially the History, National Geographic, Discovery channels. Innumerable books have been written on this and related subjects by very best and prominent professors from major U.S. universities. In fact, a whole section of the library (220-232) and in bookstores is dedicated to "General Christianity." Once Vince saw the first program and read the first book on this subject, he could not watch and read enough on the subject of these "Lost Gospels." He read so many books, saw so many programs, he threw his hat into the ring, decided to put all these sources together, and prove the underlying common thread that because of Emperor Constantine almost unilaterally threw the emerging Christianity off its Founder's intended course.

Vince had done teaching, speaking, and writing in his previous career as an International Banker on Wall Street in New York City, so he took his laptop and began to write a book. With so much great information available, Volumes I and II are still only the "tip of the iceberg"! Please take this journey as it promises to be very interesting, informative, eye-opening, and educational, as well as being extremely controversial.

Printed in the United States
By Bookmasters